D1564247

Transaction Books by Michael Novak

Belief and Unbelief

Catholic Social Thought and
Liberal Institutions

Choosing Presidents

The Guns of Lattimer

Unmeltable Ethnics

SECOND EDITION

Politics & Culture in American Life

MICHAEL NOVAK

With a New Introduction by the Author

Transaction Publishers
New Brunswick (U.S.A.) and London (U.K.)

Second printing 1997

New material this edition copyright © 1996 by Transaction Publishers, New Brunswick, New Jersey 08903. Originally published in 1971 by Macmillan Publishing Co., Inc. Chapter 11 originally appeared in *The Center Magazine* (July-August 1974): 18–25. Chapter 12 originally appeared in the *Harvard Encyclopedia of American Ethnic Groups* published by The Belknap Press in 1980. Chapter 13 was originally presented as the keynote address at the Governor's Conference on Ethnicity, Pennsylvania Heritage Affairs Commission, June 8–9, 1990. Chapter 14 originally appeared in *Soundings* (Spring 1973): 1–20. Chapter 15 originally appeared in *The American Scholar* 43, no. 1 (Winter 1973–74): 113–21. Chapter 16 originally appeared in Hastings Center *Studies* 2, no. 3 (Autumn 1974): 37–44.

This book is printed on acid-free paper that meets the American National Standard for Permanence of Paper for Printed Library Materials.

Library of Congress Catalog Number: 94-38251
ISBN: 1-56000-773-7
Printed in the United States of America

Library of Congress Cataloging-in-Publication Data

Novak, Michael.
    Unmeltable ethnics : politics and culture in American life / Michael Novak, with a new introduction by the author. — 2nd ed.
        p. cm.
    Rev. ed. of: The rise of the unmeltable ethnics. 1972.
    Includes bibliographical references and index.
    ISBN 1-56000-773-7 (alk. paper)
    1. Minorities—United States. 2. Ethnic attitudes—United States. I. Rise of the unmeltable ethnics. II. Title.
E184.A1N65   1995
305.8'00973—dc20   94-38251
                                                                  CIP

To the great-grandparents of our children:
Stephen Novak, Johanna Kaschak, Ben
Sakmar, Anna Timchak, C. B. Laub, Anna
Graf, John Swenson, Dora Carver, who
journeyed westward in their youth

Contents

PART IV: ETHNICITY IN THE SEVENTIES AND BEYOND

Introduction to the
Transaction Edition

1. *"The New Ethnicity, Si! Multiculturalism, No!"*

IT IS hard to believe that twenty-four years have gone by since the long summer of 1971 when I was writing the first edition of *Unmeltable Ethnics* (originally published in April 1972 as *The Rise of the Unmeltable Ethnics*). The world has changed a great deal since then. Some of the goals I set out to promote in this book came to pass. For example, my subtitle announced "The new political force of the seventies." It can surely be said that the word "ethnic" (used of white ethnic Catholics, especially from Eastern and Southern Europe) entered public speech at that time, and that by their voting power the newly identified "ethnics" reached out and grabbed the attention of politicians as seldom before.

Moreover, reporters slowly began to pay unaccustomed attention to these "ethnic" voters and to the leaders who were rising from their ranks, such as Mario Cuomo in New York, Richard Celeste and George V. Voinovich in Ohio, Dennis DeConcini in New Mexico, Peter Domenici in Arizona, and Barbara Mikulski in Maryland. In 1974, President Gerald Ford initiated an office of ethnic affairs at the White House under Ukrainian-American Myron Kuropas. Jimmy Carter opened his September 1976 campaign celebrating "family days" in white ethnic neighborhoods of Newark and Pittsburgh, flanked by Joseph Califano and Monsignor Geno Baroni. In 1980 I was both surprised and pleased when the sunny Californian Ronald Reagan showed an unerring instinct in speaking the language of those who, after his two unrivalled landslides, came to be called "Reagan Democrats," and also when he chose as his campaign slogan symbols that could have been taken directly from the last pages of this book ("Work, family, neighborhood, peace, strength").

In fact, I learned much later, Reagan's pollster Dick Wirthlin picked those symbols up from an article of mine addressed as a challenge to both Democrats and Republicans, tested them in his polling, and recommended them to the future president. Like many other "ethnics" (if on these grounds I may so include him), Ronald Reagan had started his political life as a labor-oriented Democrat and then, feeling more and more abandoned by the cultural Left of his own party, became increasingly conservative. Much of the rest of the country, including that other stout pillar of the Roosevelt coalition, Southern and Western evangelicals, began to do likewise. Reagan had the capacity to cast this "revolution" as a *re + volvere* (a revolving back) to this nation's founding principles. He portrayed a new progressive vision—not a socialist or statist vision, but one based on limited government and self-rule. It inspired many of us, and it infuriated the cultural Left.

The publication of this book in 1972 marked my own declaration of independence from the cultural Left, at that time the preeminent force watching over what could be said and what couldn't in American culture. As readers will see firsthand in this new edition (which leaves unchanged most of the original text), I was still writing as a man of the Left, certainly a man of the anti-capitalist Left. But I was, in truth, departing from leftwing orthodoxy in singling out cultural issues, rather than economic issues, as the primary neuralgic point in American (and not only American) life. I was defending—no, calling into political and cultural self-consciousness, and trying to inspire—those whom the elites liked to picture as paunchy fascists in undershirts, bigoted and unwashed. I was repelled by "the bigotry of the intellectuals" and the unworthy prejudices of the cultural Left. At a time celebrating the "liberation" of the swinging singles, I thought intellectuals ought to be stressing the importance of family, even the psychological differences between "family people" and those who find the unencumbered self a more fundamental reality. They ought to admire the latent strengths of traditional values and ethnic neighborhoods (even ethnic suburbs). To say the least, these ideas were premature. At the time, they were regarded as reactionary. They were said to be—the insult our elites hurl when they are being unmasked—"spreading hate."

Secretly, of course, I wanted very badly in those days to be accepted by the cultural Left, the gatekeepers all aspiring young writers must pass if they are to be allowed into the national dialogue. I wanted to be seen as offering a necessary and helpful corrective to mistakes being made in progressive politics, mistakes that were alienating the Democratic party from its base and even from its traditional tacit commitments. Naively, I thought this difficult analytic effort would be greeted with gratitude. I did not then know the fury of the Left when it marks someone down as beyond the pale of acceptability. I had never before understood how secular excommunication works: how effectively one can be banished from the innocent banter of old circles of trust, how even old friends change the flow and tone of a conversation when one approaches, signaling with a certain chill that one's presence is no longer desired. All this is a good thing to go through when one is young. One will need the toughness later.

I have to confess here, however, that the many vivid anticapitalist sentiments I sincerely expressed in this book saved me from the full fury of rejection that was to be my lot when, a decade later, I published *The Spirit of Democratic Capitalism.* In the circles in which I travelled in the late seventies, not to be sympathetic to the motives and spirit of socialism, at least democratic socialism, was a very great sin. To be positively in favor of capitalism was a sacrilege so great that to seek forgiveness was useless. Even friends who continued to agree with me, I couldn't help noticing, would in their writings distance themselves from me even when taking positions close to mine. I would xii *Introduction to the Transaction Edition*

have been alone except for the fact that about the same time a handful of other former leftists was beginning to agree that the death of the socialist idea, at least in economics, was the most under-reported fact of the late twentieth century. After 1989, many more began to concede the point. And the problem for the "progressive" Left became, as a poster on Manhattan's West Side put it in 1991, What's Left of the Left?

Culture was left. The Left occupied most of the commanding heights of American culture by that time, in Hollywood, in the chief national television and newspaper news departments, in the most influential national magazines, in the universities, in the prestigious publishing houses (one or two excepted), in the great foundations such as Ford, Rockefeller, MacArthur, Pew, Mellon, and others, and even among most corporate executives who were likely to sit on the boards of symphonies, museums, operas, and theaters. Dinner table conversations in elite circles of American culture were likely to be in the grip of the latest animosities, enthusiasms, and hygienic speech codes of the Left. What *not* to say lest a dinner party be thrown into an uproar was always somehow clear.

I had begun noting in 1971 that people on the Left increasingly lived in one culture, people on the Right in another. (This process only got worse in the 1980s, and still deteriorates.) Certain exceptions are made for persons of proven social graces. A few on each side are allowed on certain polite conditions to penetrate the circles of the other. A few mischievous persons, knowing exactly where the limits are, could always light fuses by saying with feigned innocence in a leftwing crowd something kind about Reagan, the religious Right, Jesse Helms, or pro-life demonstrators; or, at a rightwing table, about Teddy Kennedy, Tip O'Neill, feminists, and how this country is taxed too little.

In the circles of the Left during this period, guests from the Right would feel like social climbers admitted to the inner sancta of this culture's movers and shakers. In the circles of the Right, guests from the Left would usually feel as though they were slumming. Reagan with his Hollywood glamour changed that a bit, but not much. The contempt for him at the heights was wonderful to behold. (Not that this really mattered. Clare Boothe

Luce once explained that a movie star who became president had an occupational advantage: Early in his career, a Hollywood veteran like Reagan had learned the difference between box office and the critics, and being secure in the former could cheerfully be kind to the latter.)

And yet something funny happened to *Unmeltable Ethnics* on the way from its basic thesis about the "new ethnicity" of the 1970s to the "multiculturalism" and "diversity" of the late 1980s. My friends in the university began to send menacing dispatches from the front saying that I had to do something, my book was being cited in favor of some of the absurdities they were now witnessing on campus in the name of "multiculturalism." From having been excoriated in 1972 for daring to divert attention from "blacks, women, and the poor" to such forbidden subjects as cultural diversity and "ethnics," by about 1992 I was being quoted in roughly the same quarters in support of that new beast called "multiculturalism." Setting aside the "honor" of the attribution, I abhor the new thing and disavow the allegation of paternity. A few important distinctions should not have been missed.

2. *The Culture Wars*

After the collapse of real existing socialism behind the Berlin Wall, "progressive" forces around the world had few alleys down which to retreat except cultural politics. They also had to confront the socialist miseries of many ill-conceived third world economies. (The third world economies that were not socialist were anticapitalist, without respect for law, and unfree.) Even their flirtation with "progressive" regimes that expressed contempt for democracy had to yield to the cold reality that, for all its faults, democracy is better at protecting the rights of the vulnerable than dictatorship, even when it is called socialist dictatorship. The bloody experiences of the twentieth century seemed to show conclusively that capitalism works better for the poor than socialism, and that democracy is safer for the poor than dictatorship. Having lost the economic and political argument, where's a progressive to turn? Culture is the only remaining broad boulevard, and it has the historical advantage of being still the monopoly of the Left, especially in the arts.

xiv   *Introduction to the Transaction Edition*

A top leader of the Socialist party in Chile explained this to me circa 1991: "Gramsci was right, to have based socialism on the bad economics of the nineteenth century was a mistake. The true politics of socialism is cultural politics." He asked me if the Socialist party of Chile could publish *The Spirit of Democratic Capitalism* under their imprint, to signal that the capitalist-socialist argument over economics is a thing of the past.

For the cultural Left, feminism, gay rights activism, and environmentalism arrived on the historical stage just in time. At root, radicals in such movements conceive of themselves as overturning the foundations of Western culture. One current of radical feminism takes aim at the Jewish and Christian Creator, not only because of the alleged patriarchy implied by the narrative of His self-revelation, but also because of the steadfast insistence of both Judaism and Christianity that the human body, and the bodily and other differences between man and woman, are of central importance. (Such differences are clearly important to the Creator: "Man and woman He made them," He reveals right near the top of the Book.) In Judaism and Christianity, gender differences point a way to the attainment of human happiness, and help establish a sense of right and wrong. The covenant between a man and a woman joined together by God in marriage participates in the covenant between God and His people. Radical feminists and gay activists are quite right to boast that in attacking Judaism and Christianity their project involves the most profound transvaluation of values since Nietzsche's Zarathustra. But feminists believe that Christianity established patriarchy in the West, whereas Nietzsche believed it feminized the West.

Environmentalists, similarly, try to overturn the Enlightenment. They disdain its Baconian conception of knowledge as power, its "phallic" conception of objective empiricism and objective reason, and its "macho" fetish for prediction, control, and self-distancing manipulation. Radical environmentalists have a pantheistic view of themselves as swimming oceanically in the warm womb of Mother Nature, being inwardly nourished by the whole universe.

In short, feminists and environmentalists (at least the most radical and metaphysically articulate among them) are returning to gnostic worldviews that predominated in the Mediterranean basin before the triumph of Judaism and Christianity, before the awareness of God as Creator (and God as Truth) had taken hold. Before, that is, the idea that humans are made in God's image, with a vocation to try to understand and to change the world—to bring out the potentialities hidden in it—had matured, and in its maturity generated in human consciousness the idea of progress. In that earlier nonprogressive time, the myth of eternal return held sway, the repetitive cycles of history were held to be as circular as the orbits of the stars and planets, and an unending New Age of oneness with all things was going nowhere in particular.

These days, cultural radicalism makes war on every sign of a judging God, a messianic order. In some quarters, it seeks to overcome the masculine with the feminine. In this, one can still hear echoes from the old "progressive" all-out war against capitalism as phallic, patriarchal, macho, insensitive, vulgar, alienating, and hostile to nature. Now, however, the argument is laid down upon aesthetic and cultural, rather than economic, foundations.

The new progressives are by no means relativists, although they often claim to be; on the contrary, they are authoritarians quite clear about where they are going, who their enemies are, what must be censored, and what may not be allowed to be thought. They are the farthest possible thing from relativists, although they do know how to use relativism as a weapon. Relativism in hand, they attack existing establishments. Once in power themselves, they make the world over *their* way.

While the university is perfectly willing to shelter the aggressive programs of radical feminism, gay rights, and environmentalism and even to show deference to them, it by no means finds it easy to construct a whole university program around such ideologies.

But "diversity" offers many other, cognate possibilities. As one who with a few others felt like lonely voices crying out in a desert in 1972 for some needed attention to the fact of ethnic diversity in America, I have been astonished to see the speed with which major universities of all sorts began caving in to the cry for "diversity" about 1985. "Diversity" and "diversity training" have become main themes for college bulletins, speeches by presidents and deans, curricular remodelings, separate admissions tracks, speech codes, college-wide sensitivity workshops, and financial priorities. Not much happened along this line during the seventies and early eighties but then, quite suddenly, women's studies, gay studies, black studies, and third world studies linked forces in order to establish a new university-wide ideology. In a nation whose motto is *E pluribus unum,* how could anyone resist potent political pressure coming from the *plures*?

Still, it is one of the anomalies of the new "multiculturalism" that not all ethnic groups need apply. Just as they were excluded before the early 1970s, the ethnics from Southern and Eastern Europe are again today given no place in curricula about "diversity." Ethnicity doesn't seem to matter, only race, sexual preference, and gender. Intolerance is the new agenda. It never occurs to the new "multiculturalists" that ethnic differences among Europeans alone—not to mention the diverse peoples of other continents—are full of passionate power, and heavy with political significance. All this lies beyond their own narrow, politicized agenda. In this respect, among others, multiculturalism as currently practiced in most universities is a fraud. (For vivid details, see among others Richard Bernstein's *The Dictatorship of Virtue,* Dinesh D'Souza's *Illiberal Education,* and James F. Garner's *Politically Correct Bedtime Stories;* all capture the new intolerance.)

3. Nine Perversions of "Multiculturalism"

The fraudulence of much that currently masquerades under the name "multiculturalism" results from gross perversions of the new ethnicity. The fundamental principles of the new ethnicity, as many of us then understood it, will be found below in the new Part IV of this edition (Chapters 11-16), based upon six essays of mine written during the long debate after the first edition of this book. Multiculturalism is a profound betrayal of these principles. In the current culture wars on campus, an explicit indictment of these perversions may be useful.

1. *Anti-Americanism.* Since it regards the West (at least its white males) as imperialistic, and America as the most advanced

face of the West, multiculturalism expresses hostility to American traditions and institutions, while glorifying non-Western cultures, especially those inimical to America.

2. *Victimology*. Multiculturalism tends to divide the world into a privileged set of victims and their alleged oppressors, through the lens of a loose and vulgar Marxism. This Marxism is cultural rather than economic.

3. *Ego-boosting*. The aim of multiculturalism is to boost "self-esteem" at the expense, if necessary, of facts.

4. *Evasion*. The assumption of multiculturalism is that its selected favorites cannot meet universal standards because of the evil actions of others; therefore, multiculturalism regards honest inquiry as pointless. It further pretends that its privileged groups are innocent. Having no awareness of "original sin," it is merciless toward others.

5. *Tactical Relativism*. Multiculturalism pretends to be "nonjudgmental," hiding behind the myth of moral equivalence, while it is in fact based upon harsh judgments about good and evil (and the oppressed and their oppressors).

6. *Censorship*. Since it regards inquiry as useless, criticism as malevolent, intellect as impotent, and reason as nothing more than a servant of power, multiculturalism protects its wishes through speech codes, the banning of books, and the shouting down of opposing voices.

7. *Groupthink*. Blind to the complex relations of individuals to the communities that nurture them, multiculturalism approaches people only as members of groups and, afraid of the creativity of dissenting individuals, imposes thought control by humiliating dissidents in public, and encourages its partisans to look to each other before speaking out.

8. *Egalityranny*. In the name of "equality" wrongly understood, multiculturalism focusses on groups, group outcomes, and group statistical profiles—in ways destructive of individual aspiration and achievement. Equality falsely construed (as uniformity) can scarcely be imposed upon the blooming, buzzing abundance of individual vitality—except through despotic methods.

9. *Double standards*. Multiculturalism is constituted by double standards. Multiculturalism basks in the supposition that there

are no universal standards by which individuals and cultures may be judged.

By contrast, the new ethnicity also recognizes that every human being is "rooted," and that each one's social history is important—but never forgets that the unlimited drive to ask questions (implanted in each of us) impels us toward the higher standards and aspirations possible to the human species as a whole, rather than to those of our particular group or culture. For the new ethnicity, it is human to be rooted; from whichever starting place destiny gives us, it is our vocation to fulfill *universal* standards—to give play to our capacity for universal sympathies, to our unlimited drive to ask questions, and to our unrestricted desire to know. Multiculturalism is moved by the *eros* of Narcissus; the new ethnicity is driven by the *eros* of unrestricted understanding.

To be sure, the diversity of human cultures is so great, and the nuances of difference are so many, that it is probably not possible to state a common faith (or moral code) in one set of abstract universal principles. On the other hand, so many basic elements of life are common to the human condition that there are likely to be "family resemblances" in the ways in which peoples deal with such realities as these: birth, growing up, falling in love, sickness, pain, striving and failure, marriage and having children, eating and drinking, betrayal, friendship, separation, death. All communication across cultures depends on such resemblances—on the analogical method—rooted in the fundamentals of human life. The search for analogies ("family resemblances") is more fruitful than the search for universal abstract statements of principle. Of many cultures, we are one species. We thirst to recognize our common humanity. The act of recognizing analogies awakens a natural desire for transcultural standards, such as might express our ultimate unity.

For such reasons, the study of other cultures is endlessly fascinating. It is so even as a way of gaining self-knowledge, since in others one may also discover unknown parts of oneself. Similarly, it takes more than a lifetime to appropriate (Latin, *ad* + *proprius,* to make one's own), that is, to internalize the riches of one's own heritage.

For centuries, humans have suffered, and from suffering have drawn wisdom. To absorb this precious wisdom requires respectful attention to the records of the past. One learns, as well, from evils committed in the past. The past records both: sins against wisdom, and wisdom painfully acquired. Let those whose ancestors are without sin throw the first stones. Let those without sin throw the first stone at their ancestors. My father once told me that people who boast about their ancestors are like potatoes—"the only good part of them is underground." Yet he urged us all to study history avidly. He warned us not to be surprised to find that our ancestors were in some things smarter than we. (That is probably a good definition of a conservative—one who believes that his grandparents were at least as good as he.)

When and if multiculturalism embraces truth—shows genuine respect for all (including dead white males)—and ceases to be intolerant toward any but the "politically correct," it may command some measure of respect. As long as its fundamental appeal is to its own moral superiority, intolerance, and coercion, it deserves to be met with contempt by those who seek to live under standards of evidence and truth.

4. *The New Immigration*

During the 1970s and 1980s, more *legal* immigrants came to the United States, not counting the illegal ones, than in any other decade of our history except two. Through immigration, in the 1970s and 1980s alone, the United States added a new population equivalent to those of Switzerland, Sweden, Denmark, and Norway combined. Nearly all these newcomers soon found jobs; some forty million new jobs were created during that period, and by the end of it a higher proportion of American adults was gainfully employed than at any earlier time in our history. Furthermore, most of these new immigrants were nonwhite. Their rapid success proved two points to most of the American public: the United States is still a haven for peoples capable of hard work and enterprise, regardless of color. And the new immigrants, so long as they stayed off welfare, resembled the old in their strong family life, spirit of enterprise, and love for their new land. Except for one thing: They succeeded, perhaps, even *more* quickly, often in one generation.

Here again, ethnic differences showed up in differential success patterns. Peoples who migrated from entrepreneurial or market cultures showed considerable talent in starting new small businesses of their own. Among these, to mention only a few, were the Cubans, the Koreans, the Vietnamese, the Chinese, many of the West Indians, and Middle Easterners. Those who came from peasant cultures (earlier, many of the Slavs) or welfare cultures (recently Puerto Ricans are the most conspicuous) did less well. The Asians influenced by Confucianism highly valued education and succeeded spectacularly, not least in fields such as mathematics, computers, and engineering, which many Americans these days find too demanding.

The lesson of the new immigration is that for immigrants America is still a great land, filled with opportunity and open to the future. Our institutions of liberty still work, as in days of old; newcomers continue to make good use of them. Moreover, since Americans are a planetary people coming from every place on earth, people from everywhere else actually "look" like Americans. A friend of mine told me, for example, how in China small crowds will still gather around a visiting American, while little children reach tentatively to touch his white skin; whereas a Chinese relative of hers, visiting in America, asked a stranger on the street for the time, and marvelled later how he was regarded as just another American.

For most ordinary Americans, then, the recent immigration renewed their faith in the nation's institutions and in its historical self-image. But many others began to worry about porous borders and *illegal* immigration. Here, though, the real source of concern appears to be the unwise "entitlements" of the welfare state, which ensnare some immigrants in patterns of dependency, while dramatically raising costs on other citizens. These patterns of dependency run against the self-reliance, hard work, and rapid climb out of poverty of most legal immigrants, today as yesterday.

I applaud the resistance to California's Proposition 187 in California in 1994 by Jack Kemp and Bill Bennett.[1] But there is also some weight to the argument that it is unfair to ask Californians to bear the whole welfare burden, especially of the illegal immigrants, when the failure to keep order at the borders is a federal failure. Immigration to America is a great source of strength for this country, but such immigration should be law-like, orderly, and managed for the common good. Consistent with those principles, we should err on the side of more rather than less openness to legal immigration.

The new immigration, however, was sometimes used by "multiculturalists" to discredit our own national traditions, by forecasting a third world ethnic and racial composition for our future population. These *forecasts* of future diversity were then used to justify a "multiculturalism" that borrows the logic of relativism in order to assault the tradition of *unum* that is as much a part of our nation's heritage as *E pluribus*. Rare are the nations on earth that hold to both the *unum* and the *plures* at once. Yet that is the glory of this "land of immigrants." We are many peoples; we are at the same time one people. That was the premise of *Unmeltable Ethnics*. I called the new version of this old principle "the new ethnicity."

The new ethnicity was based upon respect for truth, that is, a willingness to obey evidence. Today's "multiculturalism" has only a loose relation to truth. It aims at bolstering "self-esteem" (as if self-esteem could be helped by anything but truth), and practices a flagrant disregard of fact. It undermines canons of evidence and rational standards by dismissing these as Eurocentric. It pretends to be "nonjudgmental," but the one thing about which it is judgmental to the point of intolerance is any appeal to rational evidence. It pretends to rest upon "cultural relativism." It recognizes no transcultural standards for judging cultures as more or less adequate—for the support of institutions of liberty and the development of free men and free women, for example. Undercutting its pretense to relativism, it is aggressively hostile to certain cultures, chiefly our own, with its Jewish and Christian vision of the one and the many, the different peoples of the one Creator held to the same transcendent standards.

In upholding universal standards of reason and transcultural judgment, the Jewish and Christian conviction that there is one

Creator of all peoples is superior, I hold, to the Enlightenment's
conviction that reason alone is sufficient to its own defense. The
breakdown of the Enlightenment model provides evidence supporting that argument. For many Westerners in our century, the
massacres of World War I cast sufficient doubt upon the complacency of the Enlightenment. For others, what World War I
did not cast into doubt, World War II thoroughly undermined.
The concentration camps in the homeland of the Enlightenment
are unforgettable.

Be that as it may, the point remains that the new ethnicity
teaches us a certain humility before the truth. Each of us is born
from the womb of a single woman into a particular segment of
human experience, at a time, in a place, within a language and a
particular set of cultural symbols, beliefs, rites, gestures, emotional patterns, and a not-universal sensibility. Each of us is limited, singular, concrete. We are, none of us, Universal Man or
Woman. On the other hand, by virtue of our unlimited drive to
inquire, to seek understanding, and to open our capacity for sympathy, we are each in some way potentially open to the universality of our species. We can become self-critical, not only of
our private selves, but also of the limits and faults of our own
communities. We can learn from others, adopt new and better
(or worse) ways, and grow in our capacity for appropriating cultural riches from our own past traditions and also from traditions outside our own.

My father, for example, with no more than a sixth-grade education but a lifetime habit of reading history and culture, never
ceased to instruct his children to be grateful that our family had
come under the sway of English political and civil institutions
and the riches of the English language; he wanted us also to
cherish our Catholic and Central European heritage. He considered us lucky for both these gifts, and others, too, including the
opportunity to draw as much benefit as we could from the rich
cultural diversity surrounding us in America. He encouraged us,
too, to travel and to read, as if the whole world belonged to us—
as, in truth, in a way it does.

In a sense, my father thought, the Jewish people provide the
first model for the rest of us to learn from. Aware of being

Jahweh's chosen people, Jews have always been acutely aware of their own particularity. Yet Judaism also teaches us that Jahweh is the Creator of all, the seat of human universality. Providentially, the diaspora took Jews to virtually every nation on earth, and thus meditation on "the one and the many" has been a Jewish destiny. Often accused of "cosmopolitanism," Jews have been among the most universal of all peoples in their awareness of the world. Accused of "tribalism," they have also been among the peoples of the world best able to maintain in the most varied of circumstances a sense of special identity. Individual Jews, of course, like individuals among all peoples, are free to choose how much of these two poles they build their personal life around. In one respect, each of us is thrown into a destiny we did not choose for ourselves; that said, we choose to make of our lives what we will. Each of us is provident of our own destiny; in that way, too, made in the image of our Creator.

Analogously, the term "Catholic" means universal, and perhaps it is all too natural for those of us who are Catholic to think ourselves related to peoples in every nation and every era. "Tradition," the witty Catholic writer G. K. Chesterton once wrote, "is the democracy of the dead." Pluralism is the natural soil of our minds. A mere parochialism or blind nationalism is a stunting of the Catholic sensibility. (It occurs often, of course, but it is a deformity).

Because each of us is flesh and blood, none of us is Pure Reason, merely abstract, universal, and without particularity. Because we are also given intelligence and will, in God's own image, we are made for communion with all others on earth, yesterday, today, and forever.

How do such reflections apply to the American experience? America is not accurately described as a melting pot, a stew, or a salad. Those images are too static and material for a human reality. The metaphor of a symphony is better, for it is more appropriate to the human spirit. Imagining a symphony allows us to imagine each of us keeping our own identity and playing a unique melodic line, while those different from us follow a different (but related) score, the whole forming a unity that no one person or group alone could achieve. A symphony is more like our *E pluribus unum* than is an iron vat of molten metal; the melting pot destroys particular identities as a symphony does not. A symphony is dynamic, changing, drawing on instrumental variety in changing combinations and alternating movements. A stew or a salad simply sits there, getting soggy. A symphony, representing the fluidity of the human mind, is a subtle yet vivid musical metaphor for human reality.

In order to take an oath supporting the Constitution of the United States, for example, one does not have to endure having one's past traditions, one's heritage of faith and history, and one's special cultural and familial memory burned away, melted under great heat into unified shape. As in a symphony, one may remain what one is, while becoming a loyal and patriotic member of a new *unum*. It is a great and inhuman mistake to demand that we all melt into "non-hyphenated Americans." Those who wish to do that, of course, may do so. But they should not coerce the rest of us to become like them. They have no right to do that.

On the other hand, our oath to the *unum* requires that we surrender claims to territorial separatism; and even that we make a study of the rules, traditions, and habits in which our Constitution gains its concrete expression and reality. The Constitution comes alive in our lives or nowhere at all; otherwise, it is nothing but an old sheet of parchment marked with fading ink. Our rights, Madison warned, are not defended by parchment barriers but by the habits and associations of the American people. "One people, under God, indivisible," as the Pledge of Allegiance puts it. We pledge allegiance to the flag as a surrogate for "the Republic for which it stands." Where the Germans gain a sense of unity from their fatherland, the French from their language, the English from their Queen and their history and customs, the Americans find unity in a form of government. Take away the Republic and the deal is off. In that respect, we have every reason to stress our unity. We are otherwise free to be ourselves, in our solitude or in our chosen and/or inherited communities.

Nonetheless, it must be stressed that such understandings are not available in every culture on earth. In many places, today as in the past, "diversity" is a murderous, intolerant, self-aggrandizing arrangement, the war of all against all. To maintain a peaceable pluralism is not easy. Even the ideas that undergird success in that difficult project are many, complex, and not easy to grasp. To acquire, as well, the habits necessary, not only the ideas, is a truly long-term business. Allow me to mention just one basic principle to be both learned and lived: The conviction that none of us possesses the truth, but must each strive to be possessed by as much of the truth as we can learn, places us all under judgment. This sense of being under an undeceivable judgment (the all-seeing eye portrayed on the Seal of the United States) humbles us, and invites us to search for fragments of the truth in one another, and to learn from each other. Further, it commands us to open our sympathies to others. At the same time, it prepares us to expect to find prejudices and biases in ourselves that are unworthy of our best possibilities. Finally, it instructs us to admit to others our own limits and errors and sins when we become aware of them. In all these ways, it teaches us that we need each other, and that the country is not whole as long as some groups or individuals among us are not part of the common symphony.

It will be noted that this point of view is opposed to coercive "multiculturalism," on the one side, and to coercive mono-culturalism ("No hyphenated Americans need apply"), on the other side. Arthur Schlesinger has written an admirable and in some ways devastating critique of the errors of multiculturalism in *The Disuniting of America,* for example; nonetheless, at the other extreme, he tries to impose his own personal solution to the problem of particularity and universality—a kind of melting pot Americanism—on all of us. I do not deny him his own preference for his own life, but others in similar circumstances might well choose to make a more explicit claim to their own cultural heritage than he does. It would be good for the country if many did.

5. *Some Final Points*

Running through this book like a bright red thread is an anti-capitalist animus that reflects the way I thought about the world in 1972. I took a leave of absence from the State University of New York at Old Westbury to work to defeat Richard M. Nixon for the presidency, and ended up working for George McGovern's campaign office in an attempt to keep intact the old Democratic-Catholic ethnic alliance, especially in the major cities of the Northeast and Midwest. When Sargent Shriver entered the campaign as the Democratic vice presidential candidate, I happily shifted over to his speech-writing staff, having worked joyfully for him during his long effort in 1970 to help elect Democratic congressmen around the country. In 1970, I had travelled to some 39 states with Sarge; in 1972 I was on the campaign plane with him nearly continuously from mid-August until election night, even though my wife brought into the world our third child, Jana Marya, on August 20. (I was home, all too briefly, for that happy event.) It was a time of great stress and frantic activity—and great importance in my own intellectual life. It was a time of meeting the American people in neighborhoods, plants, meeting halls, picnic lots, and motel dining rooms all across the land. It was a time of dealing daily with the press, with political activists, and with party officials of every racial, religious, and ethnic background.

I thought of myself in those days as a radical, critical of the old liberals. My ideal political leader was Robert Kennedy, for whom I had campaigned eagerly in Oregon and California in 1968—and with whom I had been invited to spend what turned out to be the last day of his life in Los Angeles. I had declined because my wife was at home in Palo Alto with two young children under the age of three. (I shall never forget the horror of that night in 1968, which we watched in shock on television, or the heavy sorrow of the funeral at St. Patrick's church in Manhattan, and the long, long day of the burial.)

In 1972, I shared fully in the anticapitalist passions that moved many of us in those days, and these pages reflect that passion. Up to that point, I had not really studied comparative economic systems. I sympathized with the great theologian of that era, Paul Tillich, whom I had met at Harvard during the early 1960s, when he wrote that any serious Christian must be a socialist. My theological mentor (through his writings, of which I tried to read every word, even the vagrant journalism he had written in such abundance), Reinhold Niebuhr, had also once been a socialist and remained until his death nearly as

critical of capitalism as in his later years he became of socialism (except of the more benign social democratic variety). I
read avidly in leftwing journals. Having become a critic of the
war in Vietnam by 1967, for "just war" reasons, I had also
fallen into a too-easy criticism of the "system" that had made
that war seem logical even to "corporate liberals." I was trying
my best to be "a man of the left."

For cultural reasons, as the main argument of this text shows,
I was becoming increasingly critical of the national Left. Doubts
were growing in my mind. Possibly for this reason, I was all the
more energetic in emphasizing the radically anticapitalist views
that still enabled me to count myself a leftist. Moreover, in reading the immigrant, ethnic literature on which I was dwelling in
preparation for this book, I wanted to represent fairly the passionate criticism of the "capitalists" so common among those
ethnic workers in the labor union movement of the immigration
period, from about the 1880s right up into my own lifetime. My
intention in 1972, which I gradually fulfilled in later years, was
to read more deeply in economic history and economic analysis.
But at this point, the main shapers of my views were the strong
critiques of capitalism common in literary history (Matthew
Arnold, John Ruskin, Coleridge); in such philosophers as John
Dewey (in *Liberalism and Social Action*), Sidney Hook, and
Stuart Hampshire; in such Protestant theologians as
Rauschenbusch, Tillich, and Niebuhr; in Catholic writers such
as Leo XIII, Pius XI, Jacques Maritain, and G. K. Chesterton;
and in such journals as *Partisan Review, Dissent,* and *The Progressive.* I had not yet stepped back from this anticapitalist tradition to form a critical view of it. Nor had I even tried to hear
out the evidence on the other side, or to read the writers, such as
Friedrich Hayek, Ludwig von Mises, and Milton Friedman, who
offered a contrary analysis of the history of liberty.

I warn the reader of this new edition, therefore, to take with a
grain of salt the vivid and energetic criticism of capitalism that
is to be found on page after page of this account. When I encounter in others today such views as I once held and recorded
here, I wince with recognition and embarrassment for myself. (I
even write here, on p. 288, that "Already forty percent of the

earth's irreplaceable resources are consumed by Americans, who
are six percent of the earth's people"—a sentence I now find so
misleading as to be absurd. What did the world mean by "energy" before the founding of the United States except the power
in the muscles of horses, oxen, and the back? Whence came the
tide of innovation that led to the use of electricity, natural gas,
crude oil, and nuclear power?) It was so costless to be anticapitalist. It did not even require fair analysis. It seemed so sophisticated and independent-minded but on both counts it was in
fact the opposite. It is only, I see now, the usual bias of literary
and humanistic elites—and, often enough, a form of bad faith, a
pose that costs nothing while increasing a false self-esteem.

What eventually woke me up, I think, was the nagging thought:
If capitalism is so bad, why did my grandparents choose to come
here (many of their compatriots migrated to Latin America, Europe, Australia, and elsewhere), and why was this system, when
all was said and done, better than any of the alternatives elsewhere? And why were we so much better off than our cousins
who had stayed in Slovakia, under real existing socialism? Something real, concrete, and familial must have so far escaped my
attention. My conception of the American "system" prior to
writing this book was far too abstract and bookish to capture
many realities I knew in my own family. *Unmeltable Ethnics*
was the beginning of my own inner voyage "home," to discover
the true down-to-earth nature of the country, and the system of
which my family is now a part, as well as its exact place in
human destiny. Sooner or later, too, I would have to study the
meaning of the American experiment for my kinfolk in Central
Europe and in the rest of the world.

Curiously, Central Europeans were in the early 1970s becoming interested in these very questions. Scholars from Poland,
Ukraine, Hungary, Czechoslovakia, and other lands were de-
scending upon research institutes in the United States such as
the Immigration History Research Center at the University of
Minnesota to learn about their own "diaspora." The United States
contained the third largest Eastern European population (one
could say "Slavic" but some, like the Hungarians, are not of
Slavic background) in the world. Even under the Communists,

the Poles issued a translation of *Unmeltable Ethnics* under a distinguished imprint; and when I travelled to Poland to lecture on the subject in 1979, in time to see the stirrings that were soon to break out in the founding of Solidarnosc, I was even given a packet of royalty payments in zlotys. This two-week visit set the stage, I now believe, for the publication of my later book, *The Spirit of Democratic Capitalism* (1982) in an illegal underground edition bravely sponsored by Solidarnosc in 1984-85. That book, I am told, led to the speed with which in 1989 the new and free Polish leadership spoke so openly of "democratic capitalism," not socialism, as their new ideal.

A second brightly colored thread runs through this book that now seems to me quite wrong. In writing it, I was undergoing a profound emotional experience, trying to trace the emotional and imaginal roots of being Slovak in America, as distinct from what I had learned, happily enough, in the process of assimilation. I was, therefore, altogether too hard on "WASPs." Although it had occurred to me, as parts of this book show, that many poor white Anglo-Saxons shared many of the same, or at least analogous, experiences as white ethnics in coming to terms with the various American establishments, I had not really focussed on that fact. H. "Brandy" Ayers, publisher of the *Anniston Star* kindly took me aside one day and began to show me how being from the hollows of Alabama was in many ways like being from a steel town in Western Pennsylvania—even to being as passionate about Alabama football as about Notre Dame, Pitt, or Penn State, and for not dissimilar cultural reasons. Friends from West Virginia—Joe Duffey was one—made similar points. They were quite right, and this would have been a richer book if I had known enough to take up such matters prior to going to press. Some of the recent "evangelical-Catholic" political cooperation rests on these similarities, no doubt.

Of course, another thing I did not anticipate in writing this book was how quickly the so-called WASP establishment (which E. Digby Baltzell and others had helped me to understand) would soon lose its nerve and capitulate to the counterculture.[2] If I had had the faintest notion of how weak the WASP establishment actually was I think I would have rushed to shore up their resolve, written more kindly, even thanked them for the very good things they had done for all our sakes. In fact, in lecturing on the ethnic theme in the years after publication, I often found myself doing just that. For many students of white Anglo-Saxon background found themselves being attacked from all sides, under a constant battery of emotional intimidation, and were completely unprepared to handle it. Previously, their status in America, especially their moral status (to them, as perhaps to everyone, the most important form of status), had been unquestioned and needed no defense. Never having needed defenses before, they now lacked them. Too often, they were reduced to well-behaved but unpleasant silence, while the younger and less strong too easily pleaded guilty to whatever they were accused of. For all involved, this was unbecoming, intolerable, and morally repulsive.

Say what you will, the traditions of politics, discourse, and manners that all of us inherit from the British settlers of this nation are without equal in the civilized world. My father was always grateful that his father had chosen to bring his family under the sway of such civilizing traditions, and into a language as vivid, concrete, rich, and beautiful as English. What other "establishment" in the world carried within itself so many blessings of liberty rightly understood? In which are daily customs and the common law more commonsensical, and the manners more civil?

Even in the strenuous effort to discern what differentiated being Anglo-Saxon from being ethnic, I was taking for granted the great virtues of the Anglo-Saxons. At the time, it did not seem necessary to make that explicit; it seemed, rather, in order to get a hearing at all, and in order not to seem fawning, that I needed to keep silent about such virtues. In retrospect, soon after writing the book, I began to feel as though I should have praised Anglo-American culture more clearly and fully, even if I did not dwell on it. Fairness demanded it; truth demanded it.

A third matter. On not a few occasions in this book, I forced myself to insert some fairly crude passages and locutions. Ripped out of context, as occasionally reviewers have ripped them, these passages embarrass me. In fact, even in context they embarrass me. Still, they were there for a reason, or rather, two reasons. One fault of upper-class Anglo-American speech, if it is a fault, is that it is so given to circumlocution, the avoidance of pain and unpleasantness, and repugnance at the direct expression of vulgarity and crudity. That this is not true of lower-class English speech is plain in theater and fiction, and even more so at a soccer match when the "hoodlums" have too many beers. But it is upper-class English manners that govern an American sense of propriety, not lower-class. Listening to the radio one day, my eleven-year-old daughter once asked me: "Daddy, are all English people rich?" "What makes you say that?" I asked. She nodded toward the voice on the radio: "They all talk like rich people."

The immigrant experience, by contrast, was quite raw, bodily, vulgar, even coarse. To be sure, mothers and aunts, school teachers, nuns, and educated men worked overtime to raise the levels of immigrant manners. But the crudity remains vivid in memory. And it had its plain, down-to-earth value. Many a scene in American literature after the arrival of the immigrants has an immigrant who knows better erupting in some verbal tirade or indecent act in order to run a bull through the China shop of stuffy upper-class decorum. Such a tirade is meant to shock. It is meant to be a declaration of independence. It is meant to announce, by a jiu-jitsu of manners, a certain cultural superiority: "We are closer to earth than you! Take that, you effete palefaces! This is how redblooded Indians feel passion, and don't you wish you could!" Obscurely, I felt then, in writing the first edition, that without this note my account would not catch an entire dimension of experience. The fact that it still embarrasses me indicates that children of immigrants live between two worlds. But so also have Jacksonian Democrats and frontiersmen of all backgrounds lived between two worlds. America, like all other nations, *is* two worlds, upstairs and downstairs.

I recommend to anyone who would like a taste of the earthy language of western Pennsylvania even today the novels of the pseudonymous mystery writer, K. C. Constantine. For a vivid account of life in Pittsburgh two generations earlier, read Book-of-the-Month Club author Thomas Bell (Belejak), *Out of This*

Furnace (University of Pittsburgh Press). For an account of the worst massacre in American labor union history until that time, at Lattimer Mines (the home of Jack Palance), near Hazleton, in 1897, I recommend without feigned modesty my own study *The Guns of Lattimer* (Basic Books, 1976, new edition from Transaction Books, forthcoming).

There are other faults in this book that I trust readers will overlook, or treat generously, in discerning its central theme: the growing alienation of liberal elites from the masses of liberal voters who once gave them their great Rooseveltian majorities. Of the three pillars of the Roosevelt majority that governed America for the sixty years after 1932, only the Jews (mostly) remain comfortably Democratic. As I note in this book, already in the early 1970s the Catholic ethnics were being pushed aside by arrogant elites and were well on their way to becoming "Reagan Democrats." In the 1980s, the Southern evangelicals—the so-called Christian Right, which used to be known as "yellow dog Democrats" ("I'd rather be a yellow dog than vote Republican")—were beginning to vote Republican. The liberal "superculture" that I first tried to delineate in this book has succeeded in isolating itself in its high positions of cultural power, precipitating the "culture wars" that now sweep our fair land. Much of this could have been avoided. But, then, cultural arrogance would have had to be set aside, and that doesn't happen often in human history.

At the heights of cultural power in the United States—the television networks, the major national newspapers and news magazines, the movies, popular comedy, pop music, the universities, the worlds of art—liberal power is pretty well unchecked. Since the worldview and sensibilities of "sophisticated" elites are still splitting ever farther apart from those of less connected Americans, including white ethnics and evangelicals, the main thesis of this book remains valid, perhaps even more so than in 1972. That thesis is twofold: first, that such a gap is destructive to the country, and second, that ordinary Americans have much to teach their putative betters. Our elites are out of touch, in a world of their own.

It cannot be said, finally, that I did not heed my own advice. After completing this book, I set out to understand this country better and, in particular, to try to see it from the point of view of the experience of ordinary people, including an appreciation for what they so admire in it. Being an intellectual in America meant for quite a long time joining what Lionel Trilling called an adversarial culture. Beginning with this book, I was becoming ever more suspicious of the adversarial culture which still had a powerful hold over me. Many sentences in this book display the sort of learned disdain I cherished for many American institutions. Nonetheless, I had begun to move in a new direction. I was obscurely trying to imagine a new politics of family and neighborhood and what were to become known as "mediating structures." I was trying to close the gap that would later become known as the "culture wars." I was trying to awaken the Democratic party to the coming disaffection of the soon-to-appear "Reagan Democrats." In all these fumbling attempts, I was making many mistakes of analysis, which I trust readers today will be able to discern as well as I.

It is quite true that this book, and others like it at that time, did awaken later in the 1970s far more attention to "roots," to the planetary composition of the American people, to the diverse riches of our pluralistic culture, and specifically to the Catholic "ethnics" themselves. Major companies, such as AT&T, began to run television ads depicting the diverse nations around the world to which real American families are tied by family connections. American blacks began referring to themselves in ethnic rather than racial terms as "African Americans." The effort of a few backlash politicians like Mayor Frank Rizzo of Philadelphia were foiled in their attempts to drive a wedge between the races during the 1970s, when white ethnic and black leaders joined forces to thwart them under the umbrellas of the new ethnicity and pluralistic coalition-building. The Project in Group Pluralism sponsored by the American Jewish Committee, ably led by Irving Levine, played a great role in this, as did the National Center for Urban Ethnic Affairs led by Monsignor Geno Baroni (later Assistant Secretary for Housing and Urban Development under Jimmy Carter).

Meanwhile, even more so than in the 1970s the Catholic ethnics remain the most potent swing vote in American presidential politics. By historical accident, they are concentrated in the ten largest states in the electoral college. They are regular voters, voting in higher proportion than any other group but the Jews (whom they outnumber nearly ten to one). And in statewide races for presidents, senators, and governors they swing back and forth between Democrats and Republicans in unusually large proportions. In many of the largest states the Protestant vote dominates in the small towns and rural areas, while the Catholic vote is strongest in the urban and surrounding suburban areas. In order to win in most of these states, Republican candidates don't have to win the Catholic vote outright—all they generally need is to keep the Catholic vote below about 56 percent. In presidential elections since 1952, for example, here are the winners and their proportion of the Catholic vote: in 1952 Eisenhower (44); in 1956 Eisenhower (49); in 1960 Kennedy (78); in 1964 Johnson (76); in 1968 Nixon (33);[3] in 1972 Nixon (52); in 1976 Carter (57); in 1980 Reagan (47); in 1984 Reagan (61); in 1988 Bush (52); and in 1992 Clinton (44). (In 1992, Perot took 20 percent of the Catholic vote, Bush 36 percent.)

Both for cultural and for political reasons, therefore, the significant body of Americans who have cultural roots in Catholic lands—Irish, German, Italian, Slavic and other central or eastern European, and Latin (French, Hispanic, Portuguese, Caribbean)—are worth studying. Their ties with the history of Western civilization, as well as with important world populations today, are of great benefit to the United States. Indeed, Alexis de Tocqueville suggested that the Catholic peoples in America might one day be of extraordinary importance to the articulation and defense of this nation's founding ideals. As my friend Richard John Neuhaus puts it in *The Catholic Moment,* that time may now be arriving. To fulfill Tocqueville's hopes would be a splendid way for "the ethnics" to express their gratitude for this blessed land.

MICHAEL NOVAK

Washington, D.C.
Presidents' Day, 1995

Notes

1. Proposition 187 was a referendum on the ballot in California that banned illegal immigrants from receiving nonemergency social benefits from the state. It was symptomatic of a growing resistance to immigration in some quarters.
2. I had never heard the term "WASP" before arriving at Harvard Divinity School in 1960, and there it was not used pejoratively except perhaps in self-mockery. It has become an ethnic slur in some usages.
3. In the three-way race of 1968, Nixon lost the Catholic vote to Hubert Humphrey by a margin of 59 percent to 33 percent, but managed to squeak out a victory, since much of the Southern Protestant vote went to George Wallace. In 1972, however, Mr. Nixon's 52 percent broke the Democratic lock on the Catholic vote. All percentages are from Gallup, except those of 1988 and 1992, which come from the exit polling of the consortium of the four major television networks, the Voter Research and Surveys.

Preface
to the
Paperback Edition

"The ethnic problem within the United States at some point has to emerge simply because we were lied to, accepted the lie, and there is no greater danger to a man than when he fools himself. We expect the opposition to fool us; but when we fool ourselves we are in deep trouble. We consistently have fallen for the old melting-pot concepts. But there never was a melting pot; there is not now a melting pot; there never will be a melting pot; and if there were, it would be such a tasteless soup that we would have to go back and start all over!"
—Bayard Rustin (April, 1972).

By coincidence, James T. Farrell, the novelist, and Alfred Kazin, the critic, lectured jointly in New York about the time this book was published. Mr. Farrell exclaimed: *"The melting pot was essentially an Anglo-Saxon effort to rub out the past of others* and turn Europe into a place where people didn't speak English . . . . *Before Sherwood Anderson, who first celebrated the beauty of difference, everything was judged by the norm,* and characters in literature did not 'talk different' from the genteel WASP tradition." Mr. Kazin added: *"Ethnicity as a something larger than self, making the self a bridge to the*

past, is very important . . . . culturally the ethnic groups
are now the richest and most interesting. If any group is
to be pitied, it is perhaps the 'WASPS,' who find their
books reviewed in the back pages of the *New York Times
Book Review*." [Emphasis added.]

During 1972, every major magazine carried long analyses of "the ethnic vote." New magazines concerned with
ethnicity are springing up; new ethnic museums and
archives, new ethnic curricula, are under way.

Movies like *The Godfather* fascinate huge audiences,
not solely by their violence (for it is easy to fill a cowboy
movie or a cops-and-robbers movie with uninteresting
violence). They fascinate because of the "glimpse behind
the curtains": a look into what it is like to live a different
way of life, to perceive oneself and the world in a different way—complete even to a distinctive system of honor
and justice, a "brotherhood" *within* a large and diverse
ethnic tradition. The movie revealed aspects of American
life never before glimpsed by the public—and it revealed,
incidentally, some of the ways in which Anglo-American
systems of justice and power excluded other ethnic groups
and led some of their members to fall back on their own
resources. It revealed a thick and dense family life, so
different from the Anglo-Saxon cult of the individual. It
revealed concepts of loyalty, honor, direct violence, and
obedience not Anglo-Saxon.

The Swedish movie, *The Emigrants*, indicates that
many scholars and artists abroad are beginning to wonder
what led some of their own people, years ago, to leave
for America; and to inquire who left, why, and what happened to them here.

So something new, and large, and deep is happening—
and not only in this country.

Reactions to the hardcover edition of this book abundantly proved its point. Some reviewers and some of the
radio and television announcers who kindly invited me on
their shows really *hated* the idea of the book. To some,
ethnicity is dirty. They think of it as a source of evil.

(They themselves were in almost every case not happy to recall their *own* ethnicity. They had fought their way out of backwardness and inhibition and were, happily now, members of that enlightened "superculture" that is beyond any subculture. "All that's behind me," they seemed to say. "The world I'm in now is better.")

The point of the book is to raise consciousness about a crucial part of American experience. Its aim is to involve each reader in self-inquiry. Who, after all, are *you*? What history brought *you* to where you are? Why are you different from *others*—have you noticed the ways in which you *are* different?

There is no such thing as *homo Americanus*. There is no single culture here. We do not, in fact, have a culture at all—at least, not a highly developed one, whose symbols, images, and ideas all of us work out of and constantly mine afresh; such "common culture" as even intellectuals have is more aspired to than accomplished. There is the *appearance* of sameness, because we dress the same, are subject to the same national media, seem to speak and look and walk the same. Standing in front of a crowded lecture hall, a speaker can scarcely single out ethnic differences. *Such differences as we have,* apart from race, *are mainly internal.* And not so much in our *ideas* or even in our *words,* but in our affections and imaginations and historical experiences: in those concrete networks in which ideas and words are given concrete reverberation, rootage, and meaning. The word "quota" has a different history among Jews, Blacks, and Poles. Attitudes of soul like "rebellion," "obedience," "morality," "loyalty," have a different shape in different cultural traditions: contrast George Meany's use of such words with George McGovern's.

In marriages between members of diverse ethnic groups, important emotional cues are often missed. He's silent; *she* interprets that as coldness, while he thinks it's manly self-restraint. He rages and screams; she's terrified, not knowing that he's not even disturbed, merely immediate and expressive. She broods; he becomes anxious, not knowing that womanly pensiveness, restraint, and "bearing burdens in silence" were taught her by every woman around her in her childhood, whereas in his family women yelled. So it also happens in labor union negotiations, in job interviews, in humor and irony, in death or in times of trouble, in anger or in lovemaking, in childbearing, and in political symbols: ethnic cues that are almost totally unconscious lead us to misunderstand one another.

The new ethnic consciousness embodied in this book delights in recognition of these subtle differences in the movements of the soul. It is not a call to separatism but to self-consciousness. It does not seek division but rather accurate, mutual appreciation.

Our personal likes and dislikes, our signals of delight and warning signals, our inhibitions and expressiveness—these are developed in us not only by our individual effort, but also by the social and cultural traditions in which we were reared. Even our rebellion is shaped by its inherited nemesis. Long before the individual *chooses* such things, he or she is being led into them both consciously and unconsciously by family and others.

Most often Americans are taught that differences are *bad*; that we should refuse to be *stereotyped*; that each of us is a unique *individual*, and *not* merely a member of a group. So the new ethnic consciousness makes many uneasy. "I guess I'm just not very ethnic," some say. "I'm just your ordinary run-of-the-mill nothing," others say. "I don't see why all these people just can't become Americans like everybody else," George McGovern is reported to have said in exasperation, at a meeting of ethnic leaders in Cleveland . . . . But the more one thinks about it, the more obvious America's diversity becomes: the more obvious it becomes that you yourself, dear reader, are part of a tradition, part of a culture, not infinite and not universal but incarnate, limited, of modest scope.

Many British-Americans, I have found, are just as alarmed at the perishing of British-American culture in America under the pressures of the superculture as are members of any other ethnic group. But other British-Americans simply take it for granted that the customs, language, and school curricula of this country are mainly British-American; this, to them, isn't "ethnic," it's natural. No one has ever pointed out to them their own ethnicity, and its varieties.

Other Americans have suffered historical amnesia; consciously, at least, they are rootless, without cultural memory, loyal to no tradition or project; their purpose in life, so far as they know, is to please themselves. Still others (especially the highly educated members of superculture) have been diligently taught that ethnicity is the source of evil and so they should be as universalist as possible, stressing not human diversity but human unity, struggling to attain a liberal, enlightened attitude of "openness" and "love."

Here "the tradition of enlightenment," a kind of cosmopolitanism grounded in the disciplines of education (especially higher education), creates a specific, distinctive state of soul, very *like* that of a new sort of ethnic group. It engenders a cast of mind, a set of cues, an historical memory, a set of approved stories to live out. Even so, ethnic differences remain telling: contrast English and French philosophy, for example, or "the Jewish novel" in the United States, the Anglo-American novel, the Irish-American novel. As for prejudice, the feelings of the "enlightened" toward the "unenlightened" often preclude discussion.

Thus the consciousness of the enlightened can properly be expanded. Diversity is not the major threat faced by the human race, or by America. One may still be enlightened *and* recognize ethnic diversity (one's own included). Then one will even be *more* enlightened. The view that we shall all become one by becoming *like* each other, more "Americanized," is not really an enlightened view; it requires a system of inhibitions and emotional repressions. The view that we are all *individuals*, and that it is what we do as individuals that matters, flies in the face of social science, not to mention daily experience. Of course, each individual is unique; what each does with his or her ethnic heritage is up to each; but well before such choices are made, the individual finds himself or herself already *thrown*: fate has provided many inescapable givens. These are not occasions for despair. They are gifts. They are roots. They are our material, our concrete limits, our purchase on a finite, real, *earthy* earth—our liberation from the land of pure spirits, disembodied presences, and gnostic hoverings. Through flesh and blood we are conceived in one single womb, thus given earthly and finite shape, launched in a particular cultural tradition. We are given incarnation.

Ethnicity is not a matter of genetics; it is a matter of *cultural transmission*, from family to child. *The new ethnicity is a form of historical consciousness.* Who are you? What history do you come from? And where next? These are its questions.

I wish I had done some things better in this book. For one thing, it surprised me to find out from others that I was hard on British-Americans. (At the Harvard Divinity School, about 1960, I first heard the term "WASP," and then it was a good word; recently, it has begun to hurt— like other ethnic nicknames. I wish I had realized that in time and had used "British-American" in its place.) Re-reading my words as British-Americans would read them, I see that I should have been much more gentle. Still, I was writing down emotions I had not known I shared, not personal feelings either, but general, cultural ones, and it seemed to me important to record those as part of the ethnic consciousness that is my theme. Many Southern and Eastern Europeans have told me how they share these sentiments, long repressed: not personal bad feelings, but the result of cultural collision. It is well for their existence to be known, and their shape to be accounted for. I do not find, so far, that any of my specific judgments require revision; in every case brought to my attention the words are clear and sufficiently modified in context. It is the accusing *tone* that troubles many; but the words, in their literal qualification, stand.

It must be hard to be a British-American male, and have Indians, blacks, women, and now even white ethnics voice long-repressed grievances. That must be the last straw.

Secondly, I wish I had said more about the Irish—and different kinds of WASP (Georgia sharecropper, Iowa hardware-store owner, Massachusetts carpenter, Pennsylvania farmer)—and the Scandinavians—and Germans—and Hasidic Jews—and many others. When I wrote the book, the word "ethnic" was a pejorative word, or else it meant "colored minorities" (Indians, Blacks, Chicanos). I didn't even want the publisher to use it in the title. But, suddenly, it's an "in" word. Everybody wants to be one. Everybody complains that I left them out.

Well, really, the Irish *are* amply present in this book. Father Greeley tells me I don't understand the Irish very well. The Irish don't understand me very well, so that's all right. But, as I say in the text, politically speaking, the Irish are in some respects in the same situation as the Southern and Eastern Europeans on whom I concentrate. Indeed, many of the best interpreters of this book have been Irish: they see exactly what I mean, perhaps all the more plainly because I am not talking about them. Since Andrew Greeley was already at work on *That Distressful Nation*, I saw no need to attempt what I could only do imperfectly. Besides, among other Catholic immigrants, the Irish have had a triply blessed inheritance: the English language; a brilliantly useable literary tradition; and a thousand-year experience in penetrating the dissimulations of Anglo-Saxon politics. I felt there was no point in competing with William Shannon, Daniel Moynihan,

Jimmy Breslin, Pete Hamill, Joe Flaherty, and even John Leonard (*Crybaby of the Western World*)—not to mention James Farrell's *Studs Lonigan,* Edwin O'Connor, J. F. Powers, Thomas Kenneally, Tom McHale, Elizabeth Cullinan, and over yonder, James Joyce, W. B. Yeats, Brendan Behan, Conor Cruise O'Brien, Sean O'Faolain, and Frank O'Connor.

It is, rather, the Southern and Eastern Europeans who are most neglected in American consciousness. My shelf of Italian-American literature is growing rapidly; and my favorite there is Mario Puzo's *The Fortunate Pilgrim.* The Slavs—and some others—remain virtually silent. Besides, to render their experience, one who has shared it is required. No doubt this is why the more inward-looking passages in this book, autobiographical or quasi-autobiographical, have been the most highly praised.

On the other hand, autobiography wasn't enough. One day on a platform, an American Indian was telling a group of Polish nuns and me what our ancestors did to *his* ancestors. I tried gently to remind him that *my* grandparents (and theirs) never *saw* an Indian. They came to this country after that. Nor were they responsible for enslaving the blacks (or anyone else). They themselves escaped serfdom barely four generations ago—almost as recently as blacks escaped slavery. Their experience of America is not the same as that of Blacks, or Jews, or Indians, or Germans, or Swedes, or the Irish, or Welshmen, or Scots, or Chinese. *Each* group has come to a different America, and each brought with it a different history. The tides of those differences still move in our blood and glands and stomachs (to speak metaphorically; for these are but symbols for imagination and sensibility and affections). So I had to do some historical exploration, too (Chapters Three and Five).

So painful and shattering was the break from loved ones in Europe, so ugly the long crossing in small, crowded ships, and so humiliating the early attempts to learn a new way of life and a new language and new

forms of emotion (in public, at least), that many descendants of immigrants suffer from cultural amnesia. Their
relatives do not speak often of "what it was like." Each
year, more and more witnesses go silently into the grave,
unheard. In school, one learns almost nothing about the
cultural traditions of one's own family. Even in anthropology classes, one is likely to study the cultures of New
Guinea but not the cultures of Hamtramck or Lowell, of
Hasidism in Williamsport, or of the Italians of Newark.
No wonder, for so many, education is unreal, about
"others," irrelevant.

So a certain new approach to American history is
called for.

Then again, besides autobiography and history, analysis
of the present sociopolitical situation was required. I desperately wanted the Democratic party to recognize that
in between the "old politics" of the ageing bosses and
union leaders and the "new politics" of the college educated there is a vast body of voters who believe in an
American dream (whose benefits they have *experienced*);
who know that that dream has not yet been fulfilled; and
who are vigorously ready for a new progressive politics.
They do not believe the "new politics" is progressive. They
believe that McGovernism (or whatever other-ism another leader of the new politics would have given us) is
basically a cover for class interests and self-aggrandize-
ment.

The new educated class—or, at least, its Left Wing—
would like to run the country *its* way. It thinks it knows
what is best, most enlightened, most humane for all of
us. But others perceive its faults as well as its virtues; and
they do not trust the new class. Of course, this new class
has defined all issues in such a way that if you are not
for them, you are not for humanism or even for humanity.
They supply many loyalty tests and purity tests. At Miami,
in 1972, they threw Mayor Daley out—*he's* not a pure
enough Democrat for them. Well, okay, if *he* isn't a
Democrat, let the purists win it by themselves.

I had hoped the Democrats would avoid this unnecessary insult to their most steadily progressive, most loyal constituency. More than that, I had hoped that the leaders of the new politics would be intelligent enough to see the class basis of their ideology, and would recognize in time that they were deluding themselves and others. All their talk about morality, humanism, and conscience is a cover for their own interests and way of life—fair enough. But they, above all, should have the perspicacity to criticize themselves and to be more generous in their approach to national politics. At least, if they want to lead the whole nation. They were mesmerized by favorite images—the image of the radical student, of the vulnerable flower child, of the militant black—and defined the political situation from this most biased angle. All those who did not agree they called forces of fear, irrationalism, and racism. Even after the election, George McGovern did so, as well as Anthony Lewis and Jack Rosenthal of the *New York Times* and countless others.*

To my chagrin, Richard Nixon seemed quicker than the Democrats to identify effectively the enormous political vacuum in urban ethnic America—in all the great cities that normally send our most progressive congressmen, senators, and presidents to Washington. George McGovern made the election a referendum on the new class and its sympathies for the counterculture. The effective symbols of the new class were expressed in the dress and bearing, for example, of Gary Hart, McGovern's campaign manager, who at times was seen more often on television than the candidate; expressed, too, in the casual, mod organizational style of the McGovern "machine"; and, on a day-to-day level, expressed in the dress, manner, and inexperience of the young men and women who served as his "advance persons." The election was decided

---

* On matters of current comment, my regular column in *The Commonweal* gives a clearer, fuller statement than I can make here.

by the process of nomination. It was child's play for Nixon to draw a broad contrast, both in deed and in speech, between most Americans and the superculture (and its mirror image, the "counterculture").

Still, by every measure, people did not like Nixon, trust him, or in voting for him support either his vision of America or his party. Many reported that he was "the lesser of two evils." Forty-five percent of the voters did not vote. Democratic candidates at every other level did unusually well. The results, in a word, confirmed the argument of this book: *viz.*, that the urban ethnic is basically progressive, in national politics independent, and alienated from both the corporate power of the Right and the media power of the Left. He feels abandoned, in a vacuum, with no one to speak for him. He waits for leadership—and perhaps for a party.

George Wallace, too, recognizes this vacuum. As a protest candidate and a gutsy man willing to face the superculture toe-to-toe, he wins support he could not win if the political vacuum were not there. His British-American and rural ways, his anti-labor record, his lack of sophistication—all these in a non-primary election, make his support among urban ethnics wither. There are political tracts that refer to some urban ethnic congressional districts as "Wallace country," because in 1968 Wallace received some 9 or 13 or 18 percent of their vote; in the same election, Hubert Humphrey received 58 or 68 or 78 percent. Except for widespread bias against ethnics, these districts would properly be called "Humphrey country" or "Kennedy country." Almost always they are far to the left compared to most American districts. It is benignly overlooked that most of Wallace's support—even in Wisconsin, Michigan, and Maryland—is nativist American.

McGovern himself talked about "the Wallace voters" as if they were responsible for his defeat. But one out of three Wallace voters voted for McGovern. Nixon's total margin çannot be accounted for by his margin over McGovern in the Wallace vote. The Left thinks it is anti-establishment. But urban ethnics think the Left is the establishment—or one major wing of it. Thus urban ethnics saw no one to whom to give their vote with enthusiasm, no one speaking to their needs, no one enunciating a politics that would make their lot better. McGovern seemed much more Protestant and rural and out of touch than Nixon did. So they gave a weak vote for McGovern, refused to vote at all, gave a reluctant vote for Nixon, or (in some few cases) converted to Nixon. Some urban ethnics, of course, especially among Italians, have long been Republican.

So now the decks are cleared again. The new ethnic consciousness extends to many more issues than to those of partisan politics. It includes every other ethnic group besides those I concentrate on here. Still, either the Democratic party or the Republican party—or some new Christian Democratic or Center or other party—will some day create a politics that strengthens the family and the neighborhood; that is serious about the civil rights involved in being safe in life and limb; that rewards integration rather than punishes it; that gives dignity and respect to laborers and service workers; that promotes a practical dollars-and-cents coalition between working blacks and working whites; that defines political issues like busing in terms of class rather than in terms of race; and that makes the economic practices of this nation, in taxation and welfare and wages and insurance and prices, more equitable. Some party will do these things because they must be done, because millions want them to be done, and because they are right.

Thus will the cultural movement of the new ethnicity— a movement primarily of personal and social identity— also become a political movement of major importance in America's history.

MICHAEL NOVAK

December 7, 1972

Preface

THE DECISION TO go ahead and write this book caused me several months of internal struggle. It is so much easier in America to forget one's ethnic past, to climb upwards into an elite culture, to become a "new man" without connection to a past. Who wants to become known as a "Jewish" writer, a "Catholic" writer, a "Slovak" writer? Lurking in such epithets is a concession of failed generality.

Why, too, ally oneself with many who are uneducated, virtually inarticulate, prejudiced, and prejudiced against? Is not the chief political battle of our time drawn up between the enlightened and the unenlightened?

I decided, finally, that the time had come. Polarization has gone too far. Prejudices and misperceptions wound too many people.

Many of us will have to step into this new no-man's land. My experiences around the nation with Sargent Shriver during the congressional elections of 1970 convinced me that many people were hungry for a new politics, and that that politics would entail a new direction for the Left.

Many misunderstandings will arise. I have tried my best to anticipate them. It was impossible to deal with every possible misunderstanding at each assertion; some clarifications had to be put off until a later context. I urge the reader to push on to the end before letting out a scream. Experience indicates that prejudice runs very deep.

Many of good will seem almost deliberately to misperceive. Many others have never noted the contours of their own ethnic tendencies.

Educated liberal Protestants are the most deprived in this respect. They take their own power, status, and sense of reality for granted, as no others in America can. As I write, I see the faces of friends and associates I much admire. I do not want to assert that *all* WASPS show the characteristics I am going to mention. I do not even wish to assert that *any* WASP allows these characteristics to dominate his conduct. My assertion is only that a distinctive set of attitudes competes with other attitudes in most WASPS, a set of attitudes that non-WASPS have learned to detect in WASPS as in no others, a set of attitudes which perhaps many WASPS are aware of and try to control or dissipate. These attitudes have great positive value. They also have an underside that is not so lovely, not so pleasant for those on the receiving end.

I recognize that in the last few years WASPS have been under heavy fire. I sense much suffering from self-doubt, intimations of past guilt, uncertain allegiance to previously solid ideals. In the search for a new identity, WASPS have been reduced to equality with other ethnic groups. And all WASPS are not alike.

WASPS often struggle to moderate the ill effects of their best qualities; namely, their strong moral sense and their vulnerability to guilt feelings. There is in WASPS a vein that urges some to make their latest revelations normative. They try so desperately to be moral that they easily confuse their earnestness with morality itself. When they become relativists or situationists, that, too, becomes a criterion others now must meet. When they at last come to see the sins of America, they must confess them loud-

est. Thus we have the spectacle of quite marvelous Quaker
ladies, the paragons of early America, now hissing their
disdain for the nation's corruption—as if to dissociate
themselves from it. Whatever is moral, *that* WASPS thirst
to be. Seeing that others are less morally concerned, they
cannot hold back too long an irrepressible condescension.
In moral competition, WASPS always win. Ethnics, for
example, who were once not American enough, are now
too American; WASPS are consistently correct.

It is a mixed tribute to educated liberal Protestants that
one can count upon them to recognize some new guilt in
themselves almost monthly, annually at least. Pilgrim's
progress never ends. My own feelings toward them are
hopelessly complex—tangled admiration, compassion,
friendship, and dismay. I know in advance that persons
of their generosity will try to see my point and be converted accordingly. Of no other group, perhaps, is such
self-criticism and plasticity to be expected; there seems to
be no limit to their willingness to "update" their moral
sensibilities. On the other hand, *plus ça change, plus la
même chose.* Subtly, those who have recognized the new
insight become superior to those who haven't. Suscepti-
bility to feelings of guilt is unchanging.

Martin Marty has described the history of America as
that of "a righteous empire." This righteousness characterizes liberals, conservatives, and radicals across the American spectrum under a variety of regional, denominational,
and ethical styles. A sense of moral superiority is signalled
in a thousand ways. Only through perceiving them can one
learn how to interpret Protestant insights and concerns.
Equally, one must discern one's own sensibilities.

My long-term aspiration in the field of religious studies
is to present it in a systematic treatment—a contemporary equivalent of what used to be called "systematic
theology." The nugget of my systematic idea has been
with me as long as I can remember. It is to attend to the
imaginative, perceptual, and affective sides of human
consciousness, to what I have called "intelligent subjec-

tivity."[1] Over the years I have been slowly working out a language, poor and inadequate at best, for talking about what happens when human beings act. I am fascinated by instincts, emotions, images, hardly articulable ways of feeling, the movements of the stomach, habits, traditions: the organic networks of actual human life transmitted from generation to generation. Intelligent subjectivity is not only private; it is social.

To understand a person's moral choices, one has to look at them, as Erik Erikson has pointed out, over a span of at least three generations. It is best, I have learned, if one can go *backward* two generations, as well as *forward* two. To learn the habits, instincts, and aspirations of a person's grandparents is to discern the emotional and imaginal weight of much in that person's life that otherwise seems inexplicable. To see the patterns of life adopted by a person's grandchildren is to discern more clearly the organic implications of the choices and efforts launched two generations earlier. Emotions, instincts, memory, imagination, passions, and ways of perceiving are passed on to us in ways we do not choose, and in ways so thick with life that they lie far beyond the power of consciousness (let alone of analytic and verbal reason) thoroughly to master, totally to alter.

We are, in a word, ineffably ethnic in our values and our actions.

The present work is consistent with all the philosophical and theological investigations I have conducted to this point, and consistent as well with my lifelong ambition. One might think of it as a struggle to discover the contours of my own sense of reality, stories, and symbols through setting forth the ways in which the official renditions of the American experience do not quite speak for me. But that would be to miss the larger point.

It is not my self-discovery that is of interest. The task is to discover what America is, or might yet be. No one, of course, can address that larger issue without coming to terms with his own ethnic particularity. No one ethnic group speaks for America. Each of us becomes aware of her own partial standpoint. For it is in possessing our own particularity that we come to feel at home with ourselves and are best able to enter into communion with others, freely giving and receiving of each other. The point of becoming ethnically alert and self-possessed is not self-enclosure; it is genuine community, honest and un-pretending.

The politics I want to recommend requires a new cultural pluralism. It draws from resources other than Anglo-Saxon history and values.

Readers of my earlier work will best be able to understand how the momentum of my thinking inevitably toppled my resistance to the present project. I did not want to enter a field so ominously bordered with taboos. But now I have enjoyed the risks. I look forward to the criticisms. They will be passionate.

A Note of Appreciation

Without the research assistance, calm, endurance, criticism, and prodding of Margaret Geib, once a student of mine at Stanford, later a lecturer at Trinity College in Washington, and a visiting scholar at St. Edmund's House, Cambridge, this manuscript would never have been completed nor liberated of a least those long lists of flaws she daily presented me. All further flaws must be attributed to her exhaustion, and to mine.

My editor, Clement Alexandre, prodded me when I was fearful, supported me with faith, and provided an advance, which in America is actual grace.

I also want to thank, for their encouragement and advice at critical moments, Irving Levine and Judith Herman of the National Project on Ethnic America at the American Jewish Committee; Monsignor Geno Baroni of the National Urban Ethnic Center; and the Reverend Andrew M. Greeley of the University of Chicago, and one of the first analysts of the new ethnicity.

The best secretary on Long Island, Judy Lally, one of the foundresses of the Conservative Party of Suffolk County, insists that not all the views presented here have the endorsement of the typist.

Carol Christ once again offered valuable criticisms. So did Gene Novak and Joan Tross Novak—long lost cousins —who at first resisted, then delighted in, the theme of ethnicity. Karen Laub Novak offered sweeping suggestions for revision, correctly. So far there has been no lack of one thing concerning this manuscript: criticisms. It has been interesting to note their ethnic character.

MICHAEL NOVAK

September 29, 1971

Acknowledgements

The author is indebted to *Harper's Magazine*, in whose pages part of Chapter Two appeared; to *The National Catholic Reporter* where "The Price of Americanization" once ran; and to the following sources for permission to quote from copyrighted material: to Harper and Row for *Laughing in the Jungle*, by Louis Adamic; Atlantic-Little, Brown and Company for *Race and Nationality in American Life*, by Oscar Handlin (Copyright © 1948, 1950, 1953, 1956, 1957); G. P. Putnam's Sons for *Advertisements for Myself*, by Norman Mailer (Copyright © 1959 by Norman Mailer); Oceana Publications, Inc., for *Workingman's Wife*, by Lee Rainwater, Richard P. Coleman, and Gerald Handel (Copyright © 1959 by Social Research, Inc.); and Jossey-Bass, Inc., for *People in Pain*, by Mark Zborowski. I depend as well on Garry Wills' brilliant *Nixon Agonistes* (Houghton Mifflin Co.) for the section on Agnew, and on other sources duly noted in the text.

The Price of
Being Americanized

*My grandparents, I am sure, never guessed what it would
cost them and their children to become "Americanized."*

*In their eyes, no doubt, almost everything was gain.
From the oppression experienced by Slovaks at the hands
of the Austro-Hungarian empire, the gain was liberty;
from relative poverty, opportunity; from an old world,
new hope. (There is a town in Pennsylvania, two hundred
miles from where they now lie buried, called "New
Hope.")*

*They were injured, to be sure, by nativist American
prejudices against foreigners, by a white Anglo-Saxon
Protestant culture, and even by an Irish church. (Any
Catholic church not otherwise specified by nationality
they experienced and described as "the Irish church.")*

*What price is exacted by America when into its maw it
sucks other cultures of the world and processes them?
What do people have to lose before they can qualify as
true Americans?*

*For one thing, a lot of blue stars—and silver and gold
ones—must hang in the window. You proved you loved
America by dying for it in its wars. The Poles, Italians,*

Greeks, and Slavs whose acronym Msgr. Geno Baroni has made to stand for all the non-English-speaking ethnic groups—pride themselves on "fighting for America." When my father saw my youngest brother in officer's uniform, it was one of the proudest days of his life . . . even though it (sickeningly) meant Vietnam.

I don't have other figures at hand. But when the Poles were only four percent of the population (in 1917–19) they accounted for twelve percent of the nation's casualties in World War I. "The Fighting Irish" won their epithet by dying in droves in the Civil War.

There is, then, a blood test. "Die for us and we'll give you a chance."

One is also expected to give up one's native language. My parents decided never to teach us Slovak. They hoped that thereby we would gain a generation in the process of becoming full Americans.

They kept up a few traditions: Christmas Eve holy bread, candlelight, mushroom soup, fish, and poppyseed. My mother baked kolacky. Pirohi, *however, more or less died with my grandmother, who used to work all day making huge, steaming pots of potato dumplings and prune dumplings for her grandchildren. No other foods shall ever taste so sweet.*

My parents, so far as I know, were the first Slovaks in our town to move outside the neighborhoods traditional for our kind of people and move into the "American" suburbs. There were not, I recall, very many other Catholics in the rather large, and good, public school I attended from grades two until six. I remember Mrs. S., the fifth-grade teacher, spelling "Pope Pius" with an "o" in the middle, and myself with gently firm righteousness (even then) correcting her.

What has happened to my people since they came to this land nearly a century ago? Where are they now, that long-awaited fully Americanized third generation? Are we living the dream our grandparents dreamed when on creaking decks they stood silent, afraid, hopeful at the sight of the Statue of Liberty? Will we ever find that secret relief, that door, that hidden entrance? Did our grandparents choose for us, and our posterity, what they should have chosen?

Now the dice lie cold in our own uncertain hands.

Ethnic Assertion in the Seventies

Not only the general public but American social scientists, who pride themselves on fact-finding and objectivity, preferred to avoid the suggestion of unequal rights in the word "minority." They used instead such terms as "subculture." . . . No one thought it necessary to invent a parallel term for the majority—such as "superculture," perhaps.

—BEN HALPERN, *Jews and Blacks.*

CHAPTER ONE

The Seventies:
Decade of the Ethnics

1. *Colombo Discovers America*

JOSEPH COLOMBO, SR., was beaming. It was a happy, even an exultant, occasion. Green, red, and white streamers crackled in the wind like the sound of rain. It was June 28, 1971, Italian Unity Day in Columbus Circle—his circle, Joe Colombo's. *Circolo di Colombo.*

In the past year, Joe Colombo had raised two million dollars for the Italian Unity League. He was gaining a reputation as an organizer without equal, a fundraiser without peer, a charismatic leader, a man of power, a saint. He saw the enormous vacuum of leadership as ethnic distress spread unnoticed in widening circles. Today, he hoped, 250,000 Italians would pour into the Circle because he had invited them.

Joe Colombo had never gone to high school. He had learned in the same school as that of the Molly Maguires, the other armed terrorists of the American past, the ethnic gangs, and the Black Panthers. Italians have been symbolic villains in the American imagination ever since the puppet shows that Huck Finn went to see: those swarthy characters in black puppet capes, with thin mustaches, so threatening to milk-white maidens. Joe Colombo was tired of the mockery. He sensed that Poles, Sicilians, Italians, Greeks, Armenians, Croats, Serbs, Portuguese, Russians, Spaniards, Lithuanians, and others were also losing the sharp lust to "become American." They looked around; the prospect did not enchant. One by one, hundreds and then thousands were deciding not to continue trying to become what they are not, can never be. They were beginning to love themselves a little better. "Kiss Me, I'm Italian" the buttons proudly said.

As best as Joe Colombo knew how—because no one else had the vision to enter the hungry, sucking vacuum of need and anger—he tried to begin a new movement and a new era in American politics. He wanted nonviolence, and he wanted a hardheaded alliance with blacks. He wasn't a professional politician. He wasn't a social organizer. What he would do with his accumulating success wasn't plain.

I watched Joe Colombo with fascination. He was (I thought) the wrong man for the job. But who else was doing it? The blacks had heroes who had been criminals, no doubt about it. Perhaps Joe Colombo would yet become a full hero, of a sort that Americans (even intellectuals) might easily admire if their prejudices would allow them; for American admiration, once released, is awe-inspiring.

It was 11:40 A.M. Mr. Colombo was checking details: some people to see, minor trouble caused by some vendors, liaison with police. The platform was already thick with distinguished people and the press.

Colombo tried to move toward his left. A gracious and charming young black loomed in front of him and asked to take some pictures. His pretty young companion, in an Afro, was smiling, too. It was a happy occasion. Joe Colombo saw the press badge; he paused obligingly. Then he pressed past the black, Jerome Johnson, a handsome youngster of twenty-three who hardly realized he had less than five minutes to live. In the crowd, dropping his camera and pulling out a pistol, Johnson swung past Colombo, and left-handed, from less than three feet away, rapidly fired three shots into Colombo's skull. Almost instantly, other shots rang out and Johnson clutched his chest. Guns clattered to the street—policemen later collected three. Johnson's camera disappeared. Colombo lay on his back, blood streaming from his neck, head, and mouth.

It was Martin Luther King, Jr.; it was Bobby Kennedy. *Once again.* Not because Colombo was yet that great or had proved himself. But because a living hope was stunned by blood. *Once again.*

At home, waiting for the noon radio report about the rally, exultant at the prospect of a massive rally that might at last tell New Yorkers to awaken before it is too late, I heard the initial, sickening details. I felt confusion. Rage. Bitterness.

A black! Would there be open race war? Was the ethnic resurgence going to be forced into a channel that there was no need, or will, to take? A cynically planted telephone call to the Associated Press, claiming that the dead young assassin was a member of a "black revolutionary attack team," added a macabre note of insanity. Did blacks think *Colombo* was their enemy? Couldn't they distinguish a fellow sufferer under Nordic prejudice from a WASP?

At regular intervals, almost as if timed, Aldo Tambellini, who was recording the scenes on video tape for the League, saw blacks enter the crowd at strategic locations. They were set upon by a few persons in an otherwise quiet crowd. Was that, too, planned? An "underworld" 'of confused motivations, perceptions, allegations, and fantasies surrounds the day.

The police later theorized that Colombo was gunned down by a rival gang. His rivals didn't want him entering ethnic politics, didn't like publicity, thought he'd lost his balance. So the police suggested.

I am not a fan of gangs. But neither am I certain that

the celebrated Yankee shrewdness involves less violence than the methods of the honored society. It is, however, less direct. The rules of the Yankee game are rigged. People on the inside do legitimately what those on the outside cannot. Gangsterism is a shortcut to wealth, power, and fame. It is despicable. Even more so than absentee landlords, or the way in which huge banks like Chase Manhattan use their power to help those within the privileged circle? How much more so, God may judge.

I am not among those who admire unreservedly the "nonconformist New England conscience." The original Brahmins had a way of getting rich. In my hometown, a number of now-respected families grew very rich from donations made to victims of the Johnstown flood.[1] Financial success, I have come to believe, is a poor guarantor of good conscience. On the contrary, success invites suspicion of evil done; it puts one on one's guard.

2. *The Famous "Social Issue"*

Scammon and Wattenberg believe that a new voting issue became paramount in the 1960s. They call it "the social issue," and they note that it is larger or more complex than race or crime. First, the movement of muggings and robberies into formerly middle-class areas spread alarm. Secondly, perceptions of blacks began to change. The more liberal attitudes that millions were growing accustomed to were jarred by images of lunch-counter protests, urban riots, looting, and young blacks carrying rifles from a building after a "take-over" at Cornell. Then young people showed contempt for purposes, styles, and feelings of older Americans. "Values" were called into question: pornography, new sexual codes, priests marrying, sexual education in the schools; there was contempt for hard work, obedience to law, and decency. Jeering, hooting, mockery, and violence came to be associated with the Vietnam war protestors.

All these elements acted on one another and on the American voter. The Social Issue was in full flower. It may be defined as a set of public attitudes concerning the more personally frightening aspects of disruptive social change.[2]

The social issue as Scammon and Wattenberg define it is not new in American politics. Nativist Americans have constantly appealed to it in resistance to other ethnic groups. The Ku Klux Klan arose around the social issue.

The question is, Can ethnic Americans be persuaded to side with nativist Americans in an "emerging Republican majority"?

Many of the political left, misreading both the issue and the popular reaction to it, feared an era of repression. Many of the political right chortled, sensing a clear turn of affairs their way. But both groups were probably premature . . . and very probably wrong.

As it stands now, at the beginning of the 1970s, the Social Issue appears up for grabs in the decade to come . . . the Social Issue is not a straight right/left or liberal/conservative issue . . . it may well be that the party and the candidates that can best and most intelligently respond to the social turbulence that is presently perceived by American voters will be known by the simple word: winners.[3]

Leaders on the Left are making several mistakes in dealing with the social issue. In the long run it is not enough (although it helped in the congressional races of 1970), for Democrats to shout "law and order" louder than Republicans. It is not enough to button a flag in one's lapel. A policy that will guide the party and the nation for thirty years—that is what we need.

First, then, many liberals and radicals have not noted their own biases. Why do educated partisans of a rational, modern, mobile culture support "change"? Because change is in their own self-interest. The breakdown of families and neighborhoods clears the way for sweeping social programs, for the mobile way of life of experts, and for the dreams of utopians. The "constituency of conscience" should get off the hobbyhorse of its own purity. The conjunction of "politics" and "conscience" properly raises eyebrows.

Second, the phrase "white racism" has become for the Left what "communism" was for Joe McCarthy: an indiscriminate scare word designed to prevent clear thought and apt strategy.

Third, prejudices against ethnic Americans have seldom been challenged on the Left, as prejudices against blacks have been. An alliance with ethnics was rejected by John Lindsay in New York—it was his major mistake—not out of political acumen but out of thoughtless prejudice. The ethnics (Italians, Irish, even lower-class Jews) were prematurely written off as backward. Lindsay propelled them in a conservative direction.

Fourth, real grievances of the lower-middle-class ethnic groups were overlooked. When muggings and robberies reached the educated and the affluent, some finally recognized that cries for law and order are not identical with "prejudice."

Fifth, reformist bureaucrats have neglected ethnic diversity (it would "wither away"). The political resources of ethnic diversity were overlooked. The recent increase in Black, Chicano, and Indian consciousness left other ethnic groups in a psychologically confused state. They are unable to be WASPS; they have lost confidence in being themselves.

Sixth, major programs in the last decade had as their symbolic message: "for blacks only." Thus the urban coalition, poverty programs, Head Start, Black Studies programs, busing, integration, and other major initiatives seemed to exclude others, despite their need. This was true in the public mind, even if not in fact.

Seventh, and above all, commitment to mechanical

images of society blinded experts to the actual moving forces in social life. Experts spoke a language of "program," "function," "machine," "input," "plug-in," as if society were a machine, not a living organism. They disvalued precisely those vitalities most prominent in the lives of blacks and ethnics—the family, the neighborhood, and the local community. Functional imagery is finally bureaucratic. It paralyzes organic thinking.

Eighth, the "social issue" is a different issue with every ethnic group, for each group perceives the individual, society, the family, political strategy, and morality in a different light. Scammon and Wattenberg's failure to notice the ethnic differential in the "social issue" makes their analysis gross and impractical.

If we run counter to each of these mistakes, a significant new politics for the future comes into view: the politics of cultural pluralism, a politics of family and neighborhood, a politics of smallness and quietness. Such a politics is not without weaknesses. But it also has major, firm, and fundamental strengths.

No one has yet contrived an image, let alone a political system, for living in a genuinely pluralistic way. The difficulties are obvious. How can each cultural minority be true to itself without infringing on the liberties of others? How can each person belong to a given ethnic group to the extent that he or she chooses, and be free as well to move into other groups?

I begin with four propositions:

First, if you explore your own ethnic identity, the effort will not blind you to the subtle, provocative ways in which others differ from you. To understand what it is to be a Jew or an Italo-American is to gain some insight into the differences implicit in being Afro-American, into black pride, into black politics, and the reverse. The white-black polarization is gross. There are many cultural streams among both blacks and whites. There are even many streams among WASPS. Each has human and political usefulness.

Second, if each American becomes aware of how he or she differs ethnically from others, no damage will be done to our capacity to design a nuanced, pluralistic foreign policy. To deal with Vietnamese is not to deal with Chinese. North Vietnamese and South Vietnamese are of significantly different cultures—not unlike North and South Italians. Ethnic awareness is not a liability in the conduct of international affairs.

Third, persons who are secure in their identity act with greater freedom, greater flexibility, greater openness to others. People who feel inferior or unacceptable lash out in anger.

Fourth, a politics based on family and neighborhood is far stronger socially and psychologically than a politics based on bureaucracy.

Let us explore some possibilities.

3. *The Catholic Assertion*

In early 1971, Norman Podhoretz, editor of the distinguished magazine of the American Jewish Committee, made a prediction to the *Washington Post*:

> Just as the black assertion set the climate for the '60s, I think you'll find a comparable Catholic, white-ethnic assertion in the '70s. You have 40 million Catholics in the United States. They've never been organized as a political bloc around their resentments. . . . You have an enormous potent force here, in this Catholic minority. It could result in the reconstitution of the Democratic Party as a relatively permanent majority. A Democratic Kevin Phillips could work this out.

He continued: "The lower-middle classes cannot help but push for the redistribution of wealth—that's one Marxist idea that I think remains valid. There are dangers—the hardhat mentality, know-nothingism. But they could be moderated. This Catholic assertion will set the agenda for the 1970s."

Podhoretz stresses the Catholic assertion; I would stress its ethnic character. The Italians and Slavs are no admirers of either the Irish or the Irish church. The Irish, for their part, give much devout respect to the church and then do in politics what they must; their political impulse is tougher and harsher than anything they hear in church. More than any other institution (the public schools, say; or the universities; the press; the bar associations; etc.), the church gave the immigrants cultural reinforcement and a sense of dignity; a feeling of belonging; support in the hours of being born, and dying; and comfort in the anxieties and disasters in between. But what is likely to happen in the seventies is independent of the hierarchy of the Catholic church.

The church in America, not least among conservatives and traditionalists, has become Protestant, individualistic, and pietist in character. It is largely Irish in tone and the Irish (alcohol aside) easily absorb Calvinism and its ethic of work, decency, and moral indignation. Except in churchy affairs (censorship, abortion, birth control), the church's record in American politics has not been one of leadership. (In 1891 Cardinal Gibbons of Baltimore barely persuaded Pope Leo XIII not to condemn, but instead to support, the cause of labor.) The church taught the immigrants to work hard, to obey the law, to respect their leaders, and to concentrate on private, familial relationships. On the other hand, beginning with a flock largely poor and often illiterate, the church moderated prejudices and hostilities more successfully, perhaps, than any institution in American society, not excluding the public schools.[4] Its chief social-political instruction was defensive rather than generous: condemnations of atheistic communism, deep suspicion of Harvard atheists in the State Department, and general criticisms of the "materialism" in which the church itself so notably shares.

"The church blinded us," a Polish tugboat operator in Baltimore said vehemently during the congressional campaign of 1970. "The church betrayed us. They told us to obey the law, to be respectable, to trust the politicians. They betrayed us." The citizens in his neighborhood could not find a single local politician to help them in blocking a proposed four-lane expressway which was about to cut their seventy-year-old neighborhood in two. The expressway would service a new factory three miles away; business interests were behind it. "The church didn't teach us to be critical. It taught us to obey."

In 1971, against enormous opposition, the tugboat operator's neighbors ran Barbara Mikulski for a seat on the City Council on a progressive ethnic platform, and she won. Steve Adubado, on a similar platform, beat Anthony Imperiale in his own ward in Newark. Gary and Cleveland will be seeing similar elections soon, and organizers will be out in fifteen major cities by mid-1972.

Political sophistication is coming late to the PIGS. When it comes, it is not likely to come through the church. The higher officials of the church, the ecclesiastically conservative bishops, are locked into cozy arrangements with mayors, news media, and realtors. Their political program can be summarized succinctly: "Do nothing unrespectable. Have faith." Faith in *them?* Faith in *politicians?* Such faith is not a sufficient (or even a necessary) condition for political effectiveness; nor for salvation.

Moreover, even the most intelligent leaders of the Catholic church sometimes have a peculiar ethnic blindness. Thus Father Theodore M. Hesburgh, president of Notre Dame and chairman of the President's Civil Rights Commission, told a convention of Catholic educators: "One thinks of the Catholic-educated who stoned nuns and priests in Chicago because they were marching for integrated neighborhoods and equal rights for blacks. One thinks of the very few blacks we have educated in our schools and, even worse, the very few Chicanos who, as Catholics, had an even closer claim on our apostolic efforts. I do receive a surprisingly large number of hate letters from Catholic ethnics every time I put in a good word for blacks or Chicanos. . . . But the young, thank

God, largely do not share these ugly prejudices of their elders."[5]

No large step of intellectual sympathy is required to see that the situation of ethnics vis-à-vis the blacks on the one hand, and establishments like universities on the other, is not an easy one. Ethnics do not usually have historic feelings about nonwhites whom they never met before arriving here.

Mike Royko catches many of their feelings in *Boss*; but he judges ethnics and blacks according to a different standard. For the former he has contempt. His account is valuable because typical. He describes ethnic neighborhoods in Chicago as petty, self-enclosed states:

> The ethnic states got along just about as pleasantly as did the nations of Europe. With their tote bags, the immigrants brought all their old prejudices, and immediately picked up some new ones. An Irishman who came here hating only the Englishmen and Irish Protestants soon hated Poles, Italians, and blacks. A Pole who was free arrived hating only Jews and Russians, but soon learned to hate the Irish, the Italians, and the blacks.[6]

Martin Luther King came to Chicago as if its symbolic structure were the same as Alabama's. He miscalculated. Ethnic Catholics have felt the accusing, jabbing finger of Protestant moralists since their arrival in this nation. There are few quicker ways to stoke smoldering resentment and to awaken an unendurable inner hatred than to look down upon others from some moral height. In Alabama, by contrast, even the poorest whites have a populist tradition to validate their patriotism and moral worth. King could turn against them the honeyed, moralistic rhetoric with which they constantly anoint themselves. For poor white Alabamans, blacks are genetically inferior; the difference between white and black has almost a religious intensity of many generations' standing. Competition for jobs and neighborhoods is not the immediate issue. In Chicago, ethnic whites have vast insecurities

about their own way of life. Competition for jobs and housing is an immediate, tangible, primary issue. The issue is
in many ways more bitter, but less symbolic. Racism in
Alabama and racism in Chicago are two quite different
phenomena, requiring different analyses and different
remedies.

A protest march is a moralizing finger jabbing into a
neighborhood sick to death of being moralized. Royko
describes the event:

> The first march went into Gage Park, on the far South-
> west Side. Many of the people in Gage Park had for-
> merly lived in Englewood, Woodlawn, and other areas
> that had slowly turned black. They were Lithuanian,
> Polish, Italian in ancestry. They were blue collar in
> occupation, and they were haters. It was an ugly event.
> King was hit in the head with a rock.[7]

Royko also describes the neighborhood in which Mayor
Daley has lived, in the same narrow house, for thirty-two
years, a neighborhood divided among Irish, Lithuanian,
Italian, Polish, and German whites, each group more or
less keeping to itself. In the summer of 1965 blacks and
sympathizers staged another demonstration "of conscience."

> Bridgeport's reaction was predictable. The second night
> the marchers showed up, the neighborhood mob grew
> to almost a thousand. The marchers were showered
> with eggs and tomatoes, firecrackers and rocks. Women
> came out of their houses to turn on lawn sprinklers,
> soaking the marchers as they walked by. The neighbor-
> hood echoed with the chants of "two-four-six-eight, we
> don't want to integrate," and hundreds of voices joined
> to sing: "Oh, I wish I was an Alabama trooper, that is
> what I'd really like to be-ee-ee. Cuz if I was an Alabama
> trooper, I could kill the niggers legelly [sic]."
> Daley sat in the house, out of sight, but giving orders
> to the corner police station by phone.[8]

My point here is not to defend Daley. It is not to side with the ethnics. It is to suggest that the tactic of demonstration is inherently WASP and inherently offensive to ethnic peoples. You do not accuse people who are insecure. You do not intensify guilt. They cannot tolerate that. Far more can be won from people if you congratulate them for their loyalty as Americans, praise them for their habits of hard work, see how their morality looks to them from their point of view—and, in brief, extend to them the same cross-cultural understanding as one extends to blacks.

There are, at present, no social rewards for integration, only penalties. When blacks begin to move into an area, city services should be upgraded; garbage should be collected one extra time, schools should be improved, streets should be more carefully repaired. Instead, everything begins to decline. Even the family that decides to stay hears a weekly knock at the door. The realtor says: "I offered you fifteen thousand last week. I'm afraid I can't go higher than fourteen-seven now." He mentions another family that has moved out. The homeowner then goes to the Savings and Loan to borrow money to build an addition, to make sure his property's value stays up. Everything goes smoothly until the banker checks a street map. "We're not making loans in transition areas." The man sells to a realtor at fourteen thousand, the incoming black family pays seventeen thousand. Everyone feels bitter. In the next district, in five to ten years, the pattern will be repeated. There is no citywide or statewide plan to stabilize the economic equity in homes, the reliability of services, the vision of a better future.

In my conversations with ethnics in Chicago, Baltimore, and elsewhere, I have not found one who does not agree that blacks get the worst deal in American life, and that the number one injustice in America is the treatment of blacks. But their persistent question is why the gains of blacks should be solely at *their* expense. They themselves have so little and feel so terribly constricted.

Thus Father Hesburgh himself would be more convincing to ethnics if he showed less moralizing and more appreciation of their reality, and if his reference group were not liberal intellectuals. When the Civil Rights Commission attacked the housing and zoning rules of upper-middle-class communities around Baltimore (including Agnew's), Hesburgh gained in credibility. Intellectuals at the University of Chicago are more open than ethnics to integration; but the structure of their values, their incomes, their mobility, and their opportunities is not equal to that of ethnics. By integration, intellectuals lose nothing at all. It is for them a moral gravy train.

The idiom of resentment in America is racist. But the latent meaning of racist expressions may be far different from the surface meaning. They may be the cries of people who are desperate and do not know how to get anyone to listen. To call PIGS racist may be mistaking an unfortunate and American idiom for a more profound malaise.

Even otherwise astute political commentators can be biased in a fateful way. Thus pollster Louis Harris, in a speech to the American Newspapers Publishers Association, spoke of a major "shift to the Left" in American politics and the emergence of "a new coalition." And who does he see forming this new coalition for a new politics? Professors, students, and educated middle-management people on the one hand; and the nonwhite and the poor on the other. Who are left out of the coalition? The lower-middle-class, blue-collar workers—the ethnics.[9]

That is an unnecessary, tragic mistake. There is no need to concede the ethnic voter to the conservative movement.

4. *Resentment Left, Right, and Ethnic*

Kevin Phillips argued in 1969 that the Catholic ethnic groups are drifting in a Republican direction. The success of James Buckley in New York in 1970 makes this thesis plausible. The issues in Phillips' mind come down to three: ethnic rivalry, especially with blacks; cultural (as distinct from economic) conservatism; and anticommunism. I think the matter lies deeper: there is also the issue of "soul." Generosity lies deeper than resentment.

Samuel Lubell predicted in 1951 that one day "we may look back upon today's Democratic era as an adventure in social unification, in the creation of the kind of nationwide social structure which an industrial civilization requires."[10] Lubell's "nationwide social structure" put enormous pressure on old values and old ways of life. Southern Democrats resisted nationalization; what they wanted economically conflicted with what they wanted socially. Ethnic Catholics were ambivalent toward Roosevelt's Left: what they wanted economically also conflicted with what they wanted socially.

Thus, despite the Ku Klux Klan, despite resentment toward WASPS, Catholic voters in New York (especially among the Irish), have entertained historic dalliance with southern and western WASPS. Phillips believes that Barry Goldwater won a majority of the middle-class Catholic vote in New York City, and "perhaps 40 per cent of the city's total Catholic vote." He adds:

Catholic New York is an early and accurate litmus of Northeastern Catholic politics. New York Irish support of Tammany Hall helped mold the Jeffersonian coalition to which the then small Catholic population rallied; the Gotham Catholics of Andrew Jackson's day helped forge his new majority to which inflowing Catholics adhered; and the Al Smith revolution, born in New York's Irish "Gas House" assembly district, brought Catholic America into the future New Deal coalition even before the Depression. In all of these upheavals, Catholic New York took up its position with a Southern and Western alliance. Even in defeat, the embryonic reemergence of this alliance was a major message of the 1964 election.[11]

Catholic resentment—nothing characterizes Phillips' argument so much as resentment—is not now directed at southern and western WASPS. Protestant Fundamentalists and New York Catholics are linked, a little uncomfortably, by a peculiar feeling of comradeship, populism; social conservatism, anticommunism, and "patriotism." Phillips' resentment is most chill toward "socialities," "Jewish intellectuals," "Ivy League graduates," morally superior "Brahmins" who waft with the vogue of idealism from Republican to Democratic politics. Teeth can be heard grinding in the background as Phillips quotes from Marietta Tree, the "older stateswoman of *salon* liberalism." She is describing her family, the Peabodys of Massachusetts:

The people who built and administered the schools, universities, boys' clubs and hospitals. They were the sinews of society. They gave generously of themselves for the public good and prudently lived on the income of their incomes. They valued educated women as well as educated men; daily exercise; big breakfasts; President Eliot; beautiful views; portraits by Sargent; waltzing; Harvard; travel; England; comradeship between the sexes; Patou dresses for "swell" occasions; long correspondence with family and friends; J. P. Morgan; mahogany and red plush; and, most of all, they believed that if you tried hard enough, you could make the world a better place. And you *must* try.[12]

·The liberal establishment since 1932 has not been composed chiefly of old-line families turning liberal. Its real strength sprang from a new social class with new interests. "A new collectivity of research, scientific, consulting, internationalist and social interests which, benefiting from the expenditures and activities of big government, propagated an ideology which promoted big government."[13]

Manual workers have a nose for the self-interest of idealists. George Wallace, loud and clear:

Now what are the real issues that exist today in these United States? It is the trend of pseudo-intellectual government, where a select, elite group have written guidelines in bureaus and court decisions, have spoken from some pulpits, some college campuses, some newspaper offices, looking down their noses at the average man on the street, the glassworker, the steelworker, the auto worker, and the textile worker, the farmer, the policeman, the beautician and the barber, and the little businessman, saying to him that you do not know how to get up in the morning or go to bed at night unless we write you a guideline.[14]

Liberals and radicals do not seem to grasp that phrases like the "power elite," "the ruling classes," or "those in power" (whom, presumably, basic social changes will sweep away) are applied by ordinary people to *them*. Intellectuals still talk as though businessmen held highest power in American life. Ordinary people see the money pouring into universities, research, and expertise of all sorts, and conclude that *intellectuals* hold highest and most visible power in America. Anti-intellectualism has a new face in America. It is not anti-intellectualism in Hofstadter's sense only, it is a bitter resentment of unchecked power and influence: it is anti-establishment.

The resentment of social class, economic privilege, and educational advantage is a pervasive emotion among Catholic conservatives. When young John Kerry, fresh from Vietnam, testified on behalf of Vietnam Veterans for Peace, and faced his crew-cut Catholic counterpart from Texas, former naval officer John O'Neill, comparison was immediately drawn between Kerry's Yale pedigree, good looks, smooth speech, powerful connections, and the limited resources, plainness of manner, ordinariness of O'Neill. Class resentment was tangible. So also was the utter conflict between worldviews and moralities.

But this particular class warfare finds the upper classes rhetorically on the side of revolution in values and structure, and the lower classes rhetorically on the side of stability, slower evolution, and loyalty. Rhetoric is not the same as reality.

Assume that the widely accepted premise is true: the Left is exhausted; it has no more to offer. Blue-collar workers, middle Americans, the Italian Unity League, Blacks—everyone is in rebellion. At what? The bureaucratic rule of experts. Lower-middle-class whites are particularly angry. At what? "Exactly those things to which the established political Left historically is committed: centralization, bureaucracy, the planned or mixed economy, economic growth, the scientific-technological direction of society. No wonder, then, that the parties of the Left are in trouble." Thus William Pfaff.

The parties of the Left do not understand that their "revolution" has already occurred and exhausted its usefulness.

As for further fundamental reform—structural change, basic change—they are at a loss. The thrust of modern protest goes against them; it seems to incorporate old conservative themes. Their great tradition has been to define political issues in economic terms; yet the new anxieties seem to be moral, communal, issues of identity and value, not things which will respond to economic treatment.

There is an impasse, "because the ideas of the Left have served their use. The new anxieties in our society contradict too much of what the Left has always believed about power and progress. The new ideas and movements which take the place of the old Left remain inchoate; yet we sense that they are outside the established categories of both 'Left' and 'Right.' "[15]

People are tired of new "eight-point plans." Politicians sound like engineers. Besides, to ethnic peoples the style of the Left seems decadent. What ethnics mean by authenticity, morality, decency, and trust, and what intellectuals mean, diverge dramatically. .

The question of style is complicated. In 1968 Robert Kennedy won ethnic support in every primary he entered. In districts which had earlier given large percentages to George Wallace, Kennedy's margins were especially impressive. Ethnic voters trusted Robert Kennedy. His bantamlike toughness, his large family, his intimate knowledge of personal suffering, even his sometimes choppy and almost inarticulate speech (especially when he came close to the edges of deep emotions) struck chords that ethnics recognized. They did not hold it against him that he also had overwhelming support among blacks, Chicanos, and Indians. That was the company they felt at home with: those outside the establishment, the prejudiced against, the struggling.

The very elements in Robert Kennedy which grated against the style of educated liberals and intellectuals—his toughness, his emphasis on law and order, his insistence that life is tough and that everybody has to play by the same rules—reassured ethnics. Some commentators said he used code words. To ethnics, Kennedy's words were as plain as a pikestaff in an Italian sun: laws of life, true at all times and places, true whether diverse races exist or not, as true in the nations of their origin as here.

There is not much evidence that the liberal wing of the Democratic party respects the culture, the values, the dreams, the hopes of ethnic peoples. On the contrary, in recent years the threat to ethnics is as perceptible as the arrival of missionaries on South Sea islands, their hands full of brassieres. Intellectuals want the ethnics to become *enlightened*, to "become converted and live." And if the ethnics don't wish to become like the intellectuals?

Groups often do not recognize how much they insult one another's most cherished values and infringe upon one another's liberty of soul. Television, for example, offends some by being bland and moralistic, and others by being decadent. Caught as it is between factions that prefer shocking honesty and factions that prefer public decency, it often flirts, teases, leers—like Bob Hope praising solid family values while ogling the bazooms of girls in bathing suits; or like potential Miss Americas, displayed like sides of beef and gushing sentiments to warm the hearts of moms.

Style aside, the real issue falls in between classical political conceptions. As always, the sine qua non is economic; there needs to be a redistribution of social burdens and rewards. But not all the burdens, not all the rewards, are directly economic. Identity, dignity, liberty from assault, a sense of generosity and steady hope, pride in self and respect from others—these elements of "the social issue" are more fundamental than, and at the very least run a strong second to, economics. Economics depends upon morale. The precedent-shattering affluence of the 1960s did not lay to rest bitter social issues; on the contrary.

The establishment of systems of identity and self-respect is as crucial for whites as for blacks. During the past decade, an upsurge of morale has transformed the black community. It is one of the most stirring stories in our nation's history. The faces of blacks, as one watches them in the streets, are purposive, resolute, often radiant. The whole nation needs a burst of such morale.

The Republicans, with whom Phillips would join the ethnics, offer only negatives: nothing real, nothing economic, no new self-identity, no vision of the future. Mr. Nixon exudes a tired WASP morality. The words and images are wrong, all wrong. Resentment is a powerful force in politics. It does not feed the family or justify the agonies of immigration.

5. *The Squeeze Is On: Some Statistics*

Let us suppose that in the 1960s the blacks and the young had their day in the sun. They had maximum publicity. And now it is the ethnics' turn. Perhaps the ethnics can carry our society further, more constructively, more inventively.

Three sets of figures set the political dimensions of the possibilities. There are seventy million Americans in families whose income falls between $5,000 and $10,000 per year. These are 40 percent of all Americans. Secondly, there are seventy million descendants of immigrants from Ireland, Italy, Spain, Greece, Armenia, and the Slavic nations. Thirdly, there are nearly fifty million Catholics.[16]

These three abstract segments overlap considerably. Most Catholics are descendants of such immigrants. Most (it appears) are also in lower-middle-class families by income.

Such persons have special characteristics, needs, and dreams. Their symbolic life, rhetoric, and ways of perceiving are unique. They form a formidable electoral bloc.

In 1960 the percentage of first- and second-generation immigrants in the major cities (larger than 500,000) of the United States was as follows.[17] If one counts the third generation, figures would presumably be larger:

RANK	CITY	%	RANK	CITY	%
1	New York	48.6	12	Philadelphia	29.1
2	Boston	45.5	13	San Antonio	24.0
3	San Francisco	43.5	14	San Diego	21.5
4	Chicago	35.9	15	Baltimore	14.8
5	Buffalo	35.4	16	St. Louis	14.1
6	Los Angeles	32.6	17	Washington	12.6
7	Detroit	32.2	18	Cincinnati	12.0
8	Seattle	31.4	19	Houston	9.7
9	Cleveland	30.9	20	New Orleans	8.6
10	Pittsburgh	30.3	21	Dallas	6.9
11	Milwaukee	30.0			

Other reflections on statistics are in order. In 1969 the median age of the American population was 27 years and 8 months. In 1910 it was 24. In 1985 the median American will be six months older than he was in 1969.[18]

According to Scammon and Wattenberg,[19] six out of seven voters are over 30. The median age of voters is 47. Younger voters, whose maximal numbers will lower the median age only slightly, may very well vote Democratic in larger proportions than their elders. But their fundamental values may be opposed to those of the liberal intellectuals. Conceivably, a politics which turned in a new ethnic direction would be closer to their own search for meaning than the classical politics of the Left. It might be possible to invent a political language and a political program that appealed simultaneously to young students and young workers, to those attracted (whether they go to them or not) to communes, and to those attracted (whether they remain in them or not) to ethnic neighborhoods. It is possible that Anglo-Saxon political creativity is exhausted, and that at last America is ready for a substantive contribution from other cultures.

By 1985, only 14 percent of Americans will be graduated from four-year colleges.[20]

Over 60 percent of young people between 18 and 22 are now *not* in college.[21]

Take the lower half of American families, by income— only one-fourth of the young people in college come from them.[22]

In some urban areas the rate of working-class whites who drop out of school runs to almost 30 percent. Of these 20 percent are out of work in the autumn following the year they drop out of school. The great majority of high-school dropouts are not from among the poor but from the working class, white and black.[23]

When one says the word "youth," therefore, one ought to think of the sons and daughters of the working class first, and of college students second.

Only one out of four high-school seniors (males) desires blue-collar work. But almost half of the jobs in our economy are blue-collar. Much frustration![24]

About half of Irish, Polish, and Italian households are in blue-collar work.

Most white ethnics have been to high school; about 30 percent have been to college.

In 1968, twenty-two million Americans were certified as poor. Fifteen million were white (66 percent).

Two out of three persons in Detroit are either black or Polish.

Chicago has more Poles than any city in the world, including Warsaw.

One out of six persons in New York is Italian. Only 14 of 165 deans in the City College system are Italian.[25]

In 1965 the average industrial worker with three dependents took home $88.06 a week; in 1969 he took home $87.27, after price adjustments due to inflation.[26] That would not satisfy a lowly instructor in a college, a journalist, a newscaster.

Between 1965 and 1970 the real income of workers has declined by 3 percent.[27]

The median price for housing in the United States is now $27,000, according to George Romney. He notes, too, that an income of almost $14,000 per year is needed to buy and to maintain such a house. Fewer than 20 percent of American families make that much. Five years ago, 40 percent could afford comparable housing.[28]

Forty percent of lower-middle-class husbands and wives both work. Even adding their salaries together, their median income is $10,700.[29]

.Statistics are difficult to assimilate. Still, nothing in the above suggests that lower-middle-class families are living in an age of affluence. Nothing suggests that they have room for economic relaxation. Nothing suggests that they have much freedom, or flexibility, or mobility. The overwhelming picture is one of constricted possibility; of frustration; and of humiliating, grubby concern about dollars.

The life of professors, businessmen on expense accounts, and journalists—mobile, swift, exciting (in the view of those who must stay at home)—supplies the image of what "modernity" is supposed to mean. It hasn't arrived yet for most Americans, except by report. They sit watching their TV while life passes by. From time to time, as a white railroad worker in Chicago put it: "Some young punk screams at me on television he's going to burn my house down."

6. *The Felt Quality of Ethnic Life*

What is it like to visit the homes of the ethnic working class? If you come as an emissary from the larger, richer, more educated world, you feel ill at ease in the doorway. The woodwork is old-fashioned in design and color. Wallpaper is flowered patterns; lace and doilies; shiny framed pictures of sons in uniform and white-haired grandparents; reproductions of the Last Supper or, in dark blue and violet, of Jesus in Gethsemane; large, soft, old furniture, with one new recliner or a sofa in a style that matches something else in the room; a television set; narrow rooms and low ceilings; old chandeliers; furniture polished, floors dusted, curtains stiffly laundered; a scent from years of furniture polish and wax—old, clean—as if windows were closed all day to keep out the heat—such are likely to be your impressions of old structures in East Baltimore, East Kensington (Philadelphia), the Bronx, Corona, Connecticut's Stamford, Mayor Daley's Bridgeport.

Mementos from the older family unit (framed pictures, a comfortable chair) accompany a family into a new home in the suburbs. Even the new house will probably have a few tiles out, or water spots on the plaster, because the construction was so cheap; and there is likely to be a barbecue pit built by the man of the house, or a boat, or a homemade backboard for basketball.

Ethnics spend most of their hours of free time with their families.[30] Many visit their parents at least once a week. (By contrast, the Irish tend to visit brothers and sisters rather than parents.) Almost always, ethnics have relatives as best friends. Their greatest celebrations are family get-togethers. Large families mean frequent weddings. The whole clan arrives. The family wits keep everybody laughing; the old men make the young girls blush; wives cluck and giggle; the old women talk about dreams, and deaths, and mysterious occurrences.

Workingmen belong to few associations outside the family. They are seldom gregarious in that sense. Their lives are not political or social so much as familial and centered in the neighborhood. At work the men meet fellows from other neighborhoods, other nationalities, other races; but mostly they meet people just like themselves.

Workingmen's families have an overpowering modesty and shyness. The wife will apologize that the home is so normal—just like anybody else's, nothing fancy; it's too small, but it's all they can afford; it'll do.

They are nervous in the larger social world, wouldn't know what to do in it, are easily intimidated by people of education or know-how. They make excuses. Workingmen's wives comment on women's clubs:

I don't think I'd be very good at a club. I'm too self-conscious. I've been thinking of joining, maybe that will help me.

I'm ashamed to say I'm not in any clubs—it's usually the very social type of person who joins clubs and I'm not that type. You have to have the knack for getting in those organizations and becoming officers in them. I'm not smart enough to hold an office. I read a lot about clubs in the newspapers. There's really no reason why I'm not in any club, except that I'm not the going type.

There's too much politics in clubs. Everybody is trying to get ahead of everybody else—and I'm not that ambitious.

Clubs tend to be made up of catty women who don't accomplish anything but a lot of talk. The women just talk about one another. Some of the women go just to hear the dirt so they can peddle it around.

You have to have an interest and be a pusher to be in clubs. I like to be told what to do. You have to be good at public speaking and I'm too nervous for that. You also have to be a good hostess—as there are times when you may have to give a tea or bridge party.[31]

Middle-class women, of course, join many more clubs; they like the social life. But it isn't only the personality conflict that is different. Workingmen's wives lack cars, time, personal freedom:

My husband comes home tired and he's worked long hours so he doesn't like to be left with the children.

I don't drive for one thing—and it is awfully inconvenient.

My husband wants me home—I don't think my husband appreciates clubs. But if that's the way he wants it, it's OK by me. I think husband and home should come first.

My husband dislikes them. He doesn't want me to be gone when he's home—and most things are at night . . . if most husbands felt like mine, I wonder who would ever get things done.[32]

Middle-class women often take pleasure in the individuality and original accomplishments of each of their children. They "come up with something new every day." A mother in a worker's family tends to see the children as a daily struggle. It is the wearing effect on her patience that she notices. There isn't space at home, or places of escape, or help. Even if she shares wonderment at her children's learning, her culture encourages her to talk mostly about the difficulties they bring.[33]

Working-class families have no bright or altered future to look forward to. Day after day is the same. Their husbands almost always reach an earnings plateau at about age thirty-five—just when the first children begin to cost the family more for recreation, clothes, and school, and just when the family has probably acquired a home of their own.[34] Their economic future cannot get better. It might get worse. Realistically, they can nourish none of the confidence of the middle class that promotions or new careers will make the future more exciting. Little in the experience of the lower-middle class promotes living for the future. They put little confidence in insurance; a small savings account is more immediate, tangible, concrete. Here are various workingmen's wives:

> He'll be working as a truckdriver the rest of his life, and it's hard to tell what he'll be making. It'll probably be about the same though. An office job just isn't for him. He tried it once and couldn't stand being cooped in.
>
> He's been doing the same kind of work since he was 15. He started as a busboy and now he's a cook. I sure hope he makes some more money in the future, but I'm not counting on it—I sure don't know.
>
> Maybe we won't be so poor in the future. I don't want much out of life. Just enough to get by on. But my husband's a bricklayer and we keep being afraid that there won't be any work. God be willing, we'll still be living here in this house. Maybe if we get some of these bills paid off I'll be more contented.
>
> They give small raises, but it's not enough to make any difference.
>
> He better be making more. I'm definitely not satisfied on his wages now. My kids need so many things. I do hope there'll be a change, although I don't think so. I don't know whether or not he'll ever make any more—and neither does he. It all depends on how the economic situation keeps going.
>
> He'd better make a little more money. He's just about got to make more money, what with three kids to take care of.

By contrast, middle-class women live in the future. They make a fetish of present discontent; it is a measure of future happiness.

I'm quite sure my husband will be earning more money. He's extremely intelligent. He's advancing in his work, and there's no reason why he shouldn't keep earning more.

My husband is going to school now, getting a master's degree because he wants a better job. He is a person who will never be satisfied to stand still.

Obviously we expect to make improvements and changes in our standard of living during the next 10 years.

Once my husband completes his medical training—he's interning now—and gets established in his profession, I expect our standard of living to zoom right up. I certainly imagine that we'll have a nice home and beautiful furniture and all that sort of thing.

I always say that as long as I want things and am not completely satisfied with what I've got I'll continue to be happy. I'm always wanting something more or different or new.

Are we ever really satisfied? I think you might as well make a long-range plan even if it does get upset. I want to spend more money in the future on things like the theater or a few more luxuries than we have now. I want to do more reading and maybe I'll take some courses at the university here in cultural subjects.[35]

Workingmen's wives are convinced that significant action originates from the world outside them, and that the world outside is mainly unchangeable, massive, uncharted, indecipherable. Each seems grateful for the smallest signs of guidance. The world beyond her neighborhood seems to her "chaotic and potentially catastrophic." She cannot influence the world; she doesn't even have an organized view of it. Reality is, "in its ordinary presentation to her, flat, unvarnished and not highly differentiated." Dullness is the overwhelming reality.

The authors of *Workingman's Wife* showed various women a picture of a young woman in a doorway with her chin in her hand looking off into space. The respondents interpreted:

> It looks like a mother after a hard day's work. She isn't quite done and wondering what to do next. It is the story of motherhood. There is no outcome. The work just goes on.
>
> This reminds me of a mother after a hard day with the kids. Thinking what's going to happen next, and wondering how she can make them behave better.
>
> Probably a mother that has been working all day. Been wondering about meals, washing, ironing, and just sat down for a rest before starting in again. There is no end. Just work.[36]

The potential drama is almost always of a world collapsing. Fundamental deprivations may arise: brawls, desertion, loss of income, illness. All these things *do*—and *may* occur. (It is not surprising that the story of crucifixion so matches their experience.)

Another picture, this time of a little girl in the doorway of a cabin, makes lower-class women think of solitariness, bruises, brokenness:

> Looks like a lonely little girl, sitting at the doorway watching for somebody. It looks as if her family have gone away and left her. Well, the somebody who cares for her is not going to show up.

By contrast, middle-class women stepped outside this picture, and described it as a minor problem in human relations. One suggested, for example, that the picture meant that too much idleness isn't good for children. An upper-class woman felt no anxieties:

> This is a girl at a summer camp. She sees chipmunks and squirrels near the door and she is sitting real still so as not to frighten them away. If she watches long enough, they will come up and take some food from her.

Workingmen's wives are markedly afraid of loneliness. Ties with others bring no permanent haven. A picture of a young woman · standing with downcast head, her face covered with her right hand, elicits these stories:

This looks like there might have been a quarrel between her and her husband. It looks like she's pretty depressed by it. I get the feeling of—wonder if he'll come back or is he definitely gone. Doesn't look like a case of family grief for there would be others around her. It's a quarrel between the two, I guess. She's waiting at the door wondering if he's coming back in, or the door is closed definitely.

Looks like a woman just got some bad news. Maybe her husband left her or died or went away. She's beside herself and heartbroken. She will just have to go on, that's all.

She's crying because her husband left her with two kids. Another woman, yeah, it's another woman. He's no good, anyway. This woman got a divorce in the end. He drank too much—too many times—too often.

That, I don't know. Unless something has happened. Maybe she lost her father. Or her mother. Or her husband. Some sorrow. I don't know how it will come out. I don't know how it will come out. You got to look—let it work out for them. That is best.

This one looks like she's been hurt or something. Some tragedy or something and she's crying. Either that or she's just had a fight with her boyfriend. She may have been out on a date and talked to some other boy and her boyfriend didn't like it (How come out?) Oh, she'll probably make up with him and they'll get along fine until the next time. Could have been a lot of things.[37]

Working-class women, much more than middle-class women, exhibit a desire "to continue to be with people, to nurture them, to be nurtured by them, or to have power over them." Middle-class women tend, by contrast, to seek escape or contentment within themselves. The life of the working-class woman is elemental: birth, illness, accomplishing the duties and chores of daily life—these are far more her central preoccupations than they are of middle-class women. Moreover, the working-class woman hates to give endings to stories or to make predictions; her world is uncertain and unstable. She does not believe that life can be defeated; but one can endure against it, brighten certain moments of it, summon up wishfulness to ease one over the hardest moments. Reluctant to given an ending to a story, one woman responded to further prompting:

> Oh well, a happy ending. I do not like endings to be unhappy. Not in the movies or anything. There is too much of that in real life to have it in stories or movies. I definitely want happy endings.[38]

Determination to keep going, the researchers find, is constantly in evidence. The workingman's wife is realistic and practical. No use giving up. Concerning another picture:

> She looks like she is thinking or very worried. Something must be troubling her. I look like that sometimes when I don't know what to fix for a meal. She might figure it all out or just go on working and skip the worry.

The workingman's wife is psychologically "passive." She accepts things as they are given. She has little energy for, or interest or skill in, stepping back from daily life and probing into things for herself. She tends to regard thinking as uncomfortable. Thinking cannot help, and usually hinders.

> Looks like a girl deep in thought; doesn't seem to be too happy.

> They are feeling fine; not thinking anything.

Thinking deeply, a little sad.[39]

She doesn't believe that she herself can be effective. Whatever her worry or her efforts, not much seems to change. She survives.

The working-class woman is afraid that her own emotions are volatile and intense. She isn't as well-organized as the middle-class woman. She feels that her emotions might run away with her, that she might be easily seduced sexually. She strives hard to ·be good and to remain in control, but she knows she needs frequent forgiveness for her outbursts, her angers, her sadness, her vivid moods.[40]

The world of the working class, here reflected through its wives and mothers, is, from the side of its men, a tough and violent world.

A young man in the industrial work force responds violently to himself and his job and his community because he is forced to live violently. In 1970 an estimated 15,000 workers were killed on the job. Twenty-five million were seriously injured; but the greater tragedy is the indecency of the life style we force on those who continue in the marketplace. I really don't believe that I or anyone, for that matter, can explain what it means to work on an assembly line. How does it feel to start your day at 6:00 A.M. Spend eight hours in a dirty, filthy, hot environment lifting 85-pound tires onto wheels at 30 second intervals, five days a week, 52 weeks a year for 30 years.[41]

No labor movement in any country suffered so much violence during its history as that of America. Police, troopers, and guardsmen murdered, beat, fired into crowds, charged with bayonets.[42] The use of violence in America is not merely racial. American upper classes have frequently and regularly turned to violence, against whites as well as against blacks. They are distinguished among other ruling classes not by their reluctance to use violence, only by their wish to disguise from themselves the immediate effects of what they do: more, say, than Yugoslav land-owners or Italian nobility, they moralize. They read declarations about "justice," but when their own interests are threatened, their cry becomes "order."

The phrase "government by laws rather than by men" shuttles back and forth between two usages. To legitimate the real power of the established, it is an appeal to a justice transcending any one man or group. To protect the present interests of the established, it is an excuse for enforcement of the order from which they so notably benefit.

Thus the phrase "law and order" has one meaning to a Rockefeller or a Reagan, another to ordinary workers. The latter resent the liberties, privileges, wealth, and securities of the professional elites based in the universities. They also resent the actual, daily contacts of their own culture with black culture. No amount of good will, theory, or ideology blinds them to the actual experience of that contact: it is very often characterized by economic penalties for both whites and blacks, by rising violence and conflict, by insolence and insult, by mutual stereotype and prejudice.

The ethnics believe that they chose one route to moderate success in America; namely, loyalty, hard work, family discipline, and gradual self-development. They tend to believe that some blacks, admittedly more deeply injured and penalized in America, want to jump, *via* revolutionary militance, from a largely rural base of skills and habits over the heads of lower-class whites. Instead of forming a coalition of the black and white lower classes, black militants seem to prefer coalition with white intellectual elites. Campus and urban disorders witness a similarity of violence, disorder, rhetoric, ideology, and style.

When ethnics say "law and order," many do so thoughtlessly, looking for any leader who will honor their own values and give them support. That is what makes the cry "law and order" potentially so demagogic. But increasing numbers of young leaders among ethnics and among workers have become more sophisticated. They see that the same economic and social elites who pollute their air, ignore their neighborhoods, send their sons to war, squander the hard-earned money they pay in taxes (often one-third of their entire $10,000 yearly income), and in other ways demean their lives, injure lower-class whites and blacks equally. Simultaneously, many black leaders see that the weight of drugs and crime falls upon the black community far harder than on any other. Law and order *must* come to the black community, or too many families, too many lives, will be destroyed. Drug traffic must be halted. Police forces, ideally derived from the community itself, must be strengthened and made effective. Liberty of life and limb is a condition for all other progress.

The phrase "law and order" can therefore be a code word for further injustice to both blacks and whites at the hands of established elites. Or it can be a cry for elemental rights to life and limb and property, without which neither blacks nor whites shall ever share genuine liberty. The overwhelming fact is the burglary, the holdup, the murder, the beatings, the barred windows that are turning urban (and even suburban) neighborhoods into medieval fortresses. Senator Henry Jackson was wildly cheered in New York in the summer of 1971 when he said: "I am a liberal Democrat and I am not soft on law and order." He said that the rich are protected from criminals, "but who protects the working man? If he cannot look to liberal Democrats, where in heaven's name can he look?"[43] Democrats in the sixties took too much inspiration from those who did not feel the weight of crime; they lost touch with real experience.

The felt quality of ethnic and working-class life in 1972 involves a world of experience as worthy as any other in America, as much in need of sympathy and support as any other. There is a race on to see who will speak best for the ethnics and the workingmen.

7. *The "Saturday Ethnics" from Professional Elites*

Not all ethnic feelings are confined to those in the working class. The culture of the American professional elites,
with its high emphasis on specialization, objectivity, and
technical proficiency, is notoriously sterile for the emotions,
the instincts, the imagination. The rebellion of the elite
young against "corporate liberalism" was in large measure
a revolt in the name of instinct: "All power to the imagination." One may regard the momentary flash of the youth
culture as irrationalist or as nihilist. One may take seriously its own pop-Freudianism ("Paranoia is true perception") and pop-Marxism ("Oppressed of the world,
arise!").[44] But we may also see in the youth culture a
profound starvation for a denser family life, a richer life
of the senses, the instincts, the memory. No other group of
young people in history was ever brought up under a more
intensive dose of value-free discourse, quantification, analytic rationality, meritocratic competition, universal standards (IQ, College Boards). What was almost wholly
neglected in their upbringing was the concrete, emotive,
even tribal, side of human nature. To that they were drawn
in a desperate way, like air sucked into a vacuum. Music,
dress, sound, sight, and feeling ran to the farthest extreme
from industrial, suburban rationality. The rise in ethnic
consciousness today is also due to disillusionment with
the universalist, too thinly rational culture of professional
elites.

The rise in ethnic consciousness is, then, part of a more
general cultural revolution. As soon as one realizes that
man is not mind alone, and that his most intelligent theories, political decisions, and works of genius flow from "intelligent subjectivity," attention to the roots of imagination,
value, and instinct is inevitable. When a person thinks
more than one generation's passions and images think in
him.[45] Below the threshold of the rational or the fully

conscious, our instincts and sensibilities lead backwards to the predilections of our forebears. More deeply than Americans have been taught to recognize, their own particular pasts live on in their present judgments and actions. Upper-class Quakers *think* and *feel* in a way that I cannot think and feel; Jewish intellectuals tend to live and breathe out of writers, concerns, and experiences I can emulate as second nature, but not as first; certain Irish Catholics exhibit emotional patterns I can follow but not find native to me. Besides a person's own private history, choices, and conscious desires, there operate in him the metaphors, memories, instincts, tastes, and values of a historical people. These traces are not simple, direct, clear, univocal. Each ethnic tradition is multiform, persons within it vary, and one generation commonly reacts against the tastes and methods of its predecessor.

The blacks have a word for those who abandon black culture for white culture—"Uncle Tom"; Italians speak of "Uncle Tomaso." But in general such terminology may be invidious. Individuals are and should be free to identify with the cultural sense of reality, stories, and symbols they prefer. After three, four, or five generations of intermarriage, or even after particularly narrow experiences in one ethnic group, many persons do not think of themselves in any other terms but "American"—mobile, cosmopolitan, not oriented toward a concrete past.[46] They are willing to lose contact with the chain of images and passions they were subtly taught before their consciousness awakened. They work with what they are aware of now, rather than searching in time and memory down the concrete, twisting route whence their psyche came to its uncontrived enthusiasms, fears, depressions, contours, energy, endurance.

Inevitably, they root their lives within a particular circle of associates and concerns, of angers and joys, of images and passions. Whether such freely chosen circles can endure, whether they will sustain more than a generation, is part of what the experiment of the "melting pot" is about. The circles of professional life—travel; career changes;

divorces; stimulants; rapid pace; whirling, solitary orbit—are notoriously draining of the simpler virtues. Some become "humane" in ideology and politics but in simple, daily living are grotesque.

No wonder, then, that many Americans who try to live in the modern, American, suburban style are restless and unsatisfied. All sorts of materials in their psyche are suppressed. The "prospering overweight sons of leaner immigrant fathers," and sometimes, too, the trim athletic sons of the overweight sons, "drive in now from suburbia to New York City's Little Italy on weekends to replenish their ever-diminishing ethnic supplies."[47] There are a great many "Saturday ethnics" in America who, like young people of the counterculture, revolt against the smooth edges of suburban life. There are, as Nicholas Pileggi puts it, many Italians who

> return, after all, not only for the bread, tiny bitter onions, bushels of snails, live eels and dried cod, but also to enjoy a weekend heritage that their education, bland wines, and the English language have begun to deny them . . . it is only with a trunk filled with Italian market produce that a Saturday Italian can face six days in the suburbs.

In everyone, not only in the working class, ethnic roots lie buried. In many the roots are so tangled through intermarriage that no one tradition dominates. "What am I?" is not a simple question. It is, in part, a matter of choice.

Still, each of us react so differently to vivid experience—to the Attica uprising, for example—that it is not idle to explore those ways in which it is not so much facts on which we differ but values, instincts, perceptual screens, imaginative structures. Often we disagree for reasons utterly different from anything we say in "rational" argument. Such reasons are almost always related not only to our personal, but also to our family and ethnic history. True, each of us stands in a new and unique relation to family and ethnicity. We are not trapped by our past, or victims of it. We are in many ways free from it, even "enlightened" from it. But we are also the fruit of it. We did not spring full-blown like some Venus from the sea.

No "enlightenment" provides a purely rational, universal form. There is no such form.

Beneath a common use of one English language, persons in different traditions have various conceptions of life and purpose and meaning. If we do not explore the range of these, we risk looking at one another wholly from outside, without sympathy. How ugly we look to one another then. Thus Professor Charles Reich, even when he is trying to be *generous* to workers, looks down a very long nose of condescension and writes sentences of unendurable contempt:

> Look again at a "fascist"—tight-lipped, tense, crew cut, correctly dressed, church-going, an American flag on his car window, a hostile eye for communists, youth, and blacks. He has had very little of love, or poetry, or music, or nature, or joy. He has been dominated by fear. He has been condemned to narrow-minded prejudice, to a self-defeating materialism, to a lonely suspicion of his fellow men. He is angry, envious, bitter, self-hating. He ravages his own environment. He has fled all his life from consciousness and responsibility. He is turned against his own nature; in his agony he has recoiled upon himself. He is what the machine left after it had its way.[48]

These words do not describe workers you can talk to in America, not if you speak to them as brother to brother, without class bias, without speaking from the height of your moral superiority. George Wallace regards the Professor, too, as "what the machine left over." Stereotype cries out to stereotype.

The psychological cosmos of workingmen and their wives is different from that of our professional elites. All through American life, one finds various cultures reacting differently to the same stimuli. A picture in a newspaper, an image on television, a speech by a president, a program presented with great publicity—each of these awakens different reactions in different American cultures. Everyone knows this. But why, then, are we so slow in developing a pluralistic manner of speech, a clear sense of each of the different cultures to which our words must be addressed, a recognized method of translation and interpretation?

8. *Ethnic Culture vs. Professional Culture*

As Marx noted, the place persons assume in the economic order deeply influences their sense of identity. A corporate executive and a steamfitter in one of his plants live, as we say, in "two different worlds," with quite divergent possibilities, hopes, and fears. Ethnic factors are also at work.

Many persons of third or fourth generation descent have availed themselves of the opportunity to become full participants in American professional life. Mike Royko, for example, has pointed out that ethnics cannot be said to be underprivileged in America when one of them is vice-president of the United States and another is a leading Democratic contender for nomination as president.[49] Several observations are in order.

Americanization exacts a price; so also does professionalization. In order to move up in the world of journalism or television, especially on a national level, it is important to be able to see the whole national picture, and to escape merely regional, ethnic, or denominational views. Persons who enter the professional elites of journalism and broadcasting, or the corporate and academic worlds, tend to think of themselves as nonparochial. But one becomes a professional only through long submission to training, discipline, and carefully criticized experience. One enters, that is, a new and not less disciplined culture. Usually, one is obliged to spend most of one's time among persons of similar training and skills. The way of life one adopts tends to be mobile. It includes travel and expense accounts, frequent changes of job and residence, sensitivities attuned to the codes of manners, and style proper to a new class. It is something of a shock, for example, to return to the neighborhood of one's birth.

For commentary on our national culture, the language and style of the northeast has been brought to a more flexible degree of universality and analytic power than that of any other region. Those born into the culture of the northeast assume its language and style as a matter of course. These are so much the native cast of their mind as to assume in them, as well, a merely parochial character. Thus people in the rest of the country often experience the northeastern style as condescending, narrow, and biased, no matter how elegant and analytic it may be. The most successful interpreters of American life are frequently those who were not born into the northeastern style, but who have learned it alongside a style of their own. A high proportion of the most successful television journalists, editors, and writers who now work in the northeast grew up elsewhere. They have at least two styles at their command.

Still, by the time a person has become a professional, a great many changes have been effected in his or her consciousness. When a young Polish-American succeeds in becoming a television commentator, he has normally had to leave "little Warsaw" very far behind.

Commonly, moreover, the professional culture into which a person moves does not allow him to express the entire range of his sensibility. There are significant differences between the images, metaphors, instincts, and energy of various ethnic groups. Each ethnic tradition is rich and allows for great personal variation. Still, John Kennedy was an altogether different sort of liberal than Adlai Stevenson or Lyndon Johnson. The metaphors and gut reactions proper to each of these men had not a little to do with the communities from which they sprang. Muskie's temper is related to his being Polish; swift expressions of anger are less repressed among a number of ethnic groups. The feeling-tone and methods by which staff members relate to one another are different in different ethnic groups. What counts as "realism" or "romanticism" varies. The threats and reinforcements people perceive tend to vary from ethnic group to ethnic group. Members of professional elites, in their adherence to "objectivity" and to standards meant to be applied universally, may develop a blindness to subtle but important social differences in themselves.[50] Mike Royko has an ethnic energy it would not hurt him to be conscious of. Stewart Alsop and Theodore White have WASP standards for what is "reasonable."

The bias of the professional classes in America, in short, disguises ethnicity. To become a professional is ordinarily to acquiesce in separation by no little gap from the people among whom one was born. One's class interests shift. One's base of power shifts. One's route to further power shifts. The professional classes in America—doctors, lawyers, engineers, academics, consultants, planners, economists, executives, chemists, architects, writers, artists— often describe themselves as a "constituency of conscience."[51] Their values, they think, are not merely the values of a class or of a region, but national, even international, and indeed equivalent to "human." They are the "human beings," others the barbarians.

Political experience teaches one to beware of the word "conscience" in politics. Who named our professional class a "constituency of conscience"? Naturally, that is what they call themselves. One looks immediately to what a group stands to gain or lose by its political commitments. The "constituency of conscience" prides itself on its concern for the poor and the oppressed in America and the Third World. But they do so in full knowledge that their own professional careers, economic security, neighborhoods, educational opportunities for their children, and summer homes are not going to be threatened, not in the least. Any likely social order needs their expertise.

And what do they have to gain? Put very simply, power. The liberal and radical "constituency of conscience" is not now in power in Washington. It is outside, looking in. A great many talented young persons are watching their youth slip away, as they while away their time in second-rate jobs. "Incompetents" run the departments of Justice; Health, Education and Welfare; and State; poverty programs; the Peace Corps, the Urban Affairs Council, etc. What route to power can the "constituency of conscience" take? They *must* mobilize young people, the poor, and the blacks if they are to outvote their rival professional elites, the conservative lawyers, industrialists, businessmen, and farmers who are the traditional backbone of the Republican party. Lucky those whose self-interest happens to coincide with conscience.

The "constituency of conscience" is no more to be trusted with the future of America than any other single group. Its moral claims need to be unmasked. Its political condescension must be checked.

The election of 1972 can differ from that of 1968 if the professional elite tries to follow rather than to lead; tries to be inclusive rather than exclusive; tries to hear voices and accents against which for too long it has closed its ears; tries to moderate its own ideologically "hot" interests for the sake of shared interests. Specifically, I hope that no new "party of the Left" is formed, and that the professional elite will revise its image of itself and the future. I hope it enters into a give-and-take with working people and ethnic interests. I hope it learns a new style of thought centered on family and neighborhood rather than on extrinsic rational planning.

"America," Barbara Mikulski says, "is a sizzling cauldron for the ethnic American." A Hungarian who arrived in Cleveland in 1965 is angry enough to say "I fought one revolution in 1956. I'm ready to start another." Even Professor Reich noted in *The Greening of America* that when the seventy million persons in America's working class become politically aware, we will see "a real explosion."[52]

The professional elites don't always realize how much they impose their own view of the world upon workers and ethnic groups. Daily they apply the full pressure of modernization. By and large, their journalism is unsympathetic to the workingmen's wives whose world is not, and cannot be, the "modern" world into which the media seem always to be prodding people. Modernization is the project of professional classes; whether it is good for children and other living things is subject to question. Behind the screen of universal values, the "constituency of conscience" is far more coercive and self-interested than it cares to admit.

9. *Pain Is or Is Not Pain*

Jews and Italians, we know, are highly dramatic people. Their self-consciousness is different from that of other ethnic groups. In each of us, the roots of perception and emotion are subterranean; we differ in fundamental movements of the psyche such as anger, hatred, desire, love. Mark Zborowski has given us a splendid study of perception called *People in Pain*.[53] (Not to mention his exquisite study of village life among East European Jews, *Life Is with People*.)[54] Dr. Zborowski interviewed male patients in a veterans' hospital. He classified them into four major ethnic groupings—nativist American, Jewish, Italian, Irish. He tried to see how they perceived pain, the hospital, disease, recuperation. The differences according to ethnic heritage turned out to be remarkable.

Such differences result in much misunderstanding and stereotyping, but also in *self*-misunderstanding. People try to be what they are not. They try to live up to a cultural type not their own. They ride roughshod over their own instinctive gropings. Self-hatred is profound.

The "Old American" in Zborowski's study doesn't believe in crying or complaining, because it doesn't help. (Practicality is his main legitimation for behavior.) The Jew and

the Italian *do* believe in crying and complaining, because
it does help. (Social drama legitimates behavior.) The
Old Americans are indignant about those of other ethnic
backgrounds:

> This fellow—he gets a lot of pain. He is Italian. He
> gets very excited. He can bellow so that you can hear
> him from one end of the hospital to the other. He is the
> fellow you ought to talk to. He ought to be psychoana-
> lyzed. [Why? What's wrong with him?] Well, he's got to
> have a lot of attention. He's only happy when there are
> two or three nurses and—uh—an attendant and a doctor
> around.[55]

The Old American believes in rational control; he likes
to feel in charge; he suffers alone. For the Italian, pain,
like everything else, is communal; he is happy when people
are around, because "life is with people." The flavor of
Old American attitudes:

> I don't cry for help, I just pull myself together and
> bite my lip. I like to control my reactions. Crying and
> screaming can't do you any good.

> I don't lay and moan. I mean, that don't get you
> nothing. It don't get you anywhere moaning about it.

> I used to have certain pains—when they first cut off my
> leg. I used to let a yell out every night. And the nurses
> used to come in there to me and say "You—you got to
> keep quiet. You are disturbing the rest of the patients."
> But—uh—I tried to do the best I could. There was
> nothing . . . that I could . . . no power I could use to
> save me from that pain that I had. The pain was
> terrible.[56]

For the Old American, disease is a "warning signal." He
imagines himself as a healthy organism in a dangerous
world full of things to avoid, under constant pressure from
potential invaders.

> The way they [the Italians] do ravioli—it's very doughy.
> And I figure on—if I eat much of it, it wouldn't digest.
> So I avoid things like that.[57]

To be inexpressive and not to need help is a way of proving his own autonomy, and also of gaining secret admiration and social reinforcement for the world-picture of autonomy. The Old American has a special concept of "resistance." If he can make his organism healthy enough, he can turn away the invaders. His body is fine; all harm is external. Dust and dirt in the environment, outside the body, are extremely dangerous. There are also countless bugs and germs out there. Everything has a cause, and so he need only be "on guard" for the early symptoms of attack. The body is more or less a machine, and the doctor is not so much a person as a man of skill. It's not difficult to believe the doctor's "probably *not* telling the truth." The Old American is himself reluctant to accept the corruptibility of his own body, so he's not sure he wants truth to intervene. He'd prefer to imagine various mechanical failures, all of which experts can manage. Pain signals which failure it is, so pain has utility. Activist in his attitude toward life, the Old American can't do enough to cooperate in treatment. It is as if health depends on his will. "Get well" is a project on which he can't wait to apply his attention.

For the Jew, by contrast, health is regarded as the exception. Each person easily sees himself as a patient and has great sympathy. Withdrawal from people is inconceivable. Pain is one of the most poignant occasions for community, sympathy, tears, caresses. Thus it helps to complain; complaint is a focus around which sympathy can flow and community be knit. Man is not alone. A wife or husband is expected to note every sign, every change of mood or attitude—*to guess,* even in advance. Attentiveness is expected to be delicate and perfect. One may imitate American restraint, but *never* the image of independence

and self-reliance. And how can one admit that tears would
be *bad*?

> I don't think I've ever cried. I've had tears come to my
> eyes—tears—but I couldn't—couldn't come out. In fact,
> sometimes I feel if I could I'd feel much better.

> I loosened down—I let out the emotion. Because I knew
> it's best to let it out than to keep it within yourself.
> Cry it out and be better off.[58]

Whereas the Old American fears diagnosis lest it destroy
his illusion of incorruptibility, the Jew delights in hearing a
precise account—his fears are invariably more total and
ominous than the event. Pain comes as a "warning signal"
to the Jew as to the Old American, but rather as the identification (at last) of the perpetual, looming enemy. His
anxieties about the future are intense and radiate in every
direction. Even slight pains are a preoccupation. They are
part of an almost cosmic drama, and every detail, nuance,
and rhythm of the pain is to be noted with the utmost precision. For the body is not a machine; it is the *self*. And
only the self knows it thoroughly. The Jew will visit several doctors. "What do *they* know?" How *could* doctors
know the self better than the self? Jews will know symptoms, diseases, drugs, and remedies with a precision and
detail unmatched by other ethnic groups. Pain is the drama
of the self in history, and the Jew loves to enliven it. Ask a
question and get a long, articulate, delightful answer. The
interviewer probes, not to provoke *more*, but to pinpoint.
The accents of Bellow, Roth, and Mailer are social poetry,
as witnessed by three patients:

> Well, I tell you what I think was pain—and to me I
> think it's a lot of pain. Do you know what a gall bladder
> attack is? Well, for eight months I took it. I rolled on the
> floor from this wall to that wall—chewing the carpet. For
> eight months! Now do you think that's pain?

> I bang my head against the wall, I've shoved my face
> into boiling water, I've taken heat lamps and gotten

so close to it as to where I've seared the skin. I have rolled around where one minute I'm lying prone and the next minute I'm up with my head buried between my legs; the next minute I'm walking around, lying down again, trying all sorts of things that might give me relief. I was laying in the house and how many times I used to roll on the floor! Many times I used to feel like jumping through the window—the pain was so severe. Another thing, I used to get relief when I jumped into the bathtub. When I jumped into the bathtub, it stopped. Not entirely, but stopped. So naturally I jumped in and out—in and out—and as soon as you get out you feel a bit chilly, and it pains again. Oh, what I went through![59]

The Irish, Dr. Zborowski finds, are almost inarticulate about pain. They don't like to think about physical weaknesses. They offer few spontaneous diagnoses, descriptions, or complaints. Their answers are taciturn, even monosyllabic, and the interviewer must probe. It's unmanly, apparently, to be as voluble about pain as the Irish plainly are on other matters. Besides, the Irishman doesn't speak of "pain," but rather of "suffering." Pain occurs in a larger dramatic context. It is not mechanical, or even a battle between germs and organism. It's a contest of the soul, a proof of stoicism and endurance. "I'm in pain," the patient says. "You better go." He wrestles with his demon alone, in privacy. He views it as a struggle—active, competitive—a process that must be undergone for the soul's good. (Whether this is a pagan stoicism or a Christian crucifixion is unclear.) "I can take it," "I can stand it"—reports from the battlefield of the spirit. Pain is for silence, loneliness, all the time it takes for the working out of a complex inner struggle.

Whereas the Old American believes pain is useless, the Irishman regards it as a priceless chance—a key to the riddle of life itself. Whereas the Old American believes it is impersonal, typical, mechanical, the Irishman treats pain as private, his, unique, and—precisely in its limited quality as pain—not worth describing to anybody else. An Irishman almost never mentions doing something to alleviate pain; the interviewer, like the doctor, must take the initiatives. Physical strength, manhood, virility are important to the Irishman's perception of pain, and also his ability to continue working. The thought of not working, or of being immobilized or disfigured wounds something very deep. Pain is not a symptom, it is a test of manhood.

> My mother is being treated right now at the Memorial. They are not sure what it is. [Did she have pain?] She did, yes. [How does she take the pain?] Very well. [What do you mean when you say "very well"?] She bore it, and she's the Spartan type. No, she never complained of her pain. [Was your father ever sick?] No, not that I can think of. He even—he is probably more hesitant about complaining about any pain than any person I've ever seen. He had a job for twenty-five years—as far as I know lost about four days in that time. He pushes himself. [Do your sisters come to see you in the hospital?] They don't know I'm in the hospital. [Why?] I didn't tell them. [How come?] I didn't think it was necessary. People have enough troubles of their own, you know, without worrying about somebody else. I have my own.

> I felt that there was a certain amount of honor, I suppose, attached to it in refusing to admit that you had pain. And occasionally I would do that, and try to force it all down and go ahead. And I'm beginning to realize that it (admitting pain) is one of the ways of expressing yourself—so that actually you shouldn't push it down too much—you should give it an expression. Yes, but there is still the degree—in there—that I haven't broken completely.[60]

The Italians, a nurse at the hospital says, are the "sweetest" patients of all; they complain, they cry, but they're like children, and they make the nurses feel useful by merely being present. For the Italian, dependency is normal, healthy, even admirable. People depend on one another, that's the beauty. There is no need to pretend to self-reliance, no need to hold back tears. "Crying is good for you." But the crying isn't just for sympathy; it's because pain is social, something to be shared. "Don't tell my wife, because she *knows*—don't bother her with it." More than the Jew, the Italian worries about the healthy partner and does not think of himself quite so fully as victim. Pain is no humiliation, an invitation to struggle, or message from the universal doom; it is a break in the daily action of joy, pleasure, food. The Italian likes to be active why not? There are so many things in life to enjoy today. *Carpe diem.* He doesn't like to "relax" as the Irishman must; he is not daily waging the Irishman's war. The Italian patient doesn't like to be alone. Thinking of past and future is not his favorite occupation; it depresses him. Pain relievers have above-normal effects upon Italians because their mood is a direct function of their pain. When pain is gone, their normal buoyancy about the goodness of life returns immediately.

Well, I get pain, but I'm the type of a fellow who ain't going to worry about it. I don't—in other words, I'm just like I was before I got hurt. This type of injury ain't going to worry me, because so what I'm going to do about it? I'm paralyzed; I get around the best I can. I get a check from the government, and I got a car to ride around with; what I'm going to worry about? Gray hair? I can meet girls; I can go out with them; I can go out to a show. Million guys worse off than me here in the hospital. What am I kicking about? I am happy. I am lucky.[61]

Take life as it comes, minute by minute, and life is sweet. The Italian has no worries about disease or being ill—those are future things. The only thing that bothers him is the present pain, which prevents enjoyment. The

Italian is not pessimistic about the future like the Jew, or optimistic like the Old American, or preoccupied with struggle like the Irishman; his consciousness stresses immediacy and joy. Worry is for him the archetypal disease. Pain is not a symptom; it *is* the disease. He couldn't care less about analysis, diagnosis, mechanics.

The Italian hates "the knife" and "the needle." He likes personal things. His parents took such constant personal interest in him that he sees the world in almost wholly personal terms. Even when the father "beat" him, he deserved it. His mother was like the madonna—or, perhaps, the madonna derives from the Italian mother:

> My mother would never punish me. She was always very good to me. When my father would beat me, she would tell my father, "Don't forget it's your son." When my father would beat me, I would cry, but I knew I deserved it. I wouldn't complain to Mother.

> When my father died, we were all crying—everybody was crying. My mother had a pretty tough time keeping us together, and she didn't remarry. She used to sew, wash dishes and floors to keep us together. She would punish us, but she didn't mean it. It hurt her more than it hurt us.

> She was sweet. Nonchalant—nothing bothered her. Hardworking woman. A real Italian mother. Very sweet person. But as sweet as she was, she knew her place. She is wonderful. She is the best mother a son could ever have. She's understanding. She's very kind—that's all.[62]

Family and food—the two great Italian joys. Food cannot possibly make anybody ill, cannot be evil. As for family, the testimony is constant:

> Oh, our family—our family is very close, very close. Now understand, I mean, we have our spats amongst ourselves and all, but still, we're very close.

I've been brought up by Father and Mother—by brothers and sisters. We were always happy together. We lived together, and we always get along well.

I love Italian families. I don't know whether you've met many Italian families. They are very happy people— very jubilant people. That's why I like my own people very much, for that reason.

My father not working for twenty years. We are supporting my father. Sure. My brother die—the one that was in the family—he die a few years ago. Now we have to support my father and mother. We are children, yes. Anything he need. One time I give him a pair of shoes and my brother a shirt. We are in business. It is nice to give him. Anything my father wants—ten dollars. He can say to the children give him. It is my duty to my father.

My mother worked very hard for us children, and we cannot do enough to satisfy her, to make her life as easy as possible now.

I never think about the future. I got my son. I brought him up right, and he can help me. If I were mean with my son, he could tell me, "My father was so mean to me, I don't care for him." But when I treat him right, the boy, he thinks about me too. Oh, he'd take care of me. That's what they say—"Pop and Mama, don't worry, because anything happen to one or the other, then I'll take care of."[63]

These different attitudes toward pain and its surrounding context are illustrative of how different a reality each of us lives in, a reality like a private cloud of meaning and significance, joining at times with other clouds, passing others by. On almost every level of moral life these differences are decisive, particularly if one looks to the *meaning* and *internal effect* of action rather than to its external, pragmatic effect. Naturally enough, the American bias is to attend to the latter. We are so different that if we waited until we all agreed upon a rationale, style, and meaning for action, we would never get started. So we usually skip the personal (communal), internal relations and concentrate on pragmatic cooperation. What we lose is a sense of who we really are and what gives meaning to our lives. We spend so much time and energy in the boiler room of pragmatic activity that we do not enjoy the cruise.

Delight comes from sharing a communal sense of reality, from being faithful to a set of communal stories, from rejoicing in communal and personal symbols. Many rootless Americans could use more delight. And, indeed, our conception of what America is, and what political action ought to be, might well be revolutionized if we take seriously our cultural pluralism; it operates within us even when we perceive a headache or an uneasy stomach. We Americans are different from each other. A strong politics might be based upon that proposition. A proportion of our widespread anomie might be healed by strengthening the organs and institutions of such differences.

The new politics is foreshadowed in the following quote:

Well, if anybody ever asks me my nationality, I'm always proud to say I'm Italian instead of—like so many people say—they're Americans. I don't see myself superior to anyone—don't get me wrong. But I think deep down inside that Italian is the best. Why? Maybe it's something inside of me which I can't identify just yet. My parents were Italian, all my friends—my real close friends. Before I got hurt I would say 90 percent of my friends were Italians. In my family we eat Italian and everything is Italian. We still at home listen to an Italian opera, and if I don't know what it means, I can always ask my father and he can always explain it to me. And if my father doesn't know, maybe my mother knows or maybe my brother knows. The relatives were always around. We had a lot of Italian friends we visited too. We usually had one of the aunts or uncles on both sides more or less.[64]

10. *What is "Ethnic"?*

When I say "ethnics" in this book, I am speaking mainly of the descendants of the immigrants of southern and eastern Europe: Poles, Italians, Greeks, and Slavs. These include, of course, Armenians, Lebanese (Ralph Nader is our favorite skinny ethnic), Slovenes, Ruthenians, Croats, Serbs, Czechs (Bohemians and Moravians), Slovaks, Lithuanians, Estonians, Russians, Spanish, and Portuguese.

The Germans, who at first were the most separatist and independent of immigrants, disdainful of American culture, were so speedily absorbed into Anglo-American life that even at the time of the Revolution Englishmen were known to observe that "they're almost like us."[65] The Nixon White House could be a cabinet for Kaiser Wilhelm: Kissinger, Haldeman, Erlichman, Ziegler, Schultz . . . as besieged WASP Russell Baker noted.

I have not fully included the Irish because, to most southern and eastern Europeans, the Irish were the first face of America. It was not at that time a pretty face. The Irish spoke English, were already well organized for political gain, and in their genial, cocky, and self-doubting way have been more than able to care for themselves. They dominated the Democratic party and the Catholic church in most of the places where ethnics arrived, and their markedly superior brokerage skills have kept them in places of dominance ever since. (They have fifty-seven percent of the U.S. Catholic bishops, only seventeen percent of the Catholic population.) The Irish, Macaulay said, have qualities that make men interesting rather than successful; his was not a good prediction. To southern and eastern European immigrants, the Irish seem remarkably cold, distant, and Anglo-Saxon. For us, to distinguish our own identity from that of the WASPS has been initially a task of distinguishing ourselves from the Irish.

Politically, however, ethnic politics is bound to include the Irish. Although their perceptions, their style, and their preferred methods differ from those of the PIGS, as Catholics we share much in common. Even Jansenism, chill and bleak and death-centered as it tended to make Irish piety (*The Portrait of the Artist as a Young Man* and *Edge of Sadness* are melancholy books), did not dim the Irish wit (*Ulysses* and *The Last Hurrah* are exuberant, ecstatic). An Irish sensibility is not as severe as the American Protestant sensibility. At least, a southern and eastern European feels more at home—although uneasy, to be sure—in Irish-American hands than in, say, the hands of Quakers. Words like "conscience," "family," "loyalty," "work," "meaning," "suffering," "sacrifice," "ideals," and even "law" have a different ring in Catholic ears than they do in Protestant ears. These things the Irish and the PIGS share. James Buckley in one way Eugene McCarthy in another, and the Kennedys have rung the changes well.

What is an ethnic group? It is a group with historical memory, real or imaginary. One belongs to an ethnic group ·in part involuntarily, in part by choice. Given a grandparent or two, one chooses to shape one's consciousness by one history rather than another. Ethnic memory is not a set of events remembered, but rather a set of instincts, feelings, intimacies, expectations, patterns of emotion and behavior; a sense of reality; a set of stories for individuals—and for the people as a whole—to live out.

Philosophers tend to speak of human action as a matter of principles or perhaps as a matter of emotional preferences. But besides the pragmatic effects of actions, there is also their intensity. Besides the principle in view, there is also the style of their execution. Besides the strategy, there is also the preferred, instinctive, comfortable ways of proceeding. Besides the tactics, there is the sense of timing, rhythm, and pace. Besides the circumstances, there are the impulses and passions. Besides the rational, discursive content, there are the gestures, winks, impassivities. Besides the agent, there is the network of others of which he is a part. Besides the calculus of interests, there are also different roles for, and ways of, experiencing pleasures and pains.

Besides happiness, or fruitful consequences, there are also the joys of doing things just for the hell of it.

The interpretive schemes according to which humans shape their actions are particular, concrete, diverse. The ethnic group is one of the chief shapers of personal action and its significance. We first learn how to act in a collective, which thereafter peoples our memory and shapes our selves. It is our human fate that, wrestle with our demons as we will, we are not solitary but social.

What is Joyce without Ireland, or Mann without the German bourgeoisie? Baldwin without Harlem, or Roth without New Jersey? You can't go home again. Nor is there any other place in which historical memory holds creative wealth. Every Jew knows it is a "complex fate."

Especially in America has the myth of homelessness been allowed to thrive, and a rootless class to grow. Industrialization thrives on rootlessness.

The realism of "enlightenment" creates a windswept vacuum in the soul, into which, finally, only naked power can rush. The enlightened ones *appear* to be more moral. But nothing prevents their children from forsaking all that they hold dear, from calling parental enlightenment darkness and sin. There is no legitimacy to the past or the present. There is nothing but liberation from roots, which is to say rootlessness. The machine meets no resistance.

PART I

You Can't
Go Home Again

Although popular rhetoric glorified the country as a
melting pot of different peoples, in actuality this
has meant melting diversity into conformity with
Anglo-Saxon characteristics. Those unable or
unwilling to accomplish the transformation have
suffered varying degrees of abuse and ostracism
because middle-class America demands conformity
before it gives acceptance.

—LEONARD DINNERSTEIN and
FREDERIC COPLE JAHER,
The Aliens.

CHAPTER TWO

Confessions of
a White Ethnic

THERE IS NO other way but autobiography by which to cure oneself of too much objectivity. It is a cure many in America might profitably indulge.

A discussion of ethnicity incites emotion. The stereotypes are not so old that they no longer injure.

While working on this book during the past year, I discovered many things about myself; my relation to my parents; my discomfort (intellectual and emotional) with a dominant conception of intellectual and professional life; my suspicion of both liberal and radical politics; my appreciation for certain kinds of writing; my unhappiness with the sterility of political debate, no less between President Nixon and his opposition than between the various epigones of the Left.

Friends of mine and critics sometimes complain that they do not know where I am, or where I am coming from. My standpoint is not fairly described (whose is?) as radical, or liberal, or conservative. So I have been trying to trace its roots.

No available public standpoint works for me. I have had to go in search of my own. A search through memory and instinct by way of history has helped. Awareness of ethnicity is not some golden thread that, taken in one's fingers and given a sudden pull, establishes the pattern of the tapestry. It is, however, an additional light for the understanding.

To understand a person's attitudes or perceptions, it is helpful to know his history. Not in order to "explain" him —for history and ethnicity "explain" nothing—but in order to estimate, against a concrete context, the weight one should assign some of his emphases. We depend on others for most of the picture of the arena in which we act. The task is to learn to see it as they see it, in order to know how to interpret what they say.

Nothing, of course, is so painful as to have one's views discounted according to some ethnic or religious stereotype. "Jews are always complaining." "A WASP *would* think so!" "You're from Mississippi, aren't you?" "New York intellectuals . . ." "That's a surprising view from a Catholic!" The knowing put-down is intolerable.

Perhaps that is why even so courageous a writer as Norman Mailer has rather steadfastly avoided Jewish materials. He tried to embrace the melting pot. When he dramatizes an encounter, central to his work, between a stud and a Jewish maid,[1] the stud is named Sergius O'Shaugnessy but given a sensibility of felt Jewishness thinly pasted over Irish. The Jewish force in Mailer is almost always hiding behind projection into Irishmen, Poles, Anglo-Saxon Texans. Mailer may want his mother's Irishness to win, but it doesn't—hardly ever. The celebrated writer's block may here have one of its sources. Meanwhile, his journalism benefits by Jewish self-dramatization. One who stands outside the usual political conflicts between WASPS, ethnics, and blacks has a fascinating alternative to the WASP style of objectivity. He gives us dramas of self and dramas of history. Sheer talent, sheer craftsmanship, divert us from the guarded core.

So the risks of letting one's own secrets out of the bag are rather real. Yet there is no other way.

1. *Neither WASP nor Jew nor Black*

Growing up in America has been an assault upon my sense of worthiness. It has also been a kind of liberation and delight.

There must be countless women in America who have known for years that something is peculiarly unfair, yet who only recently have found it possible, because of Women's Liberation, to give tongue to their pain. In recent months I have experienced a similar inner thaw, a gradual relaxation, a willingness to think about feelings heretofore shepherded out of sight.

I am born of PIGS—those Poles, Italians, Greeks, and Slavs, those non-English-speaking immigrants numbered so heavily among the workingmen of this nation. Not particularly liberal or radical; born into a history not white Anglo-Saxon and not Jewish; born outside what, in America, is considered the intellectual mainstream—and thus privy to neither power nor status nor intellectual voice.

Those Poles of Buffalo and Milwaukee—so notoriously taciturn, sullen, nearly speechless. Who has ever understood them? It is not that Poles do not feel emotion—what is their history if not dark passion, romanticism, betrayal, courage, blood? But where in America is there anywhere a language for voicing what a Christian Pole in this nation feels? He has no Polish culture left him, no Polish tongue.[2] Yet Polish feelings do not go easily into the idiom of happy America, the America of the Anglo-Saxons and yes, in the arts, the Jews. (The Jews have long been a culture of the word, accustomed to exile, skilled in scholarship and in reflection. The Christian Poles are largely of peasant origin, free men for hardly more than a hundred years.) Of what shall the young man of Lackawanna think on his way to work in the mills, departing his relatively dreary home and street? What roots does he have? What language of the heart is available to him?[3]

The PIGS are not silent willingly. The silence burns like hidden coals in the chest.

All four of my grandparents, unknown to one another, arrived in America from the same county in Slovakia. My grandfather had a small farm in Pennsylvania; his wife died in a wagon accident. Meanwhile, Johanna, fifteen, arrived on Ellis Island, dizzy from witnessing births and deaths and illnesses aboard the crowded ship. She had a sign around her neck lettered PASSAIC. There an aunt told her of a man who had lost his wife in Pennsylvania. She went. They were married. She inherited his three children.

Each year for five years Grandma had a child of her own. She was among the lucky; only one died. When she was twenty-two and the mother of seven (my father was the last), her husband died. "Grandma Novak," as I came to know her many years later, resumed the work she had begun in Slovakia at the town home of a man known to my father only as "the Professor"; she housecleaned and she laundered.

I heard this story only weeks ago. Strange that I had not asked insistently before. Odd that I should have such shallow knowledge of my roots. Amazing to me that I do nôt know what my family suffered, endured, learned, and hoped these last six or seven generations. It is as if there were no project in which we all have been involved, as if history in some way began with my father and with me.

The estrangement I have come to feel derives not only from lack of family history. Early in life, I was made to feel a slight uneasiness when I said my name.[4]

Later "Kim" helped. So did Robert. And "Mister Novak" on TV. The name must be one of the most Anglo-Saxon of the Slavic names. Nevertheless, when I was very young, the "American" kids still made something out of names unlike their own, and their earnest, ambitious mothers thought long thoughts when I introduced myself.

Under challenge in grammar school concerning my nationality, I had been instructed by my father to an-

amazon.com·

amazon.com·   1850 Mercer Rd.
Lexington, KY 40511

D5XMZg0yR/-3 of 3-/sss-us/6203807 PS

Your order of April 2, 2011 (Order ID 002-1778503-9145047)

Qty.	Item
1	**Cradles of Conscience: Ohio's Independent Colleges and Universities** James A. Hodges --- Paperback **(** E-8 **) 0873387635**
1	**Liberal Arts at the Brink** Hardcover **(** E-8 **) 0674049721**
1	**Unmeltable Ethnics: Politics and Culture in American Life** Novak, Michael --- Paperback **(** E-8 **) 1560007737**

Subtotal
Shipping & Han
Promotional Cei
Order Total
Paid via credit/c
Balance due

This shipment completes your order.

Have feedback on how we packaged your order? Tell us at www.amazon.com/packa

	Item Price	Total
	$50.00	$50.00
	$23.84	$23.84
	$24.95	$24.95

	$98.79
ling	$5.97
:ificate	$-5.97
	$98.79
ebit	$98.79
	$0.00

ging.

amazon.com

www.amazon.com/
your-account

For detailed information about this and
other orders, please visit Your Account.
You can also print invoices, change your
e-mail address and payment settings,
alter your communication preferences,
and much more - 24 hours a day - at
http://www.amazon.com/your-account.

Returns Are Easy!

Visit http://www.amazon.com/returns
to return any item - including gifts - in
unopened or original condition within 30
days for a full refund (other restrictions
apply). Please have your order ID ready.

E-mail, Print, or Mail at www.amazon.com/giftcards

Type : 1A3

nounce proudly: "American." When my family moved from the Slovak ghetto of Johnstown to the WASP suburb on the hill, my mother impressed upon us how well we must be dressed, and show good manners, and behave— people think of us as "different" and we mustn't give them any cause. "Whatever you do, marry a Slovak girl," was other advice to a similar end: "They cook. They clean. They take good care of you. For your own good." I was taught to be proud of being Slovak, but to recognize that others wouldn't know what it meant, or care.

When I had at last pierced the deception—that most movie stars and many other professionals had abandoned their European names in order to feed American fantasies —I felt only a little sadness. One of my uncles, for business reasons and rather late in life, changed his name, too, to a simple German variant—not long, either, after World War II.

Nowhere in my schooling do I recall any attempt to put me in touch with my own history. The strategy was clearly to make an American of me. English literature, American literature, and even the history books, as, I recall them, were peopled mainly by Anglo-Saxons from Boston (where most historians seemed to live). Not even my native Pennsylvania, let alone my Slovak forebears, counted for very many paragraphs. (We did have something called "Pennsylvania History" somewhere; I seem to remember its puffs for industry. It could have been written by a Mellon.) I don't remember feeling envy or regret: a feeling, perhaps, of unimportance, of remoteness, of not having heft enough to count.

The fact that I was born a Catholic also complicated life. What is a Catholic but what everybody else is in reaction against? Protestants reformed "the whore of Babylon." Others were "enlightened" from it, and Jews had reason to help Catholicism and the social structure it was rooted in fall apart. The history books and the whole of education hummed in upon that point (for during crucial years I attended a public school): to be modern is decidedly not to be medieval; to be reasonable is not to be dogmatic; to be free is clearly not to live under ecclesiastical authority; to be scientific is not to attend ancient rituals, cherish irrational symbols, indulge in mythic practices. It is hard to grow up Catholic in America without becoming defensive, perhaps a little paranoid, feeling forced to divide the world between "us" and "them."

English Catholics have little of the sense of inferiority in which many other Catholic groups tend to share—Irish Catholics, Polish Catholics, Lithuanians, Germans, Italians, Lebanese, and others. Daniel Callahan (*The Mind of the Catholic Layman, Generation of the Third Eye*) and Garry Wills ("Memories of a Catholic Boyhood," in *Esquire*) both identify, in part, with the more secure Catholicism of an Anglo-Catholic parent. The French around New Orleans have a social ease different from the French Catholics of Massachusetts. Still, as Catholics, especially vis-à-vis the national liberal culture, nearly all have felt a certain involuntary defensiveness. Granted our diverse ethnic circumstances, we share a certain communion of memories.

We had a special language all our own, our own pronunciation for words we shared in common with others (Augústine, contémplative), sights and sounds and smells in which few others participated (incense at Benediction of the Most Blessed Sacrament, Forty Hours, wakes, and altar bells at the silent consecration of the Host); and we had our own politics and slant on world affairs. Since earliest childhood, I have known about a "power elite" that runs America: the boys from the Ivy League in the State Department as opposed to the Catholic boys in Hoover's FBI who (as Daniel Moynihan once put it), keep watch on them. And on a whole host of issues, my people have been, though largely Democratic, conservative: on censorship, on communism, on abortion, on religious schools, etc. "Harvard" and "Yale" long meant "them" to us.

The language of Spiro Agnew, the language of George Wallace, excepting its idiom, awakens childhood memories in me: of men arguing in the barbershop, of my uncle drinking so much beer he threatened to lay his dick upon the porch rail and wash the whole damn street with steaming piss—while cursing the niggers in the mill below, and the Yankees in the mill above—millstones he felt pressing him. Other relatives were duly shocked, but everybody loved Uncle George; he said what he thought.

We did not feel this country belonged to us. We felt fierce pride in it, more loyalty than anyone could know. But we felt blocked at every turn. There were not many intellectuals among us, not even very many professional men. Laborers mostly. Small businessmen, agents for corporations perhaps. Content with a little, yes, modest in expectation, and content. But somehow feeling cheated. For a thousand years the Slovaks survived Hungarian hegemony and our strategy here remained the same: endurance and steady work. Slowly, one day, we would overcome.

A special word is required about a complicated symbol: sex. To this day my mother finds it hard to spell the word intact, preferring to write "s--." Not that much was made of sex in our environment. And that's the point: silence. Demonstrative affection, emotive dances, an exuberance Anglo-Saxons seldom seem to share; but on the realities of sex, discretion. Reverence, perhaps; seriousness, surely. On intimacies, it was as though our tongues had been stolen, as though in peasant life for a thousand years—as in the novels of Tolstoi, Sholokhov, and even Kosinski—the context had been otherwise. Passion, certainly; romance, yes; family and children, certainly; but sex rather a minor if explosive part of life.

Imagine, then, the conflict in the generation of my brothers, sister, and myself. (The reviewer for the *New York Times* reviews on the same day two new novels of fantasy—one a pornographic fantasy to end all such fantasies [he writes], the other in some comic way representing the redemption wrought by Jesus Christ. In language and verve, the books are rated evenly. In theme, the reviewer notes his embarrassment in even reporting a religious fantasy, but no embarrassment at all about preposterous pornography.) Suddenly, what for a thousand years was minor becomes an all-absorbing investigation. Some view it as a drama of "liberation" when the ruling classes (subscribers to the *New Yorker*, I suppose) move progressively, generation by generation since Sigmund Freud, toward concentration upon genital stimulation, and latterly toward 'consciousness-raising sessions in Clit. Lib. But it is rather a different drama when we stumble suddenly upon mores staggering any expectation our grandparents ever cherished. Fear of becoming "sexual objects" is an ancient fear that appears in many shapes. The emotional reaction of Maria Wyeth in Joan Didion's *Play It as It Lays* is exactly what the ancient morality would have predicted.

Yet more significant in the ethnic experience in America is the intellectual world one meets: the definition of values, ideas, and purposes emanating from universities, books, magazines, radio, and television. One hears one's own voice echoed back neither by spokesmen of "middle America" (so complacent, smug, nativist, and Protestant), nor by the "intellectuals." Almost unavoidably, perhaps, education in America leads the student who entrusts his soul to it in a direction which, lacking a better word, we might call liberal: respect for individual conscience, a sense of social responsibility, trust in the free exchange of ideas and procedures of dissent, a certain confidence in the ability of men to "reason together" and adjudicate their differences, a frank recognition of the vitality of the unconscious, a willingness to protect workers and the poor against the vast economic power of industrial corporations, and the like.

On the other hand, the liberal imagination has appeared to be astonishingly universalist and relentlessly missionary. Perhaps the metaphor "enlightenment" offers a key. One is *initiated into light*. Liberal education tends to separate children from their parents, from their roots, from their history, in the cause of a universal and superior religion. One is taught regarding the unenlightened (even if they be one's uncles George and Peter, one's parents, one's brothers, perhaps) what can only be called a modern equivalent of *odium theologicum*. Richard Hofstadter described anti-intellectualism in America (more accurately, in nativist America rather than in ethnic America), but I have yet to encounter a comparable treatment of anti-unenlightenment among our educated classes.

In particular, I have regretted and keenly felt the absence of that sympathy for PIGS which simple human feeling might have prodded intelligence to muster, that same sympathy which the educated find so easy to conjure up for black culture, Chicano culture, Indian culture, and other cultures of the poor. In such cases one finds the universalist pretensions of liberal culture suspended; some groups, at least, are entitled to be both different and respected. Why do the educated classes find it so difficult to want to understand the man who drives a beer truck, or the fellow with a helmet working on a site across the street with plumbers and electricians, while their sensitivities race easily to Mississippi or even Bedford-Stuyvesant?

There are deep secrets here, no doubt, unvoiced fantasies and scarcely admitted historical resentments. Few persons in describing "middle Americans" "the silent majority," or Scammon and Wattenberg's "typical American voter" distinguish clearly enough between the nativist American and the ethnic American. The first is likely to be Protestant, the second Catholic. Both may be, in various ways, conservative, loyalist, and unenlightened. Each has his own agonies, fears, betrayed expectations. Neither is ready, quite, to become an ally of the other. Neither has the same history behind him here. Neither has the same hopes. Neither lives out the same psychic voyage, shares the same symbols, has the same sense of reality. The rhetoric and metaphors proper to each differ from those of the other.

There is overlap, of course. But country music is not a polka; a successful politician in a Chicago ward needs a very different "common touch" from the one needed by the county clerk in Normal. The urban experience of immigration lacks that mellifluous, optimistic, biblical vision of the good America which springs naturally to the lips of politicians from the Bible Belt. The nativist tends to believe with Richard Nixon that he "knows America, and the American heart is good." The ethnic tends to believe that every American who preceded him has an angle, and that he, by God, will some day find one, too. (Often, ethnics complain that by working hard, obeying the law, trusting their political leaders, and relying upon the American dream, they now have only their own naiveté to blame for rising no higher than they have.)

It goes without saying that the intellectuals do not love "middle America," and that for all the good, warm discovery of America that preoccupied them during the 1950s no strong tide of respect accumulated in their hearts for the Yahoos, Babbitts, Agnews, and Nixons of the land. Willie Morris in *North Toward Home* writes poignantly of the chill, parochial outreach of the liberal sensibility, its failure to engage the humanity of the modest, ordinary little man west of the Hudson. The Intellectual's Map of the United States is succinct: "Two coasts connected by United Airlines."

Unfortunately, it seems, the ethnics erred in attempting to Americanize themselves before clearing the project with the educated classes. They learned to wave the flag and to send their sons to war. They learned to support their President—an easy task, after all, for those accustomed to obeying authority. And where would they have been if Franklin Roosevelt had not sided with them against established interests? They knew a little about communism—the radicals among them in one way, and by far the larger number of conservatives in another. To this day not a few exchange letters with cousins and uncles who did not leave for America when they might have, whose lot is demonstrably harder than their own and less than free.

Finally, the ethnics do not like, or trust, or even understand the intellectuals. It is not easy to feel uncomplicated affection for those who call you "pig," "fascist," "racist." One had not yet grown accustomed to not hearing "hunkie," "Polack," "spic," "mick," "dago," and the rest. A worker in Chicago told reporter Lois Wille in a vividly home-centered outburst:

> The liberals always have despised us. We've got these mostly little jobs, and we drink beer and, my God, we bowl and watch television and we don't read. It's goddamn vicious snobbery. We're sick of all these phoney integrated TV commercials with these upper-class Negroes. We know they're phoney.
>
> The only time a Pole is mentioned it's to make fun of him. He's Ignatz Dumbrowski, 274 pounds and 5-foot-4, and he got his education by writing into a firm on a matchbook cover. But what will we do about it? Nothing, because we're the new invisible man, the new whipping boy, and we still think the measure of a man's what he does and how he takes care of his children and what he's doing in his own home, not what he thinks about Vietnam.[5]

At no little sacrifice, one had apologized for foods that smelled too strong for Anglo-Saxon noses; moderated the wide swings of Slavic and Italian emotion; learned decorum; given oneself to education, American style; tried to learn tolerance and assimilation. Each generation criticized the earlier for its authoritarian and European and old-fashioned ways. "Up-to-date" was a moral lever. And now when the process nears completion, when a generation appears that speaks without accent and goes to college, still you are considered "pigs," "fascists," and "racists."

Racists? Our ancestors owned no slaves. Most of us ceased being serfs only in the last two hundred years—the

Russians in 1861. Italians, Lithuanians, Slovaks, Poles are not, in principle, against "community control," or even against ghettoes of our own.

Whereas the Anglo-Saxon model appears to be a system of atomic individuals and high mobility, our model has tended to stress communities of our own, attachment to family and relatives, stability, and roots. Ethnics tend to have a fierce sense of attachment to their homes, having been homeowners for less than three generations: a home is almost fulfillment enough for one man's life. Some groups save arduously in a passion to *own;* others rent. We have most ambivalent feelings about suburban assimilation and mobility. The melting pot is a kind of homogenized soup, and its mores only partly appeal to ethnics: to some, yes, and to others, no.

It must be said that ethnics think they are better people than the blacks. Smarter, tougher, harder working, stronger in their families. But maybe many are not sure. Maybe many are uneasy. Emotions here are delicate; one can understand the immensely more difficult circumstances under which the blacks have suffered; and one is not unaware of peculiar forms of fear, envy, and suspicion across color lines. How much of this we learned in America by being made conscious of our olive skin, brawny backs, accents, names, and cultural quirks is not plain to us. Racism is not our invention; we did not bring it with us; we had prejudices enough and would gladly have been spared new ones. Especially regarding people who suffer more than we.

When television commentators and professors say "humanism" or "progress," it seems to ethnics like moral pressure to abandon their own traditions, their faith, their associations, in order to reap higher rewards in the culture of the national corporations. Ethnic neighborhoods usually do not like interviewers, consultants, government agents, organizers, sociologists. Usually they resent the media. Almost all spokesmen they meet from the world of intellect have disdain for them. It shows. Do museums, along the

"Black art" and "Indian art," have "Italo-American" exhibitions or "Lithuanian-American" days? Dvorak wrote the *New World Symphony* in a tiny community of Bohemian craftsmen in Iowa. All over the nation in print studios and metal foundries when the craftsmen immigrants from Europe die, their crafts will die with them. Who here supports such skills?

2. *A Cumulative Political Awakening*

Such a tide of resentment begins to overwhelm the descendant of "the new immigration" when he begins to voice repressed feelings about America that at first his throat clogs with despair. Dare he let resentment out? Shouldn't he keep calm? Can he somehow, out of anything available, put together categories and words, and shoot them aloft, slim silver missiles of despair? The incoming planes are endless. The illusions of Americans are vast.

Allies are foes; foes are friends. A language for ethnic divergence does not exist. Prejudices are deep in social structures and institutions; deep, too, in moralities and philosophies; not shallow in families and close relationships. American politics is going crazy because of a fundamental ignorance. Intellectuals, too, are blind.

The battle is partly in one's own soul. On the one hand American, enlightened, educated; on the other, stubbornly resistant, in love with values too dear to jettison, at home neither in the ethnic community nor in any intellectual group, neither with theorists nor with practical politicians, convinced of a certain rightness in one's soul and yet not confident that others will see, can see, the subtle links in a different way of life. It is the insecurity of certainty: the sense that something of value is not likely to be understood. The planes keep droning on and on.

A Slovak proverb: When trees are blown across the road in front of you, you know a tornado's coming.

It is impossible to define people out of existence, or to define their existence for them. Sooner or later, being free, they will explode in rage.

If you are a descendant of southern and eastern Europeans, everyone else *has* defined your existence. A pattern of "Americanization" is laid out. You are catechized, cajoled, and condescended to by guardians of good Anglo-Protestant attitudes. You are chided by Jewish libertarians. Has ever a culture been so moralistic?

The entire, experience of becoming American is summarized in the experience of being made to feel guilty.

For southern and eastern Europeans, there is one constant in their experience of America—abated and relieved for perhaps the decade of the fifties only. They are constantly told to gear up for some new morality. Even in being invited to give a speech on ethnic problems (as the token ethnic), one is told chummily by the national organizer: "As far as I'm concerned, the white ethnics are simply a barrier to social progress." Catching himself, he is generous: "Though I suppose they have their problems, too."

The *old* rule by which ethnics were to measure themselves was the WASP ethic. The *new* rule is getting "with it." The latter is based on new technologies and future shock. The latter could not have existed without the family life and social organization of the former. Parent and child are now at war. In the middle—once again—are southern and eastern Europeans. We are becoming almost Jewish in our anticipation of disaster. When anything goes wrong, or dirty work needs doing, we're *it*.

I never intended to think this way. I never intended to begin writing—ye gods!—as an *ethnic*. I never intended to dig up old memories.

What began to prod me were political events. The anomaly in American publishing and television of William F. Buckley, Jr., had long troubled me: a Catholic who was making a much-needed criticism of American "enlightenment," but from a curiously Anglo-Saxon and conservative point of view. I hoped he was not a dotted line which a larger Catholic movement would fill in.

By the time of the Goldwater campaign of 1964 and the Wallace campaign of 1966, I was alarmed by the cleavage between the old WASP and the new technological consciousness. Catholics might be driven to choose, and might choose the older ways. Worse still, I began to be irritated by the controlled, but felt, anti-Catholic bias among journalists and intellectuals. Despite myself, I disliked the general American desire to believe that ethnic groups do not exist, or if they do, should not. I had nothing to do with ethnic groups myself, and no intention of linking myself to them. I was neither ashamed of them nor hostile to them; it simply seemed to me important, even from their point of view, for me to live the fullest life and to do the best work I could.

But then interpretations of the Wallace vote among Catholics in Wisconsin and Maryland seemed to me grossly false and unfair. I wasn't about to *identify* with the pro-Wallace voters. But I felt increasingly uncomfortable with the condescension and disdain heaped upon them.[6] So I found myself beginning to say "we," rather than "they," when I spoke of ethnics. It is not an entirely comfortable "we," for many ethnics have not been to college, or travelled, or shared the experiences I've had. I wasn't sure I wanted to defend them, or whether I was entitled to do so after too many years of separation from them. I couldn't be sure whether in the next decade the ethnics or the intellectuals would first abandon the path of community, diversity, integrity, and justice. Despite their internal diversity, intellectuals are by and large as capable of minority rule and a relatively narrow ideology as any other group. Meanwhile, the despair and frustration of ethnic groups might become so great that they will think only of their own survival and welfare, and close their hearts to everybody else. American life sometimes hardens. It has not yet hardened, but the present decade is (as usual) crucial.

Which group offers a better chance for social progress—

the intellectuals or the ethnics? The sixties have convinced me. The intellectuals cannot do it alone. Arrogance is their principal defect, an arrogance whose lash everybody else in America has felt. A Boston policeman gave Robert Coles the picture:

> I think the college crowd, the left-wing college crowd, is trying to destroy this country, step by step. They're always looking for trouble. They're never happy, except when everyone pays attention to them—and let me tell you, the ordinary people of this country, the average workingman, he's sick and tired of those students, so full of themselves, and their teachers who all think they're the most important people in the human race.

Then a gas station attendant gave Coles some advice to pass along to Daniel Berrigan in jail:

> And tell him he's wasting his time, because this country is run by the big industrialists, and the politicians who do what they're told to do, and the big-mouthed professors (they're all so swellheaded) who are always whispering advice to people—as if they know how the world works! That's what I say: tell the poor father to mind his own business and get out of prison and speak honestly to his flock, but stay away from politics and things like that— or else he'll start sounding like a crook himself. All politicians learn to sugarcoat the truth; they just don't talk straight from the shoulder. I guess they look down on the ordinary American workingman. I guess they don't trust us. I guess they figure they can con us, all the time con us.[8]

3. *The Flag, That Flag*

From 1870 until 1941 ethnics were told they were not worthy of America. They are cynical about authority, but they believed the dream.

The flag to ethnic Americans is not a symbol of bureaucracy or system (of which the middle classes know far more than they). It is a symbol of spiritual and moral value. It was held beyond their grasp for generations. The flag invoked asceticism, struggle, a long climb up a bitterly contested mountain. Blood flowed until it was implanted on the peak. Iwo Jima was another Calvary.

To ethnics, America is almost a religion. The flag alone proves that they are not stupid, cloddish, dull, but capable of the greatest act men can make: to die for others. The flag is not a patriotic symbol only. It is the symbol of poor and wretched people who now have jobs and homes and liberties. It is a symbol of transcendence. Many millions proved that they were men, not PIGS, by expressing a willingness to die beneath those colors. When that flag flaps, their dignity is celebrated.

Those who attack the flag attack the chief symbol of transcendence, human dignity, and acceptance available to millions of human beings.

"I AM AN AMERICAN!" How many humiliations were endured until one could say those words and not be laughed at by nativists.

Where has the dream led, in reality? While a young Italian lawyer was working with a civil rights team in Mississippi, his home city was running an expressway through the traditional homes of his family. While a young Pole was in Vietnam, his brother was laid off from work. His parents became so furious at being stereotyped as racists they are wondering why they ever came to America.

The new experiences awaken memories that are too painful. A white nativist woman in a coal town in Pennsylvania establishes the historical perspective:

Why, I would just as soon live alongside a nigger family as some of these foreigners. I think that the niggers are whiter than the foreigners are because at least they speak your own language . . . [Foreigners] might be plotting to kill you and you wouldn't even know it. . . . They remind me of these oldtime people back in the Bible.

The women would have a shawl of some kind on their head. . . . They had a different look from us . . . couldn't talk our language.[9]

Our parents "began to go out of their way in order to act American. You see, they could not stand shame, and shame was one of the means used to get them to come over and change their habits." In those dark days the flag, at least, meant pride. It was not *their* flag. It was *ours*.[10]

4. *The Itch to Modernize*

In recent years new cleavages have sprung open among the intellectuals. A few still speak for technocracy—for that alliance of science, industry, and humanism whose heaven is "progress." Others seem to be taking up the view once ascribed to ecclesiastical conservatives and traditionalists: that commitment to "growth" is narrow, ideological, and hostile to the best interests of mankind. In the past the great alliance for progress had sprung from the conviction that "knowledge is power." Both humanists and scientists could agree on that, and labored in their separate ways to make the institutions of knowledge dominant in society: break the shackles of the church; extend suffrage to the middle classes; and finally, for all, win untrammelled liberty for the marketplace of ideas. Today it is no longer plain that the power bought by knowledge is humanistic. Thus the parting of the ways.

Concerning these matters, more distinctions must be made. Suffice it now to note, as an example too plainly put, that science has ever carried with it the stories and symbols of a major religion. It is ruthlessly universalist. If its participants are not "saved," they are nonetheless "enlightened," which isn't bad. Every single action of the practicing scientist, no matter how humble, could once be understood as a contribution to the welfare of the human race; each smallest gesture was invested with meaning, given a place in a scheme, and weighted with redemptive power. Moreover, the scientist was in possession of "the truth"—indeed, of the very meaning of and validating procedures for the word. The scientist's role was therefore sacred.

In recent years, the scientist has faced Reformers. Theses have been nailed upon his laboratory doors. The stole of sacred power has fallen on the shoulders of the social scientist or program organizer, who will reconstruct society. Take it apart, put it back together. In love with change, the new social activist dreads apathy and inertia, is excited by "breakthroughs." He likes things that are "forward-looking." "Liberation" is his banner.

Imagine, then, an uncertain Slovak entering an Introductory Course in the Sociology of Religion at the nearby state university. Is he sent back to his Slovak roots, led to recover paths of experience latent in all his instincts and reflexes, given an image of the life of his grandfather that suddenly, in recognition, brings tears to his eyes? Is he brought to a deeper appreciation of his Lutheran or Catholic heritage and its resonances with other bodies of religious experience? On the contrary, he is secretly taught disdain for what his grandfather *thought* he was doing when he acted or felt or imagined through religious forms. In the boy's psyche, a new religion is implanted: power over others, enlightenment, an atomic (rather than a communitarian) sensibility, a contempt for mystery, ritual, transcendence, soul, absurdity, and tragedy; and deep confidence in the possibilities of building a better world through scientific understanding. Or, by way of reaction, the new myths of the counterculture, the new hopes of radical politics. He is led to feel ashamed for the statistical portrait of Slovak immigrants, which shows them to be conservative, authoritarian, not given to dissent, etc. His teachers instruct him with the purest of intentions, in a way that is value-free.

To be sure, certain radical writers in America have begun to bewail "the laying on of culture," and to unmask the cultural religion implicit in the American way of science.[11] Yet radicals, one learns, often have an agenda of their own. What fascinates *them* about working-class ethnics are the traces, now almost lost, of *radical* activities among the working class two or three generations ago. Scratch the resentful boredom of a classroom of working-class youths, we are told, and you will find hidden in their past some formerly imprisoned organizer for the CIO, some Sacco-Vanzetti, some bold pamphleteer for the IWW. All this is true. But suppose a study of the ethnic past reveals that most ethnics have been, are, and wish to remain culturally conservative? Suppose, for example, they wish to deepen their religious roots and defend their ethnic enclaves? Must a radical culture nonetheless be "laid on" them?

According to the sense of reality of educated people, we are living in a new age which demands a new kind of man and woman. It is *better*, *liberated*, *more advanced*, and *more mature* to fall in behind the avant-garde. Such is the modern but invisible religion.

One tenet of the new sense of reality (for that is what a religion is) is that each person is an individual; his body is his property, his personal behavior is his business. Another tenet is that society is *put back together again* rationally, cognitively, bureaucratically.

Becoming modern, then, is a matter of learning to be solitary—assuming it is normal to be alone—and dreaming of reconstruction. "New," "alone," and "alienated" are words of moral status. Those to whom they apply are to be commended. (My own name, "Novak," means newcomer, stranger, the new man who comes alone; I do not think the ancient connotations were of commendation.)

Many today express the invisible religion in their behavior. Their fundamental metaphor is atomic: they exist alone, apart. If they *join* something, the association is extrinsic. They remain encapsulated in their own hard center. Thus loyalties are temporary, marriages are contingent. Warren Bennis characterizes the most radical image for the new religion: "the temporary society." We are instructed to think about ourselves in a new way, to imagine ourselves in a different relationship to the universe and to others. Nothing permanent, everything discardable. Being temporally later in human history is assessed as being morally higher. The younger the person, the more likely he is to be pure.

So pervasive is the new sense of reality, in its conservative as well as in its radical expression, that one hardly knows how to call attention to it. We are so much *in* it; it is so much a part of the texture of our language, our distinctions, our stories, and our learned responses that we have very little distance from it. Except . . .

Except that many of us do have wives and husbands: children; close friends; sets of people with whom we spend seventy or eighty percent of our free time; relatives; and autobiographies. We have roots. A certain elite, it is. true, has fewer roots than others: those who know no neighborhood, who move a great deal—the mobile ones, the swinging atoms, the true practitioners of the new religion. Others worship only occasionally from afar.

Some people in America today are network people, not atoms; socially textured selves, not individuals; persons described more accurately as "we" than as "I." They live, now not they, but their neighbors live in them. It is the natural, normal, ordinary way of life. And in fact, the liberated, mobile ones, the atomic ones, imitate it far more than pure doctrine would allow. Like tends to marry like, to bring up children in the new way, to seek out employment with and residence near like-minded people. The patterns of freely chosen association come to resemble somewhat the closely knit communities of the sociological past. *Gesellschaft* is not, after all, so utterly different from *Gemeinschaft*. The children of the atomic ones manifest a pronounced communal spirit.

The network people, among whom are the white ethnics, find it hard to think of themselves as atoms, or of their neighborhoods as mere pieces of geography. Into their definition of themselves enter their family, their in-laws, their relatives, their friends, their streets, their stores, familiar smells and sights and sounds. Those things are not, as they are for the atomic people, extrinsic. For the network people these things are identity, life, *self*. It is not that the network people are *attached* to such things. They *are* such things. Take away such things, and part of them dies.

It is, of course, part of Americanizing the Indian, the slave, or the immigrant to dissolve network people into atomic people. Some people resisted the acid. They refused to melt. These are the unmeltable ethnics.

5. *A Liberalism of the Imagination*

The *wrong* reason to promote ethnicity is out of fear. Louise Kapp Howe expresses it succinctly in the last sentence of *The White Majority*:

> For if the error of the sixties was that the people of the white majority were never given a concrete personal reason for social advance, the clear and present danger of the seventies is that they won't be warned in time against the threat of social repression being waged in their name.[12]

In other words, attend to the ethnic because he is an ignorant vehicle of repression; enlighten him. EEEE!

The *right* reason to promote ethnicity is that it offers resources to the imagination.

America has never confronted squarely the problem of preserving diversity. I can remember meeting in my youth bitter arguments that parochial schools were "divisive." Now the public schools are attacked for their commitment to homogenization. Well, how *does* a nation of no one culture, no one language, no one race, no one history, no one ethnic stock continue to exist as one, while encouraging diversity? How can the rights of all, particularly of the weak, be defended if power is decentralized and left to local interests? The weak have ever found strength in this country through local chapters of national organizations.

But what happens when the national organizations themselves—the schools, the unions, the federal government—become vehicles of a new, universalistic, thoroughly rationalized, technological culture?

The tradition of liberalism is a tradition I have had to acquire, despite an innate skepticism about many of its structural metaphors (free marketplace, individual autonomy, reason naked and undisguised, enlightenment). Radical politics, with its bold and simple optimism about human potential and its anarchic tendencies, has been, despite its appeal to me as a vehicle for criticizing liberalism, freighted with emotions, sentiments, and convictions about humans I cannot bring myself to share. As critics noted, my radical writings (*A Theology for Radical Politics*, for example), are rooted in the social and earthy sensibility of Catholic experience. They are explicit about my dismay at "Protestant" tendencies. In later chapters (below), I contrast my views with "Jewish" tendencies.

In my guts I do not feel that institutions are "repressive" in any meaning of the word that leaves it meaningful. The "state of nature" seems to me, emotionally, far less liberating, far more undifferentiated and confining. I have not dwelt for so long in the profession of the intellectual life that I find it easy to be as critical and harsh as seems to be the practice. In almost everything I see or hear or read, I am struck first, rather undiscriminatingly, by all the things I like in it. Only with a second effort can I bring myself to discern the flaws. My emotions and values seem to run in affirmative patterns.

My interest, in fact, is not in defining myself over against the American people and the American way of life. I do not expect as much of it as all that. What I should like to do is come to a better and more profound knowledge of who I am, whence my community came, and whither my son and daughter, and their children, might wish to head in the future: I want to have a history.

More and more I think in family terms, less ambitiously, on a less than national scale. The differences implicit in being Slovak, Catholic, and of lower-middle-class origin seem more and more important to me. Perhaps it is too much to try to speak to all peoples in this very various nation of ours. Yet it does not seem evident that by becoming more concrete, accepting one's finite and limited identity, one necessarily becomes parochial. Quite the opposite. It seems more likely that, by each of us becoming more profoundly what we are, we will find greater unity in those depths in which unity irradiates diversity than we will by attempting, through the artifices of the American "melting pot," and the cultural religion of science or the dreams of radical utopias, to become what we are not.

There is, I take it, a form of liberalism not wedded to universal Reason, whose ambition is not to homogenize all peoples on this planet, and whose base lies rather in the imagination and in the diversity of human stories—a liberalism it is the task of this book to try to find.

CHAPTER THREE

The Nordic Jungle: Inferiority in America

I'VE NOTICED IT in others—sometimes in Jews, just around the corner of attention. Everything is going well; they've forgotten the familiar feeling. Then something you say prompts uneasiness in their eyes, the eyes of one hunted, almost found, in danger. Swiftly it passes. Intelligence resumes its high performance.

You can generate that uneasiness in the eyes of almost any American, except a wealthy WASP: in Poles, Italians, Chicanos, Blacks, in Greeks, Armenians, the French . . . Unworthiness was stamped upon their souls. Red-hot branding irons singe a calf's new skin. The trauma can be traced, reopened . . .

1. Not a Melting Pot—a Jungle

Louis Adamic grew up in a small village in Carniola, Slovenia. It is not Slovakia, but it is as close a parallel as I can find. All through his childhood—he was born in 1899—his imagination was fired by America. His parents did not want him to go. His father's farm was small but adequate; he looked forward to help from his children, of whom Louis was the oldest. (Over the years, the number of children reached nine.)

As Louis grew up, he saw many men come back broken from America. Some had diseases no one had ever heard of: rheumatism and asthma. Many others had gone to America and disappeared like stones in a deep, dark well. No one ever heard from them again. News of horrible accidents in which others were involved came back frequently: many died in mills or mines. His mother had a special dread concerning those who worked and died underground.

Louis was not a very religious boy. He was an observer rather than a participant in life—cool, detached, often moved with affection. He loved the almost pagan religion of his mother, her joy in life and fatalism in disaster. He did not see in Catholicism—although he did not like it— what its American critics saw. The feeling for religion among Slavic and Italian peoples is almost totally different from the feeling of WASPS or Irish Catholics: more pagan, more secular, closer to earth, aesthetic rather than moral, meditative rather than organizational. Adamic describes his mother:

In common with many peasant women in Slovenia, mother was not deeply religious in the ordinary sense. I believe that she scarcely concerned herself with the tenets of the Catholic faith. She was innately pagan. In her blood throbbed echoes of prayers that her ancestors —Old Slavs—had addressed a thousand years ago from their open-air sacrificial altars to the sun and to the wind—and thunder-gods. What largely appealed to her in Catholicism, although, of course, she was not conscious of the fact, were the ritual and the trappings. She loved the vestments that her brother and other priests wore at mass. She loved the solemn processions with bells tolling long and sonorously on big holidays or on hot, still days in midsummer when drought threatened to destroy or harm the crops. She loved the jubilant midnight mass at Christmas. She relished the incense, the smell of lighted candles, the pictures, the stations of the Way of the Cross, and the statues of saints at the main and side altars, and the organ music on Sundays. She sang in the choir with a strong and clear, although untrained, voice. Sometimes, when she sang solos, her fellow parishioners from Blato said they detected a ring of laughter in her singing. She did not care for sermons, not even her brother's; at least, so far as I know, she never praised a sermon; but I think it was deeply satisfying to her to see Uncle Martin stand in the pulpit and read the Gospel and preach . . . And some day, perhaps —perhaps, I, her son, would stand in the pulpit at Zhalna and preach! She would be so proud of me. All the people of the parish would be proud of me, just as they were proud of Uncle Martin, who was also a native of the parish, and a peasant's son.

The faith of his father, whom he also was later to leave behind when he sailed for America, was not far different:

In my father's life, too, religion was of no great moment. He was essentially a practical man who had serious and constant business with the ancient earth. He went to church on Sundays and prayed to God every evening with his family, but I think he did so more because that was the conventional thing to do than because he felt it necessary. Basically, like most peasants in Carniola and elsewhere, he was a hard realist, a practical man, a fatalist, possessing a natural, amost biological good sense and a half-cynical earth knowledge older than any religion or system.[1]

Louis was restless on the farm. His father sent him to school in the city. There the Yugoslav Liberation Movement was urging young Slovenes not to go to America. A widely read novel *The Land of Promise* depicted America as a brutal place where men cruelly sought riches and where peasants of Europe went to bitter death. "America broke and mangled the emigrants' bodies, defiled their souls, deprived them of their simple spiritual and aesthetic sensibilities, corrupted their charming native dialects and manners and generally alienated them from the homeland."[2] The last words of the novel were imperative: *"Ne v Ameriko!"* ("Do not go to America!")

In Lublyana, at the city school, Adamic took part in a student demonstration against Austrian rule. Many in Slovenia were resentful; students expressed what others did not dare. In broad daylight, mobs of students dashed through the streets. They pulled down German signs from above the entrances to stores. They ripped the Austrian doubleheaded eagle from government buildings. They broke windowpanes. Those who got their heads bloodied in encounters with the police achieved the status of heroes and martyrs.

On one particular day in May,[3] several hundred students carried the Slovenian colors through the streets. They had no permit for their march. They sang and shouted. They carried with them a huge brass cuspidor on the top of a long pole. They intended to give the white marble statue of the Emperor Francis a suitable crown.

On a side street, a detachment of Austrian cavalry with drawn sabers waited in ambush. When they charged, one student threw a rock. The lieutenant cried, *"Fire!"* The streets were full of prancing soldiers and panicky boys who raced for doorways, cafes, turns in the street. Adamic's best friend Yanko was a step or two ahead when a bullet blasted his skull. He fell dead. Adamic sprawled over the bloody form.

Within two minutes, it was over. The toll was only half that of Kent State: two were dead, four or five wounded.

Adamic, still sprawled over the warm body of his friend, was picked up by the soldiers and thrown into jail. His dead friend Yanko became a national hero; the whole city turned out for his funeral. The Imperial Government barred Adamic from ever attending any educational institution. He was fourteen years old.

"But why did you have to be in the demonstration?" his mother asked him, as the family met him outside the jail.

"Because my friend Yanko was in it."

"And I suppose your friend Yanko was in it," his priest-uncle said, "because you were in it."

Then everybody smiled, Adamic recalls: "It was an outrage for Austrian soldiers to ride down and kill Slovenian students, no matter what we had done or tried to do."

Through the intercession of his uncle, the Jesuits agreed to accept Louis as a student for the priesthood. His mother was thrilled; his father was pleased not to have to pay for his education—it was plain that Louis would not make a farmer.

Just before entering the gates of the Jesuit seminary, however, and notwithstanding the tradition of obedience, Adamic left his father sitting in a wine shop at lunch. He felt a "cold, hard" determination in his heart. He walked all the way home. His father, returning alone by train, was furious. But mother and father now acceded to his request of many years: his father gave him the money to go to America.

Laughing in the Jungle he called his autobiography. Not "melting pot." Jungle. From 1913 until 1931 he observed all across America the destruction of the spirit of the immigrants. He saw their broken bodies. He saw American soldiers firing upon American civilians. He saw Slavic pride in hard work frozen into steel and concrete buildings.

Even in his native village, when Louis was ten, a man of broken health had pointed to a picture of New York.

I—we helped to build these buildings—we Slovenians and Croatians and Slovaks and other people who went to America to work. We helped to build many other cities there, cities of which you have never heard, and railroads, and bridges, all made of steel which our people make in the mills. Our men from the Balkans are the best steelworkers in America. The framework of America is made of steel. And this smoke that you see here—

it comes from coal that we have dug up; we from the
Balkans and from Galicia and Bohemia. . . .

Three times I was in accidents. Once, in Colorado, I
was buried for four days three thousand feet underground. There were seven other men buried with me—
three of them Slovenians like myself, two Poles, one
Dalmatian, one American. When they dug us out, the
Dalmation and I were the only two still living. Once, in
Pennsylvania, a rock fell on me in a mine and broke my
right leg. The leg healed and I went back to work. I
worked two months, and another rock fell on me. It
almost broke my left leg.

Then his friend told him of walking the streets of New
York just before sailing for home:

I looked up, and can hardly describe my feelings. I
realized that there was much of our work and strength,
my own work and strength, frozen in the greatness of
New York and in the greatness of America. I felt that,
although I was going home to Blato, I was actually leaving myself in America.[4]

America is a jungle. That's how Adamic was warned to
think of it. "American industry uses you, then casts you
off."[5]

Adamic records the histories of some who survived the
jungle, and some who did not. In San Pedro, California,
the Slovenian who was "the most American" among those
Louis had met in America died by violence one night. He
was running a rum-runner through the darkness and
smashed directly into the looming side of an unseen
freighter. In the gas explosion that followed, he was
trapped in the wooden cabin for two minutes, was broiled,
and died on his way to shore. His wife Josie, in her eighth
month, had a miscarriage.

Mrs. Tanasick, Adamic's housekeeper for a short time,
was nearly dead when she came to him. She had married
four times in America, and had had seven children. Six of

the children were dead, the seventh (dead or alive she did not know) disappeared after the Armistice. Her first husband was found in a ditch during a mine strike, shot in the chest by company killers. Her second husband (like her first son) was crushed to death in the mines. Her third husband, an IWW radical, became converted to Tolstoi and the simple life. He left her, and walked all the way from Arizona to New York, refusing to cooperate with modern industry by riding a train, and went by fishing boat to Croatia—just in time for the war. He refused to serve in the Austrian army. He was shot. Her last husband paid for the funerals of the three of her children striken with influenza and infantile paralysis. Although too old, he found work as a stevedore. Something fell on him, he was crippled terribly. Mrs. Tanasick didn't want to die before he did, lest he die unattended in his own filth.

She came to Adamic's house with a "death-calm fatalism," a "tragic aspect, which was the dominant aspect of her figure." (How the image enlivens my memory of my grandmother, of the dozens of black-draped women I recall at church in my childhood, who, like presences from some other, terrible world, made me nervous.)

> There were no old-woman exaggerations or exuberances about her. She was drudgery incarnate; going through certain definite motions; a drab, cold woman, almost unliving, hovering on the edge of existence, undisturbed by emotional demands or vital communal sympathies. She seemed beyond all that. But presently her very drabness, like that of a banal, bleak old house, abandoned to collapse by itself, offered a sort of beauty and dignity.
> Aided by memories of peasant women I had seen in the Old Country in my boyhood, I tried to imagine her as she had probably been in her younger life in Croatia —stalwart, full-built and hard, of the type of women I had watched carrying gracefully and with surety great burdens on mountain roads or working long hours in the fields with a careless, even cheerful, fatalism, yet whose

whole beings seemed at the same time fixed upon a purpose of inconceivable importance; decisive, ready, and
capable, their faces flushed from the sun, with the honor
of freedom and poverty in their words, glances, and
gestures.

She evidently had been in America a long time.[6]

During the trek from Mrs. Tanasick to the suburbs of
the 1970s, many memories have been blotted out. When
one thinks of the bones of workmen encased in the concrete of dams and bridges; the bodies interred in ten thousand underground caverns; the limbs sheared off by gears,
wheels, cutters, lathes, chains, pulleys, carts, spindles, fly-
wheels, cables—the mounds of fingers, forearms, legs, ears,
heads—one's heart sinks about America. What wealth has
been based upon human misery. "Dung," Adamic reports
the immigrants were called, dung to fertilize the rapidly
growing tentacles of *species Americanus*.[7] Many delivered
their bodies to make the plant grow.

"Life was too cruel here. America is big and terrible,"
Mrs. Tanasick spoke as she lay dying. "America *must* become great . . . We all came over from the Old Country to
help America become great and terrible."[8]

2. *Nordic Prejudices: Race and History*

The eyes of others, Hegel noted, are mirrors in which we
learn our own identity. The first eyes into which the immigrants from southern and eastern Europe looked were
Nordic eyes, the eyes of "old Americans," or "nativists."
The immigrants were made to feel, as Adamic records, like
dung. Behind the eyes of nativists, however, there appeared
in the 1960s the eyes of intellectuals. Two forms of prejudice stamped the immigrants. Both had a peculiar "northern" quality: one was racial, the other "progressive."
According to one view, it was his race and religion that
made the southern European inferior. According to the
other, it was his social and political backwardness. The

first bigotry drove the ethnics to the Democratic party. The second is tempting them toward the Republicans.

A man named Procaccino declared himself a candidate for mayor of New York. At a dinner in New Haven, a well-known professor said aloud: "If Italians aren't actually an inferior race, they do the best imitation of one I've seen." Everyone at the table laughed.[9] The professor didn't make that kind of joke when Bobby Seale was on trial.

When Louise Kapp Howe was editing *The White Majority*, she asked assistance from intellectuals "of genuine compassion." She knew they would be the first to avoid any easy generalization about blacks or youth. Their animosity surprised her. They viewed the ethnic as "a boor and a bigot, a racist and a fascist."[10] Among the educated, eyes are always on the lookout for the emergence of "authoritarian" tendencies. The march of the hard hats in early May 1970 was an educated liberal's dream come true. *Real fascists*. With flags. In the streets. Breaking heads. *Blood*.

Under the whiplash of such attitudes, many descendants of immigrants for many years withered into silence about their identity. Many suppressed the instincts of their flesh, the impulses of their sensibilities, and perhaps even the signals from their genes. (Teachers made Italian boys sit on their hands all morning long, to make them stop gesticulating.) A great many try desperately to *be all alike*, to look the way Americans do in the magazines, and movies and streets: to make it, to pass.

Be warned. There is less and less reluctance about letting go. The days of racial and political bias against the ethnics are drawing to a close.

The impact of one race upon another is never simple. Until the late nineteenth century, the general pride which Americans took in their Anglo-Saxon heritage had not acquired a hard, racial, biological edge. Early Americans boasted about the English parliamentarian tradition which, against the powers of the king, had quoted ancient Teutonic texts on the freedoms of the people. Partisans of the Eng-

lish Enlightenment cited universal values and were grati-
fied by English leadership.[11] Romantics stressed human
variety, and in particular, the superiority of the Anglo-
Saxons. They emphasized that they valued the Teutonic,
rather than the Norman, side of the Anglo-Saxon heritage.

When the immigrants from southern and eastern Europe
arrived in America industry was unregulated and capitalism was cruel. The native workers were suffering from
episodic economic decline, from cruel conflicts between
management and labor, from gross exploitation. The new
immigrants from southern and eastern Europe were welcomed by industrialists as new (and hopefully more docile)
sources of labor, and also as irritants within the labor
movement.

> In the course of relying increasingly on the new immi-
> grants, industrialists perfected a system for mastering
> them. Employers of large immigrant forces learned to
> "balance nationalities," in other words to take advantage
> of the diversity and tensions among the many peoples of
> southern and eastern Europe. By judiciously mixing
> many nationalities, the employer could keep them di-
> vided and incapable of concerted action in their own
> behalf.[12]

Sometimes the industrialists' motives and treatment were
humane, sometimes not; almost always they were paternal-
istic. Whole villages of Slovaks, for example, were brought
to work at the shoe factories of Endicott and Johnson,
New York. The presence of immigrants anywhere set off
waves of cultural electricity.

Many of the new immigrants intended to return to
Europe as soon as they could raise capital to purchase
land. During the decade before 1914, one out of four
immigrants from southern and eastern Europe did return.[13]
Thus few of those who had been farmers in Europe sought
permanence on the land in the United States; mostly they
gathered in the cities. Social problems multiplied.

Often it was America that taught them they were ethnic.[14] Immigrants from Italy did not think of themselves as Italians but as *Calabrese* or *Siciliani*. The state of Czechoslovakia was chartered in Pittsburgh. Usually the immigrants came without ethnic organization or plan. Language and "network feelings" drove them to seek their own kind, to group together, to acquire self-awareness.

The great influx into the cities of the northeast and the midwest altered the feelings, the mores, and the administrative patterns of daily life. "Old American" families and groups of earlier immigrants faced an identity crisis; they felt the threat of competition. The new immigrants were for the old Americans the double threat that the blacks have become for ethnics today. A pattern of racism and superpatriotism was held over the heads of the ethnics.

In part, the ethnics were stamped "inferior" because they aroused straightforward social and economic fears. The *health* of America generated the resentment they received. For America is a land in which heterogeneous groups can find a toehold, a land changeable enough so that elites in power quite accurately feel threatened when rules of economic life and vectors of power change. But in part the ethnics were stamped "inferior" because of racist views sharpened for the occasion. The *sickness* of America was another source of the resentment they received. For America is a land in which pride in the English heritage gradually became pride in the Anglo-Saxon-Teutonic heritage, and the latter was all too near to pride in Nordic race.

The ethnics were the victims of "white racism." The immigrants who arrived after 1880 struck the American imagination as a dark, swarthy, inferior race; they were drawn into the orbit of the associations linked to "black." Their habits of life, their mores, their passions were what condemned them. Winthrop D. Jordan in *White Over Black* nails the background:

In England perhaps more than in southern Europe, the concept of blackness was loaded with intense meaning. Long before they found that some men were black, Eng-

lishmen found in the idea of blackness a way of expressing some of their most ingrained values. No other color
except white conveyed so much emotional impact. As
described by the *Oxford English Dictionary*, the meaning
of *black* before the sixteenth century included, "Deeply
stained with dirt; soiled, dirty, foul. . . . Having dark or
deadly purposes, malignant; pertaining to or involving
death, deadly; baneful, disastrous, sinister. . . . Foul,
iniquitous, atrocious, horrible, wicked. . . . Indicating
disgrace, censure, liability to punishment, etc." Black
was an emotionally partisan color, the handmaid and
symbol of baseness and evil, a sign of danger and
repulsion.

Embedded in the concept of blackness was its direct
opposite—whiteness. No other colors so clearly implied
opposition, "beinge' coloures utterlye contrary"; no
others were so frequently used to denote polarization:

Everye white will have its blacke,
And everye sweete its sowre.

White and black connoted purity and filthiness, virginity
and sin, virtue and baseness, beauty and ugliness, beneficence and evil, God and the devil.[15]

Such feelings about color are not solely English; they
characterize peoples in Asia, Latin America, and all over
the world.[16] A hand-lettered sign makes a different impression upon beholders if it is lettered in pink or lettered in a
vigorous blue; the mere color generates a different emotional response. Gestures, sounds, and timbre of emotions
in the voice, discipline or looseness in the body, spatial distance or the touching of flesh—all our routes of perception
are heavily laden with affect. Man is primordially biological, and his body reacts to other bodies in spite of his
mind or his beliefs.[17]

A famous passage in Jerzy Kosinski's *The Painted Bird*
indicates that victims of color prejudice exhibit it as well.
In advance of the Red Army, a Tartar detachment sweeps

into an eastern European village on clattering horses. The Kalmuks are Russians but they hate the Reds and fight for the Germans, who send them to punish uncooperative villages. While the deaf-mute hero of the story watches in stupefaction, the Kalmuks slash, whip, burn, torture, and commit astonishing feats of rape. The furious, passionate, bestial side of East European life, so much less repressed than in the West, is dramatized in a fantasy not uncommon in Slavic fiction:

> In the middle of the square some Kalmuks displayed their skill in having intercourse with women on horseback. One of them stripped off his uniform, leaving only his boots on his hairy legs. He rode his horse in circles and then neatly lifted off the ground a naked women brought to him by the others. He made her sit astride the horse in front of him, and facing him. The horse broke into a faster trot, the rider pulled the woman closer making her lean her back against the horse's mane. At every lunge of the horse he penetrated her afresh, shouting triumphantly each time. The others greeted his performance with applause. The rider then deftly turned the woman around so that she faced forward. He lifted her slightly and repeated his feat from the back while clutching her breasts. . . .
>
> I crept deeper into the bushes, overwhelmed by dread and disgust. Now I understood everything. I realized why God would not listen to my prayers, why I was hung from hooks, why Garbos beat me, why I lost my speech. I was black. My hair and eyes were as black as these Kalmuks'. Evidently I belonged with them in another world. There could be no mercy for such as me. Some dreadful Devil had sentenced me to have black hair and eyes in common with this horde of savages.[18]

The terror the Polish villagers felt when they saw the swarthy faces of Tartars—a terror linking sexual licence and unbridled animal nature with darkness of skin—is mirrored in the terror that nativist Americans came to feel for Poles, Italians, Greeks, Armenians, and other immigrants after 1880. Oscar Handlin describes "the racist beliefs, freely expressed in the 1890s, that the peoples of the Mediterranean region were biologically different from those of northern and western Europe and that the difference sprang from an inferiority of blood."[19] On the Statue of Liberty, the new immigrants were greeted with something less than a compliment: "wretched refuse."[20]

Many Americans believed that the immigrants might not be capable of freedom. Genetic and psychological theory was spawned in the last decades of the nineteenth century to establish Nordic superiority "on a scientific basis." The tradition for doing so was not young. Even the English skeptic David Hume was able to write in 1748:

> I am apt to suspect the negroes, and in general all the other species of men (for there are four or five different kinds) to be naturally inferior to the whites. There never was a civilized nation of any other complexion than white, nor even any individual eminent either in action or speculation. No ingenious manufacturers amongst them, no arts, no sciences. On the other hand, the most rude and barbarous of the whites, such as the ancient GERMANS, the present TARTARS, have still something eminent about them, in their valour, form of government, or some other particular. Such a uniform and constant difference could not happen, in so many countries and ages, if nature had not made an original distinction betwixt these breeds of men. Not to mention our colonies, there are NEGROE slaves dispersed all over EUROPE, of which none ever discovered any symptoms of ingenuity; tho' low people, without education, will start up amongst us, and distinguish themselves in every profession. In JAMAICA indeed they talk of one negroe as a man of parts and learning; but 'tis likely he is admired for very slender accomplishments, like a parrot, who speaks a few words plainly.[21]

Thomas Jefferson is symptomatic of the tensions involved in progressive views at an earlier stage in history. He enunciated the fundamental equality of all men in the Declaration of Independence; but he owned slaves—and he also felt acute emotional ambiguity about the attractions and repulsions of black skin. Indians he could accept; for him red, like white, was an ingredient of beauty. Negroes desired sexual relations with whites; the orangoutang preferred black women. Thus the chain of preference was a chain of superiority.

> Embedded in [Jefferson's] thoughts on beauty was the feeling that whites were subtler and more delicate in their passions and that Negroes, conversely, were more crude. He felt negroes to be sexually more animal—hence the gratuitous intrusion of the man-like ape. His libidinal desires, unacceptable and inadmissible to his society and to his higher self, were effectively transferred to others and thereby drained of their intolerable immediacy.[22]

The Negro male, Jefferson imagined, had a freedom he himself lacked: "They are more ardent after their female: but love seems with them to be more an eager desire than a tender delicate mixture of sentiment and sensation."[23]

The ladies of Charleston, Alexander Wilson writes in 1809, "hardly even speak or smile, but dance with as much gravity, as if they were performing some ceremony of devotion. On the contrary, the negro wenches are all sprightliness and gayety; and if report be not a defamer . . . [*here there is a hiatus, probably not his own, in his letter*] which render the men callous to all the finer sensations of love, and female excellence." The white women must practice their "cold, melancholy reserve" in order to avoid any resemblance to black women. The proper function of white women "was to preserve the forms and symbols of civilization—they were, after all, bearers of white civilization in a literal sense—and to serve as priestesses in the temples . . ."[24]

Jefferson himself, restless about his own attitudes, turns to a metaphor which is much used as the nineteenth century wears on. "The circumstance of superior beauty, is thought worthy attention [sic] in the propagation of our horses, dogs, and other domestic animals; why not in that of man?"[25] Human genetics is like animal husbandry. How do you keep a superior stock pure? Select your mate carefully, store up the strength of your seed through abstinence, spill it only for procreation. Weaker races are softer, more indulgent, sensual, unrestrained. Nature sees to it that they pay for their lack of discipline with a weaker strain.

Science came to the aid of nativist Americans toward the end of the nineteenth century. The story of Adam and Eve stood across the path of any suggestion that the human race is not one.[26] But suppose science could show that there is not one human race, but four or five, each as different from the other as is man from ape? Then stray, ambivalent, worrisome feelings were legitimated; concrete, tangible experience had scientific vindication. Then science, politics, aesthetics, history, heritage, and emotion could weave a seamless jacket for the soul.

By the end of World War I, old Americans and early immigrants lost faith in the strength of their own purity. They wished to stop the flood of immigration. Congressman Vestal said that southern and eastern Europeans "have not been of the kind that are readily assimilated or absorbed by our American life."[27] Others noted how they would "contaminate the race of the brave and the free."

Psychological tests, constructed within the prevailing sense of reality, led to the conclusion that "the intellectual superiority of our Nordic group over the Alpine, Mediterranean and Negro groups has been demonstrated" (Yerkes, Brigham, and McDougall, 1928).[28] The nation was divided into Nordic and "dangerous."

Why dangerous? "Precisely," records Oscar Handlin, "because they were inferior. They were sensuous rather than spiritual by nature, and their women were tyrannized by ignorant fathers and husbands. Their large families were evidence that they exercised no self-restraint, just as their poverty was evidence that they were being punished for their animal qualities. At best they were childlike and irresponsible; at worst, their brute passions erupted in frightful outrages."[29]

The most striking aspect of Nordic racism was its scientific support. *Science* magazine, for example, commended Madison Grant's often reprinted *The Passing of the Great Race* (1916) as "a work of solid merit."[30] The author, an anthropologist at the American Museum of Natural History, wrote solemnly:

> The native American has always found and finds now in the black men willing followers who ask only to obey and to further the ideals and wishes of the master race, without trying to inject into the body politic their own views, whether racial, religious or social. Negroes are never socialists or labor unionists and as long as the dominant imposes its will on the servient race and as long as they remain in the same relation to the whites as in the past, the Negroes will be a valuable element in the community but once raised to social equality their influence will be destructive to themselves and to the whites.

Except for "the foreign laborers," he adds, America would have remained "exclusively native American and Nordic."

> These new immigrants were no longer exclusively members of the Nordic race as were the earlier ones who came of their own impulse to improve their social conditions. . . . the European governments took the opportunity to unload upon careless, wealthy and hospitable America the sweepings of their jails and asylums. The result was that the new immigration . . . contained a large and increasing number of the weak, the broken and the mentally crippled of all races drawn from the lowest stratum of the Mediterranean basin and the Balkans, together with hordes of the wretched, submerged popula-

tions of the Polish Ghettos. Our jails, insane asylums and almshouses are filled with this human flotsam and the whole tone of American life, social, moral and political has been lowered and vulgarized by them.

These immigrants adopt the language of the native American, they wear his clothes, they steal his name and they are beginning to take his women, but they seldom adopt his religion or understand his ideals. . . .

. . . it is evident that in large sections of the country the native American will entirely disappear. He will not intermarry with inferior races and he cannot compete in the sweat shop and in the street trench with the newcomers.

One thing is certain: in any such mixture, the surviving traits will be determined by competition between the lowest and most primitive elements and the specialized traits of Nordic man; his stature, his light-colored eyes, his fair skin and light-colored hair, his straight nose and his splendid fighting and moral qualities, will have little part in the resultant mixture.[31]

The Ku Klux Klan was not exactly a silent majority. But in the 1920s it rose to a membership of almost six million, which is a lot of sheets. Catholics, Jews, and Blacks are plainly not Nordics. *The Fiery Cross* warned on February 8, 1924:

Old stock Americans have become restless. . . . They are dissatisfied with the denationalizing forces at work in the country. There is something wrong and the American people know there is something wrong, and they are talking among themselves as to where the trouble is. They know . . . that the Romish church is not in sympathy with American ideals and institutions . . . they know the facts as to Rome's opposition to the Bible in our public schools and to our public school system itself. They know she is opposed to a free press, free speech, and to other democratic principles.

These old stock Americans are coming to believe that the Jews dominate the economic life of the nation, while the Catholics are determined to dominate the political and religious life. And they have apprehensions that the vast alien immigration is at the root an attack upon Protestant religion with its freedom of conscience, and is therefore a menace to American liberties. . . .

They are afraid of the race groups that adhere to their own language and race prejudice and religious superstitions, and have no sympathy with our Americanism. They have their forebodings as to the union of Jews and Catholics. . . .[32]

Just imagine, though, if Jews and Catholics and *Blacks* form a union.

3. *The Seven Seals of Americanization*

There were many reasons for Nordic racism in America. When the government itself undertook the Immigration Reports of 1911 (the Dillingham Commission, 42 volumes) the controlling question of the key volume was succinctly stated: "whether there may not be certain races that are inferior to other races . . . whether some may be better fitted for American citizenship than others." The outcome of the report, as Oscar Handlin shows,[33] was predetermined. Its conclusions flew in the face of the disconcerting facts it recorded.

There was a myth, for example, that the old Anglo-Saxon immigrants came as craftsmen—skilled, literate, and virtuous. Recently, even Margaret Mead compared the idealism of the early American immigrants to the crassness of the later immigrants, for James Baldwin's benefit. Ordinarily we think of Miss Mead as a woman extraordinarily without prejudice. But when she talks about the idealism of her Anglo-Saxon forebears, as contrasted with the barbarity of those who came later, she shows she is as human as the rest of us. She writes:

I think you have to discriminate between the people who came here early for political and religious reasons—the ones whom we still think made the country and whom we still talk about and use as ideals, and who did come here to live their kind of life the way they believed in—and the great many millions of immigrants who came here in the 19th century—simply because they were driven out at home and they would have starved if they stayed there.

And she tells James Baldwin:

I don't have as good rhythms as you have, but my rhythms go back ten generations to England. The culture in this country that is so limited, is most limited, is that of the second and third generations away from Europe. They have lost what they had and aren't ready to take on anything else. They are scared to death and so busy being American . . . yes, because we have this enormous number of people who came here for only economic reasons . . . they have all the land-hungriness and all the worry of the European peasant.[34]

Unfortunately, the 1911 reports showed that Nordic immigrants like "the Germans and Scandinavians among the old immigrants boasted fewer such skilled laborers than such new groups as the Armenians, Bohemians, Hebrews, and Spanish; and the Irish were lower in the list than the South Italians."[35] Moreover, less than twenty percent of the Nordic immigrants ("the old immigrants" from 1899–1909) were skilled laborers, Handlin notes, and "the percentage in earlier periods [the British migration] was probably smaller still."[36]

Disconcertingly, too, the figures seemed to show that crime rates, notably for serious crime, were higher for "native Americans" than for the new immigrants. Insanity was higher among the non-Nordic than the Nordic races; but among the foreign-born the Irish, the Germans, and the

Scandinavian rather than the newer immigrants had the largest relative proportion. According to the data summarized by Handlin, neither in talent, skill, wealth, social accomplishment, literacy, learning, or speed in acquiring English (where relevant) were the "new" immigrants of southern and eastern Europe inferior to the "old" immigrants of Nordic lands.[37]

The crucial question is why it was so important to "old Americans" to put down the new Americans? Serious economic, social, and political dislocations were involved. But cultural differences were of highest interest. What was the American-Nordic norm, to whose dimensions the new immigrants were supposed to chop or stretch themselves? How did an "old American" think about himself, imagine his situation? What was his "feel" for life and destiny?

The subject, of course, is too vast. Crèvecoeur, de Tocqueville, D. W. Brogan, Commager, and others have tried to state it. But our interest is special. How did the "old American" appear *in the eyes of the new immigrant?* What new aspects of the American character were brought out by the immigrants from southern and eastern Europe?

Closure, certainly. The restrictive immigration laws of 1917, 1921, 1924, and even 1952.[38] The explicit boldness of Nordic racism: certain races are more "American" than others.

It is the springs of this racism that we must now explore. I am not eager to increase the quotient of Anglo-Saxon guilt. One of the most winning traits in the American character is its willingness to hear criticism of itself, take that criticism to heart, to try more earnestly still to *become perfect.* Nothing is easier than to play upon the guilt feelings of Anglo-Saxon Americans. The ideals to which they are committed are so high.

Moreover, we must make certain distinctions. At best, we shall be able to describe the ideal-typical norm, the secret set of expectations implicit in American culture as the immigrants faced it. Only toward the end of the nineteenth century were the "old Americans" themselves beginning to become aware of their special identity.[39] The very word "race" was just beginning to take on a modern meaning. Differences between English and American character were ever more strongly felt. The prospect of an America not dominated by "old American" consciousness was just being faced. The enormous revolution of bureaucratization was creating havoc in the self-identity and values of Americans, especially in the cities. Lacking the feudal traditions of Europe, Americans tended to believe, genuinely believe, in their own equality one with another. But the unchecked excesses of industry were generating a sharp conflict between management and labor, and the first profound stirrings of class consciousness were being felt. The aftermath of the Civil War occasioned deep guilts and repressions concerning the relations of blacks and whites. The economy oscillated wildly between panic and prosperity.

For our purposes, let us set to one side the intellectuals of the period 1880-1924. Their attitudes toward the immigrants were ambivalent—at times enormously sympathetic (Jane Addams at Hull House in Chicago), at other times distressed.[40] In any case, the immigrants seldom met them.

Mostly, the immigrants encountered the factory owners and the workers, the farmers, and the people of the small towns in the northeast and the middle west. They met three levels of WASP culture: the established, educated, wealthy, and middle-class culture of the cities; the "older" American culture of the small towns; and the tough, direct culture of the farmhands and laborers. When, for example, they heard the word "Protestant," it meant all three. In the interstices, more often than not acting as political brokers, were the Irish. For most immigrants, the word "American" was first applied to an Irish neighbor. Ralph Perrotta, a young lawyer who served in the Civil Rights Division of the Justice Department, recalls a feeling still powerful in the 1930s: "You're brought up with a feeling that you're not quite American and develop feelings of self-hatred. One of my earliest recollections is mother referring to the Irish families on the block as 'the Americans.' "[41] It is a recollection almost every ethnic American shares.

Although Catholic, the Irish seemed to share a WASP disdain for swarthier peoples. Even today, an Irish bishop in Pennsylvania will not scruple to refer to part of his flock as "hunkies" and another part as "dagos." Not untypically, he will regard the Irish as deeper in the faith, more devout, richer in vocations. As the "others" are not quite fully American, so they are also not quite fully Catholic. How, statistically, the Irish rate southern and eastern Europeans I do not know. But to many of the latter the way it *feels* is not liberating or encouraging; the feeling tone generates the self-hatred Perrotta speaks of. The ethnic animosity within the Catholic church has scarcely been given tongue, let alone explored.

But the American Irish have also suffered from "Americanization."[42] "No Irish Need Apply." They, too, have quite profound feelings of resentment toward native Americans, feelings that are extremely important in American politics. Kevin Phillips in *The Emerging Republican Majority* voices his resentment indictment by indictment.[43]

What were the pressures that generated this resentment? The character of "the old American" was in certain respects very different from anything that the Catholic immigrant, even the one from Ireland, had ever known before. It would be easy enough to recount the familiar characteristics: the incredible mobility, the hucksterism, the fervid evangelism of the frontier, the pragmatism, the moneymaking schemes, the reduction of metaphysics to a single test: success, the confidence men, the greed, the righteousness, the free speech. The old Americans of English stock believed that the English, as the proudest flower of the Teutonic race, had been given certain skills in self-government and certain defenses of individual liberties unequalled by any other race. This the immigrants were usually delighted to discover, to revel in, and to be re-made by. Mary Antin wrote in *The Promised Land* (1912): "I have been made over. I am absolutely other than the person whose story I have to tell."[44] Andrew Carnegie dedicated his *Triumphant Democracy* (1887) "to the country which has removed the stigma of inferiority which his native land saw proper to impress upon him at birth, and has made him in the estimation of its great laws as well as in his own estimation (much the more important consideration), the peer of any human being who draws the breath of life, be he pope, kaiser, priest, or king —henceforth the subject of no man, but a free man, a citizen."[45]

America was an intoxicant. *"America! America!"* cries Elia Kazan in 1961. Yet the price was steep: the reconstruction of the self. More like a religion than like a nation, America required conversion of soul. As I recapitulate them in the experience of ethnic Americans, seven seals must be broken, seven barriers overcome, by those who aspire to "the new paradise."

First, the new immigrant had to learn loneliness. To be sure, men often came to America in advance of their families. Most came alone. But what was different about America was that loneliness was encouraged; it was a way of life. Industrialization even in Europe meant that the "network people" of the countryside were atomized. Men no longer worked with their sons. They came home exhausted to their wives. In America, however, men were not *supposed* to value family or ethnic or neighborhood community more than their own independence and advancement. It was assumed that older people and older ways were less "American," and that with every generation a new and better type of man was steadily emerging. The moral relationship of men to the past and to the thick organic roots of their communities was reversed from what it had always been. The pre-Americans gave moral leverage to the past; the Americans gave moral leverage to the young, the coming race. Parents prepared themselves to be abandoned by their children.

Even the prayers of Protestants were different. "Because we discover in our solitude our need of thee, O Lord, we call upon thee." Italians and Slavs did not think of themselves as solitary; would not need to "discover" that solitariness would make men needy; associated God not with experiences of solitary anguish but with the surplus energy, compassion, and affection of families and communities. "*Ubi caritas et amor, ibi Christus est:* Where there are charity and love, there Christ is."

Max Weber, of course, had already made the point that Protestant individualism is a necessary condition for the growth of capitalism and industry. What was borne in upon the Catholic immigrant becoming American was that he must henceforth learn to imagine himself as a solitary atom. Resentments grew between parents and children. Quarrels multiplied. Hurts were given and received. Expectations about life, on the part of parents, were violated by the understandings of their children. Moral authority tipped toward the latter.

Oscar Handlin stresses the feelings of loneliness induced by the symbolic ocean crossing, the landing on a strange land in strange cities, the novelties of moving farther and farther from roots and families and friends so that one could imagine oneself dropping from sight without a trace. The loneliness, I suspect, was such a violation of primordial biological needs for community that Americans also acquired a new and distinctive sort of guilt. They were "foreigners" on earth, a new type of human—and there was pride in that. But they were also trespassing ancient boundaries. There was an ominous sense of possible retribution. In any case, Americans have long had a novel and overwhelming need to be reassured that they are a moral and good people. American soldiers give chewing gum to little children. We *need* to think of ourselves as good, in a manner distinctively American. It is as though affection, once bonded to family and tribe but now cut loose, floats free: America needs to be reassured that fellow-feeling has not vanished.

Moreover, as the ancient sense of the past was cut free, the American psyche was afflicted with the terrors of enormous space, the feeling of emptiness, that oppressive sense of a vast impersonal sky which O. E. Rolvaag described so powerfully in *Giants in the Earth*. In total migrations of the past, home was not disrupted: family and home and tribe were part of the movement. The American migration was atomic.[46] We have been since the beginning a "lonely crowd." From the beginning until 1900, countless individual Americans had the experience of entering a wooded cove, crossing a mountain, moving beyond a horizon—pushing themselves out into a world physically strange, distant from their fellows, cut off from civilization. "To them in their aloneness," Handlin writes, "there was one pre-eminent danger, the emptiness of the country about them. The world of familiar objects in their place had disappeared; the wilderness remained. No church, no town or village, no judge! Where was religion or law or morality?"[47]

What first struck later immigrant consciousness, therefore, was the solitariness of Protestant consciousness. In order to become American, one had to learn to be alone. One had to learn to *value* being alone. Separate bedrooms, separate TV, separate auto—the contemporary centrifugal forces of American life were splitting apart the later immigrants' internal networks from the very first.

4. *Machine, Mastery, Self*

The second seal to be broken was faith in a beneficent world. In southern and eastern Europe, one could believe that God is good, that life is sweet, that earth is poignantly beautiful; but one also anticipated hardship, heavy work, disaster, and repetition. In America, one had to learn not only hope but optimism; one had to learn social Darwinism; one had to learn that ancient limits no longer bounded the dreams of man: "The sky's the limit!" The hucksters and the con men prospered; the audacious and the dreamers enriched themselves. Those who allowed themselves to be limited fell behind.

When Locke defended private property, his sense of the finite limits of England operated as a guarantee that the distribution of wealth would not be, could not be, grossly unequal.[48] In America the Lockean sense of limits was shattered by two fundamental historical shifts. American wealth was from the beginning tied not only to land but also to money; no limits bound an individual's accumulation of the latter. Secondly, America lacked both feudal and aristocratic traditions; social limits knew no bounds—there was too little *noblesse* to dictate *oblige*. It was "wide open" country. Hence there was a contradiction at the heart of the consensus on which America was based. According to the Lockean tradition, if each person pursued his own personal interests without any thought for the common good or for social goals, the latter would take care of themselves. The economic-political order is so beneficent—guided by an Invisible Hand—that "ultimate questions" need not be attended to.

Immigrants had to learn, therefore, that it was *all right* just to think of themselves, to go after exactly what they wanted, to give free rein to avarice and ambition. It was *all right*. The social system would turn private selfishness into public beneficence. They were being pressured to purge themselves of that symbolic understanding of action according to which each action had ultimate moral and religious significance, and to adopt a new symbolic understanding of action: pragmatism. Europeans like Louis Adamic's father could, of course, be shrewd, practical, and realistic. Still, American pragmatism was different from anything known before. It was not a hardheaded concession to immediate necessities; it was a new metaphysical vision, a *celebration* of practicality, a claim that the *real* world works best if men just take small, practical steps and allow the "big picture" to adjust itself. The world is not fundamentally a world of drama in which each person acts out his destiny with regard to the *quality* of his own acts, but a world of practicality in which the good man acts with regard to *results*. There is no necessary contradiction in these viewpoints, but the distribution of emphasis may lead to a wholly different orientation of energy. Thus the Catholic clergy could preach against "materialism" and urge that the older dramas not be forgotten, and those who listened might sincerely try to heed. In America, however, the socially reinforced drama is *results*. And not even the clergy could bring themselves to quarrel with success. The beneficent world gradually received clerical blessing.

The third seal to be broken was that of mastery. The solitary American imagines his own organism, atom that he is, to be a healthy, hard center of resistance and responsibility. The universe pivots on his solitary heart. His task is to make the hostile world suit him. He wants to impress his will, his signature, his trademark, his moral vision, upon history. That is his *duty*. (H. Richard Niebuhr provided the most thorough and gracious rationale of this worldview in *The Responsible Self*.) His task is to master a continent, to conquer nature, to bring outer space within his purview, to sell light bulbs to India, to send his institutions of personal freedom in the wake of those "shots heard round the world" at Lexington. Even in questions of illness and pain, the "old American" is alone against the world.[49] The cowboy, the outlaw, the gangster are favorite fantasies of the "old American" psyche.[50] Such heroes assume that the social order, the cities, the economy, manners, and conventions are "the enemy." Even the law may be against them. Their final, fundamental value is the will of the solitary self. In the end, the forces of society win: "crime doesn't pay." But the struggle against enemies is the central drama and must continue.

As Jean-Paul Sartre did not fail to notice, the cowboy was the first existential hero: the stranger, the outsider, living by an absurdist code that—though his fiancée pleads with him—could only end in death. For his ambition to master the earth, his need to snap the primordial bonds of family and community, his identification of freedom with the restless itch to "move on," sprang from his secret love for the infinite, which finite earth cannot contain. The lover of the infinite must inevitably be killed.

Implied in the American dream of mastery is the ominous imagination of disaster. Thus Norman Mailer, surrendering himself to the contradictions of the national psyche, glorifies the American search for purity of mood, even in film:

> ... those sequences of footage where the event has been innocent of script and yet resonant with life? Of course! We are talking of nothing other than movie stars in frames where the mood has been pure. . . . So we search for the pure in film as we search for the first real tear of love. We are a Faustian age determined to meet the Lord or the Devil before we are done, and the ineluctable ore of the authentic is our only key to the lock.[51]

The authentic has fled from most of our contacts with one another as, poor atoms, we pass fleetingly in our planned orbits. Surcease comes in film, which all of us in darkness share together, more brotherhood in mood than families ever had—*out there*, on the screen—while we exit again as strangers, not even wanting our comments overheard by strangers. Faustians, yes, anticipating doom.

The fourth seal that immigrants needed to open was the myth of self-help. People who had learned in life that nothing is done without family, without community, without loyalty, without cooperation, had to learn that the right way is to count only on yourself. The Slavic immigrant had no fear of hard work; he expected it; he felt good when he was involved in it. Work was the natural expectation of men; it was their lot; it was their pride. It was not, however, an exorcism. They were not trying to purge their guilt through it, or to show results that would prove superior moral worth. To have the best-run farm of any of one's neighbors was for them a source of satisfaction, but not a proof of God's blessing, not some vindication via Darwinism. It was what it seemed: the fruit of hard work. The notion, then, that a "self-made" man has some particular moral stature had to be acquired. President Nixon, he himself reports, marks important decisions in his life by making himself suffer: not eating, going without sleep, working restlessly. Unless he feels the anguish, the decision lacks for him some moral legitimation.[52] Catholics, cherishing other superstitions, allow a great deal of room for grace, for serendipity, for sudden revelations, and unearned flashes of light. (Wasn't that the lightness of the Kennedy era?) They lack an instinct for sweaty and muscular moralism. They have to acquire it. It is the American way.

Catholics, as everyone knows, tend to be more corrupt, less duty-bound, more sensuous, less formal, more casual, less responsible, less ambitious than Protestants. It is hard for them to believe that their future depends on them, or that the future course of history is their responsibility. They are not so easily mobilized by appeals to conscience, responsibility, civic duty, social crisis, and causes appealing to abstractions like social justice, peace, or equality. Eugene McCarthy used the modern language of a modern Catholicism that does speak to abstractions such as these; but he did so in a Catholic way, for Catholic reasons, and to the utter bafflement of those whose context for such words is different. McCarthy entered New Hampshire, he said, because people cannot be moved by abstractions; abstractions need to be personified (incarnation, sacrament). Moreover, lightness, jokes, and an easy manner are required, because people don't like—and shouldn't like— crusades based on generating guilt.

McCarthy lacked the evangelical fervor that even hardheaded reporters have come to expect as the symbol of what America should be. He also resisted the "hardheaded," grubby details of planning a campaign, resisted the sweaty, muscular moral exertion that might make him worthy of the office—resisted it because it is more symbolic than realistic. The activist frenzy of American campaigns, he thought, has more to do with Puritan consciousness than with doing quietly what actually needs doing. (The incredible telephone bills run up by a staff phoning all around the country—assuaging personal restlessness, or truly practical?) He may have underestimated the real strength of Protestant symbols in this nation. He may not have been fully Americanized before 1968.[53]

The myth of self-help has deeply divided America, perhaps more deeply than war or race. The feeling is strong that each man should earn by himself whatever he has; that's the only fair way. In the beginning the lack of feudal traditions made it plausible: everyone but blacks started virtually even. Industrialization, however, changed the rules. Do it yourself—or accept corporate rewards? Many chose the corporate route. Events beyond their control could do more for them than what they could do for themselves. The nation itself placed its resources behind the partisans of industrialization to the detriment of the agrarians. Bigness, largeness, impersonality, national patterns of thought, and national methods began to reward men of a different social type than those who had been rewarded earlier. As between the ideology of self-help and the ideology of corporate teamwork, the nation gradually placed its power behind the latter—without ever admitting publicly that it was doing so.

Thus Spiro Agnew told a Republican meeting in Tulsa on May 9, 1969: "As the son of an immigrant to America, I can tell you that the opportunity to 'make it'—aided by a public education and earned through personal application —is all a man can ask."[54] But among the millions in America whom life has rewarded far beyond their personal application, Spiro Agnew must rank among the highest: a dropout from college where to studying he preferred good times. No great success as a young lawyer, he preferred to go back into the army. He was rescued again and again from 1960 to 1968 by wealthy and influential advisers. Building contractors took him in tow; a vacuum and lack of competition made him president of his Rotary club, county executive, governor, and vice-president of the United States in eight dazzling years—none of it planned, none of it earned. The rising of "stars" within corporations is today far more due to gift than work.

Still, immigrants coming to America learned a certain vulgar assertiveness. "If you don't push yourself, who will push you?" They learned that to become fully American one had to have dreams of success (and nightmares of failure). "Think big." "Even *you* can be president!" What an expansion of horizon many underwent, and what liberation of primitive energies and abilities heretofore unknown. Immigrants were encouraged to become "new men" with a different image of themselves than before. Many hastened to acquire the terrible equivalence of personal success and personal worth. For that was the true equivalence—stripping men of their radical dignity—hidden beneath the rhetoric of personal *effort* and personal worth. Success is, after all, not the same as effort.

The original Calvinist method of bringing "works" under the umbrella of "grace"—by teaching that "success" is a sign of God's predestined favor—was transmuted into a sheer contradiction. Much more than Catholics, Protestants emphasized the ascetical value of works. But the actual operation of the American system was a boondoggle of favors from government to "captains of industry." (One thinks of the fortunes made on railroads, canals, roads, oil, metals; of troops supporting factory owners against the workers.) America was socialism for the entrepreneurial classes, capitalism for the rest. "It's not what you know, it's who you know" was the wisdom of the streets, even while the public homiletics filled pantheons with supposed "self-made" men. Everywhere, hustlers looked for "angles."

The immigrants struggled to adapt their souls to the public rhetoric, even while their native cynicism taught them how *in fact* men "got ahead" in America. But in general the Catholic soul finds it difficult to value success. Success in America often requires great mobility, huge commitments of time, and separation from one's family. It is not so much a matter of hard work—hard, physical work—as of frenetic activity. Mayor Lindsay found it difficult to attract Italian community leaders into his staff, Nicholas Pileggi reported in *New York Magazine*,[55] because they did not like the hectic, family-less lives that Americanized staffers cheerfully accept.

5. *Civic Responsibility, Internal Repression*

The fifth seal that immigrants had to break in order to be Americanized is the equation of America with the Kingdom of God. According to the underlying Catholic drama of human life, every action ought to be weighed *sub specie aeternitatis*. A social system is to be judged by its *goals*. But in a peculiar way the fully Americanized mind holds that to think of long-range goals and ultimate visions is wasted energy. One properly concentrates upon practical next steps; one thinks of the future in *short-range, administrative* terms.[56] One does not question the goals of the entire social or economic system; one takes for granted its automatically benevolent purposes. Growth is good. Progress is happening. This American faith in movement is so strong that no "leap" is required. Progress is palpable; the air is electric with it. *Run, Sammy, Run.* It all works out best for everyone. Seek your own interests and you help mankind in the bargain. Grace has seldom come so cheap.

The instinctive Catholic view runs so counter to the American ethos that it is not surprising that ethnic Catholics even to this day show signs of being content with second best, of not running as hard as others, entertaining guilts and doubts about themselves even at the pinnacle of success. Was life intended for this?

On the other hand, of course, and paradoxically, Catholics who pride themselves on being religiously conservative and utterly orthodox tend most easily to confound orthodox Americanism with orthodox Catholicism. As successful businessmen, proud of the American way of success, they find no incompatibility between the story of

Horatio Alger and the story of Jesus Christ. They fiercely defend the requisite pieties of each.

Immigrants from Catholic countries tend to have less sense of civic responsibility than Anglo-Saxons: they join fewer civic associations, contribute less to programs of civic action. The usual interpretation of this difference suggests that the Protestant tradition of voluntary associations and the Protestant tradition of "building up the Kingdon of God on earth" are in this respect richer than the less civic-minded traditions of Catholic nations. But I think there are other reasons stirring in the Catholic breast. For one thing, America is Protestant; it is "their" country. Civic-mindedness is enlightened self-interest for the established. For the unestablished, it is unreal. Catholics still tend to be preoccupied with solidifying their own social and personal position against the exclusivism of certain industries, walks of life, country clubs, and other unstated barriers: "Non-Masons Need Not Apply." Insofar as the civic order is not theirs, in style or in substance, Catholics have little incentive to enhance it. Civic-mindedness—or public-regardingness, as Professor James Q. Wilson calls it—is a function of wealth, status, and education: *noblesse oblige.*[57]

Moreover, even if one compares like to like—for example, a Catholic associate professor at a state university with his Quaker or Episcopal counterpart—their style and language of "conscience" tend to diverge. The less Americanized the Catholic, the more he tends to think of civic responsibilities as a function of realistic political judgment rather than of moral judgment; the more skeptical he tends to be of those who use moral language about political matters; and the more likely he is to be slightly cynical about theories of progress and "forward-looking" positions. The long history of Italy and medieval Europe tends to be closer to his consciousness. He does not immediately concede that what is called progress is progress. He imagines that for every step forward somewhere there will be slippage backward. Social life is more a matter of "trade-offs" than "a march of progress." Those who claim to be avant-garde have their own tastes, interests, and prejudices. Although their self-image is priestly, they do not always represent the humanity of others.

I do not mean that such a Catholic is not himself a "progressive" in some different sense. For forty years the *Commonweal*, a weekly magazine edited by Catholic laymen, labored to establish a liberal Catholicism, in the conviction that a Catholic could assimilate the liberal tradition. But Catholic liberalism is liberalism with a difference. The Catholic, so long as he is not fully Americanized (has not become, shall we say, Anglo-Saxon Protestant), *does* tend to think about society's long-range goals; is concerned with the integrity of a person's life and values independently of results; is willing to accept "dirty hands" and does not imagine that politics is pretty, and on the other hand does not fully trust pragmatism; is prepared to think that politics is ultimately a realm not of results but of witness. Every day on the Catholic calendar is a saint's day; almost every day a witness is represented who gave his or her life for values not subject to compromise. A Catholic can hardly escape that antipragmatic pressure. And thus there is a Catholic instinct that has not yet found full expression in theories of American politics: an instinct suspicious of the pragmatism of Dewey and even of Reinhold Niebuhr; an instinct suspicious of the utopianism of the new Marxian and the old Enlightenment Left—and falling somewhere outside the secular categories "liberal" and "radical," as well as outside the category conservative."

The educated Catholic is often, then, inoculated against Americanization. The less educated are no less, perhaps even more, resistant. This "Catholic difference" is valuable. It weighs against the myth of personal success both by its sense of communal interdependence and by its holistic sense of society. In its view, society is not a machine composed of individual atoms, but an organism giving life to families, and through them, to persons. A society must show concern for its own goals and its own procedures; it

is an organism heading somewhere. It cannot merely allow
the self-interested actions of individuals to agglomerate
through some impersonal calculus, with faith that all will
turn out for the good. The latter is the "protestant" Anglo-
Saxon conception; it wrenches the Catholic mind. "The
'protestant' industrial economy," Daniel Bell notes in *The
End of Ideology*, "cannot adopt the system of 'family
wage,' to be found in Italy and other countries where
Catholic social doctrine applies, whereby a man with children receives more wages than one who has none, though
both do the same work."[58] In Poland as well, peasants
were paid in proportion to the size of their families.[59]
Protestant-American myths of personal success and self-
help required immigrants to change their conception of
themselves, their families, and society.

The sixth seal the immigrants had to break is a new
system of internal repression. Catholics tend not to trust
individual conscience. *Nemo judex in causa sui*: No one is
a good judge in his own case. Honesty is the most difficult
of all virtues; the human heart is a jungle of ambivalences
and contradictions. The Catholic prefers, as it were, a system of "checks and balances" both in the external forum
and in the intimate psyche. On the one hand, there ought to
be public officers of moral judgment, who assess one's behavior from their external point of view: the confessor,
the counselor. On the other hand, final judgment lies between God and the person—the confessor or the pastor
may well be mistaken, just as the person concerned may
also be. In the end, only God judges.

In principle, therefore, Catholics tend to value the existence of moral authority; in practice, they tend to be
cynical regarding the actual performance of such authority
and cavalier even in their respect for external law. Americans of Protestant traditions are deeply shocked to learn
that their government lies to them, as in the Tonkin Gulf
affair or that of the Pentagon papers. Even uneducated
Catholics tend to have a different response: on the one
hand, they tend to come to the defense of the authorities

in principle; on the other hand, after two thousand years of experience with authorities, they should be surprised that authorities lie? Original sin afflicts persons in authority even more grievously than it afflicts others; this was Lord Acton's point in comparing the Catholic and the Protestant sense of liberty.[60] "Absolute power tends to corrupt absolutely," he wrote, suggesting that enlightened Protestant theories of personal perfectibility and personal liberty tend to end, paradoxically, in a social vacuum in which absolute power gains unparalleled force.

But it is the internal repression that is most fascinating. Even colonial Americans thought of themselves as more innocent, more reasonable, more calm, more reserved than other species of men—here was being built a pacific republic of reason, in contrast with the jungles of Europe. The whole history of America can be understood as a drama of the psyche in which reason and the mild sentiments were to master the dark passions, while, externally, men with their industry and laws mastered a wild, primitive continent. "The frontier" is the frontier of cool reason, objectivity, pacification. The American destiny is to extend the light.

The early Americans had enormous faith in the reasonableness of the individual, provided he was not too crowded or harried, as well as in the structures and values implicit in a world of nature subdued by agriculture. The Anglo-Saxon image of the world is that humans in the depths of their hearts are good, and evil comes from the outside-in. The problem of life, therefore, is to achieve self-mastery first (let the good triumph within) and then to impose that internal order on the wild, primitive world. For that task, space and time are required. Order is required. Many confusions are frightening. One solves problems one by one, in isolation: isolate the evil and eliminate it. Here lay the significance of "the frontier"—it granted time and space. Thus Jefferson:

Educate and inform the whole mass of the people . . . they are the only sure reliance for the preservation of our liberty. . . . This reliance cannot deceive us, as long as we remain virtuous; and I think we shall be so, as long as agriculture is our principal object, which will be the case, while there remain vacant lands in any part of America. When we get piled together upon one another in large cities, as in Europe, we shall become corrupt as in Europe, and go to eating one another as they do there.

And again:

Before the establishment of the American states, nothing was known to history but the men of the old world crowded within limits either small or overcharged, and steeped in the vices which that situation generates. A government adapted to such men would be one thing; but a very different one, than for the man of these states. . . . Everyone by his property, or by his satisfactory situation, is interested in the support of law and order. And such men may safely and advantageously reserve to themselves a wholesome control over their public affairs, and a degree of freedom, which, in the hands of the *canaille* of the cities of Europe, would be instantly perverted to the demolition and destruction of everything public and private.[61]

The Anglo-Saxon fears overpopulation and crowding.[62] The Anglo-Saxon claims to trust human beings and to trust as well the benevolence of nature; he abjures the darker, tormented, pessimistic views of Europeans. The Anglo-Saxon relaxes in a clean, orderly, neat, virtuous world; he has a terror of noise, confusion, dirt, human density, tangled emotion. (Contrast a New England Congregational church with a Spanish chapel or Jesuit baroque.) But the terror is not clearly stated. The Anglo-Saxon trusts the human heart and the benevolence of nature only under certain conditions: when both are under the control his own will has imposed. The Anglo-Saxon is not "at home" in this universe; he must master it. Fundamentally, it terrifies him.

Not so the Italian, the Slav, the Spaniard, the Greek. Southern and eastern Europeans have a far more "pagan" attitude toward life. Their passions are kindled by nature; they love the earth. Religion for them is, so to speak, an earth religion rather than the religion of a sky-god. Thus to Anglo-Saxons, they seem "less religious." What Anglo-Saxons mean by religion is control, propriety, conscience, order, mastery—all their symbols run in the patterns of dominating reason. For that reason alone, technology and science and hospitals are natural expressions of Anglo-Saxon culture; they are the soap-and-water experts of the world. If cleanliness is next to godliness, soil is next to satan: soil, germs, bare feet in the wine presses, sweat streaming from the arm pits, unsightly hairs—disgusting things.

The Irish are a special case. Their natural tutors are the English, and the Irish are rather easily Americanized. Still, there is an untamed wildness in the Irish breast, a rebellion against neatness and order, an underlying Celtic rage, flash, imagination. The Irish are pagans like the Slavs, the Italians, the Greeks, but pagans who have allowed their church to make Christianity an agent of order and cleanliness, rather than an agent of mystery, ghostliness, fear, terror, and passion, which at its best it was. An "edge of sadness" attends the Americanization of the Celtic clergy. The Irishman (like the rest of us) tries to repress his Celtic turbulence in order to appear worthy of the ordered religion of modernity. His drunks, his wits, his poets, protest with all their power. By and large, the Irish church—against its own instincts—is an agency not of the earth-god but of the sky-god: the distant, aloof, clean, orderly God, not the God of blood and death, love and loss. At their most beautiful, the Irish can be counted on to rebel against those who betray and tame the Celtic passion.

In the fairy tales of Europe, the forest was alive with primeval instinct: unspoiled, unrepressed, uncivilized. It was the home of goblins, witches, temptation, rape, folly, death, escape, hideaway. Imagine, then, the delicious ambivalence awaiting the first Anglo-Saxons in America. No forests like America's were known to Europe. The forests dominated the American imagination, ominous reminders of what lay hidden in the human heart. Oscar Handlin describes the feelings of the first Americans:

> They themselves were now to be swallowed up in the darkness, to become themselves beings of the woods. The awesome thought came to those who were alone: no reckoning of right or wrong could find them out here. They were helpless at the sight of the mysterious path or unknown growth, at the sound of the unfamiliar. Yet they had the power enjoyed by no king on his throne: they could act without control. No authority could find the secret out. That was the horror.[63]

The American soul has been riven from the first between its commitment to self-control and its longing for a life completely unrepressed.

The Anglo-Saxon system of social control depends heavily on personal internal repression. Catholic immigrants discovered that there were many taboos in America, whole ranges of words one "did not say," actions "one doesn't do," restraints, and euphemisms. The charge always ready at hand for use against the immigrants—one that Theodore White wings toward Agnew like a poisoned arrow in *The Making of the President 1968*—is "coarseness."[64] In American movies and on television, no one calls things by their names. The language of the streets, of the army, of construction workers, is seldom heard. The agonies and antagonisms of daily life are (except on the news) seldom voiced. People in America *do* call one another Hebes, Polacks, Spics, Dagos, Spades, Niggers—but not in the movies, not on television, except with a sort of preciousness and self-protection. Anglo-Saxon censors sanitize the air. The moral pressure on ordinary people is intense. Implicitly, the media teach them what they must repress, what they cannot say. No wonder so many hate the media, and take delight in the "courage" of Wallace or Agnew: brave men who violate the liberal taboos.

In Catholic countries there is a sharp difference between the culture of the clergy and culture of the people. In general, the sexual attitudes of ordinary people in Italy or Greece or the Slavic countries are amply suggested by the life of Tolstoi, by "Zorba the Greek," by Fellini's films. For unmarried persons to make love is to violate something sacred, but in the name of something healthy, attractive, and wholly expected. The violation of the sacred adds to the enjoyment. It is *wrong* to fornicate; but it is delicious, and surely not worse than many other sins. One expects that even clergymen committed to celibacy will sometimes "fall"—it is no great shock. One does not expect human beings to be strong, masterful, iron-willed; one anticipates "human weakness." Forgiveness and compassion are values highly prized; persons easily offended by the sins of others are widely considered guilty themselves of "spiritual pride." Isn't the "laxness" of Catholic morals a scandal to the Protestant world? It is, instead, a quite different set of morals.

Moral indignation is, if not a Protestant, at least a bourgeois attitude.[65] The assumption behind it is that the guilty party need *not* have fallen, *should* not have fallen, fell not from weakness but from ill will; and a fiercely determined, truly virtuous person would *not* have given in. Moreover, moral indignation protects an utterly fundamental self-image. To concede that human beings are regularly weak is to suggest that evil lies, not in our environment, but in ourselves. It is to insinuate the conviction that humans are, that *I* am, ambivalent in my heart and already corrupt. It is to maintain the fiction that the self is healthy, only the circumstances evil. The sinner, therefore, *betrays* his kind; he is a traitor; he deliberately allowed the outside in.

People of all nations tend to xenophobia; but in the United States xenophobia arises not only from an instinct for national self-interest, but from an unusual psychic predisposition to imagine all evil outside the self.

Immigrants from southern and eastern Europe had to learn how to be shocked at new places and on new occasions. They had to learn order, discipline, neatness, cleanliness, reserve. They had to learn to modulate emotion, to control passion, to hold their hands still, to hold the muscles of their face placid, to find food and body odors offensive, to quieten their voices, to present themselves as coolly reasonable. "It takes three generations to make a gentleman." But being "civilized" in America is worlds away from the passions and complexity of Hungarian archdukes, Italian counts, and Yugoslav guerilla leaders—not to mention from the passions of artists and writers. In all God's world is there anything as cool as a Yale lawyer across the carpeted office of a major philanthropic fund? How could any other race ever fashion its psyche to that style?

6. *And the Seventh Seal Was Sex*

The seventh seal entails a new relationship to sexual fears. In America, sex has different symbolic meanings than elsewhere. One does not a expect a Yale lawyer to throw himself in front of a train because of an unhappy love affair; one does not expect three college boys to avenge their sister's "loss of virginity" by murder. The passions surrounding illicit sex in America are curiously lacking in high, doleful, and tragic romance such as one can still discover elsewhere. (Where else are there romances like those of Americans in France, Italy, Spain, or Greece?) A high premium is paid in America for rationality, practicality, "maturity." It is important not to act "like a kid," to "keep one's head," not "to make a fool of oneself," and to affect the offhanded, cool, matter-of-fact manner of the long-experienced. Though it is true that there is a cult of titillation, and even a cult of the orgasm, one cannot avoid being struck by the demystification of sex. As much as possible, both Puritans and partisans of sexual liberation seem to see their essential task as the expansion of reason, the advance of light, the triumph of spirit. Those who are for pornography and those who are against seem to share the same fundamental goal: to make larger the realm of light, smaller the circle of darkness.

There is sometimes a meanness in the southern and eastern European approach to sex, which I do not mean to deny: a vindictiveness, hostility, and condemnation harsh beyond measure. But there is also lyricism, freedom, naturalness, trembling, and the cultivation—not of techniques—but of communion. By contrast the Americanization of sex is grotesque. The subject is too large to treat in full, but perhaps a few notes on the history of sex in America will suggest what the immigrants had to learn.

Suppose that one's self-image requires a sense of internal health. And that this, in turn, means: reasonableness; the preeminence of the mild and sweet passions over the violent, fiery ones; moderation; sobriety; equanimity. One is likely to say then that true love is spiritual and ethereal, and perhaps to say as well that women understand it better than men.[66] Next, it is only a step—based on concrete experience—to suggest that woman's nature is more refined and higher; man's, more coarse and sensual. An ambiguity then arises concerning the word "natural." Is a man's more coarse and sensual nature merely a challenge to his nobility, an obstacle whose overcoming is the call of his own "true" nature—a good woman, then, being his divinely appointed helpmate in his struggle? Or is his more coarse and sensual nature shameful and irremediable? If his task is defined as the subduing of his "baser self," still, how can he not wonder whether he would be better off just *being* his baser self—redefining himself, as it were, and calling his instincts not "coarse" or "sensual," but "honest" and "authentic"? Another solution is to divide himself in two, with one part of his life "noble" and the other part "authentic." Behind the famous "double standard" is a double sexual identity, particularly on the part of men.

The threat of the American forests heightened the American's horror of his own perplexing nature. The red man did not live by the standards he did; neither did the black man. Red and black "lived in their bodies" differently; moved differently; showed a different mold, tension, and relaxation in their muscles. What, then, was "natural" here in the forested New World? Should Old World notions be abandoned? Far too strong was the overriding Anglo-Saxon imperative to "civilize" and "subdue" the continent—as a mirror, of course, of his own self-mastery. (The Spanish and French explorers, by contrast, seem to have lived much more frankly and naturally with the Indians.) Hence the Anglo-American's battle with sexual instinct was welded early to his battle with his total environment. "Purify Your Thoughts—Keep America Clean" might be the inner paradigm behind America's "manifest destiny" to set this hemisphere, and then the whole world, in order. The war on "dirt" is the central war in the American heart.

It is, I want to insist, a very long jump from the notion of sin to the notion of dirt. Peoples can believe that extra-marital sex is sinful without believing that it is dirty. Sinful and delightful is different from sinful and dirty. Biologically and psychologically, sexual activity can, without contradiction, be construed as healthy and attractive but socially wrong under certain conditions. It requires a much longer step to assert that sexual activity is *inherently* demeaning (even though socially necessary). But it was, in fact, this much longer step that Anglo-Saxon culture took in America under two quite different but related pressures.

First, there was the already alluded to conception of the human person as a creature of reason, calm sentiment, and control; and of love as a refined, mature, and reasonable passion.

Secondly, there was the growing body of primitive scientific and genetic theory which, in the nineteenth century, was coalescing as an overarching background for the linking of sex, race, and Nordic superiority. Procreation should ideally occur at intervals of three years.[67] "The generative powers would be much greater and better if the organs never had more than monthly use." During pregnancy and lactation, total abstinence was in order. Handlin records the advice that during such periods a husband sleep in a separate room in order to safeguard for his wife "one half or more of the natural supply of oxygen which God, in his Providence, had designed for her." This was, recall, *scientific* and not religious advice.

The scientists went on to explain that there was not one human race, but several. It was necessary to keep the advanced and superior race "pure." Even in 1923, the author of a government study warned his colleagues about overlooking the genetic and biological realities: "We in this country have been so imbued with the idea of democracy, or the equality of all men, that we have left out of consideration the matter of blood or natural inborn hereditary mental and moral differences. No man who breeds pedigreed plants and animals can afford to neglect this thing."[68] The whole weight of civilization fell to the responsibility of well-bred ladies. The finer instincts of women became the strict and final arbiters of the purity of the race: the future of civilization lay in their hands. (Not by accident were schoolteachers in America mostly women. Men "won the West." But women pacified the men —taught them, eventually, to grow their hair long, to put away guns, and to signal V for peace. From Henry Fonda riding toward the West, to Peter Fonda riding easy East: the womanization of the West.)

What was to become of "coarse and sensual" men obliged to live in sweet reasonableness? For one thing, they rode West. For another, they desperately sought images that would explain their turmoil.

In a primitive land, drawn toward races more primitive, less disciplined, poorer, loosely clothed, often within the orbit of his own power, what would a man of a superior race and a higher degree of civilization do? Self-hatred dogged him at every turn.[69] His need to prove that he was moral and righteous was powerful. By disdain for more lustful and relaxed races, he vindicated his fidelity to purer ideals than others were able even to imagine. He dreamed an impossible dream, struggled with an indomitable foe, imagined himself ennobled by a battle he could never win. Merely so to struggle proved he was good.

An enormous rationalization of his treatment of Indians and blacks, Orientals and Chicanos, was available to the white man at the end of the nineteenth century, as it had not been before. They were not only at his mercy, but they were morally unworthy; and they were a genetic threat to the welfare of mankind. "Who were the victims?" Handlin writes. "They were Negroes and Indians, but also white men—Jews and Slavs and Italians—an indefinable host. For the victims were chosen to be such, not by virtue of their distinctive characters, but out of the agonized need of their oppressors."[70] The victims were those sexually and socially less controlled.

What course lay open to the victims—Indians, Blacks, Orientals, Chicanos, Jews and, in our context, Poles, Italians, Greeks, Slavs? How desperately many tried to prove they were proper, reliable, chaste, self-disciplined, controlled. How earnestly they worked against their instincts, impulses, gestures, feelings, drives, and perceptions. How urgently they worked to find sex "dirty." The melting pot was a cauldron of lead for the purging and the encasement of passion. If one could not be a WASP, one could make oneself into a good metallic soldier.

7. *Many Kinds of WASP*

Growing up in America is a series of new social-cultural explorations. The undifferentiated "them" beyond one's own family; neighborhood; ethnic, religious, and economic group turns out to be exceedingly various. One evening in Boston I attended a party with black families in Roxbury; went for cocktails and dinner at the home of an assistant to the governor in a sheltered, quiet, sylvan hideaway in Cambridge; and finished up with dessert at the small suburban home of a genial Irish lawyer (a federal attorney) who had moved out from an Irish neighborhood to Wellesley. The manners, vocabulary, interests, courtesies, jokes, speech patterns, facial expressions varied from place to place.

When I first came to New York, general schemes like "Jews" shattered in my hands. I wasn't prepared for Jewish cab drivers or Jewish poverty; not for militantly conservative Jews in a teachers' union; not for countless factions, classes, political views, and neatly elaborate hierarchies of status. High in one status did not mean high in another; Jewish disdain—escaping from compressed lips—is crisp. A relatively small number of Jews in New York and Los Angeles set a style for Jewishness that may be foreign to Jews in Cleveland or Utica.

Just as clearly it has become plain to me that there are many different kinds of WASP. In the West Virginia hills there may be bitter hostility to Catholics or indeed to all outsiders, and four or five generations of residence are required before one is accepted as other than an interloper. But West Virginia WASPS would have an attitude toward Boston Brahmins or Wall Street bankers very much like that of Catholics in Dorchester, or Okies in the Southwest. WASP history is often internally tragic and bitter. Poor, forgotten, excluded persons abound.

In a brilliant short study of a single Massachusetts town, Stephen Thernstrom opened my eyes to the poverty and degradation exercised by upper-class WASPS for lower-class WASPS. He helped me to see more vividly how threatening to poor WASPS cheap immigrant labor must have been. One can sympathize with their terror. Thernstrom also shows how the image of a small-town community, where everyone knew everyone, slipped from uneasy reality into sheer fantasy two centuries ago. Far from being free and egalitarian, early American culture was severely based on class power, authority from on high, and little or no participation by the poor:

In the 18th-century community the political structure encouraged habits of obedience and deference, habits promising stability and unity. Parties were abhorred, "fashions" despised. Repeated unanimous votes in their town meetings revealed the powerful centripetal influence of local political institutions.

At mid-century the town meeting disappeared, the size and complexity which made Newburyport a city demanded a more rationalized, impersonal form of government. Voting became an anonymous act, and social constraints supporting political deference were thereby weakened. Party competition was now fierce and chaotic.

The competing political parties were not sharply polarized along class lines in 1850, and both were controlled by respectable middle-class citizens. . . . Not a single laborer was included on an 1852 list of the 72 members of the Democratic vigilance committees in the wards. The lower class was politically passive; laborers and operatives exercised their franchise less frequently than citizens of higher status.[71]

The extent to which upper-class WASP convictions rest upon high authority, distance, and direct application of force runs so contrary to the stated ideology of the Constitution, the Declaration of Independence, and the Gettysburg Address that the swift dependence of silver-haired establishmentarians on brute force always jangles one's mental images forcibly. Upper-class WASPS picture themselves as defending uniquely Anglo-Saxon liberties and a distinctive egalitarianism. Still, in the eyes of many of them, they are clearly defending order, *their* order, and they believe in beating down challenges swiftly and efficiently. The White House, GOP leaders assembled, and the Republican governors meeting in San Juan speedily came to Governor Rockefeller's defense after he had bloodily crushed the prisoners' rebellion at Attica. He did "what he had to do." They commended his "forcefulness."

The old WASP family, like other ethnic families, had a tradition of subjection. Thernstrom notes: "The seventeenth-century Puritan family had been not only 'a little church and a little commonwealth,' but also 'a school wherein the first principles and grounds of government and subjection are learned.' Every member of the community had to belong to some family, the agency through which social stability was maintained."[72] This tradition of stability, subjection, the severe internalization of order, seems to lie behind a certain WASP suspicion of other looser ethnic groups, and gives historical depth to our perception of the symbolic meaning of "law and order." The point of force is "to teach a lesson" that was, unfortunately, not learned in the family. People of good families, meanwhile, seldom feel the weight of the law even when they err, for there are many testimonies to their "good character" and "upbringing." (The support of David Rockefeller for William Bundy as a suitable editor for *Foreign Affairs* is a classic of upper-class WASP solidarity. How could anyone impugn the character of "one of us"? Similarly, the Yankee grandmother of a young lawyer wanted for allegedly passing a gun to George Jackson at San Quentin tells a television audience that whatever the young man did, "he did from conscience.")

Upper-class WASP traditions of democratic liberty depended very highly on strict family discipline and internalized order. They flourished best in small towns and rural environments, where families could be in stricter control of their offspring. As *social* conceptions, these traditions have been under enormous strains, even among WASPS, for over a century.

Things *never had* been as rosy as the myths about small-town America in the 19th century would suggest: already in the 1850's: "We don't know each other"; "we have been gradually losing that social knowledge of each other's residences and occupations"; we must "renew the spirit of former times"—these became commonplace utterances as the forces of change reached into quiet villages and towns across the land. The

warmth and security of a vanished organic community
was an attractive image to set against the realities of
the present—the factory, the immigrant, the reign of
the market.[73]

But there were other English conceptions, dear to a
whole line of liberal thinkers, waiting to take up the slack:

The rise of the city and the spread of the factory across
America was accompanied by a new social creed. According to this complex of ideas, American society was
a collection of mobile, freely competing atoms; divisions
between rich and poor could not produce destructive
social conflict because the status rich or poor was not
permanent. If society was in a state of constant circula-
tion, if every man had an opportunity to rise to the top,
all would be well.[74]

English conceptions of order, decorum, social planning,
the free marketplace (of goods and of ideas), friction-free
consensus, etc., dominate American life so thoroughly that
most WASPS seem unaware of them as ethnic preferences.[75] For them, such matters are so much a part of
their sense of reality, so integral to their own life story, so
symbolically familiar, so inherently self-validating, that
charges of partiality and bias must seem to them faintly
insane. *Their* conception of sanity is, in fact, in question.
They are being obliged to see themselves as ethnically
one-sided for perhaps the first time. What used to be regarded as dignified reserve is now mocked as uptightness;
what used to be regarded as good character is analyzed
now for its "hangups"; the individualism of the Marlboro
man, once a cherished aspiration, is regarded as alienation; the smooth-talking managerial style of liberal WASP
authoritarianism is hissed as manipulative and venal; com-
petitiveness is laughed at by those to whom it is closed.
American cultural pluralism, fed by Jews, Blacks, Indians,
and other ethnic groups, has thrown WASP ideals into a
new and unflattering light.

The recent rise in ethnic assertion is due in large measure to the discrediting of traditional WASP styles in the face of Vietnam, a revisionist history of Teutonic-Nordic prejudice against other races and ethnic groups, and the failure in the cities of WASP conceptions of social planning and social reform. For years, WASPS could comfortably comment on the distant progress of others in "Americanizing"[76] themselves, that is to say, in making themselves into WASPS. Nowadays, the glamor is gone. Who wants to be a WASP? Not even WASPS are certain.

Still, one ought not to be too hard on others. All ethnic groups have their own confusions. All acceded for far too long to the pressures of Americanization—which was really WASPification. Many individuals eagerly accepted it. All have found some good and beautiful things in it.

Besides the many regional varieties of lower-class WASPS, moreover, we should also distinguish between two WASP elites who mutually, it appears, disdain each other: the WASPS of "the northeastern establishment" and the newly rich WASPS of what Kevin Phillips calls "the Sun Belt." The industrialists around Ronald Reagan, the oilmen and new technology of Texas, the booming real estate of Florida—over against the oak-panelled rooms, quiet voices, collections of art, and attachment to civil rights of the Rockefellers, Harrimans, Lodges, and others—may draw the contrasts in power and style clearly enough. And in between these two groups is a third: those small-town lawyers of little class, wealth, or power, whose armpits sweat and whose keys to Playboy clubs compensate for the strict morals of the midwestern Bible Belt, whose legwork is the backbone of Republican power across the land, and whose epigone is Richard Nixon—Nixon the outsider, the nonestablishmentarian, shifty, hardworking, fiercely controlled internally, making himself suffer to convince himself he's on a right path, tough, moralistic, "the last liberal," and president of the United States.

In the country clubs, as city executives, established families, industrialists, owners, lawyers, masters of etiquette, college presidents, dominators of the military, fundraisers, members of blue ribbon communities, realtors, brokers, deans, sheriffs—it is the cumulative power and distinctive styles of WASPS that the rest of us have had to learn in order to survive. WASPS have never had to celebrate Columbus Day or march down Fifth Avenue wearing green. Every day has been their day in America. No more.

CHAPTER FOUR

Spiro T. Anagnostopoulos: Remembrance of Humiliations Past

AND YET, by an odd turn of events, Spiro Theodore Anagnostopoulos is now the chief defender of the WASP ethic. What does one say of a fifty-year-old son of a Greek immigrant, whose great uncertainty in 1958 was whether he could be elected vice-president of his suburban Kiwanis club; who, ten dizzying years later, in 1968, is elected vice-president of the United States?

Richard Nixon is the son of a grocer, born into a suffering Quaker spirituality, adding up day by day his pluses and minuses, making himself over little by little, accumulating a total self-mastery. Only occasionally does he explode jerkily, unsteadily, catching himself, just enough to reveal resentments rolling like the San Andreas Fault just below his thin surface of control.

Anagnostopoulos, by contrast, is ethnic through and through. The son of a restaurateur, he has always been easy-going, shiny-haired, fit. He has, for certain, been keen-eyed for opportunity: a most un-Protestant story, completely unlike Horatio Alger.

It is as if in 1959 or so he tripped a hidden lever and America—cornucopia—poured out on him abundance that fell unstoppably, uninvited even, from the hands of the gods. And he ("Ted Agnew"), wide open to the chances and occasions overtaking him, was quick enough to pull out his Arrow knit pullover from his sleek stomach and catch the streaming miracles: improbable election as county executive, improbable chance to become Republican governor, improbable nominee as Nixon's vice-president, improbable folk-hero to the nativists: *Spee-ro, he-ro*, household word and hottest populist from Florida to Oklahoma since George Corley Wallace.

What attracted Nixon to Agnew, made him elevate him to the role of Vice-President of the United States, Keeper of the Establishment, and Defender of the Faith? Nixon first met Agnew at a party in New York six months before the convention in Miami. What impressed him so warmly? In Nixon's words: "There can be a mystique about a man. You can look him in the eye and know he's got it." Garry Wills adds:

> Agnew is a believer; his faith in the Establishment (as he proudly calls it) fairly shines from him, as does his horror for its critics. The year 1968 was to be a time for law and order. Nixon, just embarked on his own campaign in the New Hampshire primary, must have sensed this man could voice that theme with a fervor and innocence, a lack of racist nuance, impossible in most campaigners.[1]

That sons of grocers and Greek restaurant owners can become presidents and vice-presidents of the United States is a not altogether ugly fact about America. A price is exacted.

1. *"We, the Establishment"*

In Agnew's case, the price was high. Many in the media see him as buffoon. His assigned role was, play Nixon's Nixon; draw off hostility; attract the barbs and jokes; be "blowtorch," "divider," fall guy. It was a role most acutely difficult. Immigrants from southern Europe receive no lack of insults, have small internal margin for accepting ridicule. Spiro's father might have seen such editorials as the following in New York at the time of his arrival from Greece:

> The flood gates are open. The bars are down. The sally-ports are unguarded. The dam is washed away. The sewer is choked . . . the scum of immigration is viscerating upon our shores. The horde of $9.90 steerage slime is being siphoned upon us from Continental mud tanks.[2]

From the mud tanks, a man's son can rise to be vicepresident. But does the son forget, ever forget, who called his father "scum"? "Predictably," the authors of *An American Melodrama* wrote in another context, Agnew "reacts most vigorously when his sense of personal status is assailed."[3]

Agnew's talent had never been accomplishment, or power, or wealth. It was status: a mirrorlike capacity to show back to people what they wished to see, an uncanny ability to learn roles and gestures and intimations, an actor's talent for absorbing background and atmosphere. Men looked at Agnew and saw their own attitudes reflected. He was one of the most meltable of ethnics, an easy number to Americanize. His father made the move from Anagnostopoulos to Agnew, and he himself went from Spiro to Ted, from Greek Orthodox to Episcopalian, from struggling young lawyer to builders' protegé, from a Greek neighborhood to suburban Loch Raven, from Democrat to Republican. Paul Sarbanes, the young Greek congressman from Baltimore, is partisan: "Agnew never did anything for the Greek community in Baltimore except leave it at the earliest opportunity."

Few ethnics have been so thoroughly assimilated. "Pragmatically," Agnew can say, as he told Pennsylvania Republicans in October 1969, "the rules of America work. . . . We are a melting pot nation that has for over two centuries distilled something new and, I believe, sacred." He can say, as he told Wisconsin Republicans in September, 1970:

More generally, my mission is to awaken Americans to
the need for sensible authority, to jolt good minds out
of the lethargy of habitual acquiescence, to mobilize a
silent majority that cherishes the right values but has
been bulldozed for years into thinking those values are
embarrassingly out of style.[4]

But behind Agnew's colorful phrases, lurking in his
voice, has been a remarkable listlessness. One can feel
resentment sizzling. During the campaign of 1968, Nixon
stayed farther and farther from Agnew. He did not mention Agnew in his victory speech. He did not meet Agnew at the plane or talk to him when he arrived at Key
Biscayne afterward. During Nixon's dramatic announce-
ment of a new China policy, Agnew was on a humiliat-
ingly trivial golfing expedition abroad. Agnew is assigned
the dirty work. When he has drawn to himself enough poi-
son and ill-will, he can be dropped.

Kevin Phillips argued in *The Emerging Republican Majority*, as Murray Chotiner had long instructed Nixon,
that voters don't vote *for,* they vote *against.* And the tall,
lanky Phillips held that the resentment ripest for plucking
by Republicans was that of ethnic Catholics who, in
Phillips' acid scheme, had come to hate Jews and Negroes
more than they hated WASPS. Nixon had decided on Agnew as a running mate ten days before the Republican
convention; he hinted in advance that the man he would
choose would help him to court ethnic voters, whom Republicans had long ignored. Agnew would be used in three
ways: as a fresh, new believer in the American system;
as a focus of ethnic resentment; as the voice of America's
millions of outsiders.

The last of these made Agnew credible. Against traditional Eastern money and the liberal establishment centered in the universities and the media, the two
establishments most powerfully fixed in the public imagination, Agnew (and Nixon) can present the image of
envenomed and determined outsiders—because in fact

they are. The envy enwrapping them crinkles like foil. Their public mission, in the name of millions equally resentful, is to humiliate the former great powers of American life.

And thus the election of 1968 revealed something fundamental about American society. Whereas those on the Left tend to think that a "military-industrial" alliance of the Right runs the country, those on the Right feel "bulldozed" by a value-system forced upon them by the Left. Each side pictures itself as the underdog; each is a small, faithful remnant guarding America's true morality.

Nixon has conceived his political struggle as one between national America and local America. More than any president he has taken pains to bring his case to local elites; he has bypassed the great national elites of broadcasting, television, the press, the corporations. The Nixon administration is an attempt to govern America from a web woven by the White House itself. The effort has been herculean and unprecedented.

Nixon's insight is sound. Garry Wills reflects it in *Nixon Agonistes:* Nixon is "the last liberal"; more exactly, the last Lockean. In Nixon are personified the values of the America· that was: the pattern of Americanization laid up in heaven for immigrants to follow. Nixon is the mold in which Agnew was made. If Nixon is a "used-car salesman," generations of hucksters built the West. If Nixon is a pragmatist, no other is America's true name. If Nixon is an ideologue of American superiority, he is devoutly faithful to the nation's creed. If our people are to have a symbol of their ordinary, daily spirit, Nixon's the one: he is Gopher Prairie, Main Street, "our town." *They* give him his "silent majority."

But why does one think of them as silent? Don't they run the country; haven't they set the tone for generations? Television is the window of the nation's soul, and television is not their voice. When Agnew referred to "Polacks" and called a friendly newsman, joshingly, "a fat Jap," he was (as he later said) doing exactly what people do every day in America. But *not* on television. ("All in the Family" is to reality as the Andrews Sisters are to sex.) The media are our double standard: except on the intolerable news, racism, prejudice, injustice, anger, hostility, and differences do not exist. Happy television families. Situation comedies, tapioca-bland.

Half of the genius of Richard Nixon in 1968, then, was the choice of Spiro Agnew to carry the war against television. When Agnew speaks about America, he is patently sincere; his chin says rough-and-tumble, honest, authentic common man. One cannot attribute to Agnew the self-serving motives of one who is protecting some entrenched establishment: there is a special poignancy in placing the word "establishment" upon his lips. He himself loves to savor it. "We, the Establishment," he likes to say. He told students during the campaign: "You may give us your symptoms; we will make the diagnosis and we, the Establishment, will implement the cure."

"We, the Establishment"—not by our own effort but by the grace of God. If Nixon has a Protestant attitude toward life, Agnew represents a Catholic attitude. Garry Wills captures it exactly:

> Leisurely "Ted" is not driven by Nixon's demons. He does not knock himself out; he does not even do his homework. But he is opportunistic—not cynically so; when lucky breaks come, one takes them, grateful. Man's function is to reap the fruits of our beneficent system.[5]

Agnew accepts the doctrines of Americanization, which in his case have been flagrantly disproved. He has not succeeded through hard work, self-help, atomic individualism—and not even personal success seems to have been all-important to him. His is not a story of determination and ambition; it is a story of miraculous handouts. It is not for that reason a less worthy story. On the contrary, one of the sources of America's greatness is that men need *not* earn everything they get; rather, that in America even a wish is rewarded far more than in any other place in any other time. Our nation is a living refutation of the Protestant ethic, and that is the source of our moral confusion.

The secret, effective value system in America today—as Agnew knows and rues—is preached by intellectuals and is not Protestant. The intellectuals include the creators of culture (artists and inventive thinkers) and the distributors of culture (media men and the professoriate). From such sources, "well-informed" and "enlightened" citizens await their signals—and not their signals only, but their sentiments and styles. Whatever is "in" need not be argued for, its partisans need not explain, the burden is on those who disagree. At one moment, abortion is hateful to a majority; in a very short span of months, the public is "informed." But how can industrialists or Pentagon generals or candidates for the presidency genuinely object? Everything is sold that way.

One of the weakest joints in the structure of the superculture, indeed, is its reliance on "informed public opinion." The process of informing the public turns out to be shockingly inauthentic. A very high percentage of "news" is "made" by "newsmakers." Modern means of communication were intended to move us from ignorance to light, and to a large extent they do. Yet much of the light turns out to be from mirrors. Images and illusions fly as thickly today as superstitions once did. Who really wrote the speech? What are they trying to suggest? Is that what he actually said, or was it edited in? or out? What is he really like?

Our people, meanwhile, live partly from common sense, partly from experience, partly from what their friends say, partly from what they happen to read or hear or see. A generation has the right to rely on what the previous generation learned the hard way so that not everything need be undergone again, like unending reincarnations. But when the experience of an earlier generation did not include many staples of the experience of the next—the

automobile, television, affluence—the younger generation
loses that precious right.

All over America, then, people enunciate values which
they do not, cannot, live by. This is not the fault of
intellectuals but of industry itself. In Orange County,
California, financiers and recently successful businessmen,
mortgaged and leveraged to the hilt, want to hold the
government to balanced budgets. While bewailing the
dissolution of "home, family, work and all values that
made America great," their wives and daughters wear
bikinis, sip martinis, and drive sports cars. Oilmen in Texas
complain bitterly about government "handouts." Corporate
executives cannot decide whether "individual initiative" or
"teamwork" is the driving piston of success.

The most revolutionary force in American life for the
past hundred years has been the nationalizing, standardiz-
ing superculture shaped by industry. The rhetoric has
been conservative. The actual impact upon the psyche
has been transformative. And that is the underlying contradiction in the Nixon-Agnew politics. The values they
express are not the ones their constituents practice, or
want to practice. Those in America who call themselves
conservative are the chief agents in the destruction of
what they claim to value: old America and its simple,
honest, rural values. Like it or not, industry and technology are the bearers of the new, invisible religion of
modernity. It is a religion neither Jewish, nor Christian,
nor civilized in any traditional sense. It is faith in power,
wealth, and success. Even Agnew cannot define any
"ideals" toward which our society is directed. All he can
do is specify procedures, and voice a touching faith in
the outcome:

Now it is time for an alignment based on principles and
values shared by all citizens regardless of age, race,
creed, or income. . . . America's pluralistic society was
forged on the premise that what unites us in ideals is

greater than what divides us as individuals. Our political and economic institutions were developed to enable
men and ideas to compete in the marketplace on the
assumption that the best would prevail. . . . The rules
were clear and fair; in politics, win an election; in
economics build a better mousetrap. . . . Historically,
[the rules] have served as a bulwark to prevent totalitarianism, tyranny, and privilege . . . the old-world
spectres which drove generations of immigrants to
American sanctuary.[6]

Thus the thoroughly Americanized descendant of
Pindar, Socrates, Aristotle, St. John Chrysostom, St. Gregory of Nyssa. It is ironical that Agnew should disdain the
intellectuals so, when most of them cherish values very
like his own: pragmatism, the marketplace of ideas, a
meritocracy. Crackling phrases had been simmering in
the melting pot for generations and his speechwriters
pulled them out molten: "nattering nabobs of negativism," "bands of impudent men," "effete corps of impudent snobs." No acceptance for Agnew, a son of a Greek
immigrant, in *those* quarters. No family lineage, no connections, no graces, no credits for enlightenment to *his*
name. ("No one," Wills notes, "could so effectively plead
ignorance.") The northeastern liberal establishment—
money, media, and mind—are outside looking in. Now it
is "We, the Establishment"—and, hopefully, "We, the
silent majority"—for the next forty years.

But at what price? What did "the melting pot" actually
do for Spiro Anagnostopoulos? Jokes about being Greek,
consciousness of the slickness of his hair and the olive
oiliness of his skin, shame at his family name (how many
hundred years had it endured without truncation?). Did
he feel uncertain of the proper manners and decorum as
he wandered up and down the unfamiliar rungs of America's social ladders: black militants, New York financiers,
journalists, policemen, old Baltimore families? Constantly,
the "enlightened" press mocked him, mocked his name

("It isn't exactly a household word," he conceded at first), mocked his manners, mocked his views, baited him, pounced upon his words. Resentment accumulated, like fireworks in a warehouse for the winter. The *intelligensia* turned the heat up to ignition, and Spiro exploded in the summer sky.

2. *The Decline of Superculture*

Agnew, of course, goes into orbit best when he is aimed northeast. Behind his antics, there is not such a bad insight. But it has to be disentangled from some poor ones. What Agnew's agents would like to do is break off the United States at the Hudson, or maybe the Potomac, and protect the superculture inland.

If only the superculture as a whole weren't in decline. There is a sad, last-ditch nostalgia to everything the Nixon administration does. The president every day declares some new "first" he has achieved. But one would not be surprised if some day his tongue slipped and he said "for the last time in history . . ."

There are two components of "superculture." One is commitment to the high WASP values of the land. The other is commitment to the values of modernity: to science, technology, industry. These two commitments reinforce one another. Protestantism is the culture religion of modernity. Its individualism, its sharp split between reason and faith, and its doctrine of works were almost perfectly adapted to the pressures of modernity.

The chief spiritual center of modernity is the university. The chief centers of diffusion are the mass media. One can cease being a Protestant and practice the new spiritual religion with hardly a break in stride. Except that explorers like Alexander Durrell, Henry Miller, and William Burroughs, journeying to exotic lands, criticize the narrow rationality of Protestantism. They insist upon the human importance of a larger sensuality, a freer passion, a descent into decadence.

Thus the superculture is wracked by inner tensions. Riverside Church competes with revival tents under a sudden summer rain in Mississippi. In economic power, "high" church wins; in numbers, "low" church is far ahead—and gaining in economic power, too.

Concerning modernity, progress through Dupont and Litton competes with progress through Freud and Marx. The material base on which—and the indispensable imaginative framework within which—intellectuals labor today is supplied by university salaries, cheap paperbacks, cinema, travel. Whether one construes "modernity" to mean the world of *Fortune* or the world of the *New York Review of Books,* the connections between the two are thick and tangled.

There are astonishing differences between "worlds" in America, of course. It is a giant country, full of strange and fascinating divergences. So many different patterns for perception exist here, conflict, oppose one another, and occasionally enrich. But there is also such a thing as "a mainstream." And since 1932, that mainstream has taken over the work of the old-fashioned WASP ethic. Modernity has come to figure more highly in its constitution than the old high WASP values do.

Modernity contradicts the ancient WASP ethic by celebrating teamwork rather than individual effort, social conscience rather than individual conscience, technical planning rather than biblical moralizing, sexual matter-of-factness rather than inhibition, excitement rather than sobriety, easy spending rather than frugality. It retains together with the ancient WASP ethic, emphasis upon the solitariness of the individual, rational control, a rationalistic approach to politics and society ("issues" rather than "persons"). Modernity is almost inconceivable without generations of commitment to WASP values. But it is also a process in whose course WASP values are more and more deeply called into question. What we meant by a "mature" or a "developed" people is a people that has assimilated WASP values—or at least values very *like*

WASP values (internalized controls, planning, individualism, consensus). On the horizon gather warnings that such values were, at best, a transient stage in the history of the race; at worst, a dead end.

The decline of superculture means a loss of confidence in the old high WASP sense of reality, in the modern project, and in the intellectuals. To the extent that all these forces have worked as one, there was a mainstream in America, a superculture, compared to which everything else was a sidestream, a subculture. '

What in recent years has been called the counterculture is, in most respects, a mirror opposite of the superculture: the romantic underside of excessive rationality. That is why in attacking the counterculture, Spiro Agnew found it easy to attack the patriarchs of the superculture as well. Superculture and counterculture have a family quarrel. But it's all within the same northeastern liberal establishment. Didn't *The Greening of America* appear in the *New Yorker*, where it showed one generation how they could join another without really changing a single value? Consciousness III is where I and II have been heading all along: a synthesis of WASP individualism and corporate teamwork, with a new sensuous mobility to fill up the free time purchased by technology.

Catholics and Jews may have been the first to sense the new liberties in the counterculture as contrasted with WASP decorum and rationality. But even Protestant clergymen soon found they could retain their central Lutheran "do your thing." And it was, indeed, on errant individualism, on enthusiasm, on sectarianism, and on the "myth of the Pure Protester" that the counterculture finally shattered. The inadequacies it exposed within the superculture it carried in itself.

3. *The National Network People*

The story of Spiro T. Anagnostopoulos is a parable. Some see in his story the glory of America; and there is glory in it. Some see in it the hollowness of America; there is hollowness (and tragedy) in it. What cannot be overlooked, however, is the role intellectuals on the Left play in it. Nothing Agnew says is cheered so wildly as his attack upon the northeastern liberal establishment. Resentment against the Left is electric, almost physical: Agnew conducts it, he does not originate it. The intellectual Left is dangerously out of touch with one of its chief constituencies.

It sometimes seems that intellectuals in America *define* themselves by opposition to ordinary people—and not only to Main Street and Gopher Prairie, but also to construction workers and assistant managers. Intellectuals do not make a sufficiently sharp distinction between lower-middle-class Protestants and lower-middle-class Catholics, between the "old Americans" and the children of more recent immigrants, between small-town America and unionized America. Like slums to Agnew, "middle Americans" in the eyes of intellectuals look alike. That misperception has given Nixon and Agnew an opportunity they would otherwise have lacked.

It will seem absurd to intellectuals, but for most Americans the only intellectuals they've ever seen appear on television. "Intellectuals" are not clearly distinguished from commentators, pundits, interviewers, meteorologists, men in long white coats selling aspirin or testing the cleanliness of gasoline. Intellectuals probably are not aware of it, but every time they take a precious few minutes from their harried lives to respond to importunate reporters (who ever heard of an intellectual burning up telephone wires trying to get a few free minutes to plug his name and books?), every time an intellectual appears on radio or television, or is interviewed in the press, he preaches *at* the people. He *enlightens*. He is aware of his responsibilities to "informed public opinion": he *informs*. There is a special tone of voice intellectuals have, the equivalent of a clergyman's special tone, which one shifts into, as in a Volkswagen. There are tones of voice called "writer," "professor," "commentator," "expert." In such tones, one may affect talking just like any other human being. But once the gear shift is shoved past neutral, on comes enlightenment with a roar.

Consequently, by aiming at the national media, and in particular at television, Agnew can attack the choicest symbol of superculture. Were America a religion, television would be the pulpit by which a mystic bond, a trance, a conscience, an incitement were disseminated to the faithful. The religion being transmitted is inevitably WASP, modern, homogenizing.

The very meaning of "information" is revised by television. Viewers receive far more than facts. Their soul itself is shaped (in-formed): affect, image, voice, tone, intensity are given.

Nothing, indeed, so rapidly weakens old American perceptions. In television, children have leverage against the values of their parents; the uneducated are not dependent on their ability to read. Into seventy million slits in the living-room armor of America seep lavish, slick, rapid percepts. The psyche of America is invaded as it never was before. Isolation is broken down. The "act" of watching contradicts every instinct of the ethic of work. Elitism is broken down: intelligence must make itself communicable to millions; tastes and styles are flashed equally to all. The "vast wasteland" is egalitarianism-in-act.

The family no longer functions as the sole inhibitor of the psyche—the new inhibitor is the medium itself. Values not implicit in the sea of percepts flowing on the screen are "out of style." Those who value "old-fashioned" virtues must decide between their evening pleasure and a steady assault upon what they hold dear. Older folks are more easily deceived, of course; when certain long-familiar words are spoken, they feel reassured. They don't allow themselves to believe that the medium itself melts eternal verities into disappearing dots. Bob Hope says huskily that he is proud to be American, and praises God. On Bob Hope's America, Jonathan Edwards, or even

Billy Sunday, would have called down brimstone. The sets of Lawrence Welk are wasteful and evanescent far beyond the frugality and simplicity enjoined by German Lutheran traditions. The world of television is inherently visual, rich, baroque, and Catholic; Protestant sensibility was doomed by the cathode ray.

Many of the professionals at work in television do not share the values and perceptions of those into whose homes television brings them. Courtesy demands that they be reasonably polite. But around the edges of almost every image and every intonation is a charge of libidinal energy, less repressed in television performers than in many citizens. Explicit material may be innocuous; but the effect is and is intended to be, in an old-fashioned sense, "worldly" and "suggestive." In political contexts, the objectivity of the material and the manner usually fails to disguise effects which reveal restrictions the news-caster feels. The viewer often senses his resentment at treating fairly what he thinks is stupid, at needing to speak in simple formulae, and at having to hold his personal reactions constantly in check. Were it otherwise, television would be wholly inhuman.

Television has an inevitable bias in favor of the Left. Who can halt progress? An insistence upon being modern is profitable both to the political interests of the Left and to advertisers. It is incessant on the media. Ethnics learn quickly that it is improper for true Americans to voice certain sentiments; deeply felt views, therefore, swiftly go underground. Thus it is difficult to find Americans ready to voice views that others, rightly or wrongly, will scorn as "racist." People don't willingly want to subscribe to views that are "backward" or "reactionary." Built into the descriptive terms frequently employed on television is a threefold code.

On the one hand, there are enormous pressures to be "with it," "swinging," "mod." Enormous moral coercion is applied to people whose values (family, personal loy-alty, stability, serenity, hard work, decency) are deemed

"old-fashioned," "square," "out of touch." Even the sops
—Doris Day, early Andy Williams, Lawrence Welk—
thrown to ordinary Americans are essentially nativist
rather than ethnic. Welk, for example, did not suggest the
stink of sweat, earth, and hay that the authentic polka
exudes; everything was cleaned up, perfumed, smoothed,
prettified. And yet older ethnics often found his show a
representative compromise between something from long
ago and today's deodorants. Geritol was its ideal sponsor.

Secondly, television is an inherently limited and highly
biased medium. It favors a certain type of personality
and penalizes other types. It favors the cool, reasonable,
soft-spoken manner and the placid face, full of life perhaps but firmly under control. Perfectly intelligent and
interesting people—many senior congressmen, for example—are unpleasant on television. Nervous, insistent, or
inarticulate people grate on the nerves far more on television than in real life. We did not have one before, and
now national television is our melting pot!

Its voices do not speak Italian, Yiddish, Armenian,
WASP—they speak televisionese. Even Archie Bunker
masks divergent ethnic sentiments behind an Anglo-Saxon
name and style. Few people come on as Jews, or Poles,
or Italians, or Blacks—they all come on as WASPS, the
WASPS of the northeast at that. If they don't they offend.
After all, people are inviting them into quiet living-rooms;
you don't insult your hosts.

"Reason" and the quiet emotions are favored. Proprieties are enforced. Euphemisms replace genuine speech. No
one calls anyone, as people (even presidents) do daily,
Sonofabitch! Seldom does one see anger, envy, hate.
Racial and ethnic voices do not sizzle with suspicion.
Molasses of tolerance. Poverty does not cry out in pain
or drag out in apathy. The pace is quick suburban. Television is the voice of superculture. Its very attachment to
"objectivity" biases it. Where there is calm and reason,
can liberalism be far behind? Where there is compassion-

—as in reporting the news there is likely to be—"bleeding hearts" are certain to be touched.

No wonder Agnew's choicest resentment is saved for network television. It imposes a superego more demanding than a Puritan father. It inhibits. It falsifies. People who are hurting from the edges of life detest its tubular slickness. They resent the rationality of television. It attacks them inwardly. On the other hand, real opposition is almost intolerable in its immediacy; intensity is too much to take. The quiet personality does best. A wart, a facial scar, a cold sore, shadowed eyes, a heavy beard—the realities of daily life—obtrude, offend, distract. The medium is by its limitations a fantasy imposed upon us.

The enforced simplification helps political candidates of the superculture. When Agnew made ethnic jibes, as men do all over America every day, the people of the media pretended to be—and *were*—shocked. Politicians who speak the rough language of the people are made to seem neanderthal, barbarian, corny, gross, excitable, irresponsible, unfit for public life. A national politician needs to symbolize the superculture. Mayor Lindsay gains points; but Procaccino, Rizzo, and Mayor Daley lose.

Agnew himself has mastered the art of cool delivery. He throws his lines away. He seems almost bored. But his early violation of taboos makes even his slightest gesture crackle. He claims that commentators do not treat him and the president "objectively." The truth is, it is the objectivity of the medium itself, its very coolness, that makes people feel his contrasting power—and danger. Simply to run Agnew straight, without comment, is enough. The *medium* is unfair to him. And perhaps turnabout is fair play. For in trying to bring television as the number one symbol of superculture into the Nixon corral, he did not follow the rites of purification. He did not first sign his submission to the rules.

Widespread resentment against the media, therefore, is not without foundation. If true and genuine emotions cannot be publicly expressed, enormous frustration churns in the soul. One thirsts for a few words of honest emotion. One feels ashamed and inhibited, because one cannot live up to the smooth, reasonable model enforced by the cool medium. Thus Agnew, Wallace, and several other populists provide genuine release, even to people who do not agree with their politics or would not like to see them in power. At least they break open the repressiveness of the media.

Thirdly, the symbolism acted out by television journalists and advertisers generates a new sense of reality. Television is a metaphysical instrument; it profoundly affects what we take to be real and how we perceive. Insistently, it favors the new, the modern, the latest invention, the newest study, the most recent, and thus leftist, enthusiasm. The medium is itself an almost perfect symbol of fluidity, mobility, atomization, and manipulation. One starts with tiny dots. They are activated and patterned at somebody's will. Images rush by at confusing and often deliberately dizzying speed. Real things are artistically taken apart and put back together at human whim. Nothing is stable, organic, rooted in the slow, familiar processes of nature. Television is an ultimate symbol of the triumph of History over Nature, of human will over natural objects. It is the quintessence of artifice and externality: of surfaces, excitements, diversions. Almost always, it leaves the soul untouched. It is a "wasteland" elegantly matched to the culture that produced it: the culture of the universities and laboratories, the corporations, the twin marketplaces of hardware and ideas.

A medium whose glow penetrates into the souls of children (who, on the average, adore in silence before it seven hours a day), a medium that shapes their imagination and their emotional expectations for all their years to come, is on top of everything else the number one marketplace. Buyers and sellers are noisy in the temple of our children's souls.

Are there no guardians of culture to drive the money changers from the temple, to impose standards and controls upon the floods of inanity? *Laissez-faire*. What is not good enough in the economic order we now insist upon for the human spirit. We do not admit that "autonomous intellect" is as fallacious an abstraction as "economic man." We do not see that images, affects, and values are not any more private than currency, and are for cultural health as subject to social decision as money is.

Whether one likes it or not, television is always an organ of censorship. What it chooses to exhibit is exhibited; what it rejects, or fails to imagine, is as much "repressed" (in Freud's nonpolitical sense) as images of the unconscious. There is good reason to be wary of censors of the church, or of the state. But are the censors of the economic world more reasonably to be trusted?

The radical problem of American democracy is economic. We have succeeded, by and large, in separating church and state. We have not succeeded in separating church and economy, or state and economy. Both our government and our churches are in thrall to economic powers. The same is true for those organs of the imagination which have replaced the churches in their impact on the human spirit—the media of communication and the schools. Economic power rules. "In coin we trust."

Agnew's pieties end up blasphemies. In the end, Agnew is on the side of large economic interests. He speaks in the language of the ordinary man only to deceive the ordinary man. He could not have been as successful as he has been unless the intellectuals no longer spoke for those to whom it is their vocation to give voice. The final epitaph on the story of Spiro T. Anagnostopoulos is that he rushed in where WASPS no longer tread.

PART II

The Intellectuals
and the People

One of the most noticeable features . . . is . . . scorn
and contempt, . . . positive loathing, for the
bourgeoisie. It was in this same atmosphere that I
grew up, rebelled and finally became a writer. . . .
What were our parents like? Ordinary, very ordinary.
What did our fathers do for a living? They had jobs
such as these: steam fitters, iron molders, cops,
bartenders, motormen, pipe-case makers, butchers,
bakers, shoemakers and so on. As I look back on
them, they seem subnormal in intelligence. . . .
The people with whom one grew up, what did one
have in common with them? Nothing, really;
absolutely nothing. The authors one read were one's
true friends; the musicians likewise. For the
intelligent, sensitive individual the problem was
the same all over the world.

—HENRY MILLER, Aug 22, 1971.

CHAPTER FIVE

The Intellectuals
of the Northeast

To PROFESS an intellectual life—as journalist, publisher, writer, professor, or simply as lover of ideas—is a rather sacred undertaking. Honesty, presumably, becomes more important than ambition. One speaks, or tries to speak, for truth, judgment, method, taste. One makes oneself vulnerable, like clergymen, to charges of malfeasance or betrayal. Anti-intellectualism is the anticlericalism of the modern age.

As Hofstadter has pointed out, a legacy of anti-intellectualism has run like a strong delta current through American history. In part, the excessive practicality of America was a reaction against the ideologies of Europe. (One finds the common man's practicality working up by osmosis into the early works of William James and John Dewey, for example.) In recent decades, however, American theoreticians have themselves developed so practical a bent, and have accumulated such power through arcane discoveries in new fields like electronics and cybernetics, that the reaction against them is not due solely to their ideologies. It is a not illegitimate anxiety about their power over other peoples' lives—those daily guidelines that George Wallace talks about; and it is a defense against their condescension.

1. *Managers, Aliens, and Immigrants*

If one speaks of the creators rather than the distributors of intellectual culture (in Hofstadter's terms), then perhaps the following points of view among intellectuals may be distinguished: Ivy League pragmatists and humanists (Commager, Schlesinger, White, etc.); the literary modernists (Trilling, Kampf, Howe, Fiedler, etc.); the pluralists (Glazer, Riesman, Lipset, Parsons, Herberg, etc.); the new radicals (Chomsky, Raskin, the *New York Review of Books*); the conservative liberals (Hook, Podhoretz, Kristol, etc.); the humanist technicians (Brzezinsky, Bruner, etc.); the Europe-oriented humanists (Arendt, Rahv, Bellow, Lichtheim, etc.). This way of drawing an intellectual map is not conventional, and it is as primitive as a Viking's map of America. Some persons synthesize in themselves more than one viewpoint, and perhaps everybody shares some elements of every viewpoint. But if the map suggests the complex sources of American intellectual life and gives the word "intellectuals" a disconcertingly various and self-conflicting ring, its purpose will be served. But if one speaks more broadly, larger categories are needed.

The many different kinds of intellectual gather in various "families." What makes persons intellectuals (as Hofstadter puts it) is their love for ideas, an attitude almost of play toward perception, image, and analysis.[1] What divides them into families are divergent senses of reality, divergent stories (which the family imagines itself to be living out), divergent controlling symbols.

To speak all too roughly, one may distinguish between "the managers" and "the aliens." The managers are engineers, accountants, economists, political scientists, consultants, lawyers, historians in residence, sociologists, and others who function as the experts without whose services an advanced industrial society cannot be intelligently run. They tend to value "realism," next practicable steps, and "hardheaded" analysis—quantitative if at all possible. They know the rigors both of scholarly research and of "meeting payrolls." They dislike old-fashioned, sloppy, soft-headed methods, and in this sense often find themselves in opposition to older powers in the older WASP business establishment. McNamara's "whiz kids," the Kennedy campaign workers, the McCarthy campaigners, the new young deans, are examples of new professionals.

The aliens, by contrast, generally imagine themselves to be outside the existent power arrangements. They speak of the economy, the government, and the conventional wisdom as if these were in the possession of foreign powers and inimical to the health of the human spirit. The aliens have assumed the role played by the clerical, more precisely the prophetic, class in more ancient societies. They imagine their activities to be in some way priestly, healing, purgative, redemptive. They think of themselves as pursuing authenticity and integrity, and as faithful to a more noble and demanding set of standards than ordinary people honor. They worry about "selling out."

Among aliens, however, there are distinct families. The mother family of them all consists of "paleface" intellectuals at Ivy League schools: honored; established; accomplished; serene; mostly white, Anglo-Saxon, and Protestant. The *Kenyon Review*, for example, was one of this family's organs. Dependent families consist of bands of elbow-patched, devoted faculty members and hard-working editors of journals and publishing houses at state universities and private colleges at assorted locations all over the country. Networks of print keep their sense of reality intact: they tend to keep "informed," and revivified by subscription to similar lists of journals and books. Whatever the sense of reality of the local townsmen in whose neighborhoods, perforce, they must often live, they keep their own identity burning bright by installments via the U.S. mails. They tend to live near one another as much as they can. Often, as many as eighty-five percent of their primary group contacts involve only fellow intellectuals. They intermarry almost exclusively with others of their class. They prefer small cars, small TV sets discreetly placed, and the intellectual rather than the mass media: the *New York Times* to local papers, the *New Republic* to *Time* or *Newsweek*, educational television to the networks, "camp" to middlebrow culture.[2]

Bands of such aliens have grown enormously in size since the Second World War. One new college has opened every two weeks since 1946. Highly educated experts are needed in industry and government. The market for lecturers, panelists, and poets is large. The aliens, therefore, are no longer merely "outsiders." The genteel poverty of some, especially those with large families and no inherited capital, and their generally lower incomes by comparison with other Americans of comparable education (doctors, lawyers, Ph.D.'s in industry, etc.) make them hesitate to think of themselves as affluent. But on the whole their income and status place their standard of living at the lower levels of the upper-middle class. Often they own or have access to summer retreats. They are consumers of marked refinement. They try to live with style.

Alongside such bands of aliens, there are also millions of other well-educated Americans—the aliens' students, as it were—who think of themselves in more or less intellectual terms. They, too, whatever their present occupation or profession, enjoy the play and the power of ideas. They, too, feel somewhat estranged from the generally low cultural level of American life. They think of themselves as enlightened, critical, mentally alert—a "constituency of conscience" as Senator Eugene McCarthy called them in 1968. They subscribe to the intellectual journals, buy books, attend concerts and the theater, relish the new cinema, and in general provide a market for creative work. Their numbers have grown rapidly since the Second World War. Their varying levels of discrimination have made some intellectuals fearful of a *new* "neo-philistinism." Intellectuals have with heavy hearts discerned a new obstacle in their difficult progress toward the highest standards: instant diffusion, which deprives them of guardianship of their own perceptions.

Still, despite their variety, American intellectuals tend to share certain biases. Not many have sympathy for the values, instincts, institutions, and concerns of southern and eastern European Catholics. The myth of the melting pot has dominated the social sciences for three decades; not very much is known about cultural divergences among whites in America. More than one person has noted that anti-Catholicism is—or perhaps was—the anti-Semitism of the intellectuals.

John Higham reports that the attitude of progressive intellectuals toward the immigrants of the early twentieth century was ambivalent.[3] Some feared the impact of the new workers upon trade unionism; some feared their lack of democratic traditions; some disliked their Catholicism and "superstitions"; some were contemptuous of their backwardness. In general, however, intellectuals helped oppose the enormous tide of the Ku Klux Klan—which in the 1920s reached a membership of six million (more than one-third the strength of the U.S. armed forces in World War II)—and its Americanist assault on the immigrants. They also helped to provide the critique of injustice, moneyed interests, and unfair practices which bore so heavily upon the shoulders of immigrant workers. Finally, they helped to create and to rationalize the fluid, mobile society in which assimilation and upward mobility (however one might evaluate them) became possible.

Overwhelmingly, the intellectuals were on the side of Americanization. The schools were their chief organs, as churches were the clergymen's. The function of the schools was to raise up "citizens for democratic living." Once a year, little children donned the costumes of their national heritage, carried flags over their shoulder, entered a symbolic melting pot and stood shoulder to shoulder waving American flags. (Ford workers in Detroit, enduring a similar ceremony, were made to walk into a gigantic cardboard melting pot and to emerge marching in Ford coveralls to tunes like "God Bless America.")[4] The task was to enlighten the corruptible masses before they became victims of antidemocratic rulers.

A great many immigrants were themselves radical in politics: socialists, anarchists, anti-imperialists. Many were ideologically far ahead of American academics, who for the most part seemed to live in a calm, "paleface," humanistic tradition, without much social or political awareness. Thus, uneducated and sometimes almost illiterate workers in the mills of Pittsburgh or the mines of. Montana were astute critics of the American system, effective organizers, and martyrs—without benefit of university enlightenment.[5] On the other hand, the majority of immigrants from southern and eastern Europe were often skeptical of ideology; implicitly, they understood the need for cohesion and discipline. Realism instructed them to depend upon leadership. They were inclined to hard work, obedience, docility. They did not expect life to be just. They hated many of the inequities of America, but mostly they were trying to keep their families alive and they essentially trusted America. As they had for centuries, most put their reliance upon three fundamentals: their families, their own hard work, and the church. Americanization, ironically, would entail the weakening of all three.

Or so, perhaps, the enlightened hoped. C. G. Grabo wrote in 1919: "We do not as a people make any effort to understand our immigrants or to aid them." He quoted a remark about one family in a report of a group of social workers: "Not yet Americanized; still eating Italian food." Enrico Sartorio wrote in *The Social and Religious Life of Italians in America*:

> The children of foreign extraction learn English and, as very little is done in school to make them keep up the language of their parents, they soon forget it, with the result that their home life is destroyed. . . . It is sad to

notice the patronizing attitude that the child assumes toward his father and mother after a few months of public school.[6]

Richard Mayo-Smith expressed in 1904 a dream of homogenization which many intellectuals shared. The immigrant, he noted with satisfaction, is effectively coerced to learn English.

Where he has not done it himself, his children have; and in many cases it has become the mother tongue if not the only tongue of the descendants. As soon as that happens, the man of foreign descent is irreparably separated from his former home. In some cases thickly settled communities have managed to maintain the foreign speech and the old religion for several generations. But the disintegrating forces are at work all about them. The moment the young man ventures out into the world he is obliged to learn English. The moment he aspires to the higher education or to political or commercial position he must recognize the prevailing tongue. The children learn it in the school. The parents recognize that it is desirable for the children if not for themselves. It is impossible to isolate the little community completely and it is gradually undermined.[7]

The schools, moreover, were not only Protestant; they were Anglo-Saxon. World literature was hardly touched. Italian students were not introduced to Dante, Boccaccio, Manzoni, Gramsci, Sturzo. French students were not encouraged to assume a special relation to Sartre, Camus, Gide, Claudel, Baudelaire, Pascal, Montaigne. What books by Czechs, Slovaks, Poles, and Roumanians have been translated by American scholars and brought into curricula for students of Slavic background? Education in America has not been conceived as a search into historical roots. It has been conceived as indoctrination into superculture.

Whatever the ingredients chopped, diced, and shredded into the melting pot, the recipe pleased only one taste. For nativist Americans, the design laid up in heaven was a vapid "true Americanism." For most intellectuals, it was an odorless "modernity." All the talk about diversity had unity in mind. All the praise for the "contributions" brought by each immigrant strain to the American cornucopia had no *specific* contributions in mind—nothing substantial, nothing requiring *America* to be converted. Even the most sympathetic intellectuals peered through a fuzz of complacency:

> One could talk in generalities about immigrant gifts far more easily than define them. No one even tried to discriminate what was "best" in the immigrants' past worth preserving, from what might be bad or worthless. When examples of specific gifts came to mind, they turned out invariably to be things to which Americans attached slight importance: folk dances, music, exotic dishes, handicrafts, perhaps certain literary fragments. The contributions that charmed sympathetic progressives had no bearing on American institutions and ideals. A pageant prepared for Fourth of July celebrations expressed the gifts idea neatly. In this solemn drama immigrant groups in native costumes performed their national folk dances in an "offertory spirit" before a white-robed figure of America. It was all very genteel and uplifting, and very far removed from the rough, sweaty, painful adjustments that converted Europeans into Americans.[8]

2. *The Bigotry of Intellectuals*

When the children of southern and eastern Europe survey their position in American society, they find two forms of bigotry arrayed against them. The first derives from the Nordic racism discussed in the last chapter. The second derives from the intellectuals: traditional New England WASP intellectuals and Jewish intellectuals. It is the prejudice of the enlightened against the unenlightened, the animosity of the educated against those less educated. It is the moral self-righteousness of those who regard themselves as "liberated" (and who may be the most enslaved and self-tormenting of all). In New York City, college kids swirl around a policeman. One policeman described for Robert Coles what it is like:

> Have you ever seen those college kids shouting at the police? I've never seen anything like them for meanness and cheapness. The language that comes out of their mouths; you begin to wonder whether you're in a mental hospital. I mean it; those kids go crazy when they see us. The uniform seems to trigger something in them. They become dirty, plain dirty. They use the worse language I've ever heard. They make insulting gestures at us. They talk about killing us. The girls make sexual overtures—when they're not swearing. Swearing, that's not the word for what you hear! . . . I'd even said "please" to them to be quiet and orderly. I asked them to clear away for the sake of pedestrians and cars. The nicer you are to them, the worse they get. God, they're a filthy-mouthed bunch of little bastards.[9]

One of the girls detaches herself from the crowd and comes up to a young cop. She lifts her skirt almost to her face and flaunts her blue bikini underpants. "This what you want?" she shouts. "Love, not war!"

It is difficult to think of exploitation more cruel. The college girl unwittingly mocks the policeman's wife and daughter, neither of whom, perhaps, went to college. The policeman, if he is Irish, say, or Italian, lives in a community in which the ethic of sex and the ethic of dissent are almost wholly different from those of the radical student. His ways may be "unenlightened." But they are his. To mock matters so deep in his way of life is to demean him. Would the girl mock black culture so caustically? Would she make fun of Indian culture that way?

What is the ethic of the educated classes, which the policeman has so difficult a time understanding? Marshall Berman describes it eloquently in *The Politics of Authenticity*. The intellectual has "a dream of an ideal community in which individuality will not be subsumed and sacrificed, but fully developed and expressed." It is a dream of perfect community, and yet of perfect individuality and full self-expression, too; not a dream in which all make sacrifices and concessions in order to pull together. The dream is modern, because "it presupposes the sort of fluid, highly mobile, urban society, and the sort of dynamic, expansive economy, which we experience as distinctly modern, and which nearly everyone in the West lives in today." (*Nearly everyone?*) It is an old dream, as well, for "it has been a leitmotif in Western culture since early in the eighteenth century, when men began to feel modernization as an irreversible historical force, and to think systematically about its human potentialities."[10]

The family, in which loyalty and virtue and obedience bind each member to seek "each other's holiness, usefulness and happiness," is *not* the model which the intellectual dreamer dreams of. When Huck Finn is about to be taken into the bosom of the Sawyer family, he must—in authenticity—resist. "I reckon I got to light out for the territory ahead of the rest, because Aunt Sally she's going to adopt me and civilise me, and I can't stand it. I been there before." The intellectual appears to be in reaction against the family. Almost every cause he espouses destroys the tissue of the family. Almost every idea he imagines renders life more inhospitable to the family. Almost every thought of his atomizes American society, separates persons from others, encourages the notion that each individual is and ought to be solitary, self-directed, self-watchful.

Philip Rieff describes the process in *The Triumph of the Therapeutic*: one gazes, as it were, at one's own internal belly button, seeking that inner balance in which pain is outweighed by pleasure. "Conscience" becomes an inner sweet feeling of preference. Networks binding the self to others are cut or uprooted, so that in the ultimate greening of America described by Charles Reich "loyalty" becomes one of the weakest of considerations. For who can know today what his or her feelings will say is right tomorrow? Good words like "honesty" and "authenticity" become lost in the libidinal jungles of competing desires. To *which* layer of the self ought one to be honest? *Which* feeling is the authentic I? To *which* presentation of the many-mirrored self should I be sincere? The pursuit of the true, the authentic, the sincere, the real *me* is fraudulent from the beginning if there is no such self waiting to be "liberated." The pursuit of isolated authenticity is stupid if a human is not a private but a social animal, not primarily an individual but primarily a member of communities. (Thus Sartre has left his simpler notions behind.)[11]

According to analyses made by the intellectual Left, America is sick because of the activities of *others;* businessmen, capitalists, industrial-militarists, unenlightened bigots, and fascists. One seldom hears advanced the possibility that America is sick because her intellectual classes are also sick; because what intellectuals think and feel and do is a primary conduit of disease. There is an enormous consonance (as one might suspect) between the social, economic, and cultural myths of "the American way of life" and the rationalizations of such myths presented by American intellectuals. When intellectuals excoriate businessmen and unenlightened sources of the radical Right; and when Agnew, representing corporate America, excoriates the sicknesses of radical-liberal intellectuals, it is a little like children under parental accusation pointing at each other: "It wasn't me!"

In 1955 (with a new edition in 1962), Daniel Bell published a collection of essays under the title *The Radical Right*. Most generous and genial scholars participated: Richard Hofstadter, David Riesman, Nathan Glazer, Talcott Parsons, Seymour Lipset, Peter Veirek, etc. They wrote of "the dispossessed" and "the discontented classes."

They worried about the new upsurge of anti-intellectualism in America. But it is crystal clear that what they
worried most about is the collapse of the old New England
elite. The new liberal intellectual elite, which had since
1932 acceded to the central position in American life, was
under threat. They interpreted the rising of discontent as
irrational resistance to "modernity." Bell states the theme
exactly:

> . . . the nature of the debate becomes clearer. What the
> right wing is fighting, in the shadow of communism, is
> essentially "modernity"—the belief in rational assess-
> ment, rather than established custom, for the evaluation
> of social change—and what it seeks to defend is its
> fading dominance, exercised once through the institu-
> tions of small-town America, over the control of social
> change. But it is precisely these established ways that a
> modernist America has been forced to call into
> question.[12]

Moreover, the cultural tradition within which alone
"modernity" is to be conceived turns out to be Nordic.
Again Bell: "The politics of civility . . . has been the
achievement of only a small group of countries—those
largely within an Anglo-Saxon or Scandinavian political
tradition." An Anglo-Saxon elite dominated America until
the emergence of a national culture; in the period between
the world wars, radio, cinema, and automobile national-
ized the land. According to Walter Lippmann, this elite
was "a well-entrenched community, settled in its customs,
homogeneous in its manners, clear in its ultimate beliefs."
Until the mid-1920s, Bell adds, "America in its top and
middle layers had been, politically and culturally, a fairly
homogeneous society." He quotes Lippmann:

> Those who differed in religion or nationality from the
> great mass of the people played no important part in
> American politics. They did the menial work, they had
> no influence in society, they were not self-conscious and

they produced no leaders of their own. There were some sectarian differences and some sectional differences within the American nation. But by and large, within the states themselves, the dominant group was like-minded and its dominion was unchallenged.[13]

According to this interpretation, America was, from its beginning until about 1932, "the land of the WASP." From 1932 until, say, 1962, it was "the land of the intellectual." Since 1962 the future has been uncertain. Already, in 1955, Professor Hofstadter was writing: "Today the dynamic force in our political life no longer comes from the liberals who made the New Deal possible."[14] It comes from the new rich of the "Sun Belt" and from the more or less successful children of Catholic immigrants, who together "have as their objects of hatred the Anglo-Saxon, eastern, Ivy League intellectual gentlemen." What worries Hofstadter "in a populistic culture like ours" is that we "lack a responsible elite. with political and moral autonomy." Americans lack an aristocracy and a "truly conservative" respect for elite institutions. Our right wing is only "pseudo-conservative" because of, for one thing,

... the attitude of the extreme right wing toward those institutions that come closest here to reproducing the institutional apparatus of the aristocratic classes in other countries. Such conservative institutions as the better preparatory schools, the Ivy League colleges and universities, the Supreme Court, and the State Department—exactly those institutions that have been largely in the custodianship of the patrician or established elements in American society—have been the favorite objects of right-wing animosity.[15]

David Riesman notes how the new dynamic in American politics has passed into the hands of those "who reject the traditional cultural and educational leadership of the enlightened upper and upper-middle classes." The new rich sent their children to college, but many of those children "who have swamped the colleges have acquired there, and helped their families learn, a half-educated resentment for the traditional intellectual values some of their teachers and schoolmates represented." Moreover, in combat over local school boards, many "lower-middle-class pressure groups" easily routed "the old conservative and hence intellectually libertarian elites." Thus "the discontented classes, trained to despise weakness, became still less impressed by the intellectual cadres furnishing so much of the leadership in the Thirties."[16]

One of the strangest developments in American politics, Hofstadter notes, is the polarization around the sexual adjectives "soft" and "hard." (Sexual metaphor is inescapable in Anglo-Saxon culture, not least because of its opposition between "rational assessment" and "passion.") Riesman reflects on the epithets "do-gooders and bleeding hearts," used after World War II for the intellectuals. These epithets are "the grown-up version of that unendurable taunt of being a sissy."

Interestingly enough, anti-Semitism diminishes in importance to the radical right, and so does the Negro. The Jew represents the superego goals of ambition, money, and group loyalty; the Negro represents the id of promiscuity, destruction, and looseness. But the new fear is that of homosexuality.

> How powerful, then, is the political consequence of combining the image of the homosexual with the image of the intellectual—the State Department cooky-pusher Harvard-trained sissy thus becomes the focus of social hatred, and the Jew becomes merely one variant of the intellectual sissy—actually less important than the Eastern-educated snob![17]

Bell speaks of "the exhaustion of liberal and left-wing ideology," and Riesman notes that the New Deal—the last alliance between intellectuals and people—ended in 1937, although the war concealed "this vacuum of goals."[18] The intellectual class, then, is a class caught in downward social mobility, and must be presumed to be as vulnerable to resentment as any other class. Hence, the arguments of Bell and his associates may be turned against them. The intellectuals represent a class in power which failed to comprehend the needs and desires of growing numbers of people. They have been suffering the long, slow process of rejection, not least at the hands of their own young.

One reads in vain in *The Radical Right* for signs that place the blame for anti-intellectualism, not on the American people, but on the intellectuals. (Riesman is more alert to this possibility than the others.) "Modernity" is not a heaven-blessed project exempt from the severest and most radical criticism. What these writers call "enlightenment" is an imposition of values and attitudes that may be less than humane, less than humanly satisfying, less than worthy of concrete men and women. They write with undaunted faith and unbreachable complacency. The actions of others are "rearguard actions" on the part of "small minorities." And yet these same "rearguard actions" have "seized the initiative," "furnish the new dynamism" in American politics, have moved "every argument" many degrees "to the right."[19] Liberal intellectuals themselves show signs of "inner doubt." Their "exhaustion" concerning new domestic programs has led to their focussing on civil rights and foreign policy. Such focus tends "to make intellectuals seek allies among the rich and well-born, rather than among the workingmen and farmers they had earlier courted and cared about; indeed, it tends to make them conservative, once it becomes clear that civil liberties are protected, not by majority vote (which is overwhelmingly unsympathetic), but by traditional institutions, class prerogatives, and judicial life-tenure."[20]

On the other hand, their own egalitarianism obliges intellectuals "to defer to the manners and mores of the lower classes generally." Riesman's honesty leads him to confess:

Whereas in the days of Eastern seaboard hegemony the masses sought to imitate the classes, if they sought to rise at all, today imitation is a two-way process, and intellectuals are no longer protected by class and elite arrogance (and the strategic ignorance arrogance protects) against the attitudes of their enemies. We find, for example, the cynicism of the lower strata reflected in the desire of the intellectuals to appear tough-minded and in their fear to be thought naive.[21]

In the past, the Left stood for progress through economics. Modernity required the atomization of traditional social groupings. Then, through "rational assessment," visionary planners would put Humpty-Dumpty together again in a new type of community that was rational, enlightened, and authentic. Each individual would in an unrepressed way seek freely his own satisfaction. No other constraints but those of reasonable self-interest would be placed upon him by the rational society.

Three fatal ambiguities flawed this vision. Are intellectuals on the side of the planning elites, or are they egalitarian? Secondly, is the kind of rationality intended by Bell ("rational assessment") a sufficient basis for a satisfying human life? Thirdly, are humans able to endure the Anglo-Saxon image of themselves as atomic particles—a "lonely crowd" swept up in "the pursuit of loneliness"?

The intellectual project for America—whether conservative, liberal, or radical—is radically Anglo-Saxon in orientation; that is both its glory and its tragic flaw. Philip Slater notes that no culture was ever so systematically based upon solitariness: for each child a separate room, a separate TV set, separate car, separate everything to the full extent of possibility.[22] The search for authenticity turns out to be a search for soul-scouring isolation, a guarantee of—not a cure for—alienation. Modernity requires a new and more terrifying, perhaps also a more destructive, personal asceticism than the world has ever known.

The myth of the Anglo-Saxon race in America almost perfectly coincides with the myth of modernity. Modernity unites atomic individuals through science and social planning. (The Anglo-Saxon "politics of civility" is, after all, a drawing-room handshake.) Oscar Handlin describes the feelings of the Anglo-Saxon pioneer in America in a vignette that might stand for the horror inscribed today in the heart of sociology:

> The ties, once severed, could never be replaced. The lonely man gazing out into the darkness of the forest or upon the empty prairies or down the endless corridors of the city streets saw never a monument of his belonging. Detached from his past, he could hardly be sure of his own identity. And as he regarded that posterity for which he was ever making some sacrifice, he knew in his heart that his children would desert him, as he had deserted his parents. That was the horror. All the emotions once safely embedded by tradition and communal custom in the family had now no stable foundation in reality.[23]

Intellectuals themselves are not a happy lot. Shall we not fairly describe them, too, as "dispossessed," place them among "the discontented classes," measure their "resentment" and their "unconscious hatred of our society and its ways," analyze the illusions responsible for their own "alienation"? Bell and his associates would have served us better if they had decided to argue frankly for the rights of an intellectual elite to govern a society as "fragile" as ours, either by their own hands or through vicars; if they had exposed carefully their own portrait of the good society and the good man, as one among competing faiths, with deficiencies like other faiths; and if they had spoken as openly of their own autobiographies, fears, and psychic defenses as they did of those of the "semi-educated" whom they took as their targets. Riesman comes closest to creative self-criticism:

These new groups want an interpretation of the world; they want, or rather might be prepared to want, a more satisfying life.

It is the unsatisfying quality of life as they find it in America that mostly feeds the discontent of the discontented classes. Their wealth, their partial access to education and fuller exposure to the mass media—indeed, their possession of many of the insignia they have been taught to associate with the good life—these leave them restless, ill at ease in Zion. They must continually seek for reasons explaining their unrest—and the reasons developed by intellectuals for the benefit of previous proletariats are of course quite irrelevant.

Is it conceivable that the intellectuals, rather than their enemies, can have a share in providing new interpretations and in dissipating, through creative leadership, some of the resentment of the discontented classes? . . . We have almost no idea about the forms the answers might take, if there are answers. But we do recognize that one obstacle to any *rapprochement* between the discontented classes and the intellectuals is the fact that many of the latter are themselves of lower-middle-class origin, and detest the values they have left behind—the dislike is not just one way. They espouse a snobbery of topic which makes the interests of the semi-educated wholly alien to them—more alien than the interests of the lower classes.[24]

Was Agnew so wrong, then, when he detected "an effete corps of impudent snobs"? Did he anger people by a calumny or by thudding an arrow into a bull's-eye? The intellectuals have since 1932 been a dominant ruling elite (among other elites) in America. Many are disturbed by their power. Many are also disturbed by their vision of life, as illustrated in its fruits. The girl who bares her blue bikini pants in a policeman's face may be in equal revolt against both the elitism of her professors and the values of "the pigs." She is no less the child of modernity.

For modernity has two faces. One wing of the intellectuals believes in rational assessment, planning, reliable elites, Anglo-Saxon *noblesse oblige.* Another wing believes in "authenticity"—in will, passion, impulse, individuality, personal liberation. The first wing celebrates technological Reason, pragmatism, utility, and human progress. The second wing seeks to show "the underside" of the major social forces unleashed in the modern era by the first wing. It desires to let all the dirty secrets out into the sunlight. Henry Miller and William Burroughs explored terrors that decent Americans are long prevented from reading; Norman Mailer once expressed an ambition to be the first novelist to bring the word "fuck" into print in America. The technique of the first wing of intellectuals has been to look upon ordinary Americans as backward and unenlightened. The technique of the second wing has been to deliver a slap to the face of middlebrow America: the girl lifts her skirt and asks the cop, "This what you want?"

Ordinary Americans do not distinguish between the pragmatic and the romantic wings of the intellectual class. In their eyes, "the so-called experts with the button-down collars and the thin briefcases full of guidelines" are one with the "explorers of the sewers, the sick men in the gutters." Both are constantly criticizing ordinary America, publishing exposés, heightening the general insecurities.

The severe, restrained Puritan tradition, as Bell points out, is not the strongest version of the Protestant ethic in America; the strongest version has been the fundamentalist, evangelical tradition.[25] Under the evangelical impulse, the world is neatly divided into darkness and light, sex and corruption are exposed, and feelings of guilt are mobilized in vast efforts of social change. This evangelical manipulation of guilt is effectively taken over in secular contexts by muckraking journalists, political intellectuals, and even by those olympian pragmatists who, despite their purported love for grays and complexities, still picture the world as divided neatly between the enlightened and the unenlightened.

Ethnic Americans are caught between heavy millstones. Both the old WASP style and the new pragmatically cool style of the experts are breathtakingly severe. Poles, Italians, Greeks, Slavs necessarily worry a little about their qualifications as Americans. Their recent ancestors, after all, abandoned one land; despite protestations of loyalty, might not they themselves weaken? Nationality in America is not natural and taken for granted; except for Indians and Blacks, people became Americans by conscious choice.

Worse, however, many ethnics worry that they haven't mastered the Anglo-Saxon, the utilitarian, style; that they might not be predictable enough, reliable enough; that their impulsiveness and instincts are ever ready to explode. The WASP and the utilitarian like to handle difficult political decisions politely; it is called "civility" but it is in fact a device useful for keeping power within a small circle. Its implicit violence—WASP managers pride themselves on their ability to make "hard, tough decisions" involving the use of force somewhere—is always kept at arm's length, invisible, conducted at a distance by intermediaries who merely follow orders. Ugly scenes and direct confrontations are not "civil." Other ethnic groups are not less violent, but they hide less from themselves.

The ethnic American is accustomed to direct expressions of anger; direct violence seems to him an ineradicable part of human life. Why try to pretend that violence doesn't occur, or that oneself is incapable of it? Better to see its effects at first hand and learn its horror, than to try to keep oneself pure of it through distance. Ethnic Americans respect strength and despise weakness, as Riesman suggests, out of complicated motives. There is, regrettably, a harshness, vindictiveness, and even sadism in their hearts, tutored through life's experiences. There is respect for authentic authority. There is contempt for strong men who fear their strength or are ignorant of it;

for persons in authority who lack strength; for persons of eminence who lack the conviction implicit in their status, or the honesty to do openly what their convictions require. Authority has its obligations.

It is here that ethnic Americans find jelly in the hearts of many in established positions in America: persons so in pursuit of "authenticity" that they falsify it; persons in power who intellectually are egalitarian but emotionally and by habit are elitist, and can't decide which they most want to be; persons in power who fear "the dirty hands" essential and always implicit in the exercise of power. The Anglo-Saxon conscience is out of tune with Anglo-Saxon behavior, and internally divided as well. That peculiar form of duplicity—too unconscious to be called hypocrisy—is despicable in American culture. Ethnics perceive it just as clearly as blacks do.

Professional football is a metaphor for the gap between intellectuals and ethnic peoples. The educated both fear and admire the violence, savagery, and physical readiness of Butkus, Robustelli, Deacon Jones, Katkavich. There is so much talk of "hard" evidence, "hard" decision, "tough" positions. But football is a game of maximal social discipline. Hence, one can look at the men on the construction gang, the truck drivers, the professional football stars, only to see, head reeling, the smashing blocks and tackles of discipline, cohesiveness, authority, fascism. Vince Lombardi, coach of the Green Bay Packers, was characteristically portrayed as if he were a fascist strongman. The authoritarianism of football, it is said, inhibits the "self-expression" of the individual. But professional football is almost a perfect expression, not of ethnic authoritarianism but of the superculture. It is a classic exhibition of social engineering. It has become "scientific." It is "corporate." Even Jerry Kramer's description of Vince Lombardi emphasizes not authority but mechanical technique:

He makes us execute the same plays over and over, a hundred times, two hundred times, until we do every little thing automatically. He works to make the kickoff team perfect, the punt-return team perfect, the field-goal team perfect. He ignores nothing. Technique, technique, technique, over and over and over, until we feel like we're going crazy. But we win.[26]

And Mike Garrett adds: "After a while you train your mind like a computer—put the ideas in, and the body acts accordingly." Murray Ross stresses the social unit: "Ted Williams is mostly Ted Williams, but Bart Starr is mostly the Green Bay Packers."[27] No wonder young professionals flock to watch pro football. Not only are they the only ones who can afford tickets. It's their life being dramatized.

CHAPTER SIX

The Concept of the Avant-Garde

> *"The sour truth is that I am imprisoned with a perception which will settle for nothing less than making a revolution in the consciousness of our time."*
>
> —NORMAN MAILER, *Advertisements for Myself.*

1. *The Concept of the Avant-Garde*

THE CONCEPT "avant-garde" is a military concept. It was not transferred to the field of the arts until the 1850s. In the old German dictionaries, care is taken to relate the forward segments of a marching troop to the main body: "The flung-out smaller divisions must govern themselves as to their movement according to the larger ones that follow them."[1] In the arts, however, the concept becomes a quite different sort of metaphor. In military usage, the metaphor is spatial; in artistic usage, temporal.

The artistic usage involves a myth about history: history is a moving arrow, a process aiming in a single direction. There is a very strong presumption that what is new, original, experimental is *better*. Moreover, the artistic metaphor has roots in a specific social class, the bourgeoisie. The artist is one who breaks through the forms (and the alienation) of middle-class life. Above all, he is one who breaks through the rationality and control imposed by middle-class life.

By contrast, the relation between intellectuals and people in a pre-bourgeois and a post-bourgeois order is not temporal; nor does it involve alienation. Middle-class life (whether in a socialist or a capitalist state appears to make little difference) is remarkable for its commitment to reason and order. Calculation of rational interests, planning, and the triumph of order over chance are the chief characteristics of the middle-class psyche and society. Feudal hierarchies look to the past; lower classes live in the present; the middle class invented the future.

A further crucial determinant of middle-class life is "historical consciousness." The middle class barely keeps its head above a flood of objects and products; all are "new and improved." The present drowns the past. In this context, the artist cannot count upon his work's survival into the future; it may be totally overlooked, buried. The necessity of living by his sales reduces him to the mind-set of an employee. He must be a fashion-setter, or in the train of fashion-setters. The contradiction in the notion of avant-garde is that we do not know what the future will be, while simultaneously we must justify ourselves by standing with the future rather than the present. The solution to this dilemma is "to keep up with the times"—that is, not to become lost in the tracklessness of the unknown, not to attend to the future after all.

Lenin applied the notion of the avant-garde to politics. The Communist party is the historical avant-garde of the worldwide proletariat. This political usage brings out the meaning of "garde."

Guards is the name given, other than to the bodyguards of princes, in many armies, to elite troops distinguished by excellent supplies and especially brilliant uniforms (cf. Elite); they are usually garrisoned in capitals and royal residential towns. Guard means originally an enclosure. . . . Napoleon I must be considered the actual creator of the g. Tradition puts into the mouth of its commander, General Cambronne (to be sure, without foundation), the saying, "The guard dies, but does not surrender."

The "garde" is a collective united by a common discipline, formed for purposes of combat, based upon a distinction that makes belonging to it exclusive. The "garde" is a distinguished minority. The concept makes clear sense in the *Realpolitik* of the communist world. Lenin intends the generals to travel not in the main body but with the elite. The avant-garde *tells* the main body where to go, whether it wishes to go or not.

Artists frequently have borrowed the connotations of Lenin's usage in order to add them to the connotations of the future. But in the arts and in culture, the usage of "avant-garde" is not really intended to call attention to a disciplined collective, or even to a future which we do not and cannot know. The real energy of the word suggests "freedom," "experiment," and "sheer wilfulness." Thus Hans Magnus Enzensberger:

No avant-garde program but protests the inertia of the merely extant and promises to burst esthetic and political bonds, throw off established rule, liberate suppressed energies. Freedom, gained through revolution, is heralded by all avant-garde movements.

Each of these words makes some sense only if we compare them to the oppressive rationality of O'Hare air terminal, a suburban shopping center, or the quiet asphalt road leading to a country club. Against the death which comes through a reasonable and ordered life in a middle-class world (quite different from the world of the Medici or of the peasants of Orleans), "freedom" and "experiment" may flash signals of life. But the signals are faint and possibly misleading.

Thus Enzensberger quotes from Kerouac's *On the Road*: "My style is based on spontaneous get-with-it, unrepressed word-slinging. . . . Push aside literary, grammatical and syntactic obstacles! Strike as deep as you can strike! Visionary spasms shoot through the breast. You are at all times a genius." The signals of such individual freedom are infinitely repeatable; such a *garde*, it turns out, is indeed a collective, a movement almost monastic in its rituals, its speech, and what it may approve.

Moreover, the celebration of the spontaneous is in the end a celebration of the empty center of kinetic activity: "improvisation, chance, moment of imprecision, interchangeability, indefiniteness, emptiness; reduction to pure motion, pure action, absolute motion, motoricity, *muovement pur*. Arbitrary, blind movement is the guiding principle . . ." Avant-garde movements have historically been full of latent violence, directed first at the materials of their own arts: blindly tossed paints, discordant tones, fragments of words. The dominant inner necessity is to shock middle-class rationality.

Ironically, the truly heavy word for the avant-garde is a pseudo-scientific word—"experimental." As Enzensberger notes, the word is usually accompanied by ennobling modifiers like "bold" and "courageous." But in the arts, the word has few of the operational meanings it has in science. It does not refer to an isolable process, whose variables can be controlled, whose success can be rechecked and repeated at will. A scientific experiment is normally the opposite of bold; it is almost routine, and requires collective scrupulosity, patience, precision, and concern for how others might repeat it independently. Once more, then, a key word acquires its meaning by contrast with a middle-class rationality. An artistic "experiment" aims at a pure, unique, original action. In performing his experiment, the avant-gardist accepts no responsibility for others, for the action itself, for himself. It is not intended for checking by others; it is not even egocentric, but in some curious way magical. He seeks a way to live outside responsibility. And he calls such regression—turning Nietzsche's phrase backwards—"beyond good and evil." The avant-gardist demands a life that looks bold but is essentially safe. It necessarily falls into the hands of cliques or commerce.

Surrealism is the paradigm of avant-gardist movements. In 1909 the futurist manifesto celebrated "perpetual dynamism" and Filippo Marinetti wrote:

We live already in the absolute: we have created permanent and omnipresent speed. . . . We extol aggressive motion, feverish sleeplessness, marching on the double, the slap of the palm and the blow of the fist above all things. . . . There is no beauty but that of battle. . . . Only in war can the world recover its health. [The last sentence in the original: *"La guerre seule hygiene du monde."*]

In 1924 in the surrealist manifesto, André Breton celebrated "absolute freedom": "The simplest surrealist deed consists in walking out into the street with guns in the hand and shooting as long as possible blindly into the crowd."[2]

Adolf Hitler, as Dali wrote, was the greatest surrealist of them all.

"Every avant-garde today," Enzensberger concludes, "spells repetition, deception, or self-deception." The conception of the avant-garde is an anachronism. It is itself, in its aims even, a cliché. For it was a conception fraught with contradiction even in its own time. It gained what force it had mainly by drawing upon the irrational underside of middle-class rationality.

The difficulties of the conception are poignantly felt today. These difficulties arise from three further sources. First, the conception necessarily rests upon a profound separation from ordinary, unenlightened people. Thus in 1954 Richard Chase wrote, rather sadly, in *Partisan Review:*

> . . . history has imposed upon the modern avant-garde
> the duty not only of disinterestedly cultivating art and
> ideas but of educating and leading an aimless body of
> philistine taste and opinion.[3]

Secondly, the avant-garde by 1954 had found itself
very well employed, stable, and respectable. The middle-
class economics of the university, the paperback publishing house, and the burgeoning middle-brow media brought
wider acclaim to Joyce, Pound, Eliot, Melville, James,
Hemingway, Miller, and Faulkner than the narrow circles
of the avant-garde had ever been able to proffer them.
The avant-garde was institutionalized.

Thirdly, as *Esquire* illustrated in a spread on "The
American Literary Scene" in 1964, "the literary power
structure" in America had by then escaped the custody of
elites gathered around *Kenyon Review* and *Partisan Review*. It had become the property of agents, editors, col-
umnists, interviewers, blurb writers, salesmen and critics
who occupied "the red-hot center" of the New York-
Hollywood media establishment. Salesmanship and celeb-
rity had to pass for discipline and standards. Who could
get published? Who could get talked about? Norman
Podhoretz referred to the ticker of literary reputations—a
cultural stock exchange—according to which literary
names rose and fell on a daily market. Theodore Solotaroff named our situation "the red-hot vacuum."

It was not always so. For almost twenty years,
Partisan Review had been the powerful organ of a disciplined band of writers whose spirit was that of "the lonely
urban intellectual, usually of recent immigrant stock,
whose intellectual homeland was still European." Its perspective was European Marxist and post-Marxist. It "took
for granted the separation of the artists and the intellectuals from the middle class." When the prospect of
Marxist revolution soured, other revolutionary or at least
antibourgeois thinkers like Nietzsche, Kafka, Lawrence,
Freud, Mannheim, Sartre, Malraux, and others kept its

fundamental critical perspective alive. The writers of
Partisan Review joined the radical element in modern
social throught to the experimental element in modern
literature and art.[4]

Philip Rahv was one of the guardians of this perspective. In 1952 he described the dreary optimism of many
educated Americans, their feeling of solidity and comfort
in a world he could feel coming apart, their easy reconciliation to the low standards of mass culture. They de-
precated the "negativism" and willful "alienation" of the
avant-garde.

> Now the avant-garde is of course open to criticism. It
> has the typical faults of its incongruous position in a
> mass-society, such as snobbery and pride of caste. It is
> disposed to take a much too solemn and devotional
> view of the artist's vocation. Its distortions of perspec-
> tive result from its aloofness and somewhat inflexible
> morality of opposition. But to accuse it of having in-
> vented alienation is ludicrous. For what the avant-garde
> actually represents historically, from its very beginnings
> in the early nineteenth century, is the effort to preserve
> the integrity of art and the intellect amidst the condi-
> tions of alienation brought on by the major social forces
> of the modern era. The avant-garde has attempted
> to ward off the ravages of alienation in a number of
> ways: by means of developing a tradition of its own
> and cultivating its own group norms and standards, by
> resisting the bourgeois incentives to accommodation
> and perforce making a virtue of its separateness from
> the mass. That this strategy has in the main been
> successful is demonstrated by the only test that really
> counts—the test of creative achievement. After all, it is
> chiefly the avant-garde which must be given credit for
> the production of most of the literary masterpieces of
> the past hundred years, from *Madame Bovary* to the
> *Four Quartets*; and the other arts are equally indebted
> to its venturesome spirit.[5]

In 1962 Rahv was unable to imagine any other condition besides that of an elite culture struggling against a mass culture. "But if under present conditions we cannot stop the ruthless expansion of mass-culture," he concluded then, "the least we can do is to keep apart and refuse its favors."[6]

Something is wrong in the fundamental conception here. Ordinary people are not *merely* a "mass." Their instincts and needs are prostituted, not expressed, by "mass culture." Why, then, must Rahv and other intellectuals conceive of their own vocation in priestly, aristocratic, and avant-garde terms? The underlying myth is quite profound. It is an image of history favoring the future. The future is, for intelligent people, the functional equivalent of God. To be on the side of the future (a benevolent future, safeguarding the continuous progress of man) is the equivalent of standing in the presence of God. The phrase "avant-garde" is a secular translation for "grace." Who would wish wilfully to be ranked among the backward and the unenlightened, or even among the plodding and the slow?

If one does not accept that invisible religion, however, the necessary link between the intellectual's vocation and the concept of the avant-garde is not obvious. One might even be pressed toward an alternative view. The intellectual's vocation is to be a voice of the people—to put into words what they already dimly know. His function is not to lead, in the way an avant-garde leads, or in the way planners, managers, and experts lead. His service to his people is to fashion clear and discriminating words, words which liberate what is already in the people, words which terrify and which illuminate—for not all that is in the people is admirable. The greatest compliment an intellectual can receive is not that he said something arresting, shocking, shattering, bizarre, or original. The greatest compliment he can receive is: "You've put into words something I've always felt but couldn't say."

Technical and managerial intelligence, even of impressive expertise, is not quite the same as wisdom. Wisdom is the art of making choices that "hit the mark"—that is, that take account of all elements, even those too elusive for words. The intellectual is the servant of wisdom insofar as he helps to discriminate, to clarify, and to articulate the human situation. His sensitivities lead him to aspects of experience the experts are liable to neglect. He serves people, against the experts.

The intellectual, then, is not in principle alienated from the people. He lives among them, and makes their experience a major focus of his empathy and intuition. His disciplines, skills, and crafts are beyond the reach of many who lack talent or dedication or endless practice. In that sense, his profession is elitist—it sets high standards of accomplishment. But his field of study includes the feelings, anxieties, resentments, needs, and aspirations of all his fellow citizens. His talent is given him, not that he might lord it over them, but so that he might serve them by fashioning words for their use. Snobbery and condescension are ugly in him; they are direct evidence of a betrayal of his task. In this sense, his profession is the opposite of elitist. Is a man's tongue an elitist organ? A tongue does not hold a pen or hear a girl's laughter. It merely gives voice.

Why has such a concept not long since gained ground? The villain is, perhaps, the metaphor "enlightened." There is no necessary connection between knowledge-equals-power and human good. In pursuit of power, intellectuals have 'long since believed that their mission was to reconstruct the human world in an "enlightened" way, often by the rules of knowledge-equals-power. The world they have made has, indeed, acquired power. It is also a world of expanded liberties and fruitful possibilities. But it is, finally, a world which divides humankind into the enlightened and the unenlightened, the planners and the planned-for, the liberated and the drones, the free and the constricted. It is a world of loneliness and dislocation.

Let us assume that "enlightenment" is only a masked religious claim, the functional equivalent of "salvation." Let us assume that no one is, or needs to be, "enlightened." To make such assumptions, we need not deny that some people know more than others, that some think more accurately, that some discern values more humanistically, that some articulate the gropings of the heart with surer eloquence. We merely deny that there are two classes of human beings. We place all members of the human body in a relation of interdependence and mutual service. The intellectuals give tongue to the people's pain. The people make possible the life, nature, and range of the intellectual's creativity.

When intellectuals feel "alienated" from the people, they ought perhaps to look first to their own way of life, their own habits of mind. In America, businessmen, con men, and hustlers too easily intimidated men of intellect. Hating Main Street, the intellectuals grasped too readily for the myth of the avant-garde. In England, even to this day, the gap between "high culture" and the culture of the people is extraordinarily wide. The "ordinary language" of Oxford philosophers is not the language of the Beatles. In America, WASP culture followed the same model, even though a whole host of writers chose to identify their lives and work with the common man, and sang of the butcher yards of Chicago, the workers on the railroad lines, the slingers of girders through the sky of the cities. The Jewish writer in particular, although not alone, set out to liberate the self-consciousness of Americans from WASP patterns of perception. The rise in ethnic consciousness is not merely a political matter. It is an attempt to give tongue to all those feelings, instincts, and fears which lie beneath the cool surface of superculture.

America is a land that only on its surface is a "mass culture." In surrendering themselves too easily to self-alienation, intellectuals have abandoned people who desperately need tongues, who experience the "mass culture" of the media as oppressive and deceitful, who long to voice the truth about their lives.

Needless to say, the heart of ordinary people is tangled with evil, ambiguity, violence, hatred, prejudice, and ugliness, as well as with hope, aspiration, decency, generosity. I am not asking intellectuals to abandon their own values and perceptions, nor suggesting that they pander to the popular will. I am urging that at least a few intellectuals wrestle in their own hearts with the demons in the American soul; wrestle in such a way that our people come to feel that they are not alone but have companions; wrestle in such a way that the intellectuals do not feel aloof from, above, or superior to the people, but part of them.

There is an enormous falsehood in the structure of intellectual life in America, a falsehood of both economic position and self-image. The intellectuals are perceived as, perceive themselves as, and *are*, separate from the people. To live in that way is to continue living a lie, damaging both to people and to intellectuals alike. Attention to ethnic roots, inclinations, and possibilities is one device for overcoming the lie.

2. *Mass, Middle, and High Culture*

The multiplication of intellectuals since the Second World War has diffused the avant-garde; it also gave it a political base. What television and commercialism weakened, politics reinvigorated. Exactly as the radical right had feared, the intellectuals became politicized; for many, almost all other work took second place. Theater, fiction, even scholarly work, seemed to decline. Faith in the existence of elite standards and tastes weakened. But the most remarkable phenomenon was the disappearance of a coherent board of arbiters.

The classical statement of the problems of mass culture, middle culture, and high culture is Dwight Mac-

donald's "Masscult and Midcult."[7] Macdonald's argument
is that until the Civil War both a high culture *and* a folk
culture prospered, in part because of clearly defined class
lines between the common people and the aristocracy.
However, the Civil War "destroyed the New England tradition almost as completely as the October Revolution
broke the continuity of Russian culture." There was no
other culture to take its place. The immigrants who
flooded to America between 1870 and 1910, he believes,
were all too easily "melted" into the mass culture awaiting
them. The inscription on the Statue of Liberty reminds
Macdonald that

> these *were* the poor and the tempest-tossed, the bottom-
> dogs of Europe, and for just this reason they were all
> too eager to give up their old-world languages and cus-
> toms, which they regarded as marks of inferiority. Up-
> rooted from their own traditions, offered the dirtiest
> jobs at the lowest pay, the masses from Europe were
> made to feel that their only hope of rising was to be-
> come "Americanized," which meant being assimilated at
> the lowest cultural (as well as economic) level. They
> were ready-made consumers of Kitsch.

Randolph Bourne at the beginning of the century took
a disdainful attitude:

> What we emphatically do not want is that these dis-
> tinctive qualities should be washed out into a tasteless,
> colorless fluid of uniformity. Already we have far too
> much of this insipidity—masses of people who are
> half-breeds. . . . Our cities are filled with these half-
> breeds who retain their foreign names but have lost the
> foreign savor. This does not mean that . . . they have
> been really Americanized. It means that, letting slip
> from them whatever native culture they had, they have
> substituted for it only the most rudimentary American
> —the American culture of the cheap newspaper, the
> movies, the popular song, the ubiquitous automo-
> bile. . . .

Just so surely as we tend to disintegrate these nuclei of nationalistic culture do we tend to create hordes of men and women without a spiritual country, cultural outlaws without taste, without standards but those of the mob. We sentence them to live on the most rudimentary planes of American life.

According to Macdonald, a new danger has arisen: the wealthier, middlebrow consumers of culture. Middlebrows preserve the essential qualities of mass culture. They like "the formula, the built-in reaction, the lack of any standard except popularity." The new middle culture, he notes, decently covers its tastes with a cultural fig leaf. "In Masscult the trick is plain—to please the crowd by any means. But Midcult has it both ways; it pretends to respect the standards of High Culture while in fact it waters them down and vulgarizes them." Macdonald then lists *Saturday Review, Harper's,* the *Atlantic,* John Steinbeck, J. P. Marquand, Pearl Buck, Irwin Shaw, Herman Wouk, John Hersey "and others of that remarkably large group of Midcult novelists we have developed" as examples of what he means.

Macdonald exempts some of the immigrants, especially among the Jews, from his complaints about mass culture. He quotes a Jewish immigrant published in 1902:

In Russia, a few men, really cultivated and intellectual, gave the tone and everybody follows them. But in America the public gives the tone and the literary man simply expresses the public. So that really intellectual Americans do not express as good ideas as less intellectual Russians. The Russians all imitate the best. The Americans imitate what the mass of the people want.

Macdonald comments: "A succinct definition of Masscult."[8]

The most rigorous cultural standards in American·life were maintained among the aliens by the family of New York intellectuals, almost all Jewish, clustered around Columbia University, the *Partisan Review,* and *Commen-*

tary. The group invented a powerful blend of literary and social criticism. Lionel Trilling, Philip Rahv, Alfred Kazin, Sidney Hook, Irving Howe, and Norman Podhoretz were among its leading critics. Norman Mailer and Saul Bellow were its most distinguished creators. The decidedly Jewish character of the group introduced jarringly new dimensions into a heretofore largely WASP intellectual life. They opened the way for ethnic pluralism.

The New York intellectuals stood well outside the ranks of the managers; but among the aliens they gave classic (though perhaps too-European) expression to the forms of American alienation. Genuinely and powerfully, they saw America "from outside," and yet with that passionate love common among immigrant peoples. America was, and was not, their own. The surrounding and suffocating WASP style was relatively cool and bloodless, although Melville, Faulkner, and even Hemingway suggested rich possibilities in the American experience. The New York family introduced into America some of the darkness, realism, and pessimism of Europe. More than that, they sharply criticized the comparatively easy alliance between American academic intellect, even among the aliens, and middle-class values like order, docility, technical rationality, and belief in benign and automatic cultural progress.

The Jewish intellectuals were emphatically not Nordic in their view of the world. They tended to see quite clearly the social and economic base of the WASP sense of reality and way of perceiving. A sharp eye for social and economic determinants was, in fact, their strong suit. Not only did many of them have rootage in another language besides English, or in a different set of cultural rituals and stories, so that they realized how arbitrary was the WASP view of the world; they also dealt seriously with Marx and Freud. They were more ready than most Americans to learn from the best and most profound thought of contemporary Europe—more ready to plumb the depths of the sickness of civilization. They systematically explored the ways in which social and economic institutions reflected man's torn psyche, and the hidden, unconscious tergiversations of the self. Experiences that other Americans scarcely were aware of they made it their life's work to explore.

WASP literature in America is largely a literature of affirmation. The American, as R. W. B. Lewis puts it, is Adam: new and pure and forward-looking. But secretly the Anglo-Saxon imagination inhabits so atomic and isolated a place, in so extreme a form of individualism and rationality, that terror is near. The prayers of Anglo-Saxon churches, as we have seen, make assumptions hardly made in any but a Nordic culture. Full of emptiness and solitariness, these prayers reflect the exhaustion of a soul that has tried to maintain an exemplary rational responsibility. The Anglo-Saxon imagination is radically individualistic; the imagination of most other cultures, not least the Jewish, is radically communal.

The paradox is that a radically atomic imagination is so intrinsically in terror that its conscious energies insist upon cooperation, good form, cautious optimism, inspiration, upbeat. The communal imagination faces terrors and disturbances explicitly, without faint heart, deriving peace therefrom. WASP culture *must* make reason and affirmation dominate. A recent despatch from London in the *New York Times* may dramatize the point:

They're still very polite in London. When Lady Dartmouth, chairman of the Covent Garden Joint Development Committee, explained to the press last month what the Greater London Council proposed, . . . she was not booed off the platform. After an elegant exposition notable for impeccable historical allusions and rich in the unconscious humor of patronizing assurances of what we think is best for you, no one laughed. Or cried.

The questions from the floor were bitter-edged, but mannerly. Planning in London, to state a truism that defines and separates two societies, is not like planning in New York.

In New York, there would have been protests and placards. A community group would have charged down the aisle carrying Jane Jacobs on its shoulders.

There was one Covent Garden community representative present, sporting rather more hair than anyone else. He wore a velvet jacket and a button that read "Stuff the GLC Covent Garden Plan." Lady Dartmouth refused to let him speak. Her firmness was iron. He acceded, politely. . . .

Until recently, planning has been a supreme British act of faith. It is part of the national character to believe that all problems are susceptible to sense, prescience and professional competence.[9]

The ethnic contribution to WASP beginnings makes New York more turbulent, more passional, and perhaps more profound than London—truer to the complexities of the human soul. More than any other ethnic group, the Jewish intellectuals have made it possible to say in America many things that heretofore could not be said. They have "made a revolution in the consciousness of our time."

The New York family, however, has broken up. Irving Kristol and Daniel Bell have moved in a conservative, affirmative direction with the magazine *Public Interest*. Jason Epstein has taken the *New York Review* in a radical direction, as a board of legitimation for the youth culture. Norman Podhoretz has taken *Commentary* into an adversary stance toward "radical" politics. Theodore Solotaroff tries at *New American Review* to restore a center of literary standards, a center that is ethnically pluralistic even if rather enamored, still, of the self-images of alienation and an avant-garde.

Intellectual life in the United States now has no cultural leadership. It is subject to the trends of momentary, passing, and contradictory publicity. Commercial culture has swamped Midcult and Highcult alike.

CHAPTER SEVEN

Jewish and Catholic

> *With a single kick the miller got the woman out of his way. And with a rapid movement such as women use to gouge out the rotten spots while peeling potatoes, he plunged the spoon into one of the boy's eyes and twisted it.*
>
> *The eye sprang out of his face like a yolk from a broken egg and rolled down the miller's hand onto the floor. The plowboy howled and shrieked, but the miller's hold kept him pinned against the wall. Then the blood-covered spoon plunged into the other eye, which sprang out even faster. For a moment the eye rested on the boy's cheek as if uncertain what to do next; then it finally tumbled down his shirt onto the floor.*
>
> —JERZY KOSINSKI, *The Painted Bird.*

I. *The "Revolution in Consciousness"*

WHAT DOES IT MEAN, to be "a voice of the people"? The people are often prejudiced, hostile, violent. They hold others in contempt. They are subject to illusion, perplexity, fury. Hear the voices of black militants when they talk about honkies. Hear the voices of cops when they talk about niggers. Hear the strains of anti-Semitism, hatred for Poles, contempt for the Irish, disdain for

Italians, and all the other ugly currents of hatred and anger.

"Power to the people." Yes, but who *are* the people? In the abstract, everyone loves them ("equality," "government of the people, by the people"). In the concrete, almost everyone fears them.

No group of black militants today runs any city with the thoroughness, skill, and ruthlessness with which Al Capone, even at age twenty-nine, ran Chicago. In 1928 the forces of reform had to come to *him* to plead for a fair election. Bombings occurred more than once a week. Capone complained that he shouldn't pay taxes, since he already had nearly all the police on his payroll. He made or broke politicians. He gave orders to industry. He effectively controlled the press. Just over nine hundred gangland "soldiers" were killed in the competition to run the city. Hundreds of millions of dollars were controlled by the gangs. When three men talked of betraying Capone, he invited them to a lavish, jovial dinner. Then, one by one, at the table, he beat each of them to death with a club. Scarcely a bone of any of the three was unbroken, scarcely an inch of flesh unbruised. A bullet in each of their brains sated his passion. They were dumped in a lot.[1]

Among "the people," there are many violent, direct, and ruthless persons who are ready to believe that life is essentially cruel and unfair. They believe the WASP system is hypocritical. They are unsentimental about acting accordingly.

There is abroad in the land a great awe of black militance. Otherwise sensible men are impressed by the solidarity, discipline, anger, hatred, and determination on the part of radicalized blacks. No one should underestimate the resources of a matching hatred and ruthlessness. *Every* ethnic group has turned to violence in order to gain a place in American life.[2] Yet people praise black violence, but not the violence of the United Mine Workers, the Teamsters, the syndicates. Someone must make the

argument in America, because it is true, that black militance can push some WASPS and some liberals around,
but it will *not* push ethnics around. It is essential to everybody concerned to get underlying emotions and underlying
commitments straight.

Al Capone said he was "in business like everybody else,
providing Chicagoans with the drink and games ninety
percent of them, even judges, want." Hidden desires were
his frontier. Rival gangs were his Indians. The deaths in
his wars over nine years were a tiny fraction of those
killed by Bethlehem Steel, the Santa Fe Railroad, Minnesota Mining, Ford Motors. Capone's men also had the
decency to avoid harming noncombatants; there were no
Calleys among them; the Valentine's Day massacre (the
worst) was no Little Big Horn.

There are different styles of violence. The war in Vietnam and black militance have unmasked upper-class violence. Antipersonnel bombs were not invented by men on
a construction gang; guys on beer trucks did not dream
up napalm. Ph.D.'s from universities, who abhor bloodshed, thought them up.

The proprietors of American culture mask the depth
of violence, rage, and the irrational in themselves but
also in others.

The Europe from which immigrants came to America
(not least those of Dickens' prisons) was a grim world.
The sight of human blood was not unknown. People survived with cynicism, shrewdness, and brutality, or with
hard work and cheerful faith. They survived.

The official rhetoric of America conveys almost nothing
of the sheer ruthlessness the immigrants have encountered here. "Reason" is exalted; "law and order" praised.
Miss America speaks idiocies. The innocence of Johnny
Carson's face insults the night. Even serious literature
scarcely reflects the brutality most of the immigrants
endured. Nativists are covered in *Grapes of Wrath*, midwestern pioneers in *Giants in the Earth*. But concerning
the urban experience of immigration, it is as though our

grandfathers did not live and did not count: as if they were only grains ground to tasteless, powdered meal. Consumed.

Growing up in America, the young ethnic finds names like "Jordan," "Bret," "McAlister," "Dodsworth." He comes to think that nothing in his own life is worthy of "literature." He seldom even has the small pleasure of encountering a "Rojack." The discovery of a "Portnoy" suggests whole worlds of imagination otherwise fallow and neglected in experience. Without "Studs Lonigan" and "Stephen Daedalus," indeed, he might well have died for want of air long ago, and surrendered everything to WASPS. The single most liberating contribution given him has been made by Jewish writers. Almost without help from other ethnic groups, Jewish writers have broken the WASP hegemony over the American imagination and sensibility.

It is inadequate to single out one Jewish writer alone. There is some advantage, however, to taking an author whose works are better known than those of others, and whose views by reason of their extremity illuminate the general situation most brilliantly: Norman Mailer. Naturally, my argument insofar as it concerns Mailer, with remarks as well on Roth, Raskin, and others, will not cover everything that needs to be said about the Jewish contribution to American self-consciousness. What I am trying to make plain is that Jewish writing explores territories of America no WASP writer opens up; and that beyond Jewish writing there are still areas of experience to be risked by ethnics themselves. The patterns I discern in Mailer's work are not immediately applicable to other Jewish writers. But it seemed wiser to attend to one prominent example in an extended way than to make weak and broad generalizations. Whether there is "a" Jewish imagination is not at issue; obviously, each person works out his own unique horizon.

The "revolution in consciousness" most necessary in America depends upon the shattering of the monoculture.

Concerning work, guilt, reason, sex, family, violence, the irrational, tragedy, the future, hope, piety, sacrifice, pain, ethnics do not all think or feel as WASPS think or feel. The public speech of America is enormously different from private experience. Education in America is largely education into falsehood. To create a "revolution in consciousness" is to cut closer to the rough, often raw, texture of concrete traditions and concrete lives; to break through the vapid generalities of Americanization, professionalization, and the national liberal style.

Good writing is characteristically a result of refusing the image of oneself imposed by others, in order to discover and invent a voice of one's own. Good writing in America is inherently subversive of "the melting pot." Norman Mailer, in particular, has had to struggle against the forms of the WASP sensibility, and also to struggle against an image of Jewishness he did not wish to accept. Concerning the first struggle, he has much to suggest about the shape of ethnic pluralism in the future. Concerning the second, he suggests how the ethnic struggle will be different from the Jewish struggle.

2. *"Near to Suffocate"*

Why is it, I sometimes ask myself, that I do not *feel* like a squirrel in a cage? Perhaps the Catholic, or perhaps it is rather the eastern European, sensibility makes me far more aware of the social texture of the self. Mailer, for example, has the good sense to distinguish the Catholic spirit from the Protestant spirit. Instinctively, he knows that the Catholic, despite his social and political backwardness in several respects, is psychically more the brother of the Jew than of the Protestant. Both feel the weight of the WASP.

The heart of WASP culture is the property relation. Upon property, the most easily rationalized of relations, WASP notions of freedom are founded. Even when the English pirate sailed under the banner of mysticism, adventure, and sheer exuberance, the rationalization was rather practical. The central WASP words are not *being* or *doing*. The central WASP words are *having* and *controlling*. From Locke through Hume until today, the outlook is functional. The dominant WASP ethic is based upon "utility." (Recently, as they were enjoying the view from a penthouse, an Italo-American friend of mine heard a WASP banking executive three times describe Central Park as "a marvelous machine.") The pure-white church interiors, with their clear glass and stately decorum: no home therein for the Spaniard, the Greek, the Slav, the Italian, the Jew, the Black. No expression therein of the dark struggles of the whole human spirit. Mailer once wrote in an essay on "hip" and "square":

> American Protestantism has become oriented to the machine, and lukewarm in its enthusiasm for such notions as heaven, hell and the soul. The Catholic Church can still not divorce itself as much from one of the indispensable notions of Hip, that particular one which is now unhappily codified by saying that we have a body (Catholics would say soul) which is growing at every instant of existence into more or into less, and that we begin to die at a disproportionate rate when we are not as brave as we ought to be. . . . It demands less of a shift in the style of the mind for a Catholic to become Hip than a Protestant.[3]

Protestantism, Mailer thinks, "was never that concerned to capture the private parts of a man." It is, he thinks, "not so much a religion as a technique in the ordering of communities, able to accelerate the growth of the scientific spirit. . . ." It separated the mind from the body.

Mailer is wrong about the degree to which Protestantism demands internalization "in the private parts," but he is right about the technique for ordering individuals. When, for example, Protestants like President Nixon talk about "the old values," "family values," "the high-school football coach," "the eternal verities," they do not mean what southern and eastern European Catholics mean. The latter mean by morality a kind of inner placidity, easy-goingness, carefreeness, a tough view of authority, even a bit of mischief (like Jack Kennedy, with his brashness and Irish ruthlessness). Protestants mean by morality inner restraint, "the responsible self."

Thus American society can depend upon a few police and minimal external restraint *if, and only if,* restraint is internalized by every individual citizen. A society enjoys a presumptive fairness without too many supervising agencies *if, and only if,* each member restrains himself from shirking burdens others must bear and from taking advantages others are not taking. (How Protestants resent the frank pushiness involved in getting on a bus in Italy!) A society can be atomistic and highly mobile, so that many can enjoy an untrammeled climb toward success, *if, and only if,* players abide by the basic rules of the game. More than most societies, therefore, America can have public mobility and freedom; more than most, it must have extremely high restraint in every private soul. In every generation Americans have found the internalization of restraints upon their private souls intolerable, and have moved out toward open spaces where they didn't have to take into consideration the conflicting needs of so many others.

The Protestant ethic of high internal restraint is, in fact, practical only in two circumstances: where the community is sufficiently homogeneous that all willingly accept the same restraints; and where the population is so sparse that too many people do not really desire the same things at the same time. The second circumstance makes WASPS, more than any other culture, fearful of over-population. The first circumstance gives rise to the characteristic Protestant tendency to "split." The whole history of Protestantism is a history of heresy, dissent, and the generation of new divisions. For the Protestant demand for social order is in appearance freer, but in reality far more demanding, than the Catholic. The Protestant places the restraints directly upon the structure of the soul, not merely on outer forms which may, after all, be taken with a grain of salt. When the Protestant feels restraint in society, it presses on his *soul*; he has no alternative but to get out, to move, to go West, before he chokes to death. The Protestant *needs* "land, lots of land, under starry skies above," he "can't stand fences"—because he already has quite enough fences *inside* his psyche.

Moreover, the Protestant preoccupation with "consensus" and unanimity of spirit depends upon such homogeneity of background, temperament, ambition, and interest that diversity of populations and diversity of personalities cannot be absorbed. What Protestants call democracy is pre-ordained harmony. That is why, despite extensive civil liberties, Protestant communities are so often experienced as internally oppressive. Protestantism is not as oppressive in its *laws* as Catholicism is; it is oppressive in its *attitude* toward law. The Protestant spirit really does want everyone, freely, to think alike, to internalize the law, to act with participatory consensus: its view of law coerces the soul. ("Change the hearts and minds. . . .") The Catholic spirit leaves judgment of the soul in God's hands alone, distinguishes sharply between the external forum and the internal forum, and expects its laws to cover outward conduct merely and internal conduct only insofar as the person so chooses. A priest absentmindedly mumbling the carefully restricted words of the Mass is far more free in this respect than the minister who may say what he chooses (in the Spirit, of course) but who must also *feel* it. The Catholic focus is not upon immediate and intense responsibility, but upon the long-term, quiet processes of growth. Ironically, the Protestant worries about works, and the Catholic relies on the grace that makes the forest grow even when the workers are asleep.

America is a Protestant country. Its lack of external constraints is one of the blessings for which Catholics are genuinely grateful and from which they have learned a new model of public order to appropriate as part of their own heritage. (Having learned from Greeks, Lombards, Goths, Huns, and Celts, why not absorb the American experience, too?) On the other hand, the Catholic feels oppressed, as well, but not precisely in the way that Mailer does. The difference is that Mailer leaves unspoken too many of the strengths of his own perceptions.

Long ago, "the mysteries and powers of existence" exercised a hold over human imagination; only recently could men use of society such an expression as "the social machine." Modern language about "the reconstruction" of society mediates a new experience of self and community. In imagination, society is divided into atomic units, assembled rationally, aimed towards certain goals, plugged in, given juice, and *bango!* Today we speak of "social programs" and "problem-solving." Computers did not engender our attitude. Our attitude engendered computers.

> At a price, be it said. The sense of Self was forced to retreat before the sense of the Other, the beholder, the critic, the judge. Man has grown into a brain whose powers of formal connection bear comparison to the mechanically elaborate intellections of a Univac machine, but the body which supports this brain now suffers by a cancerous alienation from the senses. If the orgy has taken on a new if nightmarish attraction to the deadened multi-millions of our civilization, its appeal may not be irrational.[4]

But to whom does an orgy appeal? To those most governed by the WASP restraints. To those, perhaps, most bitterly and obviously excluded from the wealth and power of WASP society but not from its advertising media. To those caught in the cauldron of guerilla war in Vietnam, at My Lai. But what Mailer is aiming at, more precisely, are reasonable and responsible WASPS:

It is no great secret that this drift toward the orgy is warred against (in the underground war of our time) by the managers of our society . . . the regulators, the managers, the upper classes, the unbent, for if they were to express themselves exactly as they wished, the orgy would be equal to carnage . . .

Decent, moral, and honorable men designed and executed the wars on the Indians, the degradation of the Negro in America, the war in Vietnam. Often they have justified their hardheaded decisions by fear of still worse disorders which might arise if they did not assume responsibility. They fear the dark passions of the American electorate, or its right wing, or the huge populations of China, or the darker-skinned and less-than-Nordic immigrants, or red-skinned savages. The only thing they do not fear is cool rationality. Which may perhaps in history's eyes have been the most murderous passion of them all.

Still, a Catholic can hardly identify the meaning of the word "reason" with the industrial era. The word has had many meanings in the past. To understand it properly, one must note the lived experience in which it receives its meaning. When he despairs of WASP rationality, a Catholic does not automatically unfurl the banner of irrationality. When Apollo is expressed by Houston, Dallas, Tulsa, Miami, and Los Angeles, the Catholic does not want to call immediately for Dionysus—and neither, I think, does Mailer.

When I try to imagine what it would be like to be brought up Jewish, I have to contrast it with being brought up a Catholic. The Catholic imagination has been deeply influenced by the memory of "dirty hands." The Catholic recalls, in his blood as it were, what it was like to exercise authority and to be part of a political establishment. The Catholic does not have the WASP qualms about handling power, does not feel the WASP's need to hide the exercise of power and to distance himself from its effects. Catholics are tougher, more direct—"ruthless" is, shall we say, the ethnic slur.

But—omitting the recent creation of the state of Israel —where, since the destruction of Jerusalem in A.D. 77, have Jews held political and social power? Where has there been a Jewish land, with Jewish leadership, Jewish institutions, Jewish responsibility? Where are there Jewish "dirty hands"?

Well might Mailer defend himself in advance by describing his position as "romantic idealism." The deep love of the Jewish intellectual for personal freedom; his fierce trust in the goodness of human nature left to itself and unimpeded by governments; his longing for a socialism without totalitarianism; his libertarian and often anarchic vision of a perfect society, in which maximal space would be left to the authentic self; his condemnation of civilization for the discontents it engenders and the price it demands—all these qualities so abundantly witnessed to in the writings of Mailer, Chomsky, Goodman, Raskin Barnet, and a thousand others of the Jewish Left make crystalline sense once it is grasped that the Jewish experience is distinguished among all others in the West by two preeminent qualities. The Jews have been for two thousand years a people without imperial, national, or general political responsibility. They have never exercised, they have always been on the *underside* of, institutional power. And, secondly, Jewish experience is a thickly cultural, thickly social experience, a *tertium quid* which its theoreticians inexplicably overlook in discussions of "self" and "society."

For *in between* the individual and his political-economic society there mediates the family, the neighborhood, and the ethnic culture: the sense of reality, stories, and symbols of a historical people. When the Jewish intellectual speaks of the "self," his words must be taken with a generous dose of salt. The Jew is seldom, if ever, a "self" in the way an Anglo-Saxon is a self: atomic, alone, solitary. And it is not only external events and foreign others that keep forcing him to remember that he is not alone, that he is "one of a people," that he can scarcely stand by himself; it is not a matter of stereotyping from outside, or through some internal reflection of what one sees in others' eyes. The Jewish family has been and remains immensely thick in its densities. The cultural currents of the Jewish people surviving intact through centuries of variety in economic and political systems—those cultural currents that engender so many "bright Jewish boys," thinkers, writers, poets, brooders, musicians, artists, theorists, lovers of the word—those very cultural currents are neither "self" nor "society" but something other. They are the sources of ethnic identity. Without them, the Jewish intellectual would for a certainty not be Jewish and would in all likelihood not be an intellectual, either.

The Jew comes closest to intellectual assimilation into WASP culture when he omits from his analysis of social and psychic texture precisely those primary group relations and cultural institutions that make his a different sort of self, and lead him to dream of a different sort of society—a sort that has never yet been seen on earth. No doubt the secret of this glaring omission, however hidden, can be inferred. Has there ever been an era, has there ever been a place, in which a Jew might so easily be himself, be taken for what he is in himself, think his way through problems without feeling required to carry a whole cultural people upon his back? Have Jews ever felt so emancipated and so intellectually expansive before? And in a climate in which to speak of ethnic identity was in poor taste? The Jew has been able to think and to theorize without reference to his own thickly cultural self and his own ethnic institutions because, on the one hand, he had already internalized their benefits, and on the other neither law nor custom required him to maintain explicit connection to his ethnic roots. Indeed, many *Goyim* welcomed him most warmly if he decided *not* to. For the WASP enterprise depends upon denying ethnic roots to others.

3. *The Great Unwasped*

Mailer was stung by some contemptuous words from William Faulkner in 1957. He then wrote "The White Negro" in an act of self-definition. He sketched a horizon, a style, a morality that were decisively ethnic, non-WASP, almost uniquely his own. (It was rather too "beat," too incipiently Sartrean for that.) He gave up trying to be a White Anglo-Saxon Protestant. In any contest between "cannibals" and "Christians," he would side with the former. He was not on the side of liberal intellectuals, the managers; he lumped them with the "Christians." What he liked about Kennedy was the outlaw streak in him—the first major public figure who was not WASP.

The second emotional spring of Mailer's work is the struggle not to allow himself to be "a nice Jewish boy." Philip Roth has treated this drama more directly. For Mailer it has become diffused into a more general combat between "the hip" and "the square." There is a certain characteristic oversight in the way Mailer, Roth, and certain other Jewish thinkers (Marcus Raskin, for example) treat—or ignore—the Jewish family; about that, the next chapter will be concerned. For the time being, it will suffice to note the Jewish struggle against WASP consciousness.

Long before it became fashionable to do so, Mailer was pointing to the central sickness of WASP society. The WASP way of life had made brilliant contributions to world history, but it was also profoundly sick. The WASP creed, of course, entailed muddling through, optimism, affirmation, chin up, faith that some little greening light waits up ahead. Essential to the WASP ethos is hope.

In *The Naked and the Dead*, Mailer was resolutely pessimistic. He despaired of the intelligent and sensitive liberal, the common man, the fruits of the melting pot, the approaching future. His General Cummings was confident of the correctness of Hitler's prophecy: the twentieth century would see the long, slow ascendancy of reactionaries.

Society rests upon resentment and fear from below. The men under Cummings' command do not make his views implausible. "All they knew was to cut each other's throats," a soldier reflects, "there wasn't even any pride a man could have at the end."[5]

"The Second World War," Mailer wrote in 1957, "presented a mirror to the human condition which blinded anyone who looked into it . . . no matter how crippled and perverted an image of man was the society he had created, it was nonetheless his creation . . . and if society was so murderous, then who could ignore the most hideous of questions about his own nature?"[6] The outlook is grim and pessimistic, for the individual and for his society.

Martinez, the Chicano in *The Naked and the Dead*, knows the weight of Nordic culture. Nordic identity has been branded into his tissue, into his nerves, into his bowels. Martinez dreams in the Philippines of becoming a war hero; that, at least, is a course open to little Mexican boys. "Only," he thinks, "that does not make you white Protestant, firm and aloof." When little boys in Australia call him "Yank," strange emotions compete in his heart. When another soldier calls him a Texan, "Martinez was warmed by the name. . . . He liked to think of himself as a Texan, but he had never dared to use the title. Somewhere, deep in his mind, a fear had clotted; there was the memory of all the tall white men with the slow voices and the cold eyes. He was afraid of the look they might assume if he were to say, 'Martinez is a Texan.' "[7]

Even Mailer long found it difficult to turn toward his own resources and differences. Enormous pressure on the Jewish artist (as on others) urges him to define himself according to prevailing literary forms, to see himself through the nets of American language, to dramatize those things about himself which are typical and show him to be human "like everybody else," that is, WASP. The writer has to have extraordinary courage in order to risk the failures involved in self-revelation, the failures implicit in seeming to be different, incredible, outside the expectations of those whose sensitivities are shaped by the dominant and accepted types. He is tempted simply to exclaim with Shakespeare's Shylock:

> I am a Jew. Hath not a Jew eyes? hath not a Jew hands, organs, dimensions, senses, affections, passions? fed with the same food, hurt with the same weapons, subject to the same diseases, healed by the same means, warmed and cooled by the same winter and summer, as a Christian is? If you prick us, do we not bleed? If you tickle us, do we not laugh? If you poison us, do we not die? And if you wrong us, shall we not revenge? If we are like you in the rest, we will resemble you in that.[8]

The ethnic artist has a difficult time penetrating WASP culture, the Yale "cool." WASP passions and impulses are understated, diverted into hidden channels, or perhaps (who can tell?) nonexistent. Control over feelings is high honor. (A bishop worried about his visit with Reinhold Niebuhr just before the latter's death. "He burst into tears so often." Then he defended Niebuhr: "It might have been the medication." Is it inconceivable that a brave man might so poignantly and freely face the absurd as to cry fluent tears?) Mastery of environment, mastery of self, mastery is given highest priority. The organism of the self is whole, healthy, rational; its underside—except for the general cover of "original sin"—seems to be ignored. Evil is attributed to germs, dirt, the wilderness, savages, peoples less able to control themselves. The WASP home cherishes good order, poise, soft voices, cleanliness. Insanity, strangeness, wildness are swept from sight. Thus the ethnic artist fears, at first, to introduce the WASP into his home. He will find it "colorful," "different." Alfred Kazin gently recalls a dinner in Brooklyn:

> For the first time, I had brought into our home someone from "outside," from the great literary world, and as Ferguson patiently smiled away, interrupted only by

my mother's bringing in more and more platters and pleading with him to *eat something*, I tried to imagine his reactions. We all sat around him at the old round table in the dining room—my father, my little sister, and myself—and there poor Ferguson, his eyes bulging with the strain and the harsh bright lights from the overhead lamp, his cheeks red with effort, kept getting shoveled into him cabbage and meatballs, chicken, meat loaf, endless helpings of seltzer and cherry soda; and all the while I desperately kept up a line of chatter to show him that he was not completely isolated, our cousin Sophie sat at the table silently staring at him, taking him in. In our boxlike rooms, where you could hear every creak, every cough, every whisper, while the Brooklyn street boiled outside, there was a strangled human emotion that seemed to me unworthy of Ferguson's sophistication, his jazz, his sardonic perch on Union Square. But as Sophie sat at the table in her withdrawn silence, my sister stared wide-eyed at the visitor, my mother bustlingly brought in more platters, and my father explained that he had always followed and admired the *New Republic*—oh, ever since the days of Walter Lippmann and Herbert Croly!—I felt, through Ferguson's razor-sharp eyes, how dreary everything was. My father kept slurping the soup and reaching out for the meat with his own fork; since I had warned him that Ferguson would expect a drink, he self-consciously left the bottle of whiskey on the table and kept urging our visitor all through the meal to take another drink. My mother, who did not have even her personal appreciation of the *New Republic* to regale Ferguson with, had nothing to do but bring food in, and after a while Sophie took to her room and barricaded herself in.

So the meal which I had so much advertised in advance—which I had allowed Ferguson to believe would be exotic, mysterious, vaguely Levantine—passed at last, and after he had charmingly said good-by to my parents and I walked him back to the subway at Rock-away Avenue, he studied me quietly for a moment and said, "What the hell was so exotic about that?"⁹

A WASP home, by contrast, offers culture shock to non-WASPS. Decorum and self-control. Tight emotions. WASP culture, one concludes, has paid a heavy price for its admirable tradition of personal civil rights and political liberties. The emotional space humans may inhabit is restricted. An Italian in a traffic jam in Rome jumps out of his vehicle, shakes his fists, pours out a stream of vituperation and threat, and suddenly is calm. The WASP sits in his vehicle and lets his stomach juices drip. To the WASP, the direct flow of emotion is childish; his accultur-ation requires cognitive control. It is a difficult culture for ethnic peoples to absorb into their flesh. When in despair they wish to mock it, they sometimes think that if ever the evolutionary chain is handed over to a superior race of computer-fed robots, and man becomes extinct, the history books of the future will note that even back in the dim ages of humankind there were precursors of the mechanical and rational age: WASPS and Nordics.

In a remarkable autobiographical statement, Theodore Solotaroff recalls "the practical, coarse, emotionally ex-travagant life of the Jewish middle class" in northern New Jersey which he, Philip Roth, and Mailer have in com-mon. Solotaroff describes the struggles Roth went through trying to find his own soul, his own past, his own identity, in order to write with authenticity. As a fellow graduate student, he watched Roth gradually achieve an "intricate kind of acceptance."

> Though Roth clearly was no less critical of his back-ground than I was [Solotaroff writes], he had not tried to abandon it, and hence had not allowed it to become simply a deadness inside him: the residual feelings, mostly those of anxiety, still intact but without their living context. That is to say, he wrote fiction as he was, while I had come to write as a kind of fantasist of

literature who regarded almost all of my actual experience in the world as unworthy of art. A common
mistake, particularly in the overliterary age of the late
Forties and Fifties, but a decisive one.[10]

Moreover, what Roth was eventually to discover was
that his "Jewish" feelings and his sexual feelings "were just
around the corner from each other" and that, like a creative writer's dream of fresh material come true, "both
were so rich in loot" that Roth could press on "like a man
who has found a stream full of gold—and running right
into it, another one." The psychoanalytic setting of
Portnoy's Complaint had given Roth "the freedom and
energy of language to sluice out the material: the natural
internal monologue of comedy and pain in which the id
speaks to the ego and vice versa, while the superego goes
on with its kibitzing."[11]

Roth had tried to create a novel of WASP culture and
WASP sensibilities in *When She Was Good* (1967). It
was an heroic attempt of which Roth was slyly proud. He
told Solotaroff, "There's not a single Jew in it." Roth
reminisced

> about the strangeness of imagining, really imagining a
> family that was not a Jewish family, that was what it
> was by virtue of its own conditioning and conditions,
> just as the Jews were, but which were not those of "the
> others"—the Gentiles.

In America, a huge gap separates the sensibilities of one
ethnic group and those of another. But how is one to find
the words and the structure to express it?

Can one imagine an Anglo-Saxon writer recording the
following:

> Jumping up from the dinner table, I tragically clutch my
> belly—diarrhea! I cry, I have been stricken with diar-
> rhea!—and once behind the locked bathroom door, slip
> over my head a pair of underpants that I have stolen
> from my sister's dresser and carry rolled in a handker-

chief in my pocket. So galvanic is the effect of cotton panties against my mouth—so galvanic is the word "panties"—that the trajectory of my ejaculation reaches startling new heights: leaving my joint like a rocket it makes right for the light bulb overhead, where to my wonderment and horror, it hits and hangs. Wildly in the first moment I cover my head, expecting an explosion of glass, a burst of flames—disaster, you see, is never far from my mind. Then quietly as I can I climb the radiator and remove the sizzling gob with a wad of toilet paper. I begin a scrupulous search of the shower curtain, the tub, the tile floor, the four toothbrushes— God forbid!—and just as I am about to unlock the door, imagining I have covered my tracks, my heart lurches at the sight of what is hanging like snot to the toe of my shoe. I am the Raskolnikov of jerking off— the sticky evidence is everywhere! Is it on my cuffs too? In my hair? my ear? All this I wonder even as I come back to the kitchen table, scowling and cranky, to grumble self-righteously at my father when he opens his mouth full of red jello and says, "I don't understand what you have to lock the door about. That to me is beyond comprehension. What is this, a home or a Grand Central station?"[12]

Why is sex the frontier which some Jewish writers (and not they alone) felt they had to crack before they could articulate their own experience? Perhaps because sex is so powerfully and deeply interlocked with family life, with mother and father, manliness and womanliness, conscience and freedom and reason and spontaneities. In sexual rituals and symbols, a people's sense of reality and stories and dynamics of action are locked. Moreover, sexual material is

right in front of everyone's eyes. Particularly, I suppose, guess, of the "Jewish" writers with all that heavily funded Oedipal energy and curiosity to be worked off in adolescence—and beyond.[13]

Shame attaches to such subjects; difficult bouts with public and personal inhibitions must be fought; finding the exact voice and language to pin the nuances of the soul is excruciatingly difficult. Candor is rare.

Against the controlled rationality of a technological culture, and against the controlled sentiments of WASP spirituality, Norman Mailer postulated in "The White Negro" the first tenet of a new faith: "One's orgasm is the clue to how well one is living." Such a faith slides precisely into the gap between WASP and ethnic culture. One imagines an ethnic construction worker and a silver-haired bank president as they first hear of Mailer's creed. The worker—I will bet—will smile with recognition first. Yet the refinements of technique will surely be better known to the banker.

Conjure up in mind's eye the normality implicit in a phrase like "good, healthy, decent, normal kids." Against the claims of normality, what Mailer describes must seem sick. Mailer wants to argue that it is the *normal* world that is sick, and precisely the "normal" men in the normal Rotary clubs who are sick. He is willing to accept being described, himself, as a psychopath. He is in pursuit of a new health and a new sanity.

Again, Mailer is not afraid to hate. A psychopath *hates*. He hates the constrictions of his society, the lies he is forced to live, the deprivation of his animal vitalities, the contradictions between beautiful words like "justice,", "freedom," and "community," and the realities of capitalistic (and socialistic) societies. Health lies in venting his rage, not in continuing to stand meekly in line, doing his duty and maintaining respect.

But this exploration in search of a new consciousness is not only an individualistic matter. It requires criticism of the social system. Before we even became aware that we might be able to search for our personal identity, institutions of family, church, state, and economic order have long been involving us in symbolic transactions that *tell* us who we are, must be. Hence, like others who have for some time been trying to put Freud and Marx together, Mailer can end his essay dreaming of

> a calculus capable of translating the economic relations of man into his psychological relations and then back again, his productive relations thereby embracing his sexual relations as well, until the crises of capitalism in the twentieth century would yet be understood as the unconscious adaptations of a society to solve its economic imbalance at the expense of a new mass psychological imbalance.[14]

The value most dear to Mailer is courage, the courage of exploration, the courage to risk life, by which alone life is saved. He understands quite well that courage by itself is no guide, and that "the desire for absolute sexual freedom" may form men of hatred who "are the material for an elite of storm troopers ready to follow the first truly magnetic leader whose view of mass murder is phrased in a language which reaches their emotions." But the hipster, the psychopath, the bruised saint of today "May come to see that his condition is no more than an exaggeration of the human condition, and if he would be free, then everyone must be free."

The fate of the person and the fate of society are the same: intimate life is a reflection of institutional life, institutional of intimate. And thus the quality of an orgasm is related to the quality of institutional controls. Mailer dreams of some "God-like view of human justice and injustice":

> If a capitalist society is grounded upon property relations, these relations are wed to monogamy, family, and the sexual structures which maintain them.

Mailer then proposes a second revolution in this century, beyond socialism, a revolution in which intimacy and institutions are joined. His call antedates by a decade or more Herbert Marcuse, Norman O. Brown, and "the counter culture."

Man is a flux of possibilities and energies long before and perhaps long after he is a manipulator of land, properties, and productions. A civilization from now, the vast chapter of Western expansion which was built on property and such inhuman abstractions of human energy as money, credit, and surplus value, may be seen as an ice-age of cruel and brutally slow liberations of productive, purposive, creative and sexual energies which the contradictions of inequity and exploitation congealed not only into the working habits of men, elaborated not only into the institutional hypocrises of society, but indeed drove as cancerous ambivalences and frustrations into the texture of being itself.

Unlike that first revolution which was conscious, Faustian, and vain, enacted in the name of the proletariat but more likely an expression of the scientific narcissism we inherited from the nineteenth century, a revolution motivated by the rational mania that consciousness could stifle instinct and marshal it into productive formations, the second revolution, if it is to come . . . would be to turn materialism on its head, have consciousness subjugated to instinct.

Mailer's faith in the second revolution is not a faith that promises happiness (leave that to dictators); it promises the only genuine human outcome: tragedy. But it is a creative faith in man, whose essence is

> that the real desire to make a better world exists at the heart of our instinct . . . that man is therefore roughly more good than evil, that beneath his violence there is finally love and the nuances of justice, and that the removal therefore of all social restraints while it would open us to an era of incomparable individual violence would still spare us the collective violence of national totalitarian liquidations . . .

The Second World War taught Mailer that violence is fed by modern institutional structures. Wouldn't a system that didn't coerce humans into technological rationality but allowed them to express their instincts—even their violent ones—directly, "open the possibility of working with that human creativity which is violence's opposite"?

The WASP way—the almost universal industrial way of the modern age—is to put a harsh rein upon the impulses of man's animal nature, to place him in the halter of the industrial machine, and to order him docilely *to produce*. It is a life geared to action, to "changing history," to progress. Its casualty is liberty of impulse. Its God is law, order, and industrious Reason. Against it, man's human instinct, his very flesh, rebel. In spasms, instinct lashes out in the single permitted channel: institutional violence. Nations do what individuals in their own name are forbidden to do. Men become violent without ceasing "to follow orders."

My Lai, as an action of State, is "no big deal." But any individual who achieved at least 102 murders in one day out of his own initiative would be universally regarded as an unprecedented monster. What dreams, what images, what demons coursed through Rusty Calley's blood as he squeezed, and squeezed again, the trigger of his automatic rifle, and red spurts appeared upon the bouncing bodies in that godforsaken ditch? Against whom or what was his flesh rebelling if not the entire history of a normal life?

When cool, reasonable eyes do not see, Mailer, like Kosinski's miller, leaps forward, spoon in hand.

But should he?

Poetry beats bare the track artillery will follow. Aggressive self-discovery in the West, the very poetic-religious passion to explore good and evil inwardly, which Mailer exemplifies, is acted out by military heroes. Our inner aggressions prepare maps which the brutal generals of history will follow. In 1971 Mailer still flirts with Apocalypse: "We are a Faustian age determined to meet the Lord or the Devil before we are done, and the ineluctable ore of the authentic is our only key to the lock."[15]

Unfortunately, "the authentic" turns out to be as much

a contrivance as its opposite. Not too many years after Mailer's ´apostrophe to violence, Ronald Laing and others will be claiming that insanity is the one true sanity. To be authentic is to be insane.[16]

One does not, I think, have to accept either the cheap grace of unruffled sanity or the conversion to "authentic" violence. The unspoken premise of WASP culture is violence and madness at a distance. The unspoken premise of Jewish culture is family.

4. *Hidden Grounds*

On what grounds, then, does Mailer base his fourfold "faith"—*first*, that "the real desire to make a better world exists at the heart of our instinct"; *second*, that "man is therefore roughly more good than evil"; *third*, that "beneath his violence there is finally love and the nuances of justice"; and *fourth*, that "the removal therefore of all social restraints while it would open us to an era of incomparable individual violence would still spare us the collective violence of national totalitarian liquidations, and would, by expending the violence directly, open the possibility of working with that creativity which is violence's opposite"?[17] Where, I dare to guess, but in thousands of years of Jewish experience. The Jewish family nourished goodness in the hearts of its people without benefit of state power, without benefit of ownership of land, without benefit of control over the means of production. Jews were for millennia a wandering people living by intellectual nourishment, by wit, by filling whatever interstices the economic systems at the various stages of history left open to those who were neither farmers nor producers.

Less than any other people have the Jews lived by property, or by production; more than others, by the arts of commerce and finance. Before there was a consumer society, before there was a middle class, the Jews were neither slaves, nor serfs, nor proletariat, but in some powerful way *outside* the approved institutions of society, free to define themselves *against* society, free to imagine with a kind of internal cultural reinforcement a genuine liberty which all men might share.

Unlike the Anglo-Saxon dream of liberty, moreover, the dream of the Jew was for *internal* liberty. Besides the English *laissez-faire*, besides "the freedom of the market-place of ideas," besides the freedom from social coercion, there is also the freedom internally won, the freedom of artists and voyagers of the spirit, the freedom of men who, in the words Chomsky quotes from Humboldt:

> . . . love their own labor for its own sake, improve it by their own plastic genius and inventive skill, and thereby cultivate their intellect, ennoble their character, and exalt and refine their pleasures.[18]

Marx would later call the opposite of such labor "alienation," but no formula of his improves upon Humboldt's:

> Whatever does not spring from a man's free choice . . . does not enter freely into his very being, but remains alien to his true nature; he does not perform it with truly human energies, but merely with mechanical exactness.

Martin Buber, great thinker of the present century, speaks of the struggle to bring about "the third and last emancipatory phase of human history." According to Fourier (1848) the first phase made serfs out of slaves, the second made wage earners out of serfs, and the third abolishes the proletariat in a final act of liberation that creates free and voluntary associations of producers.[19] Jewish thinkers, born of a people who for centuries were neither tillers of fields nor workers in factories, deplore the alienation of workers "driven by external authority or need rather than inner impulse." Marx expresses shock at the rationalization of labor whose techniques mutilate the worker into a fragment of a human being, degrade him to become a mere appurtenance of the machine, make his work such a torment that its essential meaning is destroyed; estrange from him the intellectual potentialities of the labor process in very proportion to the extent to which science is incorporated into it as an independent power.[20]

Concern with alienation is far from being exclusively Jewish. Still, their relative closeness to Europe gave the writers in *Partisan Review* a head start over other intellectual groups in analyzing alienation in America. Besides, it is by now a Jewish instinct to believe that history unfolds in stages, that prophets must denounce social evils, that new ages come through suffering and conflict, that the source of historical vitality lies in a concrete cultural history, in enduring people rather than in passing institutional forms.

East European Jews, perhaps, had long cultural contact with a further motif difficult for me to give credence to: anarchism. Anarchism, Chomsky writes, quoting Rudolf Rocher, is not

a fixed, self-enclosed social system but rather a definite trend in the historic development of mankind, which, in contrast with the intellectual guardianship of all clerical and governmental institutions, strives for the free unhindered unfolding of all the individual and social forces in life. Even freedom is only a relative, not an absolute concept, since it tends constantly to become broader and to affect wider circles in more manifold ways. For the anarchist, freedom is not an abstract philosophical concept, but the vital concrete possibility for every human being to bring to full development all the powers, capacities, and talents with which nature has endowed him, and turn them to social account. The less this natural development of man is influenced by ecclesiastical or political guardianship, the more efficient and harmonious will human personality become, the more will it become the measure of the intellectual culture of the society in which it has grown.[21]

Like the Catholic, the Jew is not comfortable in conceiving of liberty in purely individualistic terms; to do so runs against the grain of his experience of life. More often than the Catholic, the Jew tries to imagine liberty without fully imagining the social and political institutions—with their inevitable authorities—that would enflesh it. Such political and social necessities are not part of the Enlightenment's heritage; the stress is on the inner freedom. Bakunin portrays the ideal with unforgettable vividness:

I am a fanatic lover of liberty, considering it as the unique condition under which intelligence, dignity, and human happiness can develop and grow; not the purely formal liberty conceded, measured out, and regulated by the State, an eternal lie which in reality represents nothing more than the privilege of some founded on the slavery of the rest; not the individualistic, egoistic, shabby, and fictitious liberty extolled by the school of J-J. Rousseau and the other schools of bourgeois liberalism, which considers the would-be rights of all men, represented by the State which limits the rights of each —an ideal that leads inevitably to the reduction of the rights of each to zero. No, I mean the only kind of liberty that is worthy of the name, liberty that consists in the full development of all the material, intellectual, and moral powers that are latent in each person; liberty that recognizes no restrictions other than those determined by the laws of our own individual nature, which cannot properly be regarded as restrictions since these laws are not imposed by any outside legislator beside or above us, but are immanent and inherent, forming the very basis of our material, intellectual, and moral being —they do not limit us but are the real and immediate conditions of our freedom.[22]

Chomsky is careful to distinguish such thought—impressively close to one version of natural law theory—from primitive individualism. Those who "brush aside all fetters in human society," he quotes from Humboldt, "would attempt to find as many new social bonds as possible. The isolated man is no more able to develop than one who is fettered." Such an ideal is not finally *laissez-faire*, or "do your thing." It is inherently communal, inherently social. Neither individualist nor collectivist, it is in fact a sort of mirror image of the Jewish community through the ages: a people who without governmental or coercively structured economic institutions nourish in their midst strong persons, strong cultural selves. One Jewish dream, perhaps, is that the human race might share the internal coherence and liberating power of their own cultural system.

The southern and eastern European has not, however, been nourished by the Jewish experience any more than he has been nourished by the Anglo-Saxon experience. For centuries he has been slave and serf, and far more recently than his fellow worker in northern Europe, proletarian. For centuries the immigrants who streamed from Poland, Lithuania, Czechoslovakia, Greece, Italy, and Spain to the United States had worked penuriously in cities or toiled on the soil, both under an authority not their own and under the whiplash of exigent need. They knew in their flesh the mechanical necessities implicit in such work, had been hardened by them, and were in large measure reconciled to them: inescapable realities, the shape of life itself. In America, immigrants of professional skills were often obliged to become proletarians. Their higher skills were neither recognized, nor desired, nor rewarded in America, and many with heavy hearts turned to manual labor or took their places in the mills and factories.

The experience of southern and eastern European immigrants, in a word, makes the Jewish libertarian dream appear like idle dreaming, like "romantic idealism." Virtually nothing in their experience confirms it. Like Mailer, they may well believe that "a real desire to make a better world exists at the heart of our instinct." Unlike him, they are more likely to imagine that "better world" in strictly familial and personal terms. Little in their experience gives them any confidence that the larger institutions of society are sufficiently malleable to be made "better." Or perhaps, more accurately, the improvement they discern between the situation of their grandparents in Europe and their own in America gives whatever content they are liable to trust to a word like "better." Skeptical of utopias and revolutions whose cruel brunt the common people are regularly expected to bear, they look first to the dreamers: What's in it for Mailer? What price does *he* pay?

Like Mailer, they may share the faith that "man is therefore more good than evil," and that "beneath his violence there is finally love and the nuances of justice." Perhaps no belief about man is more deeply Catholic than that: a fundamental and radical trust in the goodness of creation, however wounded, bloodied, flawed. It is (in Catholic eyes) the Protestant who quintessentially announces the utter depravity and corruption of nature, culture, and man himself—and then, paradoxically, announces with the utmost cool extravagant plans for organizing the world reasonably, sinlessly, and spotlessly. The Protestant is forever confessing his contriteness, and then exalting his own acceptance of his "responsibilities" for changing history: building a better world through chemistry, making the world safe for democracy, defending the free world, inventing a theology of revolution, announcing a theology of hope, taking up the recent year's most moral cause, aspiring to a future more shining and efficient than the past.

The Catholic, believing in men's fundamental goodness, tends to look for that goodness in every concrete corruption, failed hope, damaged expectation, constrained contingency. "Providence" is the Catholic's word of reconciliation. Providence is not a Master Hand manipulating all

things to human benefit, but a trace of God's love in the
bitterest disappointment. Facing society, the Protestant
tends to be "concerned." The Catholic tends to be "reconciled." Nature and creation the way they are already
make the Catholic's heart sing. To the Protestant, creation
is apparently "redeemed" only through being mastered.
Protestant countries tend to be avid for modernization;
Catholic nations, "backward."

5. *A Bloody Law*

The last item of Mailer's faith is the most difficult for a
Catholic to believe. Mailer's opening phrase is, *"The removal therefore of all social restraints while it would open
to us an era of incomparable violence. . . ."* Here already
the Catholic has questions. An era of violence as in Sicily,
among the honored brotherhood? Violence like that of the
peasants in Jerzy Kosinski's *The Painted Bird*? Against the
cool rationality of the WASP, the regulator, and the
manager, Mailer can score shocking and liberating points.
But he seems to lack memory of ancient barbarity. Kosinski's mind's eye sees peasant women catching the local
slut in a field. They kick her to pulp with their heavy
shoes. They spit on her. Someone spreads her limp, bloody
legs, forces in a bottle of shit. A kick shatters the glass.
They grin.[23]
Let Mailer say that tortures, racks, burning stakes, eye-
ball gouging, knives in Florentine alleys, galley slaves
dying by the dozens, denizens of Egypt sweltering under
relentless skies upon the construction of enormous pyra-
mids—let Mailer say that all human violence flows from
alienating economic and political structures. What other
structures have there ever been, what are there today?
How Mailer accounts for the bloody history of the Jews,
how he assimilates Auschwitz, is unknown to me. But
how shall an immigrant account for the endlessly bruis-
ing history of his own people in Poland, in Slovakia, in
Greece, in Italy, in Spain, yes, and in the United States,

under every version of economic and social arrangement yet seen upon the earth? The suffering goes on; the crucifixion of the Christ in the body of his people still goes on, will continue yet some little longer, until . . . until?

Sufficient for today is the evil thereof. Better to offer a cup of water to one thirsty man than to dream of some social system never yet realized, never yet even thoroughly imagined.

There is no reason, of course, why the grandson of an immigrant from Eastern Europe should not learn, in America, a little of the WASP rationality, a little of the Jewish libertarian dream. But it would be a lie against every instinct of my flesh were I to say that WASP cool or Jewish heart register well the fever of my own experience.

Let Mailer finish, though, the creed begun above: ". . . *would still spare us the collective violence of national totalitarian liquidations . . .*" Can the leopard change its spots? Will Jews cease tomorrow to cherish the libertarian dream? Will Germans within a generation be cut from different cultural cloth, all continuity with past habits absolutely sundered?

It is extraordinarily difficult to believe that economic and political arrangements, once being revolutionized, soon alter the cultural character of peoples. It is more difficult still to believe that cultural habits—whether in tandem with, or independently of, economic and political arrangements—are less than glacial in their alteration. Despite fifty years of communist revolution, Russians are better understood as Russians than as Communists. What, then, shall we wait another fifty years before the Revolution breeds "the new men"? Transformations do occur, but even great and convulsive leaps forward are only such relatively speaking. The conversion of a single individual from one way of life to another is seldom without the most profound continuities of soul. Were we to wait until Mailer's transformation of collective styles were accomplished, how long would we have to wait? How long will it be before the WASP relinquishes his managerial desire, or until his cool heart warms to the temperature of Latin passion? Were human cultures as malleable as Mailer's psychology seems to imagine (his God's-eye view of intimacy and institutions in psychic harmony), shall we wait, nevertheless, longer than until the parousia?

The final clause of Mailer's faith, however, is the weakest of all: "*. . . and would . . . by expending the violence directly, open the possibility of working with that creativity which is violence's opposite.*" Does the direct expenditure of energy—of hatred, of resentment, of violence—finally liberate? Or does it wear smooth the path of less and less resistible explosions? Each time Calley pulled the trigger at My Lai, each mugging after a youth first smashes his fist into an old man's nose, each act by which a boss fires an inefficient worker—after each such act are greater possibilities opened up for creativity? The issue is not altogether simple, to be sure. Men long deadened to the terrors of the presence of God frequently prodded their slack flesh through the skills of temple prostitutes. They felt the hot lava of a bull's blood stream across the black curly hairs of their arms. Priests in Cuernavaca cut out the living hearts of maidens with knives shaped to a penis. That ritual acts of violence have a role in creativity who could deny? But ritual violence is not the same as random violence. Absurd violence is not creative violence. Even Raskolnikov's random and absurd slaughter of a befuddled woman was, in the doing, neither random nor absurd nor immediate nor instinctual; it was intellectual, arrogant, and as rational as a binary computer. For Raskolnikov, 2 plus 2 had to equal 4.

That is the lie buried in Mailer's existential ethic—and, indeed, in all but the most careful libertarian thinking. Bakunin's "I am a *fanatic* lover of liberty" is a warning. Not all Chomsky's protestations that the libertarianism involved in anarchic thought is tied to no one social system frees him from the charge that progressive thought is necessarily abstract and thereby dangerous. From the what-is, it all too speedily moves to the what-should-be. Experience teaches one to beware of those who come bearing programs, even programs of liberty. For liberty is an airy nothing if it is not embedded in the full, dense texture of a culture, values, friendships, needs, and institutions. To maximize the range of identities a man may explore, the constellations of values he may embrace, the number of choices he may make, is always a concrete achievement within the actual possibilities of the here-and-now. To imagine a yet wider range, still other constellations, a still greater number, is not yet a value— it is only a fantasy, and, as such, at best a *possible* value.

Whether to turn a fantasy into an actual value, whether to call a vision "good," depends upon discerning and critical judgment. Such a capacity must itself be free enough to learn from the past how to evaluate the new on its own fresh grounds. For what the past has to teach judgment is not how to continue making judgments on the grounds of the past but how to make fresh judgments on whatever unanticipated grounds. It is *judgment* that must be free if freedom is to occur at all, if novelty is to emerge at all, if creativity is to occur. Free judgment is not easy to achieve under any circumstances.

Against the frozen channels and deadened links of a judgment chilled by abstract analysis and out of touch with the juices of instinct and the flesh, some form of violence may "open the possibility of that creativity which is violence's opposite." It may also simply split flesh and instinct further still from judgment, in a schizophrenic doubling of our native alienation. It depends. Everything depends.

Among historical peoples, Catholics have not been the most scrupulous in avoiding violence. The razor Mailer has honed to slash the smooth face of WASP rationality might be dulled by leatherlike Catholicism. Just the other day, wasn't it, the *New York Times* reported that a cheap pornographic outlet held its opening day in an Italian Catholic neighborhood in Brooklyn. The phone rang, and while the proprietor was being told the neighborhood was ashamed of such a business on such a street, two bricks came sailing through the new front window. Protection paid or no, the proprietor moved out.

Or take the story of how Mayor Lindsay called on the Mafia to break up a gang war between Italian kids and young blacks over the integration of a white high school. For days, thousands of youths brawled, looted, and burned enemy territory. Larry Gallo was involved in a widely publicized gangland war when the mayor's office asked his help. His black Riviera glided toward the intersection serving as headquarters of the Italo-American gangs. Police lines parted. Excited, silent crowds gathered. Gallo opened the door, got out, approached the young toughs he knew were leaders, and told them to go home.

> "But the niggers are . . ." one young white began, and suddenly, Gallo smashed his fist into the youngster's face, sending him to the ground. The disturbances ended that night.[24]

Violence in Sicily proves nothing about creativity, nothing at all. Accounts of it—in its private as well as in its institutional forms—do not yield the exhilaration Mailer seems to desire from violence.

Why, after all, does a nice Jewish boy dream so much about violence? Take it from an ethnic Catholic, who isn't squeamish. Violence in life there is, plenty of it. Leave it alone. It doesn't need encouragement, individual or collective. If it comes to breaking heads, the side that wins isn't necessarily humanistic.

Still, WASPS have special unfilled needs. The famous, tough "Yankee conscience" assigns itself too much moral height.

No race has ever designed techniques more efficient for distancing itself from the effects of its own power. There should be (in fantasy at least) a law against that, the reverse of a blue law: a bloody law.

To wit, let every WASP lady by law, in yearly ritual, in full public gaze, strangle an abandoned cat with no other assistance but her bare hands.

Let ever WASP male wring the neck of a chicken until its head pulls bloodily free, or in some other way, sticky with felt violence, get the feeling of changing history and mastering the environment.

Let Governor Rockefeller, next time he decides not to sully his office in negotiation with prisoners and allows troops to go in shooting, practice pulling the wings from forty flies one by one in full view of the assembled Legislature and television cameras of the state.

Let men who ask women to have abortions publicly grind an aborted fetus underfoot.

Let some new ritual in Episcopal, Methodist, and Presbyterian churches, vividly sensual, make control less abstract and more tangibly bloody: an unforgettable image of the fate of the controlled.

Let everybody face physically what they would prefer to accomplish "at a distance."

CHAPTER EIGHT

Authentic? Authoritarian?

INEVITABLY ONE MUST COPE with the word "authentic." Writers are seldom completely honest when they use it. They write as if they were much more lonely, much more besieged, than they are. They keep a major premise hidden from sight. There will be great resistance to bringing it to light. It strips away the defiant heroism, the raging at the night.

An absolutely crucial move, then, is to distinguish sharply the power of WASP culture to enforce oppressive normalcy, from the more general problem of civilization and its discontents. WASP culture insists upon formality and reason in such a way that the non-WASP feels suffocated. The latter's emotions beat against constraints he has not learned to love. His rage, fury, passion, enthusiasm are parts of him for which he is made to feel ashamed. C. P. Snow reminds us that even in World War II, while condemning Nazi horror, the British were the first to build heavy bombers for the devastation of cities, well before the Germans or Russians acceded.[1] WASP culture channels private rage into public horror.

Civilization necessarily asks a high price of the individual psyche.[2] Thus Freud hypothesizes a version of "original sin." Despite the individual's desire to be perfect, free, spontaneous, godlike, he must trim his desires to communal necessities. The shape his particular civilization takes leaves its imprint upon the substance and center of his psyche. There is no pure, free, uninhibited, unrepressed place in which a human may hide. Each bears on his soul the conflicts of his predecessors. All persons suffer so; but on our culture a special burden descends.

The peculiar shape of our civilization springs from our commitment to "enlightenment." The economic base of the dream is a thoroughly rationalized industry. Our commitment to "enlightenment" is a commitment to a form of Reason never dominant in a civilization before.

In no country of the West but ours has the field of action been as clear for the dominance of industrial Reason. The French in Canada, the Spanish in Mexico, did not match the WASPS in their openness to industrialization. French and Spanish families do not accept so willingly the necessary atomization. They do not surrender their cultural bonds. Industrial Reason meets among them too many sources of resistance.

Suppose, accordingly, that basic metaphors about self, others, and world were to be altered in America. Suppose that our ideal were not "enlightenment" but "enhumanment." In that case, our aim would not be mastery through the head. It would be reconciliation to what we are, can be. "Enlightenment" suggests an individualistic bias; it stresses autonomy of self and individual will. But suppose the self is not individual but familial, and more than that, communal. Suppose, too, that authenticity is not the opposite of authority; rather, that the two concepts are correlative. Southern and eastern European immigrants know such things implicitly, in a confused and inarticulate way. An intellectual who tries to give voice to their instincts is armed against the conventional wisdom of "enlightenment."

1. *The Cultural Revolution*

Norman Mailer is fond of speaking of the two revolutions of our time: the first a political-economic revolution, the second a revolution in consciousness (particularly in sexual relations). Both revolutions are waged, so it is advertised, in the name of the individual. The underlying image is that of bursting through to liberty, independence, authenticity, and value. The manifest assumption is that one accomplishes such liberation by "breaking free"—one is always in search of new oppressors and new break-throughs. Breaking free is the predominant story line. But the unspoken premise is fidelity to the profound and pure values inculcated in the Jewish family, in Jewish religiousness, in the childhood neighborhood. When a Jew says he is "alienated," he speaks from a family context shared by no others.

The Jewish imagination, fortified by centuries of opposition to various penalizing and alien establishments, is anti-establishmentarian.

Even in security, it is watchful. But assimilation in America has made the Jewish imagination vulnerable at one chief point. The communal tradition of Jewish thought has ceded too much to WASP individualism. The importance of the Jewish family in nourishing literary and social imagination has been allowed to lapse from view. The concrete sources of Jewish intellectual life have not been stressed.

The outward presentation of Jewish liberalism has followed the paradigms of English *laissez-faire* and European existentialism. By a forceful appropriation of Marx and Freud, Jewish thinkers have extended the range of American intellectual life far beyond the WASP sensibility. But the image of liberation which governs a major wing of Jewish liberalism is fundamentally Benthamite.

The most recent expression of this view is achieved by Marcus Raskin in *Being and Doing*. A critique of it will perhaps serve as a suitable bridge from our previous discussions of authenticity to further discussion of Mailer to come. While I appreciate many of the points made by Raskin, I find his views curiously uncomplicated. I propose to add to them a counterpoint based on southern and eastern European experience.

Raskin sets out to describe "the four colonies" established in our psyches by the American way of life: the violence colony, the plantation colony, the channelling colony, the dream colony. What would a psyche be like that lacked such colonies? Implicitly, Raskin dreams of absolute liberation, absolute autonomy, the individual rising pure from the sea, above the *Dreck* of institutions. His implicit sense of reality is as follows: History is a process of moral progress, in which the past is more immoral and the future more moral. Progress consists in "liberation" from social institutions ("colonies"), so that the individual self can be self-directed and free. The latest, newest vision of personal autonomy is more moral than older versions; the young are purer than the old. (To have been longer in history is to have sunken deeper into evil: "the fall.")

It is striking to notice that these images are a sociopolitical equivalent to a Benthamite economics of perpetual growth. Growth in liberation, like economic growth, is good. Let institutions not interfere. Raskin is in this respect the Ayn Rand of the Left. He rationalizes the lifestyle of the affluent intellectual class. People who are making lots of money, who have established positions in secure professions, and whose highly educated children are freed from economic necessity, demand ever more "liberation." They try to increase the "private space" around their lives. "Let me alone."

The same criticism can be levelled at Raskin as at Rand. The human being is not, in fact, a solitary atom. There is not now, there never was, there never will be, a solitary autonomous self, apart from society. The human being is a social network, necessarily dependent and psychically interrelated, a social organism, a political animal. The self is not an "I" but a "we." A culture is constituted by meaning, meaning is mediated through language, and language is irrefragably social. What Raskin refers to as the four colonies that enchain our souls and shape our consciousness are only the current names for our age-old and ineradicable human identity. No self has ever existed outside a political system, an economic system, an educational system, and an affective-imagistic system (the media). To call such systems "colonizers" rather than "life-supports" is merely to reverse the metaphors of human finitude. We are not the gods we dream of being. We are enfleshed in societies.

Raskin seems to treat every reality that presses upon the self from outside itself as a form of "alienation." No word (except perhaps "repression") is so shabbily used on the Left today. If one assumes a faulty and distorted image of human life in the beginning, by supposing that there *is* an autonomous self to be uncovered and liberated, then necessarily most of human life must appear as alienation. It is alienation, as it were, by definition. One's sense of reality then dooms one to experience exactly what one is trying to avoid; alienation arises from one's own deliberate choice of self-image.

Thus at least two senses of liberation must be distinguished. According to one sense, institutions are *the enemy*. According to the other, institutions are limited and limiting life-systems; they are the human's *habitat*. In the first sense, to be liberated is (in imagination at least) to have "broken free." In the second sense, to be liberated is not to have escaped the limits of human life, but to have become conscious of them and to have exerted what power one can to create beauty in and around them. The sculptor invited to carve figures on a Gothic entrance made what use he could of the given portal.

There is a rough sort of empirical test for sorting out the two views of liberation. Where those who seek to be liberated become increasingly bitter and unhappy, projecting all evils outwards upon some external system, the first view is usually in operation. Where those who seek to be liberated become increasingly compassionate and joyous (even in defeat), and where they gain peaceful and accurate perception of their own and the system's inadequacies, the second view is usually at work. Have not the North Vietnamese been admirable in precisely this respect?

For human life is a network, and there is no self and no private space into which the network does not properly enter. Each human life participates in the lives of many others, and is participated in by them. All human autonomy is shared, participated, communal. It is not individual. The very word "autonomy" is a social inheritance, and the guidance it offers us for shaping our own lives is peculiarly Western and, more precisely, high bourgeois. Thus even the dream of autonomy is not autonomous but social.

A society of Marlboro men and "liberated" women (for Women's Lib, too, is infected with WASP individualism and the WASP metaphor of domination, despite its appeals to sisterhood) is condemned to being a lonely crowd. Where there are no permanent risks, no lifetimes of loyalty, there are no communities. Transiency between communes, no matter how affectionate the receptions, leaves one atomic in a very large crowd. Unless you lay down your life, you do not gain it. Unless you bind yourself, you have no liberation. The pursuit of liberation without bonds is pursuit of the unlimited, and the infinite yields itself to humans only in death. Thence, the preoccupation with death among the liberated in our society; violent, "innocent" death.

Thus it seems to me that Raskin's image of liberation is fundamentally regressive. It attempts to recreate the egocentricity and omnipotence of childhood fantasy. To guard one's virginity, even, is easier than to guard an autonomy which does not exist. No chastity belt can keep outside the self its interrelatedness with others.

Facing the lassitude of the infinite, imaginative children spontaneously create limits: lines not to walk on, boundaries to observe, oceans beyond carpets, fantasies disallowing other possibilities ("pretend the bed is a plane").

Joy and delight come from acceptance of the finite. There is no freedom without the finite. There is no freedom without "repression." The dream of a nonrepressive society is a regression farther back even than childhood: in the womb, too, there were restrictions.

Raskin overlooks the social texture of freedom. All that does not arise from the self he calls, in thickly Sartrean terms, the "beside-himself." The human's task is to break out of that. The human is unhealthy until he comes under the total, sweet control of his own will:

> At that moment, the person projects a future condition that he defines and for which he is responsible. . . . It is at such a moment that a new and more healthy relationship to the environment may develop. Through the projects which he chooses, either alone or as part of a group or movement, he is able to define himself as a subject, as an equal who is not an instrument serving as the tool of a person or a group which colonized him. But note that the individual must choose with and not be swept up—act with, and not be acted upon.[3]

Where in the whole wide world are such sweet luxuries available and not corrupting? Raskin senses the dangers. He does not really want *too much* isolation. One may choose to cooperate with others since, after all, one must:

> Take oneself as a case in point. My hard fight for space is still limited by the fact that I exist within a group. Since I am born dependent on others, I learn that my existence can only be in association with others. Whether I or others think of me as an artist, scholar, farmer or politican, I remain dependent. Because I am a human being, I seek cooperation, since perpetuation and fulfillment of self is achieved through cooperation. Yet my free actions with others now determine the kind of association which will result. It is easy to return to a colonized state either as a colonizer or colonized. But where cooperation and association is an important part of decolonization, a different basis might be laid.

But such "liberation" has almost nothing to offer construction workers, nothing to offer to farmers, nothing to offer to husbands, wives, or children amid daily necessities. It is a fantasy suitable for the entertainment of privileged, leisured classes—who read books and attend lectures. And who accept intellectual authorities at every step.

No human being is ever in a situation in which his "free actions with others now determine the kind of association which will result." The free actions of others have impact as well. To join an association, freely or otherwise, is necessarily to lose some power of determination. And for each member to be everlastingly jealous about who is determining whom is to forfeit any sort of activity except ego-games. The pursuit of authenticity is almost of necessity an "ego trip." The construction worker does not *choose* most of his associations. He does not choose his grandparents, his neighborhood, or even the kind of job he was lucky enough to find (some of his schoolmates never found them). He does not choose his foreman, the site, the design, or the amount of capital invested. He does not choose how much his wife loves him, or how well his kids respond to his attempts to be fatherly. And under no economic, social, or political situation imaginable would he have control—or would it help him, if he did— over such aspects of the human situation.

Raskin says of "the channelling colony" that it

> establishes, through the schools, achievement standards and orders of privilege and merit for young people; the most significant short-term purpose of the school is to break people in to accepting authority structures. Its inmates learn how to become bored, user-used and hollowed out.[4]

One cannot understand the New Left today without grasping its fundamentalist theology: "the system" as hell, "cooptation" as worldly corruption, authorities as "devils." But one must also understand its affluence. College students in prestigious schools endure a certain servitude, to be sure. Not all the world's youth have spent their early twenties behind walls, listening to lectures, disciplined by print. Still, it beats working in the steel mills. The financial prospect up ahead promises mobility no steelworker has; promises dinners in restaurants; promises stereo equipment; promises world travel; promises summers at seaside; promises discrimination in wines, magazines, associations; promises most of the consumption of consumer goods upon this planet.

If students are still bored, the cure is simple: empty the schools. In the feudal era, only a tiny minority went to school. Perhaps only a tiny minority—say ten percent —ever truly desire a university education. The rest might go to technical schools, or inflict themselves upon the rest of the world by wandering, or be given jobs like those of their grandparents: rebuilding the roadbeds on all the nation's railways. No other culture holds that life is intended to be exciting, glamorous, or fun. That is merely the ideology, if not the advertising, of industrial society. Life for most people, everywhere, has always been routine and "boring." Boredom, indeed, is the starting place of metaphysics.

Many things are wrong with our schools. But it is not their "channelling function." Given the choice of entering the factory or entering college, who wouldn't prefer to be bored at the latter? No one is forced into that "channel." For most, it is one more channel than their fathers had.

Since authority is no more than a decision-making device for groups larger than one, it is utterly unavoidable in human life. Someone in a publishing house had to decide whether to mobilize hundreds of persons around Raskin's book; and Raskin had to give instructions to typists. Hence schools are not needed in order "to break people in to accepting authority." Life itself does that job thoroughly. Parents often do the breaking-in before children even arrive at school, and not least the good, driving parents of future intellectuals.

Life comes to us, William James wrote, in "blooming buzzing confusion." Without some sort of channelling, there is no freedom. There is not even a political movement, or a concrete action, or one personal identity chosen from among many. Channelling is an expression of freedom, not a denial of it.

Short-term, Raskin says, the school breaks people in to authority; long-term it is different: "The schools' long-term effect is to create a consciousness among many students and professors which stimulates the need for decolonization and reconstruction."[5]

Long-term, the school "creates a consciousness"; that is, it "enlightens." It provides an institutional base for a new form of channelling, a "reconstruction." In whose economic interest will that new reconstruction be? Will it arrive in time to pay this month's bills or next year's tuition for Joe Santorra, our milkman? Raskin seems wholly oblivious to the self-interest of his own class. He is describing a politics for the few. He depends on the leisure of a class established upon a substantial institutional base by the affluence of the American economy. He says nothing about jobs, about necessary weekly paychecks, about the guy who doesn't mind taking orders so long as his family eats. Autonomy is the pleasure—and the fantasy—only of privileged elites. Even privileged elites, but surely all others, are no stronger or freer than the social bonds and structures of authority in which they participate.

2. *The Americanization of Consciousness*

Not everything about the past was admirable; not everything about the immigrant way of life should be preserved. Still . . . still! How many treasures have had to be abandoned; how many bones and broken chests strew the deserts of our memory. The first generation took with them into the stinking steamships the lives of at least four other generations. The long voyage of immigration is not completed when in the new land a man enters his first boardinghouse, or takes his wife to an apartment of their own. Immigration lasts at least a hundred years.

On a Long Island beach there sits an Italo-American girl, perhaps fifteen. Her face is pleasant as she watches two children play. Unlike the other girls, she wears a tee shirt and overalls; there is a transiency about her hour at the beach. A mood afflicts her: I think of Studs Lonigan's younger sister, and I am not prepared for the shadow that, blocks the sun.

Her mother is suddenly standing there: *"You're goin' ta get it when ya get home, young lady. You're goin' ta get it good. Just remember that. Ohh, I'm goin' ta give it to ya."* And to the two adults sitting nearby: *"I'm goin' to cure her ass good."* Louder: *"You're goin' ta get a beating like ya never got before. Remember that."*

The adults ask something and the reply is: *"Mouthpiece. A real mouthpiece. . . . And this is the girl that never said nothin'. I'm tellin' you, it's easier to control her older brother than her. I handle him easier than her. Ohh!"* She brushes imaginary problems from her vision and sits down happily.

She is serene and pleased with herself. Suddenly her voice toughens again. "Where do you think you're goin'? Where are ya goin' now?"

"For a walk," the girl whispers.

"Where are YOU GOING?"

"For a walk, I told ya, for a *WALK.*"

"Where to, where are ya walkin' to?"

"For a walk, how do I know? For a walk. Let me alone."

"You're going to get it tonight. Don't forget. Vacuum when you get home. Vacuum, you understand?"

The sun is pleasant on the face and the mother enjoys her relatives. Their conversation level drops. But soon she is calling out to a young girl down the beach.

"How do you like your new home?"

The girl lifts her head from her arm, a quizzical arch in her dark brows. "You must mean my sister Angela."

"Which one are you?"

The name is lost in the wind.

"Where's your mother? Haven't seen her in years."

"Over there. On the float."

"Tell her to come see me."

And everyone on the beach, it seems, does come to see her. Young wives are quizzed about babies, homes, neighborhoods. One swinger in a pants suit is asked skeptically: "You enjoy riding on that?" It is not so easy as once it was to disapprove of motorcycles. Every woman who comes to her kisses her on arrival and departure, even if they haven't seen her for years.

She was not born in Italy, but in America. She is only forty-five. When her face relaxes she belongs to the sun, the liquid-blue sky, the white sand; she is at peace with the universe.

One day her daughter may run away, with a group of hippies no less. She will not understand that. She did everything a mother could do—hounded her, taught her, cooked for her, showed her how, kept after her, sent her to church. And she beat her; yes, she did her duty by her. The girl's moodiness escapes her. Her stubbornness and back talk must be confronted, defeated, eradicated. Why? Because that's the way it is. That's the way parents bring up children right. That's morality. You're stiff-necked and resist at first; but once you surrender, you'll see, the world runs better that way and you'll be happier. You'll learn more and you'll be in tune.

It is not surprising that the lower-middle-class believes in being tough with the Communists. They believe in being tough with their own children. When eighty-five percent of American people approved of the way the Chicago police clubbed and beat unruly and taunting demonstrators, they were only saying that the parents of the other fifteen percent should have done that earlier. It has not escaped the attention of the lower classes that it is the children of the educational elite who are publicly rebellious, angry, and full of rage; who throw tantrums;

who resist authority. RESIST is a word that sends electric thrills through the emotions of bright students in the better schools, even if they have been treated with respect and rational persuasion by their parents—even because they have been so treated. But RESIST is an attitude that inflames the sense of reality of the lower-middle class. It is as though ancestral memories warned parents down a thousand years: "To resist is to die; it isn't worth it." And it is as though the bright children of the educated classes were cheated in their upbringing. Nothing in their parents' theories prepared them for the stupidities, absurdities, and violences of daily life.

The children of the lower-middle classes are closer to the brutal realism of European peasants. They must learn to cope with sudden outbursts of anger in their families; with violent storms of emotion no one in the families understands; with belt or hand or brush cutting into the flesh of the backside as though demons there needed crushing. The children of the lower-middle classes learn early about chance, the unpredictable, the absurd. They also learn a more direct vengeance, a more immediate violence. By contrast, the children of the educated classes learn repressed forms of violence. They prefer the effects of their aggressions to be far away, impersonal, where they do not see the face of those they hit.

I believe the quantum of violence in a human life, century to century, is fairly constant. I would not like reason, sweetness, and order to prevail in my home lest the children find no outlet for their fears, their anger, their rebellion. I would rather be decisive and oppose them and make them fight me, than let them grow up as distant from me as can be arranged; I prefer entanglement to distance. On the other hand, I love to see sparks of will, fury, and inventiveness in them; I do not want them to "surrender." It is impossible, of course, to talk honestly about the complexities of one's relationships with one's own children. But I do not entirely admire the methods of educated people; there is nothing that so infuriates me as the disguised aggressions of a Quaker. Hostility for the uneducated of the world is part of growing up enlightened. So also is an incapacity for direct emotion; so also is the bringing of concrete violence upon others, at a distance. (Violence is also brought, not least, by pacifists.) As Mailer says:

> . . . the Christians—the ones who are not Christian but whom we choose to call Christian—are utterly opposed to the destruction of human life and succeed within themselves in starting all the wars of our own time, since every war since the Second World War has been initiated by liberals or Communists; these Christians also succeed by their faith in science to poison the nourishment we eat and the waters of the sea, to alter the genetics of our beasts, and to break the food chains of nature.[6]

The immigrant coming to America brought with him a profound respect for authority. In May 1916, when Senator Pastore's father, Michele, was seized by a stroke, Mrs. Pastore opened a window and called out the name of the family doctor, who lived next door: "Williams! Williams!" Death came faster. Michele used his last breaths to chide his wife: "Call him Dr. Williams or he won't come."[7]

But he also brought with him a cynicism regarding the high claims of authority. "The peasant in me," wrote Louis Adamic in his autobiography (1931), "gave me the tendency to distrust intangible things, to rely on common sense and keep on guard against high ideals and fancy ideas."[8] The same cynicism was applied to the church. In the views of many of the enlightened, what is objectionable in Roman Catholicism are its doctrines, its strengthening of habits of authority, and its encouragement of existing social institutions. They don't appreciate the skepticism it also teaches.

The religion of southern and eastern Europeans is not, as it is for northern peoples, a matter of morality and ethics.[9] It is, rather, a way of feeling, an attitude, a sentiment. Whereas northerners tend to test the quality of religious life by the propriety of one's deeds, southerners tend to test it by the quality of one's feelings. To be sure, northerners measure internal qualities and southerners look to actions; but the distribution of emphasis is clearly different.

There is a pagan quality to the religion of southern and eastern Europe that I find beautiful. There is an activist quality to the religion of the north that I admire, emulate, but also distrust. I love communion with God through the things that are—red soil upon the fingers, white clouds across vast skies. My blood feels political and social disasters ever closing in. Earth and God are steadier beneath one's faith than social structures. In south and east, the split between secular and sacred has not been thoroughly established in the soul. To be lusty, natural, enchanted with the earth, in agony or in despair, is to be religious: everything is within God's presence, enveloped by him. To be true, authentic, fully alive, is to be more in him. To be timid, cautious, cramped, is to subtract oneself from his vitality. His transcendence, to be sure, is such that life is not constructed for human contentment, pleasure, or utility. It is mysterious, cruel, unpredictable. The point of life is wisdom and endurance. Who learns to be reconciled and to endure grows into all that a human being can become. Life, as the Buddha says, is suffering. When God revealed himself in Jesus he came as suffering love.

Consequently northern schemes for building a better, happier, more pleasant world leave me a little skeptical. When people are safe, affluent, able to do as they wish, manage their lives so that their pleasure exceeds their pain —when (in a word) they are content—how does one distinguish them from cows? Human beings do not grow by way of contentment. The compensating search of Mailer and others for authenticity, action, and heroism seems merely self-assertive: like Mussolini scraping a leather chair with his thumbnail to illustrate the jagged mark he wished to make upon the face of history. The ideology was northern—History over Nature—and when northerners took it over they pushed the amateurs aside: "If even the Italians could work such wonders with fascism, then how much more could we Germans, pure Nordics, achieve with fascism!" (1933).[10]

My intent is not to link all that is wrong with modernity to northern cultures, all right and peaceful things to south and east. I am trying to suggest felt. differences between cultural senses of reality, stories, symbols. More than in the north, in the south and east one learns to suffer. In the north, one exhorts oneself—and is constantly exhorted—to *do*. It is quite likely, I think, that northern activism has done what it could do, has run its course, in many ways to the benefit of us all (but also to our imminent danger). The planet could well use, perhaps, a thousand years of slowing down, a contemplative pace, a pursuit of wisdom through such suffering as is everywhere pressed upon us. In some ways, endurance is a form of escape; in other ways, action is a form of escape.

Which path is least murderous?

The Pole, the Italian, the Greek, and the Slav stand outside the traditions of northern Europe in certain helpful ways. Many of the cultural achievements of the Nordic peoples, becoming human property, are dear to them; it would be foolish not to accept grace wherever it is found. But they do not cough every time Nordic culture begins to choke.

The value deepest in the psyche of southern and eastern Europeans (I say yet once again) is an instinct for family and community. Through long centuries of oppression, one institution did not fail them: the family. Everything else was derivative, was distraction, was destruction. When agents of the state were seen in the village, it could only mean some form of death was on its way.

The life of southern and eastern Europeans in America is a basic life, simple and direct. They tend to resist the politicization of life. Political fashions come and go, the family remains forever. Politics is not a fulfilling, but an emptying way of life. The politician is set upon by eels remorselessly sucking from him every juice of his humanity. Politics devours the soul. Only superficial people are attracted to it—the Irish are explained that way. Glad hands, quick smiles, what would *they* know about the depth of feeling in a family? The Kennedys, by way of exception, are accepted as an *ethnic* family. (Bobby was the most ethnic of all: his suffering, quick emotions, many children.)

The closer a politician stays to family and clan, the more trustworthy he is. A man who is mobile and atomic, who lives according to a bureaucratic schedule and carries the thin attaché case of couriers and experts—such a man has no soul. His life has a tinny sound: no wife, no parents, no children, no cousins, no uncles and aunts. *Reason only. Rules. Schedules.* A man has to have a very small heart, and a very thin supply of juices, to find happiness in such a life.

To families who for centuries did not own homes, who owned no businesses, who possessed no land, the building of a home among people one loves and hates is paradise. Southern and eastern Europeans are deficient as economic or social climbers. They are often grasping and greedy, of course. They are hard, stubborn, narrow. They are vulnerable to the sirens of advancement, mobility, and status, but not nearly in proportion to their numbers. It is not so much discrimination that has held back the "new" immigrants. They build their lives around family values, and generally settle for modest economic roles.

Even regarding intellect, they are essentially modest. Slavic, Greek, and Italian intellectuals (let me mention John Lukacs, Ortega y Gasset, Croce, Cioran, Kazantzakis) characteristically prefer to the rituals of prophecy a sort of world-weary wisdom. They are not quick to believe in schemes of urgency and authenticity, promising a better world. Perhaps they were oppressed

for too many centuries; quite certainly, they consciously
cherish (unlike many Jewish and WASP intellectuals) a
cultural history antedating the Enlightenment. Modern
civilization—urban, fluid, democratic, determined to
change history—is a Nordic invention. The men of the
south and east have long been skeptical about its outcome.
For many generations they have talked quietly of *hubris*
and *nemesis*. They have "waited." Waiting has been their
primary intellectual style. An instinct for tragedy haunts
their souls even at moments of exuberant success.

Southern and eastern Europeans in America tend to
make a sharp distinction between "the masses," an invention of modern civilization, and "the people."[11] Public
opinion is a phenomenon of mass culture and is inherently
tyrannical; even at best it is unreliable. Only a culture
without soul is interested in public opinion.[12] For opinion
is the most shallow and superficial stratum of the mind.
No one *lives* by opinion. Opinion is information, image,
and sentiment, widely circulated. It measures the signals
people have received recently.

The distinction between "the masses" and "the people"
grounds two divergent conceptions of authority. Writers
like Ortega y Gasset (*The Revolt of the Masses*) and
John Lukacs (*The Passing of the Modern Age*) are sometimes accused of aristocratic bias. They do not trust the
masses, it is alleged, because they prefer cultural elites:
walking with a dog in the woods, cognac, an oak library,
leisure, *noblesse oblige.* What they mean by "civilized" is
what only aristocrats are. These objections, springing from
democratic resentment, miss the point. I am through my
family in no way aristocratic, and the advantages I have
gained are no doubt due to the unprecedented openness of
American society. Still I am not blind to the authoritarianism of America's educated elites, whose mode is merely
different from that of the aristocratic elites they profess
to mock.

Mechanical metaphors for human society are bound to
result in new power relationships. When troubles arise in

Anglo-Saxon democracies, the imagination immediately leaps to the language of "social problems," "programs," "reconstruction," "priorities," "mechanisms," "inputs," "modules," "procedures." But when you have begun to think of persons as units subject to rational schemes, you have ceased dealing with people and have begun to create masses. "People" is an organic, nongeometric, nonrational, nonmechanical concept. Historical peoples grow like hedges: concretely, contingently, thickly, in all directions, in ways that are entangled and dense and labyrinthine. A hedge cannot be taken apart like the engine of a Ford. A people carries with it prejudices, customs, habits, ways of perceiving and imagining and acting. All these can be given new shape and new direction. But one changes them only respectfully, with the love and subtlety of a true gardener. Ruthlessness is sometimes called for, if one knows the time and the season. To treat a people as a people is not, therefore, to be reactionary or to rest with the status quo. It is to respect what one would shape.

By contrast, a mass is a people whose organic, effective, habitual connections have been severed. A mass is an assemblage of discrete units. Their source of unity is given from outside, by those experts whose task is to rationalize and to manipulate social relationships. Because persons are not inert and inanimate, the experts do not completely have their will. They must flatter, cajole, or elude public opinion. Built into the language of Anglo-Saxon social work (Orwell encouraged us to scrutinize such language coldly) is a scheme of manipulation. Authority belongs to the rationalizers. The masses are expected to be grateful for plans contrived to make their lives more affluent and pleasant. The social system is a functional mechanism. Who are the parts, and who the mechanics? Even "getting screwed" may be given precise mechanical imagery.

Convictions are another matter. Convictions are nourished by communities. Convictions are bonds of loyalty between persons, so strongly cherished that they sustain one even in solitariness and desperation. Convictions are networks of trust. They are tacit pledges, dependable expectations. Convictions are nourished by families and other deep affective connections. They are neither "cognitive" nor "emotive"—only a schizophrenic culture could have invented such categories and built a technological culture upon them. (Not by accident is Nordic culture the focus of a technological way of life.)

To the ethnic thinker, what in fact happens among American intellectuals is quite different from accepted ideology. The manifest function of the politics of authenticity is to promote profound individuality—find yourself, be yourself, please yourself. The latent function is to homogenize intellectuals into a class apart, such that the vast majority of their primary contacts are not with the people of America but with each other. Moreover, intellectuals seem to accept as their *raison d'être* an adversary relationship to the very persons who actually execute the dirty, grinding work of keeping a fluid, mobile, technological society in operation. The unconscious motivating force of the avant-garde appears to be a projecting upon the middle class, whose very existence is due to the science and technology on which intellectuals once based so many hopes, their own chagrin at the results. The intellectuals live, economically and socially, in income and status, among the upper-middle class. They are—a type familiar to southern and eastern Europeans—comfortably placed clerics who batten upon the guilts they inject into the bourgeoisie.

America, wrote Mencken, is a nation of third-rate men.[13] But isn't it the point of a technological, democratic, consumer society to turn taste and power over to the masses? Intellectuals do their share of the consuming, exist in sufficiently dense numbers because of the institutional needs of a technological society, and have been the ardent champions of mass democracy. Let them reap what they have sown. To take up towards the world they have made an "adversary relation" is, like Dominicans of old, to preach hellfire to villagers of a Holy Empire. The intellectuals do not *rule* the country, but they are as near to Lords Spiritual as ever bishops were to kings: Kissinger as Richelieu, Harvard to Washington as Salamanca to Rome.

Two myths of Anglo-American political life particularly strike the immigrant thinker as false. First there is the myth of some earlier stage of full democratic participation in American life, when people made the decisions that affected their own lives, felt powerful, and were content as full partners in the political system. In what year, what era, was that? When blacks, women, and the property-less did not vote? When robber barons, local interests, Brahmins, industrialists, powerful preachers, and fiercely conformist customs were in every region of the nation the bane of daily experience? America never was a democracy of full political participation by its people. It has always been a highly structured, authoritarian, conformist, heresy-hunting, company-run network of cities, towns, and rural areas. A greater percentage and a greater variety of Americans voted in 1968 than in any other presidential election in our history. The power of local prejudices and powers to enforce local ways of life is less today than at any period in the past.[14] But today many no longer believe that "the system" is participatory, or free, or champion of authenticity, or perhaps even legitimate. Our political theory—for all our vaunted theory-less pragmatism—has long been out of tune with actual working practice. There does not exist a practical politician who could tell the public how things actually are without shattering their illusions.

The southern and eastern European learned immediately to face the facts of American equality, opportunity, power, and advancement. It was clearly not a land where value was recognized as value. No matter that in Europe you were a medical doctor, a lawyer, a dentist, an architect, a jeweler, a cabinetmaker, a professor of law or economics, a pianist: everything was dissolved. A Polish intellectual is quoted in 1917: "I do not think most Americans realize how revolting to a more or less educated immigrant is their naïve attitude of superiority, their astonishing self-satisfaction, their inability and unwillingness to look on anything foreign as worth being understood and assimilated."[15]

The immigrants soon learned that they had to organize. (One of their first needs was burial societies.)[16] Since most had come as individuals without any supporting social organizations, their energies were divided between economic survival, rudimentary social construction, and marriage and family. They were not—they could not be —full partners in a political democracy. They did not find America to be a democracy; it was constructed rather like small sets of competing aristocracies. There were only two aristocracies ready to receive the immigrants: city "machines" and labor unions. These "aristocracies of the working man," moreover, were in large measure his own creation; they were seldom WASP in inspiration.

The word "machine," in fact, is directly misleading. If anything in American politics is a "machine," it is reform politics: impersonal, procedural, moralistic, abstract, constructed by rules. If anything is human and scaled down to a size, shape, and mode of relations that people can understand, it is the person-based politics of the Irish and other Catholic groups. Corrupt and immoral? The Protestant tends to favor the abstract, the Catholic the concrete. Their outrage is ignited at different points and at different temperatures. Is reform politics, now that it has had some little history, less corrupt and less immoral than machine politics? Perhaps the question is, rather, which system more speedily demoralizes the populace, breeds malaise, and generates anomie.

Here, too, the ethnic Catholic has a second contrasting slant on American politics. According to myth, what people want (should want) from politics is self-determination. Protestants generally, as Moynihan once put it, are "suffering servants of the Lord," and they have been obliged "to perceive in the whole miserable business the morally autonomous individual struggling for salvation."[17] People universally want (should want) autonomy, power over decisions that affect their lives, participation in government, the dignity that comes from political power. Thus an enormous and disproportionate energy goes into reforming the procedure of *voting*, as though a procedure based upon the conception of the marketplace will operate by some Invisible Hand to elect the best available rulers, determine the wisest decisions, etc.

Thus Richard Nixon in 1968: "There is nothing wrong with this country that a good election cannot cure." Thus Richard Goodwin in 1969: "Somehow the crucial aspects of his environment seem in the grip of forces that are too huge and impersonal to attack." This produces a "malaise of powerlessness." Men want to "regain control of and play a real part in the enterprises of society . . . For individuals have a fundamental, instinctive need for a degree of personal mastery over their lives and environment."[18]

"Personal mastery over their lives and environment." Catholics from southern and eastern Europe have never had that; the very phrase is Nordic and Protestant. Is it, in fact, true that human beings want (should want) what the myth says they do? Observing what politics tends to do to highly politicized people, ordinary men and women do well not to associate either a rich humanity or a full morality with greater participation in politics. Goodwin writes: "If citizens are to find a purpose beyond their daily lives, it will come from having a personal share in important public causes, and the causes must be large and worthy enough to tap moral will and energy." Yes, political passions can give meaning to life—for some people, under some circumstances. But do I really wish to find the meaning of my life "beyond" my daily life, and above all in becoming a "public" agent? Even on the face of it, the proposition is implausible.

A realistic instinct suggests—and surely empirical observation everywhere confirms—that most people at most times prefer to have as little to do with politics as absolutely necessary.[19] Politics involves a great deal of dirty, grimy, irksome, unrewarding, and often bitterly frustrating work. Not everyone subscribes to the doctrine that the meaning of life is to be sought in self-punishment. The fundamental impulse in human life is not a desire for autonomy but a desire to live privately, under conditions of tolerably good leadership. Nor is the desire to "live privately" a matter, as it is in America, of fluid atomistic mobility. One prefers to live with one's family and friends; living privately is a social, and only when threatened, a political, matter.

Democratic investigators seldom conclude that the facts patently make democracy less than salvific for large numbers of persons. They seldom conclude that democracy, according to the facts in front of them, is not especially desired by ordinary people, and is not nearly all that privileged classes imagine it to be. They conclude that something is *wrong* with the people; that the people need therapy, or education; that the people need to be converted and reconstructed; that the people are dangerously ill with fascist "tendencies."

Is it true that a desire for good rulers is inherently a desire for fascism? The fact is that people, even professors, *will* be ruled. The acceptance of authority does not necessarily detract from one's own autonomy, dignity, or power; it may enhance all three. To have the good sense to study with the best teachers available, accepting provisionally and in countless subtle ways the influence of their judgments, style, direction, methods, emphases, their lived story of what an inquirer is, their favored symbols, and their sense of reality, is not necessarily to lose one's own independence, momentum, or ultimate new directions.

The theories of the Enlightenment are much too heavily weighted on the side of the individual, dissent, personal independence, and originality to account for the actual way of life even of those who accept its doctrines. We are mimetic creatures, political creatures, and every part of our lives is subject to far more authorities from outside ourselves than our limited internal capacities allow us to transcend. We are, far more than our touching and sentimental faith allows, men of our time, place, class, and origins. One does not use a theory, at best partially plausible for persons of genius who come but rarely in a century, as a description for the practices of whole legions of followers.

The actual, noble, and admirable role of various kinds of authority in our actual living practice is sadly neglected both by Enlightenment writers and by American writers generally. Many first-rate defenses of liberty, individuality, and dissent come to mind; little of quality celebrates the blessings of repetition, docility, tradition, apprenticeship, learning from masters, regularity, order, uninterrupted rhythms, the creativity and efficiency of a nonpolitical existence. A writer can scarcely avoid noticing how important to his way of life such values are. Where, though, are their praises sung?

There is not nearly so much autonomy in life as we imagine; nor is such autonomy as is accessible to us wholly private in character. It is itself a social achievement. It was given to us as an ideal in our culture, as it has not been in others. The methods for attaining it are taught us. The tests for measuring it are taught us. The techniques for thinking about it—and even for questioning its existence, value, and relationships—are taught to us. Invention, to be sure, is always a possibility and we occasionally achieve it. To think thoughts no one has ever before thought is a not entirely unimaginable feat, since it in fact occurs. But a frog's flight is not judged by the standards of birds.

It is a characteristic mistake of the enlightened to demand too much of humans and then to loathe them for falling short. That is not an ethnic mistake.

3. *Rational Authoritarianism*

Acts done under authority are not automatically unjust, untruthful, or even inauthentic and unfree. Free, authentic acts are not by that very fact just or truthful. The issue of authority vs. freedom is in most moral contexts simply irrelevant. Those who have imagined the conflict in Western civilization for almost four hundred years as a "crisis in authority" have given our attention a misleading focus. In every human community, today as yesterday, both authority and freedom are operative. The two are not opposites or contraries. They are qualities mixed in every social system and in every personal act.

Action requires a selection among various possibilities. Every action thereby limits freedom: if one has decided to do one thing, other courses of action are ruled out. The ground of authority is the need to choose. In groups, procedures for making choices are indispensable. Not even an absolute tyrant can have his will absolutely carried out, for other human beings are not absolutely malleable. Societies necessarily seek ways of "legitimating" the necessary social choices. The chief transition in recent Western history has been a transition from the legitimation of choices made through aristocratic-monarchical elites to the legitimation of choices made through corporate, professional elites. Neither elite gets its way entirely. Each must deal with a stubborn populace.

The distinctive ideology of democratic elites grants high praise to the "rational" surrender to authority A man is assumed to be free until he freely yields his consent to authority. It would, however, make as much sense to assume that a man is under authority until he freely exerts his own contrary will. Robert Dahl lists three principles whereby, according to democratic ideology, authority is rationally legitimated:

First, a process may insure that decisions correspond with my own personal choice. Second, a process may insure decision informed by a special competence that would be less likely under alternative procedures. Third, a process may be less perfect than other alternatives according to the first two criteria but, on balance, more satisfactory simply because it economizes on the amount of time, attention, and energy I must give to it. Let me call these respectively the Criterion of Personal Choice, the Criterion of Competence, and the Criterion of Economy.[20]

On all three counts, one might stand the ideological praise of democracy upon its head. For persons whose time is preoccupied with economic necessities, democracy in all but major elections might seem to be too expensive: to demand too much energy for too little return.

My intention is not to praise the failure of many ethnics to participate actively in politics. It is rather to throw light on the extent to which democracy is an ideology and a procedure which appeal most to privileged and relatively leisured elites. To succeed in democratic politics, one must have money, organizational or forensic skills, and perhaps, above all, time and energy. A truck driver who wants to run for alderman has a tough time arranging free hours, paying his way to banquets, having posters printed, etc. Democracy is an invention for the prosperous.

Ideologues of democratic life tend to overlook three forms of class bias implicit in democratic procedures. They overestimate the attractiveness of their own ideals of autonomy, freely given consent, and rational yielding to authority. Most people have fewer pretensions. Secondly, they fail to notice how many economic and educational privileges must be present before democratic procedures become a practical expenditure of energy. Thirdly, they neglect to note that their own concern for "issue-oriented" politics and issues of "conscience" rest upon full bellies, a secure economic future, and their own interests in a rationalized, reconstructed society in which their type of person dominates.

Moreover, in the actual practice of democracy, many proponents of democratic pluralism do not trust the direct, popular will. One encounters constantly in the propaganda of democracy references to the "fragility" of democracy, "our fragile consensus," the "tragedy" that lurks below the skin of democratic life. The fear is threefold. Either the populace is fickle and subject to chauvinism, jingoism, or demagogy. Or the people have been dissolved into "masses" susceptible of resentment and volatile revenge. Or coherent minorities narrowly construe their own immediate interests, do not easily rise above them, and become locked in barely manageable confrontations with other interest groups.

Thus in *The Intellectuals and McCarthy*, Professor Rogin finds a number of our most admirable social theoreticians extolling "pluralism" and "democratic compromise," but quite plainly suspicious of the popular will. They accuse the masses of "authoritarian tendencies." The remedy they propose is strong *leadership* in each interest group.[21] I call this point of view "rational authoritarianism." It is a form of rule through professional leadership elites. I am not eager to discredit it, but I would like to show that a form of class bias is transparently at work wherever such pluralists accuse workingmen of authoritarianism without calling attention to their own version of the same.

The pluralists worry about the tendencies of the American people to "reject the traditional cultural and educational leadership of the enlightened upper and upper-middle classes," that is, "the eastern, educated, Anglicized elite."[22] They speak much of pluralism and the legitimate conflict between groups. But what they have in mind is argument between "responsible leaders" of such groups. They know that the leaders of such groups tend to be more activist; liberal; better informed; checked, counter-checked, and socialized by each other. In short, "more than one road seems to suggest the elitist underpinnings of pluralist doctrine."

Enlightenment thinkers, Rogin notes, "favored a society of in-individuals uncoerced by group or traditional ties." But an atomized society generates anomie, pointlessness, and terror. It turns formerly organic peoples into an atomized, restless mass: the ground, Durkheim argued, of totalitarianism. American liberal thinkers solve this problem by relying upon interest groups mutually committed to "rational politics." Such groups provide vehicles with which individuals can identify. These vehicles are pragmatic. Their politics are "rational" in four senses:

> First, political demands are not rationalizations for underlying frustrations. Since their manifest content is what counts, they can be handled rationally. Second, people are rational about means. They seek those that will achieve their ends; they think instrumentally. Third, individuals concern themselves with short-run, self-interested goals; rationality and self-interest become synonymous here. Finally, political ends are not utopian; they can be achieved within the framework of the existing social order. The politics of those who long for the return of the traditional, preindustrial way of life are irrational on all four counts; and this desire is at the root of much political irrationality.[23]

Pluralist politics, Rogin adds, is rooted in studies of "the authoritarian personality." Unconscious psychological attitudes become the grounds for predicting social behavior. Such a procedure is dubious—and may be turned on its proponents.

What if, in fact, humans are neither mere individuals nor mere members of interest groups? What if "irrational" factors, of a highly symbolic and valuational nature, both do and *ought to* operate in political choices? A student alert to the subterranean realities of ethnic feeling, Robert Coles describes a conversation with a Polish machinist:

. . . and he has a certain background, which he proudly calls his own, even as he wonders, in an off-guard moment, precisely what he and the rest of us are to be called: "I don't know who's *really* an American. There are guys I work with, they're Italian and Irish. They're different from me, even though we're all Catholics. You see what I mean? We're buddies on the job. We do the same work. We drink our coffee together and sit there eating lunch. But you leave and you go home and you're back with your own people. I don't just mean my family, no. It's more than your wife and kids; it's everything in your life."

So, he resists our effort to fit him neatly into a category.[24]

What one takes to be "authoritarianism" may be quite complicated by a particular ethnic history. Arthur B. Shostak in *Blue-Collar Life* stresses the power of the ethnic factor:

Indeed, as one investigator concludes: "The proposition that the ethnic factor is second only to the economic factor in influencing an American's vote is unlikely to be overthrown in the near future."[25]

The economic factor may not even be strong enough, alone, to override the ethnic factor, as John C. Leggett warns in *Class, Race and Labor:*

In Detroit, increases in class consciousness fail to be accompanied by decreases in inter-ethnic hostility.

In considering the impact of class consciousness on political choice in a modern industrial town, we have seen how class-conscious workers support a pro-labor candidate when the times, the candidate, the unions, and the party demand their vote.

However, because of inter-ethnic hostility, class-consciousness has presently a limited range of political consequences. The absence of bonds of solidarity among workmen of different racial and nationality groups prevents workmen, labor organizations, and reform groups from collaborating on a sustained basis, even when faced with common problems.[26]

Many pluralists minimize the values implicit in the ethnic "bonds of solidarity." Are such values *prima facie* less worthy than those implicit in "rational" politics? For "rational" politics also depends upon the authority of an educated class. Should "authoritarianism" be ascribed only to others? Thus Shostak:

> Working-class authoritarianism goes far to explain the rigid and intolerant approach many blue-collarites take to American political affairs.
>
> Unable to understand how politics works, and contemptuous of conciliation and compromise, working-class authoritarians seek to impose on society some sort of "fundamental truth" that will liberate America from its soft-headed illusions. . . . many blue-collarites are frightened today both by the vagueness of what is being allowed, and by the inadequacies they note in the central systems of family life, police justice, and the like. Many fear that the simple virtues are being threatened.[27]

Psychoanalysis of others has its hazards. Thus Shostak must employ without explanation at least one contradictory datum: "Harboring an old-world or ethnic suspicion of authority, blue-collarites hesitate to bring government into their lives and resent the successes that such action seems to bring to Negroes."

Some of these contradictions are best understood as an ethnic rebuke to the ideology of the American Left. Democracy is not actually in practice in this country in anything like its theoretical form. Democracy does not work in most other cultures or regions of the world, either. In his remarkable study of "participation and opposition," *Polyarchy*, Robert Dahl surveys the very few existing approximations of the democratic ideal in the world.[28] He analyzes seven sets of complex conditions required before a country can approximate that ideal. Democracy turns out to be so difficult to achieve and depends upon "such a maze of factors," as Michael Harrington suggests, "that the democrats of the advanced countries should give up their fantasies," at least so far as the Third World is concerned.[29] But in the United States as well, ethnic workingmen might wish to say, political democracy is not uppermost in their experience.

Have the descendants of immigrants from southern and eastern Europe experienced America as democratic? I do not mean to be defending a nondemocratic theory, nor to be falling into the characteristically Catholic vice of extolling authority at the expense of liberty. But not all that I have learned from a Catholic heritage about the structure of social and political reality has turned out to be mistaken; some parts of it form a realism more real than the conventional wisdom of Enlightenment and American thought.

Democracy is in actual practice and in a very wide range of matters extremely fatiguing, inefficient, and a vast nourisher of illusions. Most supposedly democratic forums breed, in my experience, far less wisdom than the theory of a free marketplace of ideas and options would have us believe. Let me cite committee meetings at universities; open discussions in which large numbers of persons of widely divergent points of view, values, and interests try to psyche each other out; and all negotiations in which factors of power and interest are not kept in mind with absolute clarity.

The fact is that interest groups and minorities of various sorts, and even individuals of various temperaments, dispositions, and strength of voice, are seldom if ever equals in the actual settings in which democratic procedures are invoked. Fundamental and inevitable inequalities are, in the concrete although not perhaps in abstract theory, always present. Every experienced administrator knows that his trump card in a meeting concerned with

democratic consensus is his own actual power to carry
out or to block alternative courses of action. Discussion
can *seem* to be about "the merits of the case," but in the
end "realism" usually prevails. A very great deal of purported democratic procedure is in fact *pro forma*. It is a
quasi-religious ritual of the most superficial and degrading
sort, like a Mass perfunctorily hurried through by a distracted congregation. Its role is vaguely to legitimate an
inexorable order of events.

There are times when such rituals "explode"—that is,
really reveal their manifest power and purpose—and it is
worth preserving the rituals against that day of grace. But
unless one understands the religious quality of democracy
for the man of the Enlightenment, one misses the quality
secular theorists are least likely to face within themselves.

Democracy is usually touted as a way of life for "the
common people." In fact, however, the democratic way
of life fulfills the interests and serves the power of the
educated. Not by accident do all studies of voting patterns
and democratic values show a vivid correlation between
privilege, especially educational privilege, and democratic
attitudes. The more educated people are, the more they
cherish enlightened values—it is almost a tautology. Thus
even intelligent articles on "Working-Class Authoritarianism," like that by Seymour M. Lipset, reflect a profound
class and religious bias.[30] The religion is that of enlightenment, the class is that of privilege and education. Those
not in such a class do not tend to be devotees of that religion; they are even, notoriously, somewhat "anti-intellec-
tual." They tend to be apathetic politically, as if politics
had little to offer them. (And what, realistically *does* it
offer them, in concrete fact?) Lipset writes:

> The gradual realization that extremist and intolerant
> movements in modern society are more likely to be
> based on the lower classes than on the middle and upper
> classes has posed a tragic dilemma for those intellec-
> tuals of the democratic left who once believed the pro-

letariat necessarily to be a force for liberty, racial equality, and social progress. The Socialist Italian novelist Ignazio Silone has asserted that "the myth of the liberating power of the proletariat has dissolved along with that other myth of progress."[31]

But everything depends on what is meant by "extremist" and "intolerant." "The poorer strata everywhere," Lipset goes on, "are more liberal or leftist on economic issues; they favor more welfare state measures, higher wages, graduated income taxes, support of trade-unions, and so forth. But when liberalism is defined in non-economic terms—as support of civil liberties, internationalism, etc. —the correlation is reversed. The more well-to-do are more liberal, the poorer are more intolerant . . ." Thus, the terms used by Lipset are clearly loaded. For why is it not open to persons of the poorer strata to assert that it is "extremist" and "radical" for privileged, educated persons to pursue their own interests and to solidify their own power by neglecting the fundamental economic needs of the poor and concerning themselves with luxuries like civil liberties and internationalism?

The basic interests of privileged, educated persons in a technological society lie on the side of superculture. A rationalized social order will function more efficiently if attitudes are universalized and if local pockets of tradition, "prejudice," and ignorance are made to give way to atomistic conceptions of self, society, and happiness. The pressures for civil rights are not simply moral; they are largely technological and economic. The industrialization of the South did more to bring about progress in civil rights than did Enlightenment preaching. For both production and consumption it is more efficient if all human units are treated according to a universal scale. It is easier for the highly mobile personnel of national corporations if their sensibilities are not assaulted by widely varying local practices. When it became industrially significant to standardize, arguments for differential treatment of whites and blacks had to fall back upon "mere myth." The cry "Never!" was but the obverse of a new inevitability. For new religions triumph through personal conversion only among the few, and through the secondary effects of a powerful new social system àmong the many: a religion being nothing but a sense of reality, a set of stories to live out with one's life, a brace of symbols by which to interpret one's experience.

The "invisible religion" which Thomas Luckmann[32] sees dominant today among enlightened and educated persons is invisible only because many understand enlightenment to be enlightenment "from" religion, from popes, church-going, clergy, rituals. Religion is understood as a superrogatory set of institutions of whose services one's sense of reality, one's chosen stories, and one's preferred symbols are no longer in need. Correspondingly, many who continue attending the manifest religious services in the churches often feel a certain redundancy rather than a sharp contradiction between their church religion and their invisible secular religion. For the invisible religion has gradually been assimilated by Jewish and Christian institutions in much the same way as—but possibly with less integrity than—these institutions once assimilated other great cultural religions in their long and ambivalent past.

Lipset's well-known article provides many insights into the sense of reality of this invisible religion. "The evidence from various American studies," he reports, "is also clear and consistent—the lower strata are the least tolerant." For enlightened persons, of course, "tolerant" is a highly charged moral word. It is a little like telling Irish clergymen that "Jewish intellectuals are not chaste," when one perhaps only wants to say that chastity does not rank high in the moral priorities of one group as compared to another with a different morality. For Lipset goes on to point out, generously, that the less liberal workers may be psychologically more healthy and "the more liberal members" may well be "the more neurotic." For in such a group, authoritarian attitudes—shall we rather say, respect for and cynicism regarding authority?—is normal and expected.

Moreover, "noneconomic liberalism" (by which Lipset regularly means tolerance, civil rights, and internationalism) "is not a simple matter of acquiring education and information; it is at least in part a basic attitude which is actively discouraged by the social situation of lower-status persons." That is, the sense of reality ("basic attitudes") of such persons does not include such "realities." Tolerance, civil rights and internationalism are not real to them, not part of their "faith" or "hope" about the world. The lower strata "are *isolated* from the activities, controversies, and organizations of democratic society." So Lipset cannot be talking about a *moral* fault. He is talking about a world of experience in which what for some persons are realities—"the sophisticated and complex view of the political structure which makes understandable and necessary the norms of tolerance"—do not have enough real existence for workers to make them feel the norms arising therefrom. Do people for whom God is not real feel the normative weight of his will?

The worker, Lipset goes on, lacks "economic and psychological security." Thus there is "a great deal of direct frustration and aggression in the day-to-day lives of numbers of the lower classes, both children and adults." Meanwhile, "acceptance of the norms of democracy requires a high level of sophistication and ego security." Which would seem to argue that democracy is not a realistic option for the working class. Their behavior in unions may indicate this: they are "not at all as concerned with dictatorial leadership as are middle-class critics." They value strong leadership, personal services, a minimum of theoretical discussion or intellectual debate (which frustrates educated, idealistic leadership); moreover, even when their own instincts tend to be in some defined ways intolerant, their innate respect for authority will commonly bring them to solidarity with their leaders even against their personal views. For—in their eyes—they themselves lack the education, the experience, and the brains to make tricky social and political decisions; their best, perhaps their only, hope lies in acting solidly behind good leaders. Is such an attitude too arrogant, or too timorous—or accurate and piercing and humbling in its truthfulness?

Richard Hoggart writes in *The Uses of Literacy*: "If we want to capture something of the essence of working-class life . . . we must say that it is the 'dense and concrete' life, a life whose main stress is on the intimate, the sensory, the detailed and the personal. This would no doubt be true of working-class groups anywhere in the world."[33] Such a description—in these latter days of meritocracy, rational control, bureaucracy, professional unreality, and "newspeak"—is not altogether damning. Even Lipset is moved, although not entirely unstrung:

> It may be argued, though I personally doubt it, that this capacity to establish personal relationships, to live in the present, may be more "healthy" (in a strictly medical, mental-health sense) than a middle-class concern with status distinctions, one's own personal impact on one's life situation, and a preoccupation with the uncertain future. But on the political level of consequences . . . this same action-oriented, nonintellectualistic aspect of working-class life seems to prevent the realities of long-term social and economic trends from entering working-class consciousness, simply because such reality can enter only through the medium of abstractions and generalizations.[34]

Here, of course, is precisely where those who want to "help" come to the service of the workers. The broad masses, Lenin saw, are "slumbering, apathetic, hidebound, inert, and dormant." Left to themselves, they would never develop socialist or class consciousness, and would remain on the level of economic day-to-day consciousness. An organized group of revolutionary intellectuals must bring them a broader vision. They require, that is, "outside agitators." Kurt Vonnegut's bicycle manufacturer from Indiana put the same point a little differently in explaining why he was moving his plant to a primitive island: "The people down there are poor enough and scared enough and ignorant enough to have some common sense."[35]

Lenin understood that the working class is concerned with today rather than tomorrow, dislikes complex theories and discordancies, is frustrated and hostile, and is prone to enthusiastic hope in sudden, simple causes. He wanted the Communist party to offer them an uncompromising and unified view of the world and an immediate program for drastic change. By contrast, democratic parties were in his eyes "vacillating, wavering, unstable."

Still, the very factors of immediacy and simplicity stressed by Lenin must normally work in a conservative rather than in an "extremist" or "radical" direction, as Lipset next points out. Workers tend to want something limited and concrete today, rather than something total and simple in the remote future. They do not trust politicians or promises. They are not secure enough to gamble what little they barely have for indulgence in utopian hopes. "The same underlying factors which predispose individuals toward support of extremist movements under certain conditions may result in total withdrawal from political activity and concern under other conditions." Economics is the worker's basic reality; politics is a luxury.

Why, then, the pejorative terms "authoritarianism," "extremist," "radical," "intolerant"? Why, above all, do objective and value-neutral social scientists allow themselves to use of others words they would not like applied to themselves? Working-class consciousness seems coherent, in some respects enviable, in some ways weak, but above all appropriate to the real conditions of working-class life. The interests of the working-class are not those of the educated and privileged class. That is not among the moral faults against which one should pick up stones.

4. *Insistent Pressure from Above*

Like an iron pipe on the back of the neck, ethnics feel
the authority of the educated. Insistently, they are made
to feel unenlightened, stupid, immoral, and backward. A
new and alienating cultural style is pressed upon them.
The schools undermine their families. Television beats
upon them. In their eyes, it is hard to distinguish engineers and advertisers of General Motors from sociologists
and literary critics—both seem to insist on the atomiz-
ing values of modernity.

The confusion, however, is not merely ethnic. Are the
sons and daughters of the affluent confident about the
state of freedom in America? Are liberal senators confident that more and bigger central government is a cure
for this nation's injustices? Morton Mintz argues in *America, Inc.*[36] that, in fact, American politics is in thrall to
special economic interests. Do even radical intellectuals
genuinely believe that Mayor Lindsay's "reform government" is morally and administratively superior to Mayor
Daley's "machine"? Democracy in America is undergoing
a siege of doubt.

Ethnic politics has some solutions to offer in our dilemma. Rather, ethnic politics makes possible a new perspective and a new starting place. It is useful, however, to
notice some of the deficiencies in the ideology of democracy from an ethnic standpoint. Some new approaches
may come into view.

First, the threat today is from homogenization, a coercive sameness, a dreary standardization. The melting-pot
ideology, Professor Janes suggests,[37] may have been a
rationale for deculturizing immigrants, depriving them of
their cultural values and strength, and thus reducing
their political and economic power. If one deprives people
of their affective bonds to family, culture, and value, then
one can reconstruct them afresh. While they are confused
and without identity, one can manipulate them more

freely, telling them what they *ought* to be. One takes their souls and gives them bread and circuses. For a while— until they awaken—they are grateful.

The persistence of ethnicity has for some time been treated by sociologists as dysfunctional, since it prevents the emergence of "rational" universal values. But this charge may be turned around: the emergence of "rational" universal values is dysfunctional since it detaches persons from the integration of personality that can be achieved only in historical symbolic communities. The "divisiveness" and free-floating "rage" so prominent in America in the 1960s is one result of the shattering impact of "forced nationalization" upon personality integration. People uncertain of their own identity are not wholly free. They are threatened not only by specific economic and social programs, but also at the very heart of their identity. The world is mediated to human persons through language and culture, that is, through ethnic belonging.

The function of ethnic belonging is to integrate a person's sense of reality, the stories that tell him how to live, the symbols that move him. These are the matrix in which his conscience receives instruction. By contrast, the American system of individualization and rationalization leaves all but a certain human type profoundly deprived —deprived of imaginative and symbolic thickness, unable to function in the nonconnected way demanded by the ethnic symbols of WASPS: individualism, competition, and merely rational interest. These inform Protestant, but not other ethnics', conscience. The superiority attributed to Protestant symbols is difficult to believe in today.

Thus American democracy operates as a shield for WASP hegemony, and to reinforce a WASP sense of reality, stories, and symbols. Name a social problem in America. A thousand voices will prescribe as a cure "more democracy." Such a cure seldom touches real economic or social anguish. For democracy is not a system for resolving real differences, only a procedure for neutralizing or displacing them.

When democracy is conceived as a procedure, all the moral power in it depends upon qualities developed in persons, families, and groups prior to the employment of the procedures. Democratic procedures cure nothing; teach nothing; inculcate nothing. They are nothing but mechanical procedures. They are strictly neutral. They are, in fact, neutralizing agents; at best, they prevent certain abuses. It simply is not true that the spreading use of democratic procedures—an increase in participatory democracy—will bring people dignity, or satisfaction, or moral pride, or political potency. The sources of such values are far deeper than the advent of some mechanical procedure. One can imagine democratic procedures being used to elect Adolf Hitler, to repeal the Bill of Rights, to affirm all the evil of which men are capable.

It is not even true that democratic procedures often bring out the best qualities in people. Discussions in open meetings are not often high points in the history of human intelligence. Few spectacles are more dreary than democratic exercises in "group dynamics." Temperamental quirks, gifts of manner or style, the gaffes of one's opponents, threats, bullying, cajoling, playing to the gallery, etc., are the roads taken toward the "will of the majority." The conduct of city councils, state legislators, and even the Congress of the United States is often less comforting. Persons of forensic skills deserve our gratitude, for they get the world's democratic business done; but so do buyers and sellers.

Again, lower-status persons need contact with persons; they don't trust structures. Reform government is impersonal in conception and in execution. Elect a reformist mayor, and you elect six new agencies. To poorer people, the great value of "the machine" is that it is not a machine. It is not at all like a reformist bureaucracy, which is patently mechanical, abstract, a puzzling maze of rules and laws and fine print. The ethnic machines—Irish, Italian, Polish, Jewish, Lithuanian, etc.—are not impersonal but personal. Your street light is out? You call the

precinct captain or the alderman. The garbage men are
banging up your cans? The telephone. You get results the
same day. You feel significant. You *have* "participatory
democracy." Participatory democracy, ethnic style, is not
participation in making *rules;* it is participation in a network of people who exchange *services.* As George W.
Plunkitt, a ward politician in the early 1900s, once put
it:

> There's only one way to hold a district: you must study
> human nature and act accordin'. . . . To learn real
> human nature you have to go among the people, see
> them and be seen. I know every man, woman, and child
> in the Fifteenth District, except them that's been born
> this summer—and I know some of them, too. I know
> what they like and what they don't like, what they are
> strong at and what they are weak in, and I reach them
> by approachin' at the right side.
>
> For instance, here's how I gather in the young men.
> . . . there's the feller that likes rowin' on the river, the
> young feller that makes a name as a waltzer on his
> block, the young feller that's handy with his dukes—I
> rope them all in by givin' them opportunities to show
> themselves off. I don't trouble them with political argu-
> ments. I just study human nature and act accordin'.
>
> But you may say this game won't work with the high-
> toned fellers, the fellers that go through college and
> then join the Citizens' Union. Of course it wouldn't
> work. I have a special treatment for them. I ain't like
> the patent medicine man that gives the same medicine
> for all diseases. The Citizens' Union kind of a young
> man! I love him! He's the daintiest morsel of the lot,
> and he don't often escape me . . .
>
> Among other things I watch the City Record to see
> when there's Civil Service examinations for good
> things, then I take my young Cit in hand, tell him all
> about the good thing and get him worked up till he
> goes and takes an examination . . .
>
> What tells in holdin' your grip on your district is to

go right down among the poor families and help them in the different ways they need help . . . It's philanthropy, but it's politics, too—mighty good politics.[38]

This ethnic insight is not without substance. The actual workings of democracy in America, even in its most reformist circles, even in the highest bureaucracy, necessarily have more to do with "who you know, not what you know." To get any business through Washington today, one simply must know the appropriate persons. Human beings are so constructed that they do trust persons more than regulations. The best recommendations a bureaucrat gets come not from cold pieces of paper in a file but from people whose judgment he respects. People who "get things done" know lots of people, have multiple "connections," know "who to call," and have the political credits to risk making the call. Reformist politics protects an elite from the people. *Inside* the club, it's not what you know but who you know. *Outside*, it's not rule by persons but by law: cold and impenetrable law.

To the immigrant first arrived in America, "rule by law" is a noble phrase. It has a transcendent ring. One will be protected from arbitrary leadership. It turns out, of course, the leadership is protected from people. "Rule by law" essentially is rule by laws that protect the interests of elites. In town after town, industry after industry, national scandal by national scandal, ethnics learn that if the law is to protect *their* interests, they have to organize —and around people they know, people who understand.

A party "boss," a big-city mayor, a tough and "authoritarian" football coach, is not likely to be an intellectual, a saint, a Goethe, a Socrates, or a Jesus; but he is not *ipso facto* an enemy of mankind. On the scales of humanism, authority can weigh as much as liberty. Both are values indispensable to getting bellies fed, morale sustained, cooperation assured, dignity and justice defended, bold social choices made.

Established power and money comprise a hugely formidable foe. What the workingman has is solidarity. It is not so important to the ethnic American that he "participate" in every decision that affects his life. It is far more important that those decisions be intelligent and in his true interest.

His ethnic solidarity, meanwhile, can best be mobilized around sharp and immediate irritants: a falling real income, taxes, insurance rates, medical costs, unemployment, the defense of homes and neighborhoods. A reconstruction of the relation between home and work might not be far from his dreams. An argument about the enormous economic powers that take advantage of him will touch his instinct—but he is realistic, and does not believe in utopias.

How to break the thralldom of economic power we have hardly begun to imagine. That is the large task of the future. It cannot be forgotten that the liberal intellectual supplied the basic conceptions on which the hegemony of economic power has been constructed. "Knowledge is power," Francis Bacon said, launching the Western bias on a technological course. Not reality, not wisdom, not reconciliation, not compassion, not brotherhood or peace or justice. Power.

A philosopher friend of mine, agnostic and skeptical, tells a touching story. For years, he has begun his courses by showing kids how everything is relative, how skepticism is in order, how they ought to be suspicious. Then he would go on to show the value of precision, clarity, tests for meaning and verification, and the rest. In 1971 students loved the early sessions. When he tried to move on to standards of precision, meaning, truth, they absolutely refused to follow. "It's all relative," they shrugged. They liked it loose.

"Get with it!" "Abandon inhibition!" "Acquire power!" "Do it!" These are the fundamental messages emanating from our educated classes. They have for generations been breaking down any cultural residue that stood in the path of "modernization," that is to say, the hegemony of economic power. They have done so in the name of liberty, equality, and fraternity. Their latent message speaks so loudly one can no longer hear, or hearing understand, the sacred names invoked.

PART III

The New
Ethnic Politics

... searches for a new way to define what it means
to be an American. We embrace the American dream
as culturally pluralistic—a nation having a unity
of spirit and ideal, but a diversity of origin and
expression, a nation not of atomic individuals, but of
dynamic, interacting groups, each of which brings
forth its best to help build a just and equitable
society, free of isolation, segregation, and racism.
We believe that people who are secure in their past
and joyful in their present cannot but be hopeful in
their future. We call this the "new ethnicity."

—The Orchard Lake Center for Polish
Studies and Culture

CHAPTER NINE

Political Dreams for Every Finger of My Hand

PRAGMATISM HAS MANY VIRTUES. It distinguishes dreams from practical proposals. Of both programs and dreams we have had a surfeit in the last ten years. A new politics is announced as often as a new detergent.

Still we are a people of a dream. Politics begins in dream and ends in bureaucrats. Is it the dream that vivifies, execution that corrupts? Embodiment makes real, "dirty hands" are not to be despised, even the barque of Peter has a boiler room. Human life requires dirty work.

Southern and eastern Europeans are not dismayed by dirty work. Their approach to morality is not by way of moralizing, but by way of dream. America taught them how to dream. Many tears were in grandparents' eyes— perhaps more at the cost than at the dream, at the past than at the future—when they swore their oath and were at last counted citizens.

So I am going to allow myself to dream. It is a profession our nation honors uncommonly.

I. *The Dream of Revised Rewards*

A just redistribution of the world's resources will necessarily begin with graduates of prestigious schools: with lawyers, doctors, newscasters, full and associate professors, journalists, authors of best sellers, advertising executives, those on the payrolls of foundations, experts in consulting firms. Expense accounts are outlawed. No business done over lunch or martinis will be favored by tax deductions; refreshment itself (denied to so many fellow citizens) is reward enough. The monies saved shall serve to lower prices, reduce taxes, increase welfare payments to the disadvantaged. Political activists who write books which sell over twenty thousand copies will, by law, yield all further revenues to the families of policemen injured or killed while keeping them alive.

An income law shall be established in America, limiting a journalist's salary to that of an autoworker, a doctor's to a plumber's (fair enough?), a corporation president's to a steamfitter's, Dick Cavett's to a humble Bunny's. If the Left stands for a redistribution of the world's resources, authenticity demands beginning with the salaries paid many on the Left. Activist college students shall be obliged to pay for their college education by spending two years on police forces in high-crime areas; leaders of the YAF shall be obliged to have their skin dyed black and to shine shoes in airports.

Integration laws are passed. Children of professors shall be bussed to study with the children of hard hats. Children of intellectuals shall be admitted only to colleges of agriculture in prairie states. Schools where riots, disorders, or regular personal assaults occur shall be attended mainly by liberated girls.

Workers' sabbaticals are instituted, according to which once every seven years all Americans change jobs for a year. Writers shall work in mines, underground. The TV news shall be in the hands of a steelworker and a window-washer from the Bronx. Taxi drivers shall teach sixth and seventh grade, while football coaches shall become short-order cooks and teach philosophy classes at night schools. Politicians shall polish mirrors or perhaps (to stay in touch) deliver mail. The Teamsters Union shall manage the universities. Judges shall be jailbirds, and ex-cons shall replace the hostesses in cocktail lounges, who shall plan the charity balls to raise money for wealthy wives, who shall be picking lettuce with ex-hairdressers.

Garry Wills caught the essential idea when he wrote: "American does not honor the quiet work that achieves social interdependence and stability. There is, in our legends, no heroism of the office clerk, no stable industrial 'peasantry' of the men who actually make the system *work*. There is no pride in being an employee . . . There has been no boasting about our social workers . . . We have no pride in our growing interdependence, in the fact that our system can serve others, that we are able to give those in need 'something for nothing.' "[1] There is little of the casual acceptance of men by men in America, little joy in how, like brothers, we are caught in a common fate and in common tasks, little of the open and frank recognition of how much each of us depends upon favors, contacts, and connections—little, in a word, of the sense of charity.

This is not a Catholic country, stressing the common hard lot of all, and the common grace. (I am not praising feudalism, the Inquisition, monarchies, or clergy.) It is a Protestant country, stressing how each man must earn his own way, restrain himself, master himself, regulate himself: millions of squirrels shut up in millions of cages of their own fashioning. And it is a Freudian country, stressing how each man must liberate himself, explore himself, express himself: millions of squirrels biting their way out of the millions of cages constructed inside them (so they imagine) by society.

2. *The Dream of Two Thousand Cities*

The overwhelming fact of the last thirty years in American life has been massive migration from agricultural areas to urban areas, first to the inner and lately to the outer city. This migration did not merely happen. Three government policies propelled it.

First, the agricultural policies of the United States support the huge, heavily industrialized farmer, and drive the small farmer off the land. The number of farms in the United States shrank from over six million in 1940 to about three million in 1967. Productivity on American farms increased at astonishing rates; during the post-World War II period, farm output per man-hour went up twice as fast as nonfarm output; by 11.3 percent in 1964–65, for example.[2] Were these gains in productivity socially useful? Is "productivity" some magic and sacred standard which must be venerated? Was it good for people to be driven off the land? Did a better life await them elsewhere? I dream of *more* people on the land, of policies that make life on farms socially and economically attractive.

Second, the highway building of federal and state governments made suburban life possible, and helped to build up the huge, ugly sprawl around our cities.

Third, the welfare policies of federal and state governments drove the poor, especially the black poor of the South, in massive waves toward cities were welfare payments were more liberal. The black population of the cities increased by twenty percent in five years (1960–1965).[3]

The crises in our cities are a direct effect of government policies. Cannot those same policies be reversed?

"Modernization" is our project. Mass production, mass markets, centralized transport—everything favors dense metropolitan areas. Is "modernization" worth it? The recent history of huge cities—from New York to Rio to Saigon—is not dazzling.

Midway through the nineteenth century, large American cities were already the dumping grounds of those who could not make it in the towns or rural areas. Defeated, often unskilled and unprepared for city life, they came and found others like themselves.[4] Work of one sort or another was usually available. If not, anonymity cloaked their efforts to live as best they could. Welfare, at last, came to rescue millions from disaster—and, not least, to provide further consumer markets.

Fewer and fewer people enjoy living in modern cities. Fewer claim to *want* to live there. Eighty percent say they would escape if they could.[5] The flight to outer cities is in tide. The children of many who are loyal to the city seek communes in Vermont, Colorado, Wyoming.

Intellectuals and artists claim to love the excitement, stimulation, and variety of cities. The price of human suffering in New York seems a little high for the stimulation of so few. Especially since whole regions of the Bronx, Queens, Staten Island, Brooklyn, and Manhattan seldom *see* an intellectual. Wouldn't a small chunk of Brooklyn, the Village and the West Side suffice? Florence at the height of its creative period was a city of one hundred thousand souls. Athens under Pericles numbered forty thousand.[6]

What if there were laws making the growth of cities beyond one hundred thousand persons too unattractive to be feasible? Pollution, crime, loneliness, despair, hunger, taxes, and poor services, for example, might be imposed. Also, the costs of maintaining smaller cities would be lowered significantly if autos were banned within their limits.

If there were more cities, each limited in size, one could encourage one or two cities entirely black, real Chinatowns, a set of thorough "little Italys," three or four Warsaws, a Berlin or two. Most of the new cities would, of course, be integrated. At least one, however, could consist of the entire WASP establishment in all its purity. (It would be the cleanest city of the land.) There could be cities of evangelism, and cities of sin, gambling cities, and cities dry as Oklahoma in a drought. Divide two hundred million people by one hundred thousand and one imagines two thousand glittering pearls—livable, various, and nice to visit.

There must be policies that would encourage the migra-

tion of people out of the present houses of death. Couldn't
we establish as our goal for the next two hundred years
the building of new cities on a human scale?

The drive from Manhattan toward Binghamton con-
stricts the heart in terror: from poverty, compression,
crime, pollution, across miles and miles of green valleys
and wooded hills. Are human beings so lacking in intelligence that they would rather die like rats in uninhabitable
corners of a maze than find their way to open spaces?
Surely, human beings can imagine and contrive better
ways of life than the modern imagination has arrived at.
The centralization implicit in the pursuit of rational efficiency is monstrous.

I dream sometimes that for the next thousand years life
will slow down. This century will be regarded as a carnival, signifying nothing. People will grow some of their
own vegetables and fruits in their own gardens. Relatives
and neighbors will receive more of their attention, compassion, and mutual risk. Men and women will rejoice in
the arts of cookery and conversation. Childrearing will
involve more imagination, affectivity, and (in both parents) childlikeness. Tourism will be replaced by travel.
The pursuit of excitement will yield to quiet awareness.
The nuances of nature, people, and communities will be
noticed.

We need a politics of smallness. Think small. It is a
time for small states and quiet ways.

Our old dreams of productivity, industrialization, and
progress seem as sad as isinglass. Yet it is the success of
those dreams that makes possible our new ones. You do
not have to be a Luddite to imagine an economic order
based upon dispersed technology. Light industries—tex-
tiles, mobile homes, makers of transistors and other elec-
tronic parts—are already seeking out plant sites in small-
town, relatively rural America. Why not aim still further
out across the countryside, encouraging the growth of
towns near to fields and lakes and forests? New and well-
constructed systems of transport will make problems of

proximity to markets relatively minor. Every government policy that favors the shrinkage of large cities and the building of smaller ones, through tax incentives and assistance in construction, will be brought into play. The demographic policy of the government will encourage a return to the countryside.

The more done to decentralize industry; to bring it near the home; to weave work more naturally into the rhythms of the home; to protect the living networks of family, relatives, and friends; the more humane is the economic order. Modern communications make possible the best of both worlds: dispersion across the countryside and close ties between scattered communities. The worker who can camp, fish, own a boat, grow some of his own vegetables, have space for his children, is wealthier by far than a worker in a tacky suburb of a sprawling "outer city."

What I am recommending is not a dream, merely. The question keeps pounding in my brain: why can't welfare incentives, matched with tax incentives to light industry, attract three or four million of the most hard-pressed residents of New York City, white and black, out into the empty countryside of New York State, northern Pennsylvania, Vermont, the Middle West? Most of them have not been city people for longer than a generation. Life cannot be more desperate for many than where they now throng, seeking service jobs and welfare. It seems insane not to provide places where various ethnic and cultural groups can create a more congenial life for themselves, pluralistically or separately, with economic stability. Is it wholly impractical to try to imagine a way to attract even one million of the poor from New York to places where air is clean and there are green fields and hills, jobs and dignity? I am not sanguine about changing our present habits suddenly. Surely, Iowa would welcome three or four hundred thousand new workers and consumers. Surely, the migration toward cities is not a natural and irreversible law, against which we must fall down in adoration.

How can we slow down modern life so as to bring it

once again into human scale? Useless to pretend we are
gods, reaching beyond our abilities;—better to be what we
are. Labor must lead if management is mesmerized by
rational, inhuman schemes of efficiency and bigness.
Modern rationality has disclosed sufficient irrationality.
Enough.

3. *The Dream of New Work*

In his Labor Day address, 1971, President Nixon urged
American workers back to four qualities of soul: "the
competitive spirit," the "work ethic," "greater productivity," and "sacrifice." His only honest prescription was the
last.

As the president spoke, 6.1 percent of American workers had no work at all. On most jobs there is no one with
whom, and nothing for whom, to "compete," except the
privilege of having a job. Most jobs for working men are
dead ends so far as advancement is concerned. Working
conditions make "productivity" less and less the responsibility of workers. Experts and engineers design new machines for that. Craftsmanship and responsibility decline
all the time. The president desires incompatible universes:
the universe of small-town merchants with competitive
Protestant sweat in their armpits, and the universe of
highly bureaucratized technology, in which workers are
merely units.

The more machines take over, the lower the quality of
performance. In a true, exact sense, quality cannot co-
exist with standardization. Quality depends upon an individual's response to the individual character of materials;
quality is necessarily variable and fluctuating. Quality is
the mark of an individual's own spirit on genuine, undisguised materials. It has "character." When "quality controls" are imposed, one guarantees only that the same,
standardized product does not fall below a certain measure. No one automobile, for example, shows that the
craftsmanship of one worker is better than another's.

"Productivity" under a system of mass production eliminates the worker as much as possible.

In a fit of inefficiency, the Creator ignored standardization. He made all persons and bits of material unique. It takes heroic persistence to squeeze the unstandardization out of things. It takes imagination to make all canned orange juice taste the same, when every fresh orange is so different.

"Productivity" is an archaic fantasy. Productivity means a higher output of goods and services per laborer. The president makes it sound very simple.

As the American economy moves toward meeting the new needs of the American worker, what should it look for in return? The answer can be summed up in a single, often-misunderstood word: productivity. That word, productivity, puzzles and sometimes frightens people. It sound like the old "speedup" or some new efficiency system that drives people harder.

Productivity really means getting more out of your work.

When you have the latest technology to help you do your job, it means you can do more with the same effort. That's why we say investment in modern equipment will increase productivity.

When you have the training you need to improve your skills, you can do more. That's why we say job training will improve productivity. When you are organized to do away with red tape and duplicated effort, you can do more. That's why we say better management techniques will increase productivity. And when you have your heart in what you're doing, when it gives you respect and pride as well as a good wage—you naturally do more. That's why we say job satisfaction is a key to productivity. Those are the four elements of productivity; investment in new technology, job training, good management and high employee motivation. Taken together, they raise the amount each worker actually produces.[7]

The president didn't add a fifth fact about productivity. The gap between the United States and the vast majority of people on this planet spreads wider daily. Already forty percent of the earth's irreplaceable resources are consumed by Americans, who are six percent of the earth's people. And fifteen percent of our own people consume fifty percent of all our goods. That is, one percent of the earth's people consume twenty percent of the earth's irreplaceable goods. In return, fifty percent of the world's pollution is caused by America.

Many hidden costs—selfishness, pollution, envy, international conflict, and alienation—are lurking in the word "productivity." Productivity means thinking of the earth as a planet to be conquered and despoiled. It does not mean thinking of this planet as a web of life to be participated in, a home in which to live at peace, a park in which to play, fields and sky in which to let one's spirit roam.

If a man believes that "productivity" is good for the soul of the competitive individual, he at least ought also to ask how good it is for the other ninety-four percent of the world's people. As American goods become more expensive, they cannot be consumed by the hordes of the world's poor. The circle of humans on this planet who can consume them becomes proportionally smaller every year. Economic vision cannot rest on productivity alone.

I dream, when I am weak, that the orgies of consumption we have assumed to be "normal" will one day quiet down.

What we in America today call normal may soon resemble, looking backward, a brief "golden age," like the reign of the Sun King just before the whining of the guillotines.

Our immediate problem, however, is the anger, low morale, and alienation of our workingman. Mr. Nixon claims a "silent majority," but when he describes its values he seems to be speaking of that minority of Americans that is WASP and moral in its attitudes. Anyone who spends time with ethnic workers soon realizes how angry workers are at "the system"—although not the same "system" perceived by radical students. "Some blue-collar workers are at least as critical of the factory as students of the multiversity," writes Herbert J. Gans:

> While they have not often resorted to media-covered demonstrations and confrontations, they have probably been more effective in disrupting the assembly line than students the university, through high rates of absenteeism and turnover, wild-cat strikes, deliberately shoddy workmanship and occasional acts of sabotage.
>
> From the limited journalistic and sociological research so far available, it would appear that a yet unknown number of blue-collar workers, particularly on the assembly line, complain, like the students, that their work is inauthentic and their workplace, dehumanizing. They do not use these terms, of course, but they find the work boring; they have no control over the job; they must obey arbitrary decisions by their foremen and they cannot take time off for personal business or even a phone call. In short, they are veritable prisoners of the assembly line and the people who run it.[8]

Electricians, truck drivers, and construction crews are wearing longer sideburns. Long hair bunches out from under football helmets. Tolerance for the individuality of others is growing. Young workers by and large ignore the views of older workers. For many, jobs are not selected with much forethought or commitment. "I was looking for a job and found this one." Turnover is extremely high. The aim is to "make a little bread and split." Work a month, take off a month.

It is quite likely that over the next decade younger workers will be seizing leadership in the unions. They are likely to want a greater range of options on work hours, free time, job procedures, job conditions. Mass production is liable to grow expensive. It will surely come under intense criticism for the boredom it induces, the traffic

problems it creates for those getting to work, the noise in
the plant, the oil on the floor, the fumes, the bureaucratic
attitudes of managers and old-line union leaders, the differential in salaries between management and labor.

Older workers, whom cultural habits and experiences in
the Depression have taught to be docile and glad for
what they get, are themselves not unsympathetic to the
possibilities of a new militance. Many feel they have been
pushed around enough, from the public on the one side,
from management on the other. The rise of black consciousness in the industrial unions is giving impetus to a
rise in ethnic consciousness. A coalition based on divergent
cultural consciousness and mutual real interests has double the strength of the old union solidarity. An Italian
proud of being Italian, a Pole proud of being Polish, and
a Black proud of being Black are three times stronger
than just three more bodies in a union asking higher
wages. Management is forced to discern the distinct
accents, style, and needs of each. It is forced to regard
them as living participants in distinct cultures, rather than
as units.

May we dream that work should be imagined as part
of the tissue, network, and organism of family and
growth? If there must be large factories, perhaps schools
should be built alongside. Fathers could take their children
with them in the morning. Lunch hours would sometimes
be spent together. Industrial establishments would be required to put a certain percentage of their income into
enhancing the total environment of family and leisure.
What salary is commensurate with the purchase of a man's
youth?

Industry is not outside the texture of society. What economic institutions take as real *becomes* real. They mold
our sense of reality. They must therefore be most scrupulously prevented from making us into what we do not
wish to be.

A dream: that industry conceive itself as subject to
children and other living things.

The formation of workers' caucuses to devise ways of humanizing their work, and weaving their work more humanely into their family life and home life, will turn the attention of the labor unions away from merely economic questions to the questions of the worker's whole way of life. Why should a man sell eight hours of his energy, five days a week, forty-nine weeks a year—especially if it tears him away from his neighbors, his family, his friends, his own interests and craftsmanship? Some people are no doubt glad to sell their energies, to do their work, get it over with, and then to resume the real business of living.

But humans are not atoms, detachable from their family and friends, able to live in foreign environments like fish out of water, eight hours a day. Why must they pull up the live ends of the tendrils which tie them to others? As much as possible, work should be tied to the networks of family and neighborhood. One should not break living roots every day.

Crafts and skills, moreover, are dying of starvation in America: bronze-casting, masonry, carpentry, woodwork, stonecutting, furniture-making, weaving, leatherwork, tailoring, glassblowing, pottery. . . . The trained fingertips of a sheet-metal worker go unappreciated. The praises of the daily arts are nowhere sung. Cynicism marks the laborer's life. *That* is the radical defect of our technology, constructed as it is upon the ideology of power, objectivity, efficiency, and production.

Technology is, after all, an art. Arts should be free and open to every human being. What our experts (and ideologies) have done is to deprive the workingman of art. To confine him to crowded and noisy homes, to polluted sections of the cities, to poor and dispirited educational systems, to a horizonless income peak, to a constant stream of silent contempt—all this was bad enough. But to take from him, as well, pride in the arts of his own hands was to strip his spirit raw. When work becomes "a job," violence accumulates beneath the surface of the skin.

The immigrant did not work because some Puritan

demon goaded him, as it drives Nixon, to compete and to dominate. He worked because it is good, human, and dutiful to work. He took pride in hard work. A nativist miner long ago described his immigrant co-workers in Pennsylvania:

> I'll tell you what I mean by hard work, Buddy. When an American shovels coal and has to take a piss, he quits for a while. When a foreigner is shoveling coal and has to take a piss, he pisses down his leg and goes right on shoveling coal. That's what I mean by workin' hard. Now these foreigners are really bulls, they work like dogs.[9]

The cynicism involved in Americanization has destroyed such European habits. It has chilled the early American desire, nourished by desperate poverty, to work oneself out of misery and, at last, to death.

A cousin of mine describes a late-afternoon snowstorm on Virginia Avenue in Johnstown. He was a skinny ten. An early December warmth was in the heavy air. He heard footsteps coming up the path below a ridge of the hill. He packed a snowball and laughed as he let fly. The head of an old miner, covered with coal dust, appeared above the ridge. The man was at the end of a hard walk from the mine in Coopersdale four miles away, where he had hiked to work before dawn. For ten hours, arthritic, he had been bent over, digging on his knees. . . . The iceball hit the old man in the face. His face wore a frightening look of despair as he fell backwards in the snow. . . . Panicky, my skinny-legged cousin ran for home.

The sons of that miner, and his grandsons, do not believe in work as he had to believe in it. They do not believe in America as he believed in it. Perhaps, while Death approaches them as it did him, they are not certain they are happier than he was. Those who climbed out of the pit may have been the generation of a golden age from which the rest has been decline.

4. *The Dream of the Inevitable Coalition*

"I have a dream," Martin Luther King, Jr., intoned. "I have a dream."

What is the correlative ethnic dream?

It is based on self-interest; and on the solidarity of underdogs. It is a dream of the one inevitable, fundamental, indispensable coalition: blacks and ethnic whites, shoulder-to-shoulder. It is a dream of frank and open talk about the needs of each. Above all, honesty.

The first truth is that the hour is late. It is almost as if polarization were deliberate, as if the Left intended to condemn one social group and glorify another, assist one and penalize another, as if America had to choose between the two: black niggers, white niggers.

The degree of hatred and bitterness is sometimes breathtaking. The police officers storming Attica reportedly shouted "Nigger!" and "That's where black power gets you!" as they fired in the throng. The relative lack of education among many ethnics, their fierce sense of neighborhood and territory, their resentment of outsiders of *any* other group (Poles, for example, of Irish), their sense of oppression at the hands of the media, their deep feelings of inferiority, not infrequently erupt in hatred. The world saw the faces of Cicero, Illinois. Twisted faces, even in the young.

Nevertheless, among political emotions, hatred is not the most destructive. It is, at least, a direct and visible emotion, and its sources can be sought. It often springs from frustration and despair, from the conviction that no one understands. It arises when one faces the wall, when there seems nowhere to go, when death is preferable to escape. Blacks know hatred. It is an emotion they can understand and deal with. Hatred leads to the edge of murder. To avoid mutual bloodshed, there is nothing left except to face one another and to deal. Genuine hatred as a political phenomenon (when it appears) is easier to make constructive than feigned compassion, condescension, or morality.

Moreover, hatred is far deeper than economics. It issues from a swirling vortex of images, symbols, psychic agonies. For that reason, the new ethnicity is the nation's best hope for confronting racial hatred. A Pole who knows he is a Pole, who is proud to be a Pole, who knows the social costs and possibilities of being a Polish worker in America, who knows where he stands in power, status, and integrity—such a Pole can face a black militant eye-to-eye. A Pole uncertain whether he is American or Polish, WASP or racist, worthy or despicable, feels emotions too confused for compromise, emotions most easily discharged as hate. For generations he blunted, modulated, tamed *his* identity; now a black in Afro and dashiki calls him "Pig!" It hurts too much if he thinks it might be true. Tom Wicker may call such men "insensitive,"[10] but they no doubt perceive themselves as men willing to settle challenges with fists or guns or any force required. They perceive themselves as men. (Why were Wicker and others so moved when black prisoners cried out that they would live, or if necessary die, as men? Ethnics and blacks are alike in that.)

Honesty is almost wholly absent in discussions of race. Paroxysms of guilt help neither white nor black. I sometimes dream that no one will use the word "racist" for fifty years. At present, it is full of innuendo, intended to paralyze through guilt, contributing nothing to intelligence or strategy.

As we have seen, ethnic workers have legitimate reasons for economic, social, and cultural anxiety about the black revolution. It is not "racist" to have such anxieties. The ethnic will not say "nigger" and the black will not say "pig," when the two decide that they are not each other's enemy—and when the Left decides that in any humane political strategy both white and black must be helped together. The *enemy* is educated, wealthy, powerful—and sometimes wears liberal, sometimes radical, sometimes conservative, disguise. The enemy is concentrated power. Lower-class ethnics and blacks, who lack that power, are allies.

Ethnic Americans agree they would not like to be black in America. If they are angry, it is as much at the Left as at blacks. They don't begrudge the blacks' gains; but they smell something very *unfair*. On television, blacks are wealthier and smoother than the ones workers meet every day. "Propaganda, lies!" they think.

The theories which liberals have about ethnic emotions —sexual envy, resentment, the need for a class lower than they, irrational fear—remain to be tested by in-depth interviews. The intellectual theories are self-serving. They justify the intellectuals' picture of the world. They are accepted with very little evidence. And those who—like Robert Coles[11] and the study group of the Cambridge Institute—are trying to be as thorough in their understanding of ethnics as of any other group, report being surprised by how low a salience the strictly racial issue has in ethnic conscience. Economic and cultural conflicts with blacks rank far higher in intensity.

The source of strictly *racial* prejudice lies far more within Nordic consciousness than in southern or eastern European consciousness. The latter have their own hostilities; strictly racial feelings do not have the same psychic symbolism for them. Ethnic Americans are less prejudiced against blacks than nativist Americans. Whitney Young's Urban League released a Harris survey in 1970 which showed that "native Anglo-Saxon Protestants are more likely to be hostile to blacks than Americans of Irish, Italian or Polish descent." The study, Young told a press conference "suggests that some Americans may be projecting their own prejudices to minorities of recent origin." Young said he was "somewhat surprised by its findings since he had been led to believe that the so-called 'ethnics' provided the mainspring of white backlash."[12]

Twenty-two percent of Anglo-Saxon Americans favored

racially separate schools, compared with six percent of
the Irish, five percent of the Italians and sixteen percent of
the Poles.

Forty-two percent of the WASPS disapproved of the
1954 Supreme Court decision: an astonishing percentage.
Thirty-one percent of the Irish and Italians opposed;
thirty-six percent of the Poles.

Young attributed the figures to the fact that close to
half of all households of Irish, Polish, or Italian origin are
composed of manual workers, and thus identify with the
problems of lower-income minority workers.

Still, the moral dilemmas posed for ethnic Americans
by racial issues are acute; they need guidance and help.
Above all, they need honesty. Who today speaks honestly
about racial relations?

When blacks move into an ethnic neighborhood, far
more than a morality play is being acted out. It is quite
likely (as we have seen) that real-estate speculators are
already at work and that city services are already in
decline. It is also likely that hotheads will vent their hostilities, that friends and neighbors will debate whether to
try integration or to get out while their small property
investment is still good. What guarantee is there that the
next few years will not be marked by demonstrations,
large or small? That the neighborhood reputation will not
suffer from violently partisan conflicts? That politicians—
including liberal politicians—will not make the fate of the
neighborhood a political issue? For people who desire
stability, such terrors have a basis in reality.

Is it true, for example, that three centuries of injustice
have done battering damage to the ego of blacks, have
deeply hurt black families, have stirred deep antiwhite
hatreds? Is it true that an insufficient diet has hurt the
black child's health and intelligence? Is it true that blacks
are so angry—as pictures show on TV—that they are
ready to explode, to loot, to burn? These are the messages
which black militants, liberal intellectuals, and media men
moralistically convey on television. And if such men are to

be believed, then ought one to risk one's little children in schools to which large numbers of blacks come? Liberals cannot have it both ways: "Blacks are a badly damaged and angry people" and "Bring them happily into your neighborhood." Ethnics cannot have it both ways: "We have nothing against them, but even so . . ." Robert Coles reports the conversation of a not untypical Pole:

> He insists that "there have to be all kinds." America stands for that, its historical willingness to receive hard-pressed people, offer them sanctuary, and after a brief time grant them the political rights that go with citizenship. He doesn't want any of that changed; America would no longer be America. But even so, but even so; he keeps on adding those three words. He keeps on zigzagging. He keeps on struggling with the mixed feelings he has and he needs no visitor to point out that such is the case, that he has shifts of opinions, that he contradicts himself, goes here and there (and sometimes it seems) everywhere as he talks. In fact he is quite concerned with position. ". . . I'd be more consistent, like they want, if the world would let me be."[13]

Neither politicians nor the intellectuals offer much help to such persons: not honesty, not clarification, not assistance, not guarantees—only moralizing. Persons most in need of help are largely abandoned to their own resources.[14]

White leadership and black leadership have made eight serious strategic and tactical mistakes. It may help to sort them out.

First, they have failed to study the particular values, ways of perceiving, and moral sensibilities of ethnic cultures. Southern and eastern European cultures start with the assumption that life is cruel; survival is the first morality. Southern and eastern Europeans have strong family ideals about helping others who are in need. But they hate to ask favors; often they refuse help from government welfare programs. They believe in people banding together to help one another, chiefly in the family, but also in the social unit: the burial society, the boarding-house, the miners' union, the neighborhood. The Slavic miners in northern Pennsylvania amazed the nativist Americans because they were not individualists. They believed in solidarity. They did not admire *laissez faire*, and they made strikes succeed where strikes had not succeeded before. They did not hesitate to enforce solidarity on the reluctant, or to meet the force of sheriff's posse and militia with violent counterforce. Even the Slavic women joined in the fighting, and "Big Mary Septek" led vivid assaults upon reluctant non-Slavic strikers.[15]

Second, black and white activists do not recognize precedents in the history of ethnic resistance to WASP power. Five hundred Irishmen in northeastern Pennsylvania halted a troop train bearing draftees off to the Civil War and urged those who wanted to resist to join them. One Irishman insulted the flag at a Fourth of July ceremony in 1862, and when he was upbraided by a mine foreman, several of his cohorts beat the latter so badly that he died. The Molly Maguires lost twenty men to hangings by officials, and many others to gunshot, club, and jail in what they regarded as a legitimate "war" against nativist America.[16] In the Irish riot of 1863, between twelve hundred and two thousand New Yorkers (mostly Irish) died. Would that be called "genocide" if it happened today?

The Slavs succeeded the Molly Maguires as the organizers of northern Pennsylvania miners during 1880–1900. The sagas of violence and counterviolence, of law and order vs. resistance, read like contemporary chronicles. At the Lattimer massacre of 1897, the sheriff's posse fired directly into a crowd of men, women, and children, killing nineteen and seriously wounding thirty-nine: twenty-six Poles, five Lithuanians, twenty Slovaks. Naturally, the courts found the sheriff and his deputies not guilty. No reparations were ever made to the families. The official story was that the rioters had refused to halt and were charging forward; medical examination showed that all had been shot in the back.[17]

Third, black and white leaders can't seem to perceive that ethnic culture does not respond to appeals based on a WASP ethic. But appeals to solidarity, mutual help, and coalition with the underdog do stir ethnic memory. Sacrifice for the common good is the most noble ethnic theme. There is a difference between an appeal to guilt ("Live up to your own ideals") and an appeal to solidarity ("Life is unfair, we all must help each other out.") The rhetoric of John F. Kennedy touched ethnics deeply.

Most black militants, however, come out of a Protestant background; their Protestant moralism offends ethnic Catholics. Liberal white leaders also err when they employ the language of guilt. "Everytime I hear you speak," a Dorchester Irishman told a liberal senator, "ya make me feel guilty." The choice of guilt as the main motif of white-black relations is a most costly mistake. White ethnics refuse to feel guilty. Guilt is not their style. They react to guilt feelings with anger. They do not imagine life as an effort to live up to abstract ideals like justice, equality, fairness, reasonableness, etc.; but as a struggle to survive. The virtues of survival have most appeal to them: compassion, forgiveness, mutual help. They tend to be cynical about the language of high ideals, but open to the argument that someone else needs help.

A fourth mistake comes from a failure to discriminate what is *really* being said from what *seems* to be being said. It is as hard to understand ethnics correctly as to understand blacks—or WASPS. Ethnics, especially in the working class, have not learned the modern style of euphemism. They tend to bargain directly and to call things by their local names. In matters of mutual self-interest, their bluntness is an asset. Where white ethnics and blacks work in coalition, as in Newark, Gary, and parts of Chicago, direct talk turns out to be more reliable than the language of liberals.

Fifth, black culture and Slavic culture, in particular, are opposed to one another on issues independent of color: contrasting cultural attitudes toward money, consumption, clothes, habits, styles, for example. Slavs have an unparalleled capacity to cut back on consumer expenditures, to get by on very little, to live modestly, to save.[18] Ownership of land and home is very important to them. Conspicuous consumption is subject to social contempt. Through such habits, they are in direct cultural conflict with the general style of black culture (not of all blacks, of course).

Sixth, a difference in attitude toward family values is also overlooked. The ethnic attitude toward family is more like the black attitude in respect to the importance of neighbors and relatives; the pattern tends to be the extended family. The black family seems to be more like the modern liberal family in respect to its sexual mores. Here blacks and ethnics clash. Again, the responsibility of the ethnic male to the family circle is different in style from that of the black male. Since family values are so central to ethnic peoples, white and black leaders need to explain and to teach. It is not "racism" to be deeply antagonistic to a different family style; both ethnics and blacks are often outraged by opposing family styles, independently of color.

Seventh, the style chosen by black militants is a blend of three styles; all three have the political disadvantage of antagonizing white ethnics, whether white or black men use them. The first is the Protestant evangelical style. Fire and brimstone, Good and Evil, Paradise and Armageddon. The second is the style of pop Marxism, a very simple division between "exploiters" and "exploited," "Third World" and "Racist, Imperialist Amerika." The third is the colorful, flagrant style of threat, violence, and mayhem. Here Jerry Rubin antagonizes ethnics just as much as militant blacks do. Whatever these styles are supposed to do to "middle Americans," they could scarcely be designed more effectively to alienate ethnic whites from a cause in which their cooperation is crucial. A political style which antagonizes potential allies is its own punishment. Black militants tend to perceive whites as if they were all WASPS, and that may be their most egregious political error.

The eighth mistake is a failure to distinguish strategic, tactical, political violence from everyday criminal violence. A hundred years ago, *every* act of violence in northeastern Pennsylvania was attributed by the authorities to the Molly Maguires or (later) to the Slavic strikers. Both groups were wise enough to *disown* criminal acts, and to accept responsibility only for their own acts. The Molly Maguires opened with a prayer the meetings in which they plotted murder and they reputedly did not confess their murders as sins because they reckoned them as "acts of war." Thus ethnics cannot automatically *blame* blacks for acts of violence in accomplishing their own political ends. But ethnics have every right to abhor the major political blunder of black and white activists who say that *every* violent act committed by a black is "an act of war," and that all black criminals now in prison are "political prisoners."

There is a difference between *understanding* that political violence is sometimes necessary and deciding to *oppose* acts of violence. "Acts of war" committed against one's own welfare, relatives, friends, and children have this one property: they raise a fine ethnic temper to a heat. If a political movement wishes to succeed, it must choose its targets carefully. The effects of political violence must be calculated politically.

This point is important because the ideology of black militance is beginning to be used as a cover for the acts even of psychotic and disturbed individuals. In holdups of small stores, more and more shopkeepers are being needlessly killed, sometimes merely because they move too slowly, or simply because they are white. Commenting on a series of such killings, a veteran New York policeman said: "These are not slayings. They are public executions.

. . . New York is paying a terrible price for social integration, but nobody has the guts to face up to it."[19] Police officers are shot down from behind, ambushed, stalked. In human terms, such acts are as despicable as the murder of Fred Hampton in Chicago. In political terms, they need to be distinguished sharply from acts which have a clear political objective.

Where there is no discipline, there is no politics. Generations of injustice to blacks have created special problems of leadership, instability, and ideological heedlessness; these cannot be wished away. But those who suffer for these political deficiencies among blacks cannot be blamed for wishing to take up arms in self-defense, for wishing to crush the offenders thoroughly, for being livid at educated persons who glory in the romance of black militance while neither running its risks nor suffering as its object. The costs of social integration are more bloody, more tragic, and more sickening than believers in rational morality anticipated, or perhaps even now have the honesty to face.

Finally, the most effective way to help one social class is to sweeten the burden of their neighboring social classes, to give assistance, instruction, encouragement, and psychic strength. An ethnic class that in itself feels inferior and marginal can scarcely be asked to give of its abundance to others, for it feels in itself no abundance; it feels inadequate. Ethnic groups have ordinarily lost contact with the culture of their origin without gaining full contact with American culture and without having developed an intermediate, hyphenated culture rich enough to support their needs. They gambled a great deal on the melting pot. It did not exist.

I plead with black leaders—it is my dream—not to be too Protestant with ethnic Catholics. Don't confuse ethnics with nativist Americans. Recognize their problems with "Polish is beautiful" and "Italian is beautiful." I plead with white leaders: Help your people to find their own identity and pride, from which they can meet others without anxiety.

A coalition of blacks and ethnics will be inherently more stable than a coalition between intellectuals and blacks. For the real interests of blacks and ethnics— homes, neighborhood services, schools, jobs, advancement, status—are virtually identical; whereas the political interests of intellectuals are mainly those of a consciousness that can easily and often, as blacks well recognize, be false.

In recent years, intellectuals have been more helpful to blacks than ethnics have. As the going gets rougher, slower, closer to real interests, and as the grubby deals of actual power are made, intellectuals are likely to become scandalized or bored.

The inevitable coalition is between blacks and ethnics. To make a coalition, mutual love is not prerequisite. Mutual respect, or even mutual need, will do.

5. *An Ethnic Perception of Anticommunism*

Those who bid ordinary people to look upon world communism, not as a monolith, but as a complex phenomenon, ought to heed their own advice when they pass judgment on anticommunism. Five streams of thought are involved in it.

The first stream was articulated eloquently by Herman Melville in 1851:

> There are occasions when it is for America to make precedents, and not to obey them. We should, if possible, prove a teacher to posterity, instead of being the pupil of bygone generations . . . we Americans are the peculiar, chosen people, the Israel of our time—we bear the ark of the liberties of the world.
>
> We are the pioneers of the world; the advance guard sent on through the wilderness of untried things to break a new path in the New World that is ours. In our youth is our strength; in our inexperience, our wisdom. At a period when other nations have but lisped, our

deep voice is heard afar. Long enough have we been
skeptics with regard to ourselves, and doubted whether,
indeed, the political Messiah had come. But he has
come in us, if we would but give utterance to his
promptings. And let us always remember that with ourselves, almost for the first time in the history of the
earth, national selfishness is unbounded philanthropy;
for we cannot do good to America, but we give alms to
the world.[20]

A second stream was put in words by Max Rafferty,
former superintendent of schools in California, in a speech
called "The Passing of the Patriot." Rafferty praises
Nathan Hale, hanged before his twenty-second birthday.
He contrasts Hale, "the rope already knotted around his
bared throat and the pallor of approaching death already
on his cheeks," to "the voice of rock-and-roll, high speed,
carefree young America" and the "sickening, staggering
number of our young men just ten years ago who sold out
their fellow American soldiers, and licked the boots of the
brutal Chinese and North Korean invaders, and made the
tape recordings praising communism." Rafferty's vision of
the world is clear in the following passages:

What went wrong?
There were two things, you see, that we *didn't* teach
them. And oh! how they needed to learn these.
One was that most of the inhabitants of this big, bad-
tempered, battling planet hate our American insides.
This is hard to teach, and unpleasant to learn. It is the
simple truth, nevertheless.
The other thing . . . They would know that their
country was in danger, and that would be enough. . . .
. . . A soulless Thing slavers at us today on all continents, under all the seas, and out into the void of inter-
planetary space itself—a rotten, hateful, vicious entity.
Our national nose has been first tweaked and then
rubbed contemptuously into the dirt. The flag for which
our ancestors bled and died has been torn down and

unspeakably defiled by a dozen little pipsqueak comic-opera countries emboldened by our weak-kneed spinelessness and encouraged by our sneering Enemy. I don't know when at long last the American people will rise in all the power and majesty of their great tradition to put an end to this role of international doormat which we have assumed of late, and which becomes us so poorly.

. . . We had better not be caught witholding from the nation's children the wonderful sharp-edged, glittering sword of Patriotism. In a word, this means Indoctrination. An ugly word? I think not. But if it is ugly to teach children to revere the great Americans of the past—to cherish the traditions of our country as holy things—and to hate Communism, and its creatures like Hell—then I say let's be ugly, and let's revel in it.[21]

The third stream is given almost religious expression by William F. Buckley, Jr. He recounts how Richard Nixon once leaned toward him to whisper as the prime minister of Australia stood just in front of him: *"He's one of us."* What secret communion did Nixon have in mind? Buckley speaks of it sacramentally:

Nixon meant to say to me: Gorton is an anti-Communist. That used to mean a great deal in America, and it still means something. . . . Anti-Communists can feel one another's presence. Although it bore no national political fruit, small but important achievements were registered over the years by anti-Communists who worked together, in *ad hoc* associations, in pursuit of special objectives: socialists, conservatives, labor union leaders, professors: they had the tie in common of acknowledging Communism as the principal philosophical-strategic threat of the century. . . .

The question a great many American conservatives are asking themselves these days about Mr. Nixon is, "Is he one of us?" Or is there nothing left of—us? Or—a third possibility—does the bond of anti-Communism simply not mean anything any more? Strange, if that should be so; it was Mr. Nixon who, in the aside, invoked the bond. . . . Has he, the while in office, presided over the liquidation of the anti-Communist communion?[22]

On July 4, 1951, the *Capitol Times* of Madison, Wisconsin, sent reporters into the street to secure signatures on a petition. The petition consisted exclusively of sections from the Declaration of Independence and the Bill of Rights. Of 112 persons approached by the reporters, only one would sign. One person called the petition "the Russian Declaration of Independence." Another accused the paper of "using all the Commie tricks, putting God's name on a radical petition." Later, the *New York Post* sent out two reporters with the same petition. In New York, 19 of 161 signed. Only three recognized where the statements came from.[23]

The fourth stream depends upon a suspicion of liberty and dissent. One person's sense of reality, we have seen, is another person's myth. Melville imagines the United States as God's chosen historical vehicle. Rafferty sees this chosen vehicle imperilled, encircled, besieged by a hostile, hating world. Buckley sees participation in the instinct that communism is the principal threat of the century as a sacred communion. Still, the ordinary citizen of Madison, Wisconsin, and New York City does not recognize the philosophic tenets in whose name the titanic contest of the century is being waged. Is it all, then, power politics, global strategy? Is it all a rationalization for certain internal economic interests and certain worldwide ambitions?

The fascinating motif in these passages, particularly in Rafferty and Buckley, is the sense that the numbers of the anticommunist faithful are shrinking daily. Buckley is explicit:

. . . is what we Americans have so markedly superior to what the Soviet Union has as to warrant (1) the expenditure of $80-billion per year on the military, and (2) a foreign policy based on an explicit preference for the risk of nuclear war, over against submission? I register my unclassified opinion that this is the important datum of the sixties in America. It was the decade in which an important minority of Americans, who exercise extraordinary influence in the academy and in the opinion-making community, asked themselves the question: Is it worth it? Are atomic submarines, and ABMs and hydrogen bombs, and Minutemen, and orbital satellites—are they all worth it, given what we know about the corruption of America, as we have learned about it from our priests and poets and professors? No single datum establishes this opinion as conclusive in the intellectual world, but it is suggestive to note that when the question was asked of upperclassmen at Yale in 1963—Would you fight a nuclear war rather than surrender to the Soviet Union?—the answer was Yes, 78 percent. The same question, asked of Yale students in 1970, got the answer Yes, 37 percent.[24]

A fifth stream is an ethnic stream. Many ethnics find it psychologically difficult to voice their anguish in terms that mock their own recent past. Their rage against malfeasance in insurance companies, against medical costs, against city planners, against social engineers, against preachers, against boring jobs, dead ends, rising costs, the dissolution of their families, their overcrowded homes—such rage is now aimed at the sons and daughters of the privileged. Loyalty to nation is so central to their personal identity that they cannot tolerate abuses of the flag. They are susceptible to the other four streams of anticommunism.

It is wrong, however, to interpret ethnic patriotism as if it were nativist patriotism. The auto worker in Hamtrack and the chemist in Pittsburgh do not see in the flag what the used-car salesman in Dallas sees. It is not a boast of white supremacy. It is not a glorification of self. The nativist American is *complacent* about the flag; he and his culture come first, the flag exalts his self-image. The ethnic American is grateful for the flag; it transcends

WASP interests. He is *part* of what it represents. It is a symbol of what has been given him, and what he must willingly die for.

The nativist American looks down on "foreigners" and fears foreign entanglement, foreign encirclement. He has towards foreign affairs the same attitude he has toward health: he imagines his own organism healthy, but surrounded by dirt, carriers of disease, and sources of infection. He wants as little to do outside his own sterilized environment as necessary. His metaphors for intervention elsewhere are largely surgical: "precision bombing," "isolate the enemy," "swift incursion." (Air and sea power establish a minimum of infectious body contact.) The Anglo-Saxon lives in a clean place, surrounded by darkness and corruptions.

The ethnic American, by contrast, *is* or recently *was* a foreigner. Relatives of his still live in Abruzzi, or Spis, or Lodz, or Zagreb, or Acrostia. Foreign cultures, he knows, have a different style, outlook, family pattern, morality, emphasis. They speak a different language. They eat different foods. Their emotions and perceptions are somewhat different. The ethnic is glad to be American, and may (or may not) have confused emotions about the manners, mores, and even the politics of his motherland. Such emotions help to complicate his image of the world.

If it is communism that appears to him as the major "philosophical-strategic" menace in the world, it is not a communism learned from books, magazines, or even preachers. It is a communism learned from the experience of members of his family. It has a face, a name, an inexpungible set of dates, a list of deeds, a present hegemony. Many have gone "back home" to Poland, or Slovakia, or Slovenia, to walk in silence across the plank floors of a cottage that villagers uncertainly point out as the birthplace of a father, grandfather, uncle, aunt. They have eyed the grey uniforms and submachine guns at the borders. They have learned of marriage laws, the difficulties of churches, the pressure on family budgets, starvation for genuine news and open political conversation. Perhaps they have visited political graves. They have not returned to the United States convinced that the Cold War is merely propaganda.

The anticommunism of ethnic Americans has an earthy, real, textured side to it. It is not the fantastic image a Southern senator can conjure up for poor whites in the bayous. Thus the ethnic is capable of learning to make earthy distinctions about the many national versions of communism. Ukrainians are not friendly to Poles. Yugoslavs and Czechs have uneasy relations, which long antedate their different experiences with communism. Roumanians have a history of separateness in central Europe. It is not too difficult for inhabitants of eastern Poland to imagine that the North Vietnamese nourish a thousand-year enmity for the powerful Chinese upon their borders. An instinct for the importance of ethnicity is a powerful solvent for the simple-minded, universalist division of the world into "communist" and "anticommunist."

Moreover, those who cherish family and neighborhood, and do not regard with pleasure the growth of impersonal procedures and bureaucracies, are quite capable of seeing uncomfortable similarities between some developments in the United States and those in Soviet Russia. I have heard not a few ethnics say in anger: "We might as well be living in Russia!"

The Sovietization of the world and the Americanization look too uncomfortably alike. This perception is blocked if approached in an antipatriotic, negative tone. But if one makes it *in the name* of America, in the name of the dream that brought their grandfathers to these shores, many ethnics will seize the point swiftly. They do not like all that has happened to America these last fifty years. They look at it, not as a genuine expression of America, but as a betrayal.

The American Left, I fear, has great trouble grasping its own complicity in that betrayal. Science, reason, progress, economics, planning, strong central government, social engineering, behavior control, productivity, quantification, expertise—all such words have been heavy on the Left for two or three generations. Whatever happened, for example,'to the tag "scientific humanism"?

Before the Left can be converted from its love affair with the sources of modern restlessness, ethnics can be converted from simple anticommunism.

A steady look at a map, meanwhile, makes plain the four or five chief power centers on this planet. One does not need a theory of communist expansion to anticipate many military tensions over the next fifty years. Power corrupts. There are many goods to covet—oil in the Middle East, markets in Asia, outlets and prestige in Latin America. Cynicism learned over centuries would instruct wise men to beware of imperial powers, including their own.

Vietnam already is becoming for the Left what Munich for thirty years has been for the Right. Nothing can be written of unless it is compared to Vietnam: a prison riot, restlessness in school, childrearing, the building of an airplane, highway litter, civil service. . . . The imagination has been traumatized. As the fear of "appeasement" led to Vietnam, so our major strategic and political blunders for the next thirty years are likely to be made through desperate efforts to avoid "another Vietnam." Some day, after we *should* have acted decisively and quickly, some future Ellsberg will reveal that our bureaucrats were writing very cautious memos.

There is harsh wisdom, then, as well as adolescent foolishness, in the desire of the Pentagon to be "Number One." To seek superiority through self-congratulation, fat, and heaviness is silly. To seek it through intelligence, minimum investment, and determined flexibility is smart. The Pentagon is, however, the number one drag on American military preparedness—too fat, too heavy, too established, too·committed to real estate and·fixed installations. It is not hungry, lean, trim. America's most intelligent statesmen and strategists do not seek careers in it.

Worse, power does corrupt. It is ominous that the grandparents of so many ethnics endured forty days of seasickness to escape conscription into imperial armies in Europe; now their grandsons are conscripted to maintain the stability of American empire around the world. Ethnics did not come here to become imperial masters of the world. They did not come to dominate, to oppress, or to flaunt military power. The dream that brought them here was pacific. They did not intend their taxes to pay a million dollars for a fighter plane over rice fields far across the world (where villagers as helpless as their grandparents watch). One million dollars—just one of those downed two thousand aircraft's worth—spent in an ethnic neighborhood on the local school, might have done so much that is creative, good, frugal, and wise. Just one plane's worth.

Those who served in the army know that no one wastes money like the military. No one is quite so arrogant. It was good to serve the nation. The nation requires many kinds of service.

Old-line WASPS of the northeast have developed by now a fairly differentiated view of communism, at least in Europe. Their arrogance about America has lessened. (Thus Mr. Buckley's figures from Yale.) But they still have such disdain for ethnic peoples that they *preach* at them, do not come at issues from the ethnic side. They exude a sense of superiority. Although they have discovered ethnicity in the Soviet bloc, they have little stomach for it at home.

Jews, too, as Ben Halpern's *Jews and Blacks*[25] makes crystal clear, need foreign policy coalitions, but are culturally estranged from Catholic ethnics. The "Christian" overtones of anticommunism are too much for many Jews to take (also for some Christians). And, though Halpern doesn't say so, the "Catholic" tones of anticommunism emit terrible vibrations.

Ethnicity is a troubling concept for many Jews. For most ethnic groups, ethnicity is, at least in part, free and voluntary; but a Jew is forced into an identity by others, whether he wants it or not. Even if he is not religious, even if he is atheistic, even if he is in profession and taste and residence and habit thoroughly Americanized, a Jew is treated ethnically: he is a Jew. To call attention to ethnicity is to narrow and to harden such enforced identity. A strong stream in Jewish history encourages strong patriotism to the nation of residence, but also a strong current of anti-ethnic, universalist liberalism: fluid, mobile society of full acceptance for everyone. Out of such a tradition, Arthur Goldberg said to a group of Italians in 1970: "Ethnic politics is degrading."

The Six-Day War and the threat of genocide it symbolized; the imperialistic designs of Russia in the Middle East; and the treatment of Jews within the Soviet Union are generating strong anti-Russian caution among many Jews. But young Jews tempted by the revolutionary identity of the New Left seem to be impaled upon Third World rhetoric, whose anti-Israeli message is quite clear.[26]

A large majority of American Jews came here from Eastern Europe. Although for historical reasons they are antagonistic toward Catholic ethnic groups, particularly the Poles, there are solid reasons for a Jewish-ethnic coalition in some matters in foreign affairs. Polish peasants experienced emancipation and industrialization later than Western Europeans, and the Jewish migration eastward into Slavic countries placed many Jews in middle positions between the upper and the peasant classes.[27] Feelings today remain intense; rare is the Jew who is not bitter against the Poles, rare the Pole not resentful of that bitterness. The question now is how to make the future better than the past.

An alliance between Polish-American and Jewish sentiment regarding the power moves of Russia as an imperial nation (even independently of communist ideology) may one day be extremely important. One can deal with such issues on a frank ethnic basis.

For a start, Polish-American attacks on anti-Semitism

in Poland and the Soviet Union might be matched by Jewish attacks on the restrictions upon Catholicism in Poland. This would be a small but not unimportant start. Both Jews and Poles feel the weight of many historic injustices.

In mutual concern about Soviet power, they might also be mutually critical of the foolish uses of American power. That power is needed on this often absurd and cruel planet. Tempering, it and disciplining it require the combined energies, of all.

If highly placed WASPS and Jews in the intellectual world and the media grasped the political usefulness of ethnic perceptions which have not disappeared, many issues could be approached in a straightforward ethnic manner. Not least of these are the varied stakes ethnic groups have in the role of America in the world, and the consequent need for a larger-than-WASP formulation of public discussion.

CHAPTER TEN

The Ethnic
Democratic Party

THE FORCES PROPELLING modern civilization press us toward uniformity.

The weight of these gigantic forces was already oppressive a hundred years ago. De Tocqueville wrote that Frenchmen of his time were more alike than the Frenchmen of their parent's generation. "The same remark might be made of Englishmen in a still greater degree," John Stuart Mill observed a generation later, in 1859.

> Formerly, different ranks, different neighborhoods, different trades and professions, lived in what might be called different worlds; at present to a great degree in the same. Comparatively speaking, they now read the same things, listen to the same things, see the same things, go to the same places, have their hopes and fears directed to the same objects, have the same rights and liberties, and the same means of asserting them. Great are the differences of position which remain, they are nothing to those which have ceased. And the assimilation is still proceeding.[1]

From 1859 to 1972, what Mill feared has not abated.

1. *Against Homogeneity*

One single ideology—that practical attitude toward affairs, that instinct for what Mill called utility—does indeed characterize politicians, businessmen, religious leaders, and ordinary people all around the world. The pragmatic way of life gives access to the wealth and power by which most human beings are easily tempted. Things that used to be sacred, and different, and ancient, everywhere give place to things that are practical, standardized, and new. What we have been doing for the last hundred years is creating a planetary mold: one way of life, one way of thinking, one way of feeling, everywhere the same. In some places, the process is called "Americanization." It is the inevitable fruit of technology in China and Russia as well.

In one thing Right and Left long concurred: the progressive power of science and industry. The Right legitimized such power by invoking what Henry Adams called "the Dynamo," calling down the honeyed blessings of church, Western values, industry, civilization, and Reason. The Left legitimized such power by invoking the symbol of "the Future." It invoked the stirring language of revolution, socialist values, comradeship, and science. In both, the fundamental dynamism was the same: the process called "modernization." Indeed, the war in Indochina may be seen as a competition between two rival ways of legitimizing modernization.[2]

The Right *appears* to be more benign toward churches and organic traditions than it is; in Butte, Montana, the churches are razed along with the saloons when stripmining through the center of the town appears to promise profit. The Left *appears* to be more future-oriented than it is; in Bologna, Italy, and Bogotá, Colombia, strong Communist parties protect entrenched interests as adequately as Christian Democrats. The effective ideology of the modern world is neither socialism nor capitalism. It is pragmatism. That is the secret hidden in the heart.

In his *On Liberty,* Mill was depressed by the stagnation (as he saw it) of Chinese society—"they have become stationary—have remained so for thousands of years; and if they are ever to be further improved, it must be by foreigners." (Little did he imagine Marx toiling just then in the British Museum.) The Chinese, Mill says with irony, "have succeeded beyond all hope in what English philanthropists are so industriously working at—in making a people all alike, all governing their thoughts and conduct by the same maxims and rules." Mill despised, above all, "the modern regime of public opinion," to which he attributed the same potency as the Chinese system had shown. Europe, he feared "will tend to become another China." He ruminated:

What has made the European family of nations an improving, instead of a stationary portion of mankind? Not any superior excellence in them, which, when it exists, exists as the effect not as the cause; but their remarkable diversity of character and culture. Individuals, classes, nations have been extremely unlike one another: they have struck out a great variety of paths, each leading to something valuable; and although at every period those who traveled in different paths have been intolerant of one another, and each would have thought it an excellent thing if all the rest could have been compelled to travel his road, their attempts to thwart each other's development have rarely had any permanent success, and each has in time endured to receive the good which the others have offered. Europe is, in my judgment, wholly indebted to this plurality of paths for its progressive and many-sided development. But it already begins to possess this benefit in a considerably less degree. It is decidedly advancing towards the Chinese ideal of making all people alike.

Mill feared that diversity might not be able to stand its ground. The forces arrayed against the continuation of difference were "so great a mass." If efforts are to be made to defend diversity, he wrote, "the time is now."

It is only in the earlier stages that any stand can be successfully made against the encroachment. The demand that all other people shall resemble ourselves grows by what it feeds on. If resistance waits till life is reduced nearly to one uniform type, all deviations from that type will come to be considered impious, immoral, even monstrous and contrary to nature. Mankind speedily become unable to conceive diversity, when they have been for some time unaccustomed to see it.[3]

It is good to have a liberal and English philosopher on one's side in the struggle against homogeneity. I confess to the judgment, however, that the consideration of "the useful," which Mill so warmly recommended, entailed the homogenization he deplored. Mill hoped that "individuality" would save the day; not, that is, ethnic differences, but *the individual's* mobility and liberty.

Many sociologists have begun to doubt the conventional wisdom about American society. That wisdom was a rationalization of the WASP conception of America. As a Jew, Halpern understands the rules limpidly:

> In those not so old but nearly forgotten days, a simple conception of the way newcomers could be "Americanized" was generally accepted. The public view was that the old settlers, the real Americans, had established an open society based on the American Way of Life: on freedom of belief and opinion and free enterprise. Participation in it was open, in principle, to anyone according to his individual merit. There was no discrimination—but admission to the real America was subject to a test of individual performance.
>
> America was the New World, come to redress the balance of the Old, to replace it by something bigger and better. Everyone in it, in principle, had turned his back on the corrupt Old World; and, in order to enter, newcomers had to be willing to do the same. This was *the price* of assimilation into the real America, the preliminary test and condition that must be met.
>
> The American idea of proper social organization was not that of a totally unstratified, unsegregated, undifferentiated society, but of a society with class dif-

ferences and loose, permeable segregations, open to the passage of individuals who proved their worth.[4]

In a word, America will assimilate *individuals*. It will not assimilate groups.

The new ethnic politics is a direct challenge to the WASP conception of America. It asserts that *groups* can structure the rules and goals and procedures of American life. It asserts that individuals, if they do not wish to, do not have to "melt." They do not have to submit themselves to atomization. "Subcultures" are refusing to concede the legitimacy of one (modernized WASP) "Superculture." A black sociologist, L. Paul Metzger, puts it best:

> To abandon the idea that ethnicity is a dysfunctional survival from a prior stage of social development will make it possible for sociologists to reaffirm that minority-majority relations are in fact group relations and not merely relations between prejudiced and victimized individuals. As such, they are implicated in the struggle for power and privilege in the society, and the theory of collective behavior and political sociology may be more pertinent to understanding them than the theory of social mobility and assimilation.[5]

Not everyone, of course, is prepared to admit that white ethnic groups still have cultural cohesion in America. Thus a second tenet of the conventional wisdom is that *class* identifications are important, but not ethnic identifications. Herbert J. Gans interprets the resistance of Italians to an expressway in Boston not to anything *Italian* but to traditional working-class attitudes.[6] What is more salient among the lower-middle class, the issue is posed, that they are ethnic or that they are workers? Ethnicity or economics? Both sorts of identification are important, and sometimes one may supercede the other. But the argument in favor of placing special emphasis on ethnicity—an argument permeating every line of this book—may be summarized in three steps.

1. Patterns of perception and action are socially arrived

at, especially in the intimacy of the family and primary group relations. The profoundest elements in these patterns are assimilated in instinct and imagination, below the threshold of consciousness. Hence, fundamental attitudes regarding sex, children, authority, money, home, ambition, pain, joy, and social loyalty are derived, as it were, from chains of transmission far below the level of easy eradication or conversion. Outward behavior can be made to conform. Opinions may easily be molded. Education into a cosmopolitan culture can lead to analytic power and articulation. Still, concrete behavior may show remarkable stylistic and pragmatic variation from ethnic group to ethnic group.

2. The legitimacy of high WASP culture, of modernization, and of professionalization, is not so easily conceded today.

3. In a time of crisis and confusion, those who find resources in an ethnic history have a clear sense of reality, a story to live out, symbols about which they are clear. They are freer in meeting others, more flexible in taking chances, less inclined toward *ressentiment*. It is not surprising, then, that persons who take an active part in ethnic activities are considerably less likely to be prejudiced against others than the average American.[7]

I can understand why some old-line WASPS would be reluctant to stress a revival of ethnic consciousness. I can also understand why some Jews, though perhaps not Orthodox Jews, would be reluctant to stress such an assertion. Some are afraid that the ethnic assertion will be regressive; their interest in it is a form of preventive war. Others try hard to imagine some positive fruitfulness in the new ethnicity. It is worth stressing that such estimates will often have an ethnic form, undertow, or rationale. Out will come the documents of the Founding Fathers. Out will come appeals to universalist ethical assimilation. Legitimately enough.

Can ethnic consciousness be restored? Each person has an answer in his own autobiography. No one is so godlike

that he perceives like all other Americans combined.
Very well, then, what are the edges of the particularity
of each of us? Inescapably, there is in all but the most
mongrel, orphaned, and rootless of us a considerable
inheritance from grandparents. That inheritance colors
the eyes through which we discern what is reasonable,
fair, cause for joy, or for alarm. Each of us is different
from any other, and yet our similarities with some others
tend to cluster around shared ethnicities. It is more comfortable for us to be with people whose range of feeling,
irony, instinct, and word is like our own. Each of us finds
certain other groups offensive, puzzling, menacing, taxing.
Such findings are marks, not of our malice, but of our
finitude. No ethnic group (dearly as we each believe it) is
God's people. No individual (dearly as we each would love
to be) is universalist. It's all right to have limited perceptions. It's really all right. Self-hatred isn't necessary.

Diversity of ethnic consciousness is exciting and valuable. It is so utterly refreshing to meet people in touch
with their roots, secure in them even if long ago having
transcended them. One meets so often people who are
victims of what Mill called "the tyranny of public opinion,"
whose judgments are whatever those of their intimate
circle are, but who are dismayed at "ethnic prejudices." In
meeting others who are en route to discovering their own
inherited chains of instinct, one learns how to see oneself
from a different angle and a different depth.

Diversity of ethnic consciousness is becoming more
rare, as people uproot convictions in order to plant opinions, uproot values of substance in order to plant values
of process, uproot personal angularities in order to plant
professional sentiments. The human question is *Who?* It
is not *How?* It is a social question. Perish diversity of
groups, perish humanity.

2. *The Limits of Social Policy*

In the good old days, President Eisenhower didn't do
much. Along came Kennedy to "get the nation moving

again." It was a field day for social policy. A whole nation, maybe world, to reconstruct.

But what *is* social policy? How would you go about imagining a new politics if the American people told you, "Go ahead!" They're not about to, of course. And yet, practically everywhere people want change. They know there's a crisis. . . .

Weariness with political programs arises from unimpeachable experience: our way of thinking about social policy is inadequate. John Dewey argued brilliantly in *Liberalism and Social Action* (1935) that liberalism was historically creative because of its capacity to be transformed. In its first great moment, it championed individual rights against the king of England. In its second great moment, it championed individual initiative and creativity in industry. A third great moment, he wrote, beckons liberalism; namely, a shift from the perspective of the individual to the perspective of the whole society. Men's social skills were increasing at such a rate that only rational social planning would enable all to share in the fruits of the earlier liberal victories. In raw intelligence, he noted, an auto mechanic (or a philosopher) is not superior to a primitive man; but in the auto mechanic as in the philosopher lives a wide range of *social* knowledge and *social* skills, enabling him to do far more with the same quantum of intelligence.

Obviously, if the last thirty years of social planning are as threadworn as they appear to be, a fourth transformation is required. It is, I would guess, a turn toward the organic networks of communal life: family, ethnic group, and voluntary association in primary groups. We may imagine that for the past hundred years, a masculine attitude of prediction, control, and dominance was unleashed upon every aspect of human life. In those functions in which the woman used to be indispensable, she has been more and more replaced by professionals, experts, and bureaucracy. Food is "processed" in huge factories. Births, illnesses, and deaths occur away from home. Children are taught in "consolidated" schools. Her shopping, her daily round of chores, her working—all these are made nuclear, highly rationalized and scheduled, efficient, mechanical. The juices of human interchange, surprise, and creativity have been as thoroughly as possible squeezed out, freeze-dried, prepackaged. Only the unpredictability of children grants her a crisis or two to prove her worth.

If I were to invent a political program for the future, particularly for the poor and the lower-middle class, I would center its social focus on family and neighborhood. Its criterion would be: what helps family and neighborhood is good; what injures them is bad. The family is the center of the social universe. It is so, in any case, for the poor, if not so for wealthier classes (except insofar as wealth is inherited through families). Groups whose members are alienated from their families are doomed to seeking ersatz, transient, and ultimately anomic relations elsewhere.

More than WASPS do, ethnics seem to value family—a large family, extended through more than two adults. They were closer to Europe, perhaps, and to the poor. Richard Sennett describes their history:

> Up to the nineteenth century, European families throughout the ranks of society were an intricate web of relatives; instead of husbands and wives living alone, clusters of married couples lived together. Due to the accidents of war, disease and work, uncles and cousins often took the place of absent fathers, and as many as twenty or thirty children were tended by this network of parents. If we looked in America today for a parallel to these families, we would be more likely to find it among the ranks of the poor than among those of the middle class.[8]

In America the costs of education discriminate against large families. Activities are scheduled for age groups rather than for families. The weight of every conceivable social practice and psychological instruction is to break up extended families and to atomize nuclear families. The fission of America seems to focus upon all organic, communal links.

The rise of the small family coincided with the rise of modern industry—which suggests both its latent purpose and its symbolic base. Humans began to think of themselves as appendages of machines. The dominant value came to be that form of "reason" which cherishes practicality. The fabric of extended families is too dense, thick, and complex for reason of that sort. Industrial reason needs to atomize social groups in order to shear them apart and put them back together efficiently. The Lockean and Humean base of Anglo-Saxon thought, with its associative connections—its "social contracts"—between nomadic atoms, provides the imagery. The loneliness individuals boast of (proof of their courage, nerve, and maturity) is a precondition to their assimilation into the industrial system.

The system requires that families be small, independent, not cohesive either externally or internally: associative merely. It is more economical if no outsider lives at home and drains its resources. It should be "private and insulated." It should stress self-reliance, preparing its children to abandon their parents as their parents had abandoned theirs: abandon family in order to throw themselves into the arms of the beneficent national system. Abstract plans for the future replace concrete pleasures and immediate needs. Theory replaces feeling. "Mom" becomes dysfunctional. The nuclear family is a recent invention.

Richard Sennett argues that "children reared in such homes," according to sketchy but accumulating evidence in the social sciences, "are often less successful than children of the same background who have grown up in the old-style extended homes," particularly in dealing with the work world:

. . . there are less scholarly, more tangible signs that this kind of family is not performing as it should. These signs are the cries of boredom, of aimlessness, of discontent that children raised in such homes during an era of unparalleled affluence are making. There is a groundswell of communalism in this country among the young, and not just among the minority who are radicals; there is a widespread yearning to find some kind of intimate human association which will put behind the sense of privateness and fixed role embodied in the small, isolated family. There is a yearning for human contacts which will approximate the richness of extended family life in the past.

I believe this revolt against the narrow confines of the middle-class home is not a fashion of the youth culture that will disappear. History is too much on the side of the young; in some ways the communalism we see now appearing is a conservative reaction, in that it is trying to recapture threads of human association cut during the rise of the industrial order. Rather than a healthy, adaptive form, the small and private family seems to have been a historical fluke that destroys itself under conditions of economic stability and affluence . . . We are indeed on the edge of an immense change in the conduct of family life throughout the society; there is a longing for the kind of intimate yet complex association that has marked the West for most of its history.

No doubt this change comes too late for many ethnic families. Closely tied to parents, uncles and aunts, in-laws and cousins as many of them have remained, countless sad stories have already transpired: of bitter misunderstanding between old and young, old ways and new ways; of alienation, furious argument, silence, and the death of the elderly in faraway, lonely places. "My father had a stroke. But why didn't I go?" a New Yorker confesses. "Hell, two hundred dollars, two days, I could have gone. Think of the stupid people I had meetings with instead. I could have gone."

These are not good times for the family. Many are even predicting its disappearance. But the conception of what we have recently meant by "family" can be altered. Age-old ethnic views of family and neighborhood, given a new flexibility and governmental support, can ground a new form of political and social organization.

Nathan Glazer set the stage for new proposals in a paper pointing out "the limits of social policy." He defined his own position:

> 1. Social policy is an effort to deal with the breakdown of traditional ways of handling distress. These traditional mechanisms are located primarily in the family, but also in the ethnic group, the neighborhood, and in such organizations as the church and the *landsmanschaft*.
> 2. In its effort to deal with the breakdown of these traditional structures, however, social policy tends to encourage their further weakening. There is, then, no sea of misery against which we are making steady headway. Our efforts to deal with distress themselves increase distress.[9]

In politics, not least democratic politics, more must be promised that can be delivered. Thus people are educated to support policies which are guaranteed to disappoint them. Secondly, the passion for equality is both insatiable and self-defeating. It spreads from political rights to economic power, from social status to authority in all things. But equal treatment of individuals has *not* meant, and cannot mean, equal treatment for groups. Fairness is possible; equality is not. "To each according to his needs," is a justification for inequality, and so is "from each according to his abilities." Contradictions multiply.

Glazer also makes a larger criticism: "It is illusory to see social policy only as making an *inroad* on a problem; there are dynamic aspects to any policy, such that it also *expands* the problem, *changes* the problem, *generates* further problems."[10] The social problems of Sweden, for example, a nation far more homogeneous, more enlightened, and less military than ours, require a tax budget soaring higher than forty percent of the Swedish gross national product. "A new set of priorities" in America will not match resources to needs. It will alleviate some needs, and generate others.

A major reason, Glazer points out, is the professionalization of services. A "certain point of view is developed about the nature of needs and how they are to be met." Only certain people are "qualified" to handle these problems. Dissatisfaction develops with the large numbers of "unqualified" people. But soon those outside the profession come to distrust the "qualified," as well. Do social workers handle welfare, teachers and principals education, doctors and hospital administrators health care, policemen law and order, managers housing projects, insurance agents our disasters, community organizers poverty? Every new agency breeds a new professional interest group.

Another limit on social policy is "the paradox of knowledge." The more we know, the less confidently we can act. "A little knowledge is a dangerous thing"—but easier on the ego. In social policy as in personal life, self-knowledge turns out to be more like ignorance than like knowledge.

In the past, there was a clear field for action. The situation demanded that something be done; whatever was done was 'clear gain; little as yet was expected; little was known, and administrators approached their tasks with anticipation and self-confidence. At later stages, however. . . . we had already become committed to old lines of policy; agencies with their special interests had been created; and new courses of action had to be taken in a situation in which there was already more conflict at the start, less assurance of success, and less attention from the leaders and the best minds of the country.[11]

The knowledge of experts soon loses contact with public opinion; conflicts increase; earlier programs have to be defended—or opposed. A "bureaucratic mire" develops.

Thus insoluble factors of cost, professionalization, and ignorance dim our hopes that man is perfectible by the route of social manipulation.

> . . . every piece of social policy substitutes for some traditional arrangement, whether good or bad, a new arrangement in which public authorities take over, at least in part, the role of the family, of the ethnic and neighborhood group, or of the voluntary association. In doing so, social policy weakens the position of these traditional agents, and further encourages needy people to depend on the government, rather than on the traditional structures, for help. Perhaps this is the basic force behind the ever-growing demand for social policy, and its frequent failure to satisfy the demand.[12]

Professionalization also lies at the heart of the disaster in Vietnam. Realistic assessments, quantification, relocation of populations, nation-building, body count: human lives subject to systems analysis, human beings treated as atoms to be rearranged according to rational schemes. Vietnam sprang not from the industrial-military "system"; it sprang from the invisible religion—shared by Left as well as by Right—at purest doctrinal pitch. To see done far away and instantly what has been done over a longer time span at home was like seeing a film at too high a speed: it induced nausea. We had set out to pour the acids of our melting pot over Vietnam, to modernize and to Americanize a faraway land. Paul Mus notes that Ho Chi Minh in his early days made the same error; only when he learned to think of his own people not in the atomic forms of Western Marxism but in the network forms of Vietnamese villagers did "the mandate of heaven" point to him.[13]

Something similar is needed in America. Huxley diagnosed one unconscious source of rage and violence: "Today, every efficient office, every up-to-date factory is a panoptical prison in which the workers suffer from the consciousness of being inside a machine." Daniel Bell notes in *The End of Ideology* how the American engineer breaks units of work into a simple, comprehensive, mechanical scheme of Time and Motion. "In each instance, the striving is toward the irreducible atom, the nuclear unit which, in alchemic fashion, can be recombined into almost infinite variations, yet be encompassed within the two dimensions of a single card."[14] Human beings are imagined as monadic parts of a great social machine. No wonder that's the way they feel.

Whatever professionals touch begins to die. Even the professionalization of football destroys as much as improves the game. Professionalization is necessarily an abstraction; a person concentrates upon becoming good at a narrow sliver of life. Many interests are reduced to one. All energy goes into a single wavelength. Earsplitting distortion accumulates. Human beings become grotesque. Professionalization is the remaking of human beings in the image of machines. It is a "retooling." But human beings are not tools. If professional football were forbidden to use special units and each man had to play several facets of the game well, instead of one, we would have a game more in human scale, less destructive of knees, legs, teeth, cartilage, muscle, and bone. In its present form, however, pro football is almost a perfect symbol of our professional classes. Even the Progressive Left is torn in half its soul by the desire to manipulate—in the name of humanism and liberty, of course. The Left is strong among the experts.

I do not know how to deal with professionalism directly. Professionalism generates power. Will anyone willingly surrender power, even if it is destroying him?

A women's liberation movement, aimed at drawing the control of life back from the hands of experts, would be a cause in which both the most liberated and the most traditional might build alliance. Women's Liberation may, of course, prefer to model itself on WASP and Jewish ideals of solitary autonomy and economic competition with men. There will always be a professional world; it must become as open to women as to men. But the professional world is no longer the hope of further progress.

Whether or not Women's Liberation is interested in such a project, I propose it as the plank of an Ethnic Democratic Party. The EDP would be, at the very least, a caucus within the Democratic party. Its goal would be genuine cultural variety; strong communities of value, identity, and conscience; and strong families and neighborhoods. It would aim to convert the mechanical, functional image of society to an organic, living human image: closer to primordial preceptions and primordial strengths. It would wish to limit professionalization only to those areas in which it is absolutely necessary. It would not be antiprofessional, or antimodern, but it would intend to block excesses of professionalization, modernization, and growth-for-the-sake-of-growth.

People first. Families first. Neighborhoods first. In the last third of the twentieth century, one can safely call upon such energies without fear of regression; they are the only hope of further progress. For talented persons, women not least, work could be most attractive if not too rigidly scheduled, if close to home, if not too alienating from family, neighborhood and friends. In the old days, mothers and grandmothers were economically indispensable. They worked in the fields or in the shops with men; they canned food; they baked; they made clothes; they delivered babies and set bones; they cared for disturbed children; often they gave children their primary education; they established and governed the family budget. In our age, given the much higher educational attainments of many men and women in the neighborhood, the neighborhood and home could reabsorb such tasks with far greater competence and effect than ever before in history. Why *can't* people of talent organize for their own needs, providing for them locally? Why *can't* education

be aimed, not at "qualifying" professionals, but at impart-
ing the real skills necessary to care for the needs of one's
local communities?

The neighborhood would put many potentials and
yearnings for satisfaction to great use if it reclaimed
many of the functions now grabbed up—and made fan-
tastically expensive—by professionals. Children are better
taught in their home neighborhood by parents and friends
than by bureaucratically run public schools. Most cuts,
sicknesses, and complaints could be treated in neighborhood clinics more humanely than in hospitals. Death is
accomplished with greater dignity at home than in the
hospital. Women who have undergone the painful but
deep satisfaction of natural childbirth could bring childbirth to the home once more, were there skilled midwives
in the neighborhood—who might well be of more assistance than distracted doctors.

Investigative reporting has begun to show that the success of large professional institutions—the schools and the
hospitals, particularly—falls far below their claims. Professionals in large, rational, bureaucratic complexes are
not in scale with human feeling and imagination; much
of their work is counterproductive. The law of human
scale has its inevitable effect. Schools do not educate.
Hospitals do not heal. For many diseases, including certain kinds of heart attacks, home care does more for
patients than hospital care. How many operations,
bureaucratically diagnosed, are useless? If men and
women in the neighborhood could be paid to set up and
to run local clinics, under a doctor's direction perhaps,
the health of the nation might be enormously improved.
Training for local citizens would give them satisfying work
near home, as well as income.

This country is desperate for good craftsmen. The villages, towns, and cities of America have been visibly
decaying for forty years. Mass production has weakened a
generation in its basic skills of hand, eye, and shoulder.
Rather than giving tax breaks to huge industries, let the

government give large tax incentives to carpenters and other craftsmen. Tax deductions should be given to those who learn, practice, and teach ancient crafts.

People who hire craftsmen in their homes should also get tax credits rather than, as often at present, higher tax assessments for home improvement. A society that does not honor handiwork dooms millions to alienation, for human creativity flows through the hands. Where men cannot earn a good living through the skills of their hands, frustration is inevitable. That is a radical realism from which illusions should not blind us.

Neighborhoods are also the natural locale for the care of the elderly. Housing that includes provision for the elderly should be given favored status. Families that keep grandparents and uncles in their midst should get special support. Older citizens who take part in child care, in clinics, in local schools, should be paid rather than given Social Security. In some neighborhoods, older women have learned how to make out income-tax forms, and mastered other intricacies of accounting and legal services; they help out all their neighbors, in a relation far more satisfying to everyone than going to strangers.

In Baltimore funds were once available for finding elderly persons who were sick and bringing them to clinics. In 1969 these funds were cut off. A nurse, who for a while continued making her rounds, visited an old woman. There was a sickly stench. She asked about it. The woman was a little deaf. "It's my brother," she finally said, hands shaking. Upstairs the nurse found a man of ninety who lay in his own filth. Neither he nor his sister had strength to do better. When the ambulance attendants lifted him from his bed that afternoon, the skin of his back remained attached to the sheets. Such agonies would not occur, were neighborhoods organized.

Local neighborhoods have generosity and talent to care for their own as they did since man first walked the earth. We have so far done everything possible to demoralize our people. We tell them they are not "qualified." With support and encouragement, people could regain pride, capacity, and competence.

The EDP is dedicated to bringing human resourcefulness, political power, and social policy to the organic networks of family and neighborhood. Its every activity in organizing families, neighborhoods, and ethnic groups is a fulfillment of its platform. Its political success depends on bringing economic, enabling power back to local units. Local grievances, voiced by people themselves, are the point at which experienced organizers begin. The large professionalized system around us is a bubble. Pricking it at any point deflates its claims.

A new form of social policy will take many years to build.

3. *Dangers in the Neighborhood*

What does a politics based on family and neighborhood do to integration? What does it do to conflict and prejudice? What does it do to mobility? What does it do to bussing?

Not all ethnic groups desire to be integrated with others. The Chinese prefer to educate their own children. Poles often prefer to avoid Irish Catholic schools and build their own. Nativist Americans sometimes prefer their neighborhoods to remain "all white." If bussing were left to some neighborhoods, it would never happen.

There is no use dodging the dilemma. National culture is often more liberal than local culture. Still, the agents of national culture have displayed persistent misconceptions. For example, the main reason for bussing should not be integration of whites and blacks. The main criterion should be education of high quality. There is no special magic in "integration"; the whole point is higher quality on a fair basis. The children of white ethnics in Philadelphia, as Peter Binzen has shown,[15] are as hopelessly short-changed as blacks by the inequities between suburban and urban schools. Children in the suburbs are deprived of realistic experience of diversity and hardship. Thus bussing *can* improve the quality of education for all concerned.

On the question of bussing, it is crucial to distinguish between nativist and ethnic America. In Alabama, George Wallace has not scrupled to bus black children ten miles or more so that they can attend an all-black school. A dual school system, in which one receives resources denied to the other is an outrage against equality. In such circumstances, the notion of "neighborhood schools" is an injustice. Residential patterns are designed with inequality in mind.

"De facto" segregation in urban environments, amid ethnic enclaves, is a different phenomenon. Urban schools, white and black, usually suffer grievously by comparison with white suburban schools. Teachers, faculties, and programs in the latter are usually far superior. Between white and black urban schools, there is often not much to choose. Traditions of respect for authority among whites, and a long-repressed rebellion against rural Southern traditions among blacks, provide the most significant difference. If there is to be bussing of children in such circumstances, ethnic whites should be promised equal gains with blacks: equal opportunity for an experience in the better, more advanced suburban schools. As for the children of the suburban schools, who does not sympathize with the parents obliged to watch their children bussed downtown to inferior schools? The burden on such children must be limited. Compensation must be provided.

No mathematical formula does justice to the complexity of social needs and interests. No one principle exhausts the interests and needs involved in bussing. At least the following issues need to be defended:

1. Segregated racial education is no adequate preparation for living in a genuinely pluralistic society.

2. No child should bear the burden of going from a superior to an inferior school for his entire career.

3. To make schools superior, good teaching is the chief

ingredient; to lure good teaching into the most socially disadvantaged schools, special social and financial advantages should be offered. It is cheaper to pay for good teachers than to pay for busses. Better to pour $300,000 directly into poorer schools than to pay for bussing the children elsewhere.

. 4. Education is best when it is a combination of ethnic and universal. Every child should have an education in his own ethnic tradition, and also an experimental exposure to the ethnic traditions of others.

Many ethnics in particular do not object to school integration unless the ratio of whites to blacks falls below 60 to 40. If it does, they claim, quality and services deteriorate. National, state, or district legislation to stabilize such ratios would reduce insecurities and threats considerably.

In general, persons secure in their own families and neighborhoods are more likely to reach rational compromises than persons who feel total and unremitting threat. The establishing of such security is one aim of the Ethnic Democratic Party. The diminishing of anti-Semitic sentiment since the Second World War, the abatement of most interethnic hostilities, the general rise of blacks in their own esteem and that of others, suggest that an ethnic focus does not carry all the dangers it once had.[16]

A parallel may be drawn from the field of religion. There is a distinction between an "open church" and a "characterless church." An open church recognizes that its mission is service to a transcendent God and to all men without discrimination; it does not exist to be self-serving. A church without character simply adapts itself to the cultural religion of the day—for example, the "religion of the American way of life." There is a difference between being non-profit and being non-prophet. An open church may have harsh things to say to the society in which it lives, and it may take controversial stands. It is committed to *arguing* for its positions, perhaps also to generally accepted democratic processes like lobbying; but it does not enforce its own views upon others. Many would like to see American Catholicism become increasingly open, but not to lose its distinctiveness.

In the same way, strongly ethnic families and neighborhoods are free to construct and to defend their own distinctive ways of life, while recognizing that in a democratic and pluralistic society many compromises and accommodations must be reached.

Ethnic groups are not merely interest groups, but often they are at least that. Blacks, for example, have been so deeply penalized in education, economic resources, and political organization that their social strategy has had to be unique. Jews fulfilled their own interests as an ethnic group by excelling individually in universities, merchandising, and new industries like television, cinema, and electronics.[17] But blacks face their new possibilities with very little social leverage. It is in their interest as an ethnic group to insist on high quotas for blacks in schools and jobs, and not to accept as valid the argument that equality is only for those who "qualify." For it is exactly in their lack of preparation to qualify that many blacks have borne the weight of injustice. Hence blacks have seen fit to "change the rules." They have discovered that whites fear black rebellion and disruption. They know that whites will *not* commit genocide—that is their ace. But whites do wish the race problem would "go away"; and that is a fantasy of genocide. It is a deeply buried fantasy precisely because it is too awful, difficult, and normally impossible to contemplate. Rather than face such fantasies, whites will pay a ransom. Still, whites both hate themselves for giving in and feel guilty for their fantasies. So the taunt of genocide intensifies their desire to be generous. (The most liberal probably have the most repressed aggressions.)

Ethnics can understand the strategic interests of blacks. Hence, to place costs and needs on a frank trading basis would no doubt constitute a step forward. If blacks replace Jews in the New York school system, provision has to be made for the training of new teachers and the displacement of and reward for those displaced. If blacks move into an ethnic neighborhood, quotas may have to be bargained for or other arrangements made—such are political realities—to protect the quality of public services. If blacks demand a "black studies" program at Brandeis, a guarantee that anti-Israeli propaganda doesn't emanate from it is at the very least a decent *quid pro quo*.[18] If blacks demand "open admissions" to universities, young men and women in local white communities who hadn't thought before of a college career should publicly be invited to accept hitherto unavailable assistance. The program should be billed as an invitation to *all* ethnic groups, white and black.

If racial issues are pulled out from the mists of liberal rhetoric, and thought through in terms of their costs and benefits to each ethnic group involved, the more likely it will be that fairness and mutual satisfaction will ensue.

The new ethnic politics asks no more than a fair deal—but for each *group,* and not only for outstanding individuals. It demands a multiform ideology and culture. Not a superculture with satellite subcultures, but a multiculture in which each group supplies pivotal ideas and methods. It demands that "the American way of life" be broken open like a cocoon giving way to the burgeoning wings of a butterfly.

4. *Old Ethnic Politics vs. New Ethnic Politics*

In the old days, "practical" politicians with a flair for symbolic differences waited on the docks. Poles, Italians, Greeks, and Slavs were enrolled as Democrats before they were enrolled as Americans. The Irish were especially sensitive to ethnic nuances, as the WASPS were not ("seen one foreigner, you've seen them all" seemed to be the nativist conception of the world). They were the most successful political brokers. The Irish, other ethnics came to believe, are essentially a procedural people; substantive issues do not attract their wit as much as the problems of organizing and arranging things. Poems and contentions are what they enjoy organizing best.

Italians and Irish may both be Catholic, but their attitudes toward sex, love, pain, emotion, demonstrativeness, gestures, public exuberance, etc., could scarcely be more opposed. Rare is the Irish mother who has not warned her daughters about Italian men. Italians find the Irish hard, ironic rather than direct, morose; the Irish suggest Anglo-Saxon coolness, plus a shrewd angling for advantage. The ward politics of Joseph Plunkitt express the Irish way concisely:

> Everybody is talkin' these days about Tammany men growin' rich on graft, but nobody thinks of drawin' the distinction between honest graft and dishonest graft. There's all the difference in the world between the two. Yes, many of our men have grown rich in politics. I have myself. I've made a big fortune out of the game, and I'm gettin' richer every day, but I've not gone in for dishonest graft—blackmailin' gamblers, saloon-keepers, disorderly people, etc.—and neither has any of the men who have made big fortunes in politics.
>
> There's an honest graft, and I've an example of how it works. I might sum up the whole thing by sayin': "I seen my opportunities and I took 'em."
>
> . . . Or, supposin' it's a new bridge they're goin' to build. I get tipped off and I buy as much property as I can that has to be taken for approaches. I sell at my own price later on and drop some more money in the bank.
>
> Wouldn't you? It's just like lookin' ahead in Wall Street or in the coffee at Colton market. It's honest graft, and I'm lookin' for it every day of the year. I will tell you frankly that I've got a good lot of it, too.
>
> Another kind of honest graft. Tammany has raised a good many salaries. There was an awful howl by the reformers, but don't you know that Tammany gains 10 votes for every 1 it lost by salary raisin'?[19]

The Italians saw quickly enough that they'd have to break new ground for themselves. Many broke from the (Irish) Democrats and became Republicans, especially in Rhode Island and large sections of New York City. They also set out to take over trucking, transport, the docks, service industries, construction, restaurants.

WASP culture finds such industries slightly sinful and corrupt. Almost all of these were on the borders of politics and illicit desire, especially after Prohibition. WASP prejudice led swiftly to the image of the Italian as faintly evil. The villain in WASP puppet shows almost always has an Italian appearance: tall, thin, dressed in Continental black (with cape), a thin black mustache on an olive face, with slick black hair. In *The Marble Faun*, Hawthorne described the delicious corruptions Italians represent for the Anglo-Saxon imagination. To denigrate the success of Italian interests in accumulating wealth and power, it was a short step to the myth of a powerful Mafia. Had there been no reality beneath the myth, the American imagination was ready to invent it. Even though, in the national crime syndicate, "La Cosa Nostra" is only a colorful minor league, Americans more easily believe Italians villainous than Jews, Slavs, or nativists.[20] Even Bobby Kennedy allowed his instincts to be affronted by Jimmy Hoffa and the Mafia—as if they represented something new and un-American.

Two cinematic myths have dominated American consciousness: that of the outlaw gangs of the frontier, that of the outlaws of the great city. Beneath the myth that America is good there is a remarkable national fascination with shrewd, illegal, and violent assaults upon success. A "new world" lacked laws and standards by which to be sure how to behave. The great "robber barons," like the fighters against the "French and Indians" before them, went out and seized what they wanted to seize, creating laws afterwards. Crime is and has always been a national way of life. The bold and the strong, in almost directly Nietzschean terms, followed their own "will to power."

Success conferred upon them respectability after the fact. The great families of America almost all rode to power upon naked will operating outside the laws: the Stanfords, the Rockefellers, the Ames family, the Kennedys.

With the arrival of Al Capone and others, the American imagination could redeem itself by discharging its own guilts on others: darker of skin, Machiavellian, foreign, Catholic, untrustworthy, black-draped villains. (Poor white blond Mae West—in the grip of a huge, dark, hairy foreign gorilla in the City!) Imputing to the Mafia a corporate structure such as only Anglo-Saxon imagination could devise, with crisp organizational charts and lines of authority, and at the same time investing the Mafia with a touch of gothic horror and melodrama, Americans could satisfy the images they had nourished for generations.

In America, it is wiser for ethnic groups not to throw stones.

The *old* ethnic politics, in any case, required political leaders to show up at national picnics, endure gastronomic culture shock, say a few words (badly) in another tongue, enter into the spirit of a mazurka or a polka, wear a peasant cap, attempt some athletic or carnival feat. The idea was to show acceptance and delight. If you could *understand*, fit into the spirit, honor the symbols—and deliver one or two critical services—you might win a solid vote. By and large it was easier for Democrats than cool WASP Republicans to look comfortable through it all.

WASP politicians have their own ethnic style. They like to gather men of wealth and influence, respectable and "blue ribbon" scions, consult with a few technicians and experts, and discuss matters in solemn and solid environments. Their symbols are soft-spoken voices, handshakes, oaken panels, committee reports, and consensus around the table. They pay one another tribute as "reasonable men."[21]

The *new* ethnic politician proceeds first by way of "consciousness raising." He has to explore his own psyche to see whether he is an emissary of the superculture or a genuine representative of his own culture. (Here, as in so many matters, both by vocation and by choice, I remain on the boundary; Steve Adubado, Geno Baroni, and Barbara Mikulski are the real thing.) One's own self-identity is absolutely crucial.

For the new ethnic politics is not, in the end, interest politics. It is cultural politics. It is the seizing of one's own finite, concrete, social identity upon this huge, interrelated planet. Its ideal is, in Dostoevski's words, "humble charity." Not pretending to be universal or to speak for all groups, it closes its heart against no group. "Humble charity is the most powerful force in the universe."

The issue of personal identity is not easy to resolve, especially for a national politician. A national politician does well to have identifiable roots and a fairly sharply drawn ethnic identity; the contrast between Edmund Muskie's rootedness in Maine and Richard Nixon's rootlessness is not the least powerful symbolic difference between them. But a national politician has the further task of speaking in many accents, touching many audiences, reassuring many groups, using correctly many symbols. It would be fatal for him to seem to be the wielder of one set of symbols merely. Still, curious tensions can arise. In recent years, for example, despite his own acute political instincts, Senator Edward Kennedy tries very hard to frame everything in terms of "the issues." For it is now part of the conventional wisdom that the old politics of ethnicity and special interests is regressive, and progressive politics is concerned with ideals and rational arrangements —that is, "the issues." Enlightened voters study congressional voting records carefully. "Conscience" is identified with "issues," whereas what power is supposed to be about —interests and deals—is considered "expedience." Left politics is the last refuge of those wonderful people who brought us Prohibition.

Is Edmund Muskie really in touch with his Polish past? Any number of his instincts and moves reveal adaptations to the American scene of favorite Polish modes of action. When most Poles came to America, Poland was parcelled out to three foreign nations: Russia, Prussia, and the Austro-Hungarian Empire. A certain caution, a certain keeping of one's own counsel, a certain refusal to panic were habits required for survival. But does Muskie *think* of himself as Polish? Does his story have significance, in his eyes, because of Polish history and the needs of Poles and others like them in this country? Or, on the other hand, representing a state in which Poles are not numerous, are his concerns mainly those of keeping his steadiness and making his way through the superculture as best he can? A good man might choose either road. But for the new ethnic politician, identification with his own people makes all the difference.

Ethnic identification gives him distinctiveness, rough edges perhaps, a defined character and story. It allows him to relax in his native style of proceeding, his personal method of operating. It puts him in touch with the roots of his own emotions and images. Those who choose the route of superculture, as Muskie is sorely tempted to do— the route of the national liberal culture, the media experts, the consultants, the new professionals—are creatures of a new shape. They have not grown organically from their past, with all the deficiencies therein implied. They have been processed, with all the deficiencies *therein* implied. There seems to be a war within Muskie, between assimilation and distinctiveness. Unresolved, that war blurs his identity.

Identification with an ethnic group is a source of values, instincts, ideas, and perceptions that throw original light on the meaning of America. We have had high WASP presidents, low WASP presidents, and middle WASP presidents (consider Eisenhower, Johnson, and Nixon). And we have had an Irish president, from whom to learn a new moralism ("We can do better!"). We have not had Italian, Polish, Jewish, Black—and many other—styles of presidency, as lenses through which to see our national identity in a new light. There is a great deal yet to be discovered about America.

The new ethnic politics will prove its worth if it helps us to diminish the racial and other tensions in our cities; if it gives us a larger and more generous view of the role of families, neighborhoods, and primary-group networks in the health of social policies; and if it enables the nation to assume a more supple and accurate relation to ethnic groups in other nations of the world. The superculture around us is declining because it seems to have reached the limit of its creativity in precisely those respects.

In any case, millions of Americans, who for a long time tried desperately even if unconsciously to become "Americanized," are delighted to discover that they no longer have to pay that price; are grateful that they were born among the people destiny placed them in; are pleased to discover the possibilities and the limits inherent in being who they are; and are openly happy about what heretofore they had disguised in silence. There is a creativity and new release, there is liberation. and there is hope.

America is becoming America.

PART IV

Ethnicity in the Seventies and Beyond

CHAPTER ELEVEN

The New Ethnicity

THE WORD "ETHNIC" does not have a pleasing sound. The use of the word makes many people anxious. What sorts of repression account for this anxiety? What pretenses about the world are threatened when one points to the realities denoted and connoted by that ancient word? An internal history lies behind resistance to ethnicity; such resistance is almost always passional, convictional, not at all trivial. Many persons have tried to escape being "ethnic," in the name of a higher moral claim.

There are many meanings to the word itself. I have tried to map some of them below. There are many reasons for resistance to the word "ethnic" (and what it is taken to represent). Rather than beginning with these directly, I prefer to begin by defining the new ethnicity.

The definition I wish to give is personal; it grows out of personal experience; it is necessitated by an effort to attain an accurate self-knowledge. The hundreds of letters, reviews, comments, invitations, and conversations that followed upon *The Rise of the Unmeltable Ethnics* (1972) indicate that my own gropings to locate my own identity are not isolated. They struck a responsive chord in many others of Southern and East-

This chapter originally appeared in *The Center Magazine* (July-August 1974), pp. 18–25.

ern European (or other) background. My aim was—and is—to open up the field to study. Let later inquiry discern just how broadly and how exactly my first attempts at definition apply. It is good to try to give voice to what has so far been untongued—and then to devise testable hypotheses at a later stage.

The new ethnicity, then, is a movement of self-knowledge on the part of members of the third and fourth generation of Southern and Eastern European immigrants in the United States. In a broader sense, the new ethnicity includes a renewed self-consciousness on the part of other generations and other ethnic groups: the Irish, the Norwegians and Swedes, the Germans, the Chinese and Japanese, and others. Much that can be said of one of these groups can be said, not univocally but analogously, of others. In this area, one must learn to speak with multiple meanings and with a sharp eye for differences in detail. (By "analogous" I mean "having resemblances but also essential differences"; by "univocal" I mean a generalization that applies equally to all cases.) My sentences are to be read, then, analogously, not univocally; they are meant to awaken fresh perception, not to close discussion. They are intended to speak directly of a limited (and yet quite large) range of ethnic groups, while conceding indirectly that much that is said of Southern and Eastern Europeans may also be said, *mutatis mutandis,* of others.

I stress that, in the main, the "new" ethnicity involves those of the third and fourth generation after immigration. Perhaps two anecdotes will suggest the kind of experience involved. When *Time* magazine referred to me in 1972 as a "Slovak-American," I felt an inner shock; I had never referred to myself or been publicly referred to in that way. I wasn't certain how I felt about it. Then, in 1974, after I had given a lecture on ethnicity to the only class in Slavic American studies in the United States, at the City College of New York, the dean of the college said on the way to lunch, "Considering how sensitive you are on ethnic matters, the surprising thing to me was how American you are." I wanted to ask him, "What else?" In this area one grows used to symbolic uncertainties.

The new ethnicity does not entail: (a) speaking a foreign language; (b) living in a subculture; (c) living in a "tight-knit" ethnic neighborhood; (d) belonging to fraternal organizations; (e) responding to "ethnic" appeals; (f) exalting one's own nationality or culture, narrowly construed. Neither does it entail a university education or the reading of writers on the new ethnicity. Rather, the new ethnicity entails: first, a growing sense of discomfort with the sense of identity one is supposed to have—universalist, "melted," "like everyone else"; then a growing appreciation for the potential wisdom of one's own gut reactions (especially on moral matters) and their historical roots; a growing self-confidence and social power; a sense of being discriminated against, condescended to, or carelessly misapprehended; a growing disaffection regarding those to whom one had always been taught to defer; and a sense of injustice regarding the response of liberal spokesmen to conflicts between various ethnic groups, especially between "legitimate" minorities and "illegitimate" ones. There is, in a word, an inner conflict between one's felt personal power and one's ascribed public power: a sense of outraged truth, justice, and equity.

The new ethnicity does, therefore, have political consequences. Many Southern and Eastern European-Americans have been taught, as I was, not to be "ethnic," or even "hyphenated," but only "American." Yet at critical points it became clear to some of us, then to more of us, that when push comes to shove we are always, in the eyes of others, "ethnics," unless we play completely by their rules, emotional as well as procedural. And in the end, even then, they retain the power and the status. Still, the stakes involved in admitting this reality to oneself are very high. Being "universal" is regarded as being good; being ethnically self-conscious raises anxieties. Since one's whole identity has been based upon being "universal," one is often loath to change public face too suddenly. Many guard the little power and status they have acquired, although they cock one eye on how the ethnic "movement" is progressing. They are wise. But their talents are also needed.

The new ethnicity, then, is a fledgling movement, not to be confused with the appearance of ethnic themes on television commercials, in television police shows, and in magazines. All these manifestations in the public media would not have occurred unless the ethnic reality of America had begun to be noticed. In states from Massachusetts to Iowa, great concentrations of Catholics and Jews, especially in urban centers, have been some of the main bastions of Democratic Party politics for fifty years. The "new politics," centered in the universities, irritated and angered this constituency (even when, as it sometimes did, it won its votes). Thus, there is a relation between the fledgling new ethnicity and this larger ethnic constituency. But what that relationship will finally be has not yet been demonstrated by events.

Those who do not come from Southern or Eastern European backgrounds in the United States may not be aware of how it feels to come from such a tradition; they may not know the internal history. They may note "mass passivity" and "alienation" without sharing the cynicism learned through particular experiences. They may regard the externals of ethnic economic and social success, modest but real, while never noticing the internal ambiguity—and its compound of peace and self-hatred, confidence and insecurity.

To be sure, at first many "white ethnics" of the third generation are not conscious of having any special feelings. The range of feelings about themselves they do have is very broad; more than one stream of feeling is involved. They are right-wingers and left-wingers, chauvinists and universalists, all-Americans and isolationists. Many want nothing more desperately than to be considered "American." Indeed, by now many have so deeply acquired that habit that to ask them point-blank how they are different from others would arouse strong emotional resistance.

For at least three reasons, many white ethnics are becoming self-conscious. As usual, great social forces outside the self draw forth from the self new responses. First, a critical mass of scholars, artists, and writers is beginning to emerge—the Italians, for example, are extraordinarily eminent in the cinema. Second, the prevailing image of the model American—the "best and the brightest" of the Ivy League, wealthy, suave, and powerful—has been discredited by the mismanagement of war abroad, by racial injustice at home, and by attitudes, values, and emotional patterns unworthy of emulation internally. The older image of the truly cultured American is no longer compelling. Many, therefore, are thrown back upon their own resources.

Finally, the attitudes of liberal, enlightened commentators on the "crisis of the cities" seem to fall into traditional patterns: guilt vis-à-vis blacks, and disdain for the Archie Bunkers of the land (Bunker is, of course, a classy British American name, but Carroll O'Connor is in appearance undisguisably Irish). The national media present to the public a model for what it is to be a "good American" which makes many people feel unacceptable to their betters, unwashed, and ignored. Richard Hofstadter wrote of "the anti-intellectualism of the people," but another feature of American life is the indifference—even hostility—of many intellectuals to Main Street. In return, then, many people respond with deep contempt for experts, educators, "limousine liberals," "radical chic," "bureaucrats"—a contempt whose sources are partly those of class ("the hidden injuries of class") and partly those of ethnicity ("legitimate" minorities and unacceptable minorities). The national social class that prides itself on being universalist has lost the confidence of many. Votes on school bond issues are an example of popular resistance to professionals.

In my own case, the reporting of voting patterns among white ethnic voters during the Wallace campaigns of 1964 and 1968 first aroused in me ethnic self-consciousness. Descriptions of "white backlash" often put the blame—inaccurately I came to see—upon Slavs and other Catholic groups. The Slavs of "South Milwaukee" were singled out for comment in the Wallace vote in Wisconsin in 1964. First, South Milwaukee was not distinguished from the south side of Milwaukee. Then, it was not noted that the Slavic vote for Wallace fell below his statewide average. Then, the very heavy vote for Wallace in outlying German and British American areas was not pointed out. Finally, the strong vote for Wallace in the wealthy northeastern suburbs of Milwaukee was similarly ignored. It seemed to me that those whom the grandfathers called "hunkies" and "dagos" were now being called "racists," "fascists," and "pigs," with no noticeable gain in affection. Even in 1972, a staff advisory in the Shriver "trip book" for a congressional district in Pittsburgh called the district "Wallace country," though the Wallace vote in that district in 1968 had been 12 percent, and the Humphrey vote had been 58 percent. I obliged the staff member to revise his account and to call the district "Humphrey country." It is one of the most consistently liberal districts in Pennsylvania. Why send this constituency the message that it is the enemy?

Jimmy Breslin was once asked by an interviewer in *Penthouse* how, coming out of Queens, he could have grown up so liberal. Actually, next to Brooklyn, there is no more liberal county in the nation. A similar question was put to a liberal journalist from the Dorchester area, in Boston. The class and ethnic bias hidden in the way the word "liberal" is used in such interviews cries out for attention.

One of the large social generalizations systematically obscured by the traditional anti-Catholicism of American elites is the overwhelmingly progressive voting record in America's urban centers. The centers of large Catholic population in every northeastern and north central state have been the key to Democratic victories in those states since at least 1916. The hypothesis that Catholics have been, second only to Jews, the central constituency of successful progressive politics in this century is closer to the facts than historians have observed. (Massachusetts, that most Catholic of our states, stayed with McGovern in 1972.) The language of politics in America is, however, mainly Protestant, and Protestant biases color public perception. Protestant leadership is given the halo of morality and legitimacy, Catholic life is described in terms of negatively laden words: Catholic "power," "machine politics," etc.

There are other examples of odd perception on the part of American elites with respect to Catholic and other ethnic populations. The major institutions of American life—government, education, the media—give almost no assistance to those of "white ethnic" background who wish to obey the Socratic maxim: "Know thyself." One of the greatest and most dramatic migrations of human history brought more than thirty million immigrants to this land between 1874 and 1924. Despite the immense dramatic materials involved in this migration, only one major American film records it: Elia Kazan's *America! America!* That film ends with the hero's arrival in America. The tragic and costly experience of Americanization has scarcely yet been touched. How many died; how many were morally and psychologically destroyed; how many still carry the marks of changing their names, of "killing" their mother tongue and renouncing their former identity, in order to become "new men" and "new women"—these are motifs of violence, self-mutilation, joy, and irony. The inner history of this migration must come to be understood, if we are ever to understand the aspirations and fears of some seventy million Americans.

When this part of the population exhibits self-consciousness and begins to exert group claims—whether these are claims made by aggregated individuals or claims that are corporate— they are regularly confronted with the accusation that they are being "divisive." ("Divisive" is a code word for Catholic ethnics and Jews, is it not? It is seldom used of others: white Southerners, Appalachians, Chicanos, blacks, native Americans, prep-school British Americans, or others who maintain their own identity and institutions.) Earl Raab writes eloquently of this phenomenon in *Commentary* (May, 1974): "Modern Europe... never really accepted the legitimacy of the corporate Jew—although it was at its best willing to grant full civil rights to the individual Jew. That, for the Jews, was an impossible paradox, a secular vision of Christian demands to convert...[And] it is precisely this willingness to allow the Jews their separate identity as a group which is now coming into question in America." Individual diversity, yes; group identity, not for all.

The Christian white ethnic, like the Jew, actually has few group demands to make: positively, for educational resources to keep values and perceptions alive, articulate, and critical; negatively, for an equal access to power, status, and the definition of the general American purpose and symbolic world. Part of the strategic function of the cry "divisive!" is to limit access to these things. Only those individuals will be advanced who define themselves as individuals and who operate according to the symbols of the established. The emotional meaning is: "Become like us." This is an understandable strategy, but in a nation as pluralistic as the United States, it is shortsighted. The nation's hopes, purposes, and symbols need to be defined inclusively rather than exclusively; all must become "new men" and "new women." All the burden ought not to fall upon the newcomers.

There is much that is attractive about the British American, upper-class, northeastern culture that has established for the entire nation a model of behavior and perception. This model is composed of economic power; status; cultural tone; important institutional rituals and procedures; and the acceptable patterns of style, sensibility, and rationality. The terse phrase "Ivy League" suggests all these factors. The nation would be infinitely poorer than it is without the Ivy League. All of us who came to this land—including the many lower-class British Americans, Scotch-Irish, Scandinavians, and Germans—are much in the debt of the Ivy League, deeply, substantially so.

Still, the Ivy League is not the nation. The culture of the Ivy League is not the culture of America (not even of Protestant America).

Who are we, then, we who do not particularly reverberate to the literature of New England, whose interior history is not Puritan, whose social class is not Brahmin (either in reality or in pretense), whose ethnicity is not British American, or even Nordic? Where in American institutions, American literature, American education is our identity mirrored, objectified, rendered accessible to intelligent criticism, and confirmed? We are still, I think, persons without a public symbolic world, persons without a publicly verified culture to sustain us and our children.

It is not that we lack culture; it is not that we lack strength of ego and a certain internal peace. As Jean-Paul Sartre remarks in one of his later works, there is a distinction between one's identity in one's own eyes and one's identity in the eyes of others. In the United States, many who have internal dignity cannot avoid noticing that others regard them as less than equals, with a sense that they are different, with uncertainty, and with a lack of commonality. It is entirely possible that the "melting pot" would indeed have melted everyone, if those who were the models into which the molten metal was to be poured had not found the process excessively demanding. A sense of separate identity is, in part, induced from outside-in. I am made aware of being Catholic and Slovak by the actions of others. I would be sufficiently content were my identity to be so taken for granted, so utterly normal and real, that it would never have to be self-conscious.

The fact of American cultural power is that a more or less upper class, Northeastern Protestant sensibility sets the tone, and that a fairly aggressive British American ethnocentricity, and even Anglophilia, governs the instruments of education and public life. Moreover, it is somehow emotionally important not to challenge this dominant ethnocentricity. It is quite proper to talk of other sorts of social difference—income, class, sex, even religion. To speak affirmatively of ethnicity, however, makes many uneasy. Some important truth must lie hidden underneath this uneasiness. A Niebuhrian analysis of social power suggests that a critical instrument of social control in the United States is, indeed, the one that dares not be spoken of.

In New York State, for example, in 1974 the four Democratic candidates for the office of lieutenant governor (not, however, for governor) were named Olivieri, Cuomo, La Falce, and Krupsak. It was the year, the pundits say, for "ethnic balance" on the ticket. But all four candidates insisted that their ethnicity was not significant. Two boasted of being from *upstate,* one of being a *woman,* one of being for *"the little guy."* It is publicly legitimate to be different on any other account except ethnicity, even where the importance of ethnic diversity is tacitly agreed upon.

If I say, as I sometimes have, that I would love to organize an "ethnic caucus" within both the Democratic Party and the Republican Party, the common reaction is one of anxiety, distaste, and strained silence. But if I say, as I am learning to, that I would love to organize a "caucus of workingmen and women" in both parties, heads quickly nod in approval. Social class is, apparently, rational. Cultural background is, apparently, counter-rational.

Yet the odd political reality is that most Americans do not identify themselves in class terms. They respond to cultural symbols intimate to their ethnic history in America. Ethnicity is a "gut issue," even though it cannot be mentioned. A wise political candidate does not, of course, speak to a long-shoreman's local by calling its members Italian American and appealing to some supposed cultural solidarity. That would be a mistake. But if he speaks about those themes in the cultural tradition that confirm their own identity—themes like family, children, home, neighborhood, specific social aspirations, and grievances—they know he is with them: he does represent them. In order to be able to represent many constituencies, a representative has to be able to "pass over" into many cultural histories. He may never once make ethnicity explicit as a public theme; but, implicitly, he will be recognizing the daily realities of ethnicity and ethnic experience in the complex fabric of American social power.

According to one social myth, America is a "melting pot," and this myth is intended by many to be not merely descriptive but normative: the faster Americans—especially white ethnic Americans—"melt" into the British American pattern, the better. There is even a certain ranking according to the supposed degree of assimilation: Scotch Irish, Norwegians, Swedes, Germans, Swiss, Dutch, liberal or universalist Jews, the Irish, and on down the line to the less assimilated: Greeks, Yugoslavs, Hungarians, Central and East Europeans, Italians, Orthodox Jews, French Canadians, Portuguese, Latins and Spanish-speaking.... (the pattern almost exactly reflects the history and literature of England).

Now it was one thing to be afraid of ethnicity in 1924, in confronting a first and second generation of immigrants. It is another thing to be afraid, in 1974, in confronting a third and fourth generation. Indeed, fears about a revival of ethnicity seem to be incompatible with conviction about how successful the "melting pot" has been. Fears about a "revival" of ethnicity confirm the fact that ethnicity is still a powerful reality in American life.

What, then, are the advantages and disadvantages in making this dangerous subject, this subterranean subject, explicit?

The disadvantages seem to be three. The first one on everyone's mind is that emphasis on ethnicity may work to the disadvantage of blacks. It may, it is said, become a legitimization of racism. It may "polarize" whites and blacks. Nothing could be further from the truth. Those who are concerned about the new ethnicity—Geno Baroni (Washington), Irving Levine (New York), Barbara Mikulski (Baltimore), Ralph Perrotta (New York), Steve Adubado (Newark), Otto Feinstein (Detroit), Stan Franczyk (Buffalo), Kenneth Kovach (Cleveland), Edward Marciniak (Chicago), and others—have given ample proof of their concern for the rights and opportunities of black Americans. Many got their start in the new ethnicity through their work among blacks. The overriding political perception among those concerned with the new ethnicity is that the harshness of life in the cities must be reduced by whites and blacks together, especially in working-class neighborhoods. Present social policies punish neighborhoods that integrate: Such neighborhoods should be rewarded and strengthened and guaranteed a long-range stability.

But fears about ethnicity require a further two-part response. Racism does not need ethnicity in order to be legitimated in America. It was quite well legitimated by Anglo-American culture, well before white ethnics arrived here in significant numbers, well before many white ethnics had ever met blacks. Indeed, there is some reason to believe that, while racism is an international phenomenon and found in all cultures, the British American and other Nordic peoples have a special emotional response to colored races. Not all European peoples respond to intermarriage, for example, with quite the emotional quality of the Anglo-Saxons. The French, the Spanish, the Italians, and the Slavs are not without their own forms of racism. But the felt quality of racism is different in different cultures. (It seems different among the North End Italians and the South Boston Irish of Boston, for example.)

In America, racism did not wait until the immigrants of 1880 and after began to arrive. Indeed, it is in precisely those parts of the country solely populated by British Americans that the conditions of blacks have been legally and institutionally least humane. In those parts of the country most heavily populated by white ethnics, the cultural symbols and the political muscle that have led to civil-rights and other legislation have received wide support. Liberal senators and congressmen elected by white ethnics—including the Kennedys—led the way. Even in 1972, both Hamtramck and Buffalo went for George McGovern. McGovern's share of the Slavic vote was 52 percent. Nixon won the white Protestant vote by 68 percent.

It will be objected that white ethnic leaders like Frank Rizzo of Philadelphia, Ralph Perk of Cleveland, and others are signs of a new racism on the part of white ethnics in the Northern cities, of a retreat from support for blacks, and of a rising tide of anti-crime and anti-busing sentiment. The proponents of the new ethnicity perceive such developments as a product of liberal neglect and liberal divisiveness. The proponents of the new politics talk well of civil rights, equal opportunity, economic justice, and other beautiful themes. But the new politics, in distinguishing "legitimate" minorities (blacks, Chicanos, native Americans) from "less favored" minorities (Italians, Slavs, Orthodox Jews, Irish, etc.), has set up punitive and self-defeating mechanisms. The new politics has needlessly divided working-class blacks from working-class whites, in part by a romance (on television) with militance and flamboyance, in part by racial discrimination in favor of some against others, not because of need but because of color.

The second part of this response is that the politics of "the constituency of conscience" (as Michael Harrington, Eugene McCarthy, and others have called it)—the politics of the liberal, the educated, the enlightened—is less advantageous to blacks than is the politics of the new ethnicity. The new politics is less advantageous to blacks because it is obsessed with racial differences, and approaches these through the ineffectual lenses of guilt and moralism. Second, it is blind to cultural differences among blacks, as well as to cultural differences among whites; and sometimes these are significant. Third, it unconsciously but effectively keeps blacks in the position of a small racial minority outnumbered in the population ten to one.

By contrast, the new ethnicity notes many other significant differences besides those based upon race, and defines political and social problems in ways that unite diverse groups around common objectives. In Chicago, for example, neither Poles nor Italians are represented on the boards or in the executive suites of Chicago's top 105 corporations in a higher proportion than blacks or Latinos—all are of 1 percent or less. In Boston, neither white ethnics nor blacks desire busing, but this highly ideological instrument of social change is supported most by just those affluent liberals—in such suburbs as Brookline and Newton—whose children will not be involved.

The new ethnic politics would propose a strategy of social rewards—better garbage pickup, more heavily financed and orderly schools, long-range guarantees on home mortgages, easier access to federally insured home improvement loans, and other services—for neighborhoods that integrate. As a neighborhood moves from, say, a 10 percent population of blacks to 20 percent or more, integration should be regulated so that long-range community stability is guaranteed. It is better long-range policy to have a large number of neighborhoods integrated up to 20 or 30 percent than to encourage—even by inadvertence— a series of sudden flights and virtually total migrations. Institutional racism is a reality; the massive migration of blacks into a neighborhood does not bring with it social rewards but, almost exclusively, punishments.

There are other supposed disadvantages to emphasis upon ethnicity. Ethnicity, it is said, is a fundamentally counter-rational, primordial, uncontrollable social force; it leads to hatred and violence; it is the very enemy of enlightenment, rationality, and liberal politics. But this is to confuse nationalism or tribalism with cultural heritage. Because a man's name is Russell, or Ayer, or Flew, we would not wish to accuse him of tribalism on the grounds that he found the Britons a uniquely civilized and clearheaded people, thought the Germans ponderous and mystic, the French philosophically romantic, etc. A little insular, we might conclude, but harmlessly ethnocentric. And if it is not necessarily tribalistic or unenlightened to read English literature in American schools, just possibly it would be even more enlightened and even less tribalistic to make other literatures, germane to the heritage of other Americans, more accessible than they are.

The United States is, potentially, a multiculturally attuned society. The greatest number of immigrants in recent years arrives from Spanish-speaking and Asian nations. But the nation's cultural life, and its institutions of culture, are far from being sensitive to the varieties of the American people. Why should a cultural heritage not their own be imposed unilaterally upon newcomers? Would not genuine multicultural adaptation on the part of all be more cosmopolitan and humanistic? It would be quite significant in international affairs. The Americans would truly be a kind of prototype of planetary diversity.

Some claim that cultural institutions will be fragmented if every ethnic group in America clamors for attention. But the experience of the Illinois curriculum in ethnic studies suggests that no one school represents more than four or five ethnic groups (sometimes fewer) in significant density. With even modest adjustments in courses in history, literature, and the social sciences, material can be introduced that illuminates inherited patterns of family life, values, and preferences. The purpose for introducing multicultural materials is neither chauvinistic nor propagandistic but realistic. Education ought to illuminate what is happening in the self of each child.

What about the child of the mixed marriage, the child of *no* ethnic heritage—the child of the melting pot? So much in the present curriculum already supports such a child that the only possible shock to arise from multicultural materials would appear to be a beneficial one: not all others in America are like him (her), and that diversity, as well as homogenization, has a place in America.

The practical agenda that faces proponents of the new ethnicity is vast, indeed. At the heights of American economic and social power, there is not yet much of a melting pot. Significant ethnic diversity is manifested in the proportion of each group studying in universities, on faculties, in the professions, on boards of directors, among the creators of public social symbols, and the like. In patterns of home ownership, family income, work patterns, care for the aged, political activism, authoritarianism, individualism, and matters of ultimate concern, group differences are remarkable. About all these things, more information is surely needed. Appropriate social policies need to be hypothesized, tried, and evaluated.

Ethnic diversity in the United States persists in the consciousness of individuals, in their perceptions, preferences, behavior, even while mass production and mass communications homogenize our outward appearances. Some regard such persistence as a personal failure; they would prefer to "transcend" their origins, or perhaps they believe that they have. Here two questions arise. What cultural connection do they have with their brothers and sisters still back in Montgomery, or Wheeling, or Skokie, or Pawtucket? Second, has their personal assimilation introduced into the great American superculture fresh streams of image, myth, symbol, and style of intellectual life? Has anything distinctively their own—formed in them by a history longer than a thousand years—been added to the common wisdom?

The new ethnicity does not stand for the Balkanization of America. It stands for a true, real, multicultural cosmopolitanism. It points toward a common culture truly altered by each new infusion of diversity. Until now, the common culture has been relatively resistant to internal transformation; it has not so much arisen from the hearts of all as been imposed; the melting pot has had only a single recipe. That is why at present the common culture seems to have become discredited, shattered, unenforceable. Its cocoon has broken. Struggling to be born is a creature of multicultural beauty, dazzling, free, a higher and richer form of life. It was fashioned in the painful darkness of the melting pot and now, at the appointed time, it awakens.

CHAPTER TWELVE

Pluralism: A Humanistic Perspective

HUMANISTS HAVE NOT analyzed as closely as they should the concept of ethnicity. By and large, this task has been left to scholars in the fields of history, political science, and sociology. This essay, therefore, may appear to offer a novel view of the subject. Scholars, teachers, and writers in the fields of literature, philosophy, and theology do have resources to bring to bear upon the realities of ethnicity, not only as these have affected human life in the past, but primarily as these affect the present—and promise to affect the future—under the rubric of the "new ethnicity." These resources have not yet been fully differentiated and sharpened. Scholars in the humanities commonly work upon literary texts, public rituals and liturgies, manners, mores, and ethical practices. The empirical clarity available to social scientists is theirs only at secondhand. But what they can do—and what this essay undertakes—is to ferret out the ways by which the daily realities of ethnicity are felt and perceived in ordinary experience, and to establish the worldviews within which such experiences are daily understood.

A theory about the methods proper to the humanities may help to orient the reader. The humanities are concerned about the

This chapter originally appeared in the *Harvard Encyclopedia of American Ethnic Groups* published by The Belknap Press in 1980.

question, "Who?" They are concerned about the human person, the human subject, and thus about the experiencing, perceiving, imagining, understanding, judging and deciding of human persons. *Quidquid percipitur,* runs the Thomistic adage, *per modum percipientis percipitur: Whatever is perceived is perceived through the character of the one who perceives.* Who a person is (the range and quality of his or her experiences, imaginings, understandings, decidings, etc.) affects what a person perceives. The scientist is taught to operate in the mode of objectivity, discounting so much as is possible the factor of *whoness. Any* observer trained to the scientific mode should be able to replace the original observer, without loss of meaning. Subjectivity, so far as is possible, is eliminated. In the humanities, by contrast, students are trained to deepen and to enlarge their own subjectivity, to attempt to "cross over" and to enter into the subjectivity of others. They are taught that subjectivity is, in human affairs, important; that it is finally irreplaceable; and that it holds within it much that repays the effort to raise questions in order to understand more exactly. The work of scientists sometimes seems almost mystical to humanists, containing as it does measurements, lucid analytical models, mathematical invention of great brilliance, and refined and much-tested verbal clarity. Similarly, the work of humanists must seem, at times, almost mystical to scientists, with its indirect ways of eliciting almost unconscious senses of reality (myths), symbols, stories, viewpoints, sensibilities, images and imaginal structures. Necessarily, humanists must discuss ethnicity in a way unfamiliar to, and at least in part unsatisfactory to, the scientist. Still, the work of the humanist is valuable to the scientist, if only to provoke further inquiry by turning up surprises, puzzles, anomalies, or perhaps even wholly new paradigms within which to raise further questions. For the scientist, too, and not only part time, is a human being, a *who,* trying to make sense of his own experience.

Thus, while the present essay may convey meanings not easily translatable into scientific propositions, perhaps it can succeed in expressing a plausible worldview within which to order some of our present-day experiences concerning the phenomena of ethnicity.

I. The New Ethnicity

Ethnicity is a baffling reality—morally ambivalent, paradoxical in experience, elusive in concept. World travelers observe that cultures differ from one another in mores and manners. Diplomats recognize that even the simplest gestures, words, or behaviors may signal multiple meanings. Nearly everyone recognizes that culture affects the subjectivity of individuals as well as their outward behavior. Culture shapes sensibility and perception, expectation and imagination, aspiration and moral striving, intellect and worldview. Yet it cannot be said that most highly educated persons are well prepared to account for the multicultural experiences available to them in the present age. Our theories about cultural differences and ethnic nuances are not as deep, broad, or subtle as our experience. Some philosophical distinctions may, therefore, be useful in charting this fascinating but treacherous terrain.

"Culture" is not an easy concept, since so many institutions, rituals, and practices contribute to its shaping. Its ramifications are sweeping, subtle, and often unarticulated. Its effects upon us often lie below the threshold of words or even of consciousness. The culture that has shaped us shapes our way of experiencing and perceiving, of imagining and speaking, so deeply that it is very difficult to think our way outside it. It teaches us what to regard as relevant and what to count as evidence; it provides our *canons* of relevance and evidence. We are not "products" of a culture in the way that objects are produced by a machine. Indeed, we must make conscious and voluntary efforts if we intend to appropriate our culture wholly, to go to its depths and to master its multiple possibilities. Cultures are freely elaborated by human beings; they lie, as the German philosophers were wont to say, in the realm of freedom, and the variety of human cultures on this planet is testimony to the capacities of human liberty over and above the necessities of nature. An individual passing over from his or her native culture into a culture quite different may experience "culture shock"; may, that is, come into a set of presuppositions, expectations, criteria for perception and evaluation and behavior so different as to undermine much that was previously taken for granted.

The concept of "ethnicity" has traditionally been seen as somewhat narrower than, although related to, the concept of culture. From earliest times, distinctive social groups found themselves living under the shaping influence of a common culture. In a sense, what made such social groups distinctive were the prior shaping influences of diverse cultures. Yet one could speak of a new overarching culture—Mesopotamian, Greek, Roman— within which the concept of ethnicity pointed to less all-embracing cultural influences. It is useful to note that within a concept like "Western culture," for example, quite dramatic, pervasive, and persistent sources of cultural distinctiveness have remained vital. In philosophy, to choose but one example, there are quite different creative impulses, presuppositions, methods, standards and criteria manifested in different ethnic traditions: German, French, British, Italian, Spanish, American. In literature, theology, and in the arts it is possible simultaneously to discern characteristics that justify the notion both of a wider shared culture—Western culture—and of particular, original and vital sources of differentiation. Humanists have not so often used the word "ethnic" to describe these differences (until recently, the word has had a ring more proper to the social sciences). From early Latin times the tendency has rather been to speak of *nationes* (as at the University of Paris in the 12th century), not in the modern political sense but rather in a pervasive cultural sense, signifying the existence of divergent cultural entities.

It is important, then, to recognize that any humanist wishing to work out a full theory of ethnicity may find many already cherished texts in which, under other names, a tradition of giving cultural differences their due weight has been observed. Among such texts would be Alexis de Tocqueville's *Democracy in America* (1835), Ralph Waldo Emerson's *English Traits* (1856), George Santayana's *The German Mind* (originally titled *Egotism in German Philosophy,* 1939), and many others. More recent writings include Luigi Barzini's *The Italians* (1964), Jacques Maritain's *Reflections on America* (1958), and Hedrick Smith's *The Russians* (1976).

A major watershed in our thinking about ethnicity seems to have been reached in the period after World War II. As a result of the growth of international communication and of a worldwide infrastructure of technology and commerce, human beings almost everywhere have become more aware of cultures not their own. It was long imagined that the creation of "one world" would bring with it many homogenizing tendencies, based on the imperatives of universal "reason" and science and on the standardization of technological artifacts (from Coca-Cola to Shell, from transistors to computers). It was also imagined that the managers and intellectuals who operated the new international systems would create a cadre of leaders, or even perhaps a new managerial class spread around the globe, who would be almost equally at home in the urban technical environments of London, Tokyo, New York, Berlin, Rio de Janeiro, and Calcutta. The same methods, the same problems, and (roughly) the same living conditions, it was imagined, would accompany them wherever they went. Indeed, such eventualities have come to pass, largely as expected, as a result of many homogenizing influences. Political ideals—"liberation," "equality," "national sovereignty"—have crossed virtually all the world's frontiers. So have rock music and movies, jeans and automobiles.

Simultaneously, however, the late 20th century has also been marked by a resurgence of ethnic consciousness. In the Soviet Union since about 1950 the Jewish community has become increasingly conscious of its special identity and increasingly public in its self-consciousness—an attitude seen also among the ethnic Germans, Ukrainians, and other peoples of the U.S.S.R. In Great Britain, the Scots and the Welsh have demanded greater autonomy, as have the French Canadians in Canada. In Africa, Latin America, Asia and many other places throughout the world the self-consciousness of cultural bodies has been similarly heightened. There appear to be four components of this new self-consciousness, and in examining them, it is important to pause long enough to see clearly what is new in this "new ethnicity."

The new cultural self-consciousness is, first of all, post-tribal, arising in an era in which almost every culture has been obligated to become aware of many others. In contrast to the isolation of ancient times, each culture has met at least some of the others in actual experience, and many others via the media.

Secondly, the new ethnicity arises in an era of advanced technology. This technology paradoxically liberates certain energies for more intense self-consciousness, even as it binds many cultures together in standardized technical infrastructures. The communications media, for example, are neutral with respect to cultural differences. In the techniques required to operate them and in some of their internal imperatives (scientific knowledge, technical control, precision, order) they are clearly homogenizing in effect. On the other hand, the content of what the media express is necessarily received by audiences affected by cultural memory, cultural differences, and distinctive cultural aspirations. Communicators who had heretofore taken their own cultural identity for granted—because it was so much a part of their daily reality that they hardly needed to be aware of it— have become more sharply aware of their own distinctive tastes, needs, and hopes in using these media. They commonly find that they must become more analytical, articulate, and self-conscious about their own distinctive voice and viewpoint.

Thirdly, the new ethnicity arises in an era of intense centripetal and homogenizing forces. Great technical power has become centered in the apparatus of the state, in the central agencies of communication, and in the central distributors of technology. These new forces call into being countervailing forces, but are themselves so powerful that a wider range of diversity can be tolerated.

These new forces also generate rebellion against "mindless" and "soulless" modernism. This rebellion represents a fourth condition for the emergence of the new ethnicity—namely, a certain discrediting of the supposed moral superiority of the modern. For some generations now, high political and moral status has accrued to all things modern, enlightened, and up to date. The forces of habit, custom, and tradition have been on the defensive. Now that the fully modern type of man or woman is everywhere more visible among us, however, the secular, pragmatic style of the proponents of modernization has lost its halo and has begun to reveal serious moral flaws. In casting about for a posture that promises a higher degree of wisdom, nobility, and relevance to ordinary people, many leaders have begun to look again at the moral sources of their traditional cultures. For most, the choice is not simply dichotomous—either traditional or modern. Rather, the status of inherited wisdom has risen, while that of the modern has slipped. In order to be evaluated, this inherited wisdom, now at last to be taken more seriously, has first to be more clearly known. Thus, the examination of "roots" has attracted both scholarly and popular attention. It is probable that a general law is here being observed: in times of moral perplexity and crisis, a reappropriation of the past, a search for renewal, gains impetus. In China there have been profound cultural cross-currents, in the United States the Bicentennial renewal, and in other cultures the drive toward cultural or national awakening; all these exhibit a strong moral dimension, fed by dissatisfaction with a merely modern morality.

In a word, peoples in every part of the world, to the surprise of those who anticipated the power only of homogenizing tendencies, are becoming both more aware of others and also more aware of their own distinctive cultural identity. A heightened cultural awareness, coupled with demands for its appropriate political expression, has made of the new ethnicity a major factor in world affairs—perhaps even one of the major sources of political energy in our era.

2. Revising the Liberal Tradition

In the past, tribal consciousness was with good reason considered to be a real or potential threat to liberal and rational institutions. While loyalty, fellow feeling, and sympathy are values highly prized, they are, nevertheless, moral sentiments sometimes weakened by the propensity of human beings to limit their application to persons of their own kind. Human beings most easily grasp through shared experience, imagination, and tacit social bonding those ways of life most like their own. In his criticism of sentimental liberalism, *Moral Man and Immoral Society* (1932), Reinhold Niebuhr spelled out very clearly the limitations of such sentiments with respect to group behavior. Because of their enduring power, however, he also distrusted such counterimperatives of the modern spirit as "enlightenment" and "rationality." These were, he thought, too optimistically set in opposition to ties of kin, to "reasons of the blood," to inherited or ascribed status, and to related "nonrational" factors. The real world, he suggested, is more complex.

In his famous essay, "What is Enlightenment?" Immanuel Kant singled out two elements of great importance to the modern temper: individuality and rationality. Each individual, he argued, is an originating source of universal reason. Each individual stands equal to every other through participation in a unifying and universally distributed rationality. Kant locates reason, then, not in the group or social unit but in the individual. He holds that reason is universal in its fundamental character. In reason, persons find their individuality, their unity with all other individuals, and their dignity.

It is important in the present age to defend these basic principles of enlightenment set forth, in the language of his time, by Kant and others; the declarations of fundamental human rights embraced by the United Nations depend upon such conceptions. However, it is important, as well, to recognize that the emergence of a kind of worldwide interdependence built upon a scientific and technical base, which has been achieved since the Age of Enlightenment, has also taught us much about the diversifying impact of cultural, economic, and political systems. Such systems affect the self-consciousness of individuals. They also affect the consciousness of whole social groups. No one would deny that there is a perfectly straightforward sense in which all human beings are members of the same human family; every human being is bound by imperatives of reasoning, justification, and communication across cultural and other boundaries; and each human being is entitled to claims of fundamental human dignity. Still, it is also widely grasped today that reason itself operates in pluralistic modes. It would be regarded as "cultural imperialism" to suggest that only one form of reasoning is valid in all matters. It would be regarded as naive to believe that the content of human experiencing, imagining, understanding, judging, and deciding were everywhere the same. If anything, our age, perhaps, has learned too well the relativity of values and cultures, to the point of neglecting those things that unite all human beings as one.

It seems important for a liberal civilization today to thread its way philosophically between the Scylla of relativity and the Charybdis of too narrow a conception of universal reason. Bernard Lonergan in *Insight: A Study of Human Understanding* (1957) has suggested that it is of intellectual benefit to call attention to the difference between invariant human operations and the varying content upon which those operations work. In this way, he proposes to defend at one and the same time both the spiritual unity of the human race and that multiplicity of cultures that springs from human liberty.

Unlike other animals, the human being elaborates across space and time multiple forms of behaviors and practices. Cultural differentiation is a primary characteristic of human life, a direct expression of human liberty. As a source of originating agency, possessing a capacity to perceive, to intend, and to act in a self-directed manner, each individual human person stands in a certain sense alone. Yet in living in social units, in elaborating social institutions of great complexity, each individual human being is also a social creature. As a bodily organism, each is born, suffers, is hungry, loves, dies. Yet in various cultures these fundamental identities acquire distinctive symbolic meanings. On several levels of life, individual and social, intellectual and physical, certain invariant structures of experience cut across all cultures and unite all human beings in certain specific human perplexities. Daniel Bell has theorized in *The Cultural Contradictions of Capitalism* (1976) and in his Hobhouse Lecture at the London School of Economics (1977) that cultural systems are variant solutions to fundamental and common human perplexities such as birth, suffering, love, moral consciousness, and death.

In addition, according to Lonergan, certain invariant operations of human understanding also occur across cultures: every human being experiences, imagines, understands (both in flashes of insight and in conceptual expression), judges, decides. Moreover, these operations lead to one another, and depend upon one another, in certain invariant ways. Experiences raise questions for imagination. In the dark, one feels a presence and hears a sound; is it a mosquito, the effect of anxiety, or sheer restlessness? Examples posited in imagination raise questions for understanding. (What is it?) Hypotheses conceptualized for understanding raise questions for judgment. (Is that so?) Judgments about what really is so raise questions for action. (What ought I to do?) In every culture, by every human being, such operations as these are performed daily. The manner in which they are performed, the imaginative, linguistic and conceptual equipment with which they are performed, and the content upon which they are performed vary widely. The importance attached to one or the other of these operations also varies in different cultures. The point is that we are not entirely helpless when we attempt to find our way through the disparate cultural materials we encounter in trying to understand our shared humanity. The great intellectual work of reconciling our unity to our diversity is underway. Thus, even if we have not as yet achieved adequate methods for transcultural communication and analysis; even if our present methods of trying to order the staggering cultural variety to be found upon this globe remain at a primitive level; even if international scholarship, except perhaps in elementary scientific and technical areas, remains upon deplorably parochial and ethnocentric bases—despite all this, the task of developing a truly international intellectual perspective is not in principle beyond us.

Thus, the enterprise of constructing, as it were, a new form of "universal reason" remains yet to be accomplished. It remains a valid aim for enlightened and liberal scholarship. To be sure, the discovery by each of the world's cultures of the almost immediate presence of the others has come upon the world rather suddenly, with the advent of instant communications and rapid travel since World War II. Admittedly, too, naive and simple forms of rationality, and even the supposition that the liberal spirit itself is to be understood in one way only, have had to be modified under the pressure of the discovery of immense human variety. Still, individual human beings have been able to perform truly remarkable acts of understanding concerning cultures not their own. There is no reason to believe that the number of such explorers and interpreters will not grow.

If there was a temptation for the rationalist wing of the liberal movement (represented by Kant) to suppose a simpler and more immediate path to "universal reason" than has proved to be possible, that is no justification for refusing to embrace the possibilities of a more cosmopolitan form of the liberal spirit. If there was a temptation for the romantic wing of Western culture (Nietzsche may serve as an example) to exalt differences at the expense of the intellectual enterprise of human unity, that is no reason for conceding to despair. Different materials may be understood differently, in more than one way, by more than one method. Reasoning by way of analogy is possible. One may "cross over" from one mode of cultural experience into another, with remarkable gains in mutual understanding. It is not necessary to reduce one culture to the terms of another, invidiously or even imperialistically, in order to penetrate some, at least, of the secrets of its way of life. The way of understanding is never without trial and error. Where some explorers fail, others may do better. The enterprise of intellectual understanding and cultural sympathy stands upon firm ground and is not undercut by repeated failures.

It is a mistake, then, to hold that the new ethnic consciousness is necessarily a counterrational or illiberal force. So long as the commitment to the intellectual enterprise of mutual understanding remains firm, the new cultural consciousness need not collapse into ethnic chauvinism. Insofar as the new ethnic consciousness may prove to be a post-tribal development, it would be tragic to permit it to be reduced to merely tribal intelligence. In those cases, indeed, where that reduction has taken place, the consequences are amply displayed for everyone's contempt. Indeed, the contempt we feel on such occasions is a sign that such reductionism, far from being necessary, evinces a radical human failure.

The new liberal spirit, I propose, should rest upon two pillars: a firm commitment to the laborious but rewarding enterprise of full, mutual, intellectual understanding; and a respect for differences of nuance and subtlety, particularly in the area of those diversifying "lived values" that have lain until now, in all cultures, so largely unarticulated. In this sense, the true liberal spirit is *cosmopolitan* rather than *universalist*. The connotations of those two words suggest the difference between a liberalism that expects, and desires, a certain homogenization and a liberalism that expects, and delights in, variety. Cosmopolitan liberalism is surely closer to the heart of the authentic liberal spirit. Just as Kant was eager to defend the uniqueness of individuals (despite his tendency to imagine universal and general laws), so cosmopolitan liberalism is eager to respect the individuality of cultures.

3. The Pluralistic Personality

Culture is not only external to the individual. The individual interiorizes, appropriates, and carries culture. A culture has vitality only if it lives in the skills, disciplines, morals, and manners of individuals, only if it is carried even in the motions of the individual heart. Individuals continually re-create, modify, and enrich cultures.

In a pluralistic nation like the United States, cultural diversity plays a unique psychological role. Indeed, it appears to be bringing about the development of a unique psychological type: the pluralistic personality. Although many scores of different groups may be distinguished among the American people (the number varies with the criteria employed) this nation may not be the most linguistically and culturally diverse of nations. It is possible that the peoples of the U.S.S.R., India, China, Brazil, Canada, and other nations are at least as pluralistic as are our own. Yet, from a very early period American society was established upon three significant principles which have led to a unique experiment in pluralistic living. These three principles have provided an important measure of a civilized reconciliation of unity and diversity, for the inspection of other nations and for any future world civilization.

First, in the United States, ethnicity has not been permitted to become an instrument of territorial sovereignty, or of political exclusion in any jurisdiction. It is not permitted to become the exclusive instrument of political organization. Political rights inhere in individuals, not in ethnic groups.

Second, individuals are free to make as much, or as little, of their ethnic belonging as they choose. No one is to be coerced into a system of ethnic identification he does not choose for himself.

Third, individuals organized together in voluntary associations are encouraged to nourish such sentiments, memories, aspirations, and practices of group life as they choose. In such matters, the state is not only neutral but positively encouraging, through favorable tax laws and other legal principles. The social dimensions of individual life are thereby recognized.

It is considered something of a sin against "the American way" for persons to be made to feel that they *must* be identified by social characteristics; for the law so to distinguish them; or for individual social groups to coerce their members into such identification. Many rituals and practices have been established, from public ceremonies of representation to such political practices as the "balanced ticket," whose purpose is symbolically to include every group of Americans within the public presence of "the American people," and to strengthen in each breast the sentiment, "We are all Americans now." In this sense, the "melting pot" has been a powerful myth and an effective practice in American life. The concept of the American people is designed to include all equally, without discrimination. On the other hand, the oath of citizenship does not require any individual to renounce his or her former cultural belonging or cultural history. In order to become a U.S. citizen one does not have to cease living from and being nourished by the cultural traditions of one's native inheritance. In this sense, "the melting pot" does not entail the melting away of cultural differences among the American people.

The result of this special experiment in pluralism is that many Americans develop what might be called a "pluralistic personality." Each individual is, by right and by opportunity, responsible for choosing his or her own identity from among the many materials presented by the contingencies of human life. In a society like ours, an individual participates in the cultural life of more than one social group. We are each differentiated by such characteristics as age, sex, religion, biological and cultural inheritance, marriage, education, occupation, region, locality, personal exploration, and voluntary association. In at least such senses, everybody (or virtually everybody) participates in more than one social group and carries multiple associational identities. One person may be, for example, a New Yorker by birth, a professional humanist, a liberal in politics, Jewish, of parents who emigrated from eastern Europe, and by choice chiefly interested in associations and projects that establish his identity as future-oriented and assimilationist. Of some of these forms of "belonging," the individual in question may choose to make little or nothing, to pursue, as it were, a form of forgetfulness; while on others the individual may choose to focus his energy fully. Another individual of similar background might make a quite different choice.

Notwithstanding an individual's conscious choices, however, each person is also influenced by social factors over which he or she has had no control. We do not choose our grandparents, nor the basic lines of our early nurture. We do not choose (entirely) how others will regard us or what, even despite our best intentions, they may ascribe to us. Moreover, even the patterns of our conscious choices—our careers, successes, living patterns, educational choices, political behaviors, and incomes—may be studied by those who quantify our age, sex, religion, ethnicity, or other group-shared characteristics. Even if we do not choose to be "ethnic," in other words, even if we consciously renounce or disregard our cultural inheritance, it can hardly surprise us that sociologists or other students of social life will notice, at least in a generalized way, materials of ethnic specificity in our outward behavior. Finally, our own conscious choices with respect to our own cultural belonging may change over time, both in extension and in intensity. Personal experiences, or changes in the world around us (the precariousness of the state of Israel, for example, or turmoil in Ireland) may conspire to alter in us our own sense of identity.

"Ethnic belonging," then, is a phenomenon of human consciousness and is subject to multiple influences and multiple transformations, in ourselves and in the eyes of others. Its importance for any individual or group may change over time. Ethnicity is not a simple phenomenon; it is not easy to define in terms that apply in precisely the same way to everyone.

In a pluralistic society like that of the United States, moreover, many persons have the opportunity to become involved in many cultural traditions not originally their own, and to appropriate music, ideas, values, and even a set of intellectual landmarks not native to their own upbringing. We find that each of us can live from many diverse spiritual sources. In this respect, too, ecumenical and multicultural activities nourish in us a pluralistic personality—a personality rooted in multiple sources of spiritual power.

In the American system, then, the ideal of ethnic belonging has a special quality. It includes not only a willingness to cooperate democratically with those nourished by other traditions, but also an openness toward learning from others. It includes a willingness to appropriate from other traditions admirable traits and purposes, and fruitful sources of insight and sensibility. The notion of a wholly closed form of ethnic belonging—entirely inward-turning and wholly resistant to others—has come to seem seriously flawed. Even those within various traditions who propose the strengthening and deepening of their own cultural traditions normally find themselves working closely with others outside their own cultural group. They feel quite honored to be cited for their services to other communities or to the nation as a whole. Thus, American life provides many inhibitions against "tribalism," both within individual groups and within the culture as a whole. Indeed, the normal worry is that homogenizing and simply ecumenical influences are, if anything, out of balance, and threaten to overwhelm the influences of differentiation and cultural continuity.

As a result, individuals in our society tend to develop a plurality of cultural roots. Those of us who are not by ancestry Anglo-American learn to assimilate the values, attitudes, and practices of—as it seems to us—one of the most liberating of the world's traditions. We gladly learn its political history, its language, and its literature. From Jewish traditions, we learn both a psychiatric and sociological sophistication, a way of looking beneath the surface of the self and of society, and a sense of the long reality of Western history as it was experienced by Jews. From black culture, Indian culture, from the multiple Catholic cultures, from the cultures of Asia and of Latin America we appropriate other cherished values.

In the sense that all citizens share major national experiences—prosperity and depression, war and peace, great moral leadership, sad official lapses, and the assassinations of beloved figures—all of us participate in a "common culture." This common culture is built up, as well, by the tacit and powerful influences of a common language and the experience of common legal, economic, and political traditions. Yet the many cultures so united are vast, rich, and various, so that individuals do not assimilate all of them equally. In this sense, each individual lives, as well, from the particular cultures in which he or she was born and reared, and from which it has been his or her good fortune or free choice to learn. Thus, we each forge our own individual cultural identity, drawing (almost always) upon more than one tradition. In this sense, too, we each develop "a pluralistic personality," and are individually able to understand implicitly and to dwell with tacit ease in more than one cultural tradition.

A complicating factor in the attempt to sort out the many strands of actual American life as it is experienced from many standpoints—by a Filipino in Hawaii, a Polish American in Los Angeles, a Chicano in Chicago, a Georgia Baptist at Yale, a North Carolina black in New York—is the relative silence of the public media and of public discourse generally about these multiple differences. It is, perhaps, impossible to have a public language, especially for expression through media whose scope is national, which is simultaneously understandable by all and fully expressive of the nation's variety. Public communications are necessarily pitched to a kind of lowest common denominator. They reflect no specific subculture fully. In this sense, a public sort of "superculture" is imposed upon the top of the many subcultures of the land. Nearly everybody learns this national argot, which is in large measure commercial in its purposes and its utility.

"Superculture" is not precisely the same concept as "mass culture." For those forms of communication that are aimed at the national "high culture," the shared culture of national elites, are also conducted within it. The reporter or the commentator who speaks through the national media of communication is expected to exhibit a form of sophistication that is higher than that of "mass culture." In this sense, "superculture" is guarded by its own elite. But both superculture and mass culture aim at a level that is above the nation's pluralism. In order to develop a theory about the relations between the shared common culture of the American people and the particular cultural streams from which individuals draw their nourishment, it is necessary to notice how superculture and mass culture overlay, rather than grow out of, the many particular cultures that constitute our people. These overlays are probably indispensable to our system of national communication. They generate a form of ersatz culture, a sort of false consciousness, insofar as they arise from no particular culture but are constructed for broad communication.

A sign of this artificiality becomes apparent when one notices how many television shows—but also weighty generalizations about our national life and national character—actually represent no one neighborhood, no single culture or region, but appear rather to represent a fictional "nowhere," a construct designed on some superficial level to represent almost everyone. It is virtually impossible to refer accurately and profoundly to everyone at once, and so this flaw in our national self-understanding is no doubt inevitable. But it does require continuous intellectual correction. When one hears sentences about "middle Americans," or "typical American values," it is usually instructive to try to visualize the actual and complex variety that such sentences attempt to cover. (Do such sentences, e.g., well describe my uncle Emil?) Such reflection often brings to one's attention materials of considerable political and moral significance. Our variety confounds our need for easy generalizations.

In self-defense, then, those who try to retain their grip on reality develop techniques of translation. Privately, we learn to read between the lines of public speech and to focus upon concrete realities dear to us. In this way, we often mentally cross over from one cultural horizon to another. Some, for example, inspect public generalizations for their accuracy concerning blacks, or women, or specific ethnic groups. This capacity for accepting the common idiom, while mentally translating it into one's own horizon, illustrates the pluralistic personality at work.

The pluralistic personality has, then, a quite unique historical range and liberty. Such a personality, for all its broad experience and liberty of action, is not "rootless." Under the conditions of the old ethnicity, the consciousness of many may have been essentially parochial and isolated. Under the conditions of the new ethnicity, a capacity to enter into multiple perspectives, and to see the same matter from more than one point of view, seems to represent a clear gain for the human spirit. Without depending upon a kind of universal homogenization, the new ethnicity represents an admirable development in the liberal spirit, and a new type of social personality in human history. It is produced almost effortlessly by the sort of institutional life our pluralistic society has developed. Naturally, some individuals represent the pluralistic personality in fuller development, others in lesser. Every human being suffers from some degree of limited sympathy and limited perception. No one can claim to have a godlike capacity to understand everything about everything. The pluralistic personality discovers that learning comes by way of a certain humility, a certain hesitance to judge others too quickly, a certain generous watchfulness for possible errors in his own perceptions.

4. Ethnicity and the Soul

Such humility is necessary because the ways by which ethnic heritage affects an individual's inner life are subtle and complex, and mistakes of interpretation are easy. In the United States persons of Anglo-American stock have found their own heritage reinforced by the common use of English, continued close ties to the culture of Great Britain, the study of English literature, and the continuity of many institutional forms in politics and law. Those who stand directly in the line of these major cultural institutions may not be especially aware of their own cultural tradition; it forms so immediate a part of their daily reality that it may seem to them like second nature. Those Americans whose native traditions are not Anglo-American have had, by contrast, to adapt to new institutional and cultural forms, to learn not only a new language but also a new repertoire of gestures, mores, and manners. More deeply than that, many have had to learn new ways of thinking, feeling, and imagining. Great energy was expended in the process of assimilating this rich and liberating culture. In response, America itself changed under the impact of mass immigration. The common culture was altered by being assimilated in fresh ways. Even descendants of British Americans have had to adapt to a new common culture not identical to their own. Our common culture, then, belongs to no one ethnic group, although much of it has an Anglo-American origin, and it simultaneously allows diversity to thrive, less so in national public speech but more so in local communities of thought and feeling.

Measures of external behavior then—in education, politics, occupation, income, and other areas—continue to reflect differences among individuals that are related to their cultures of origin. The social scientists note these differences well enough, but the most neglected and unexplored dimension of ethnicity lies in the fields of the humanities: how ethnicity affects the individual spirit, in its tastes, memories, aspirations, and systems of value and meaning.

There are some major intellectual difficulties blocking the way to the humanistic analysis of such materials. It is useful to mention these first. The humanistic tradition wishes, first of all, to defend the individual. Hence, one cluster of difficulties surrounds the dangers of stereotyping. Each culture, in its institutions, its religions, and its literature, celebrates a distinctive constellation of human values and upholds a distinctive set of cultural heroes, saints, and everyday models. The ideals of the French intellectual, for example, are not identical to those of the British. The folk heroes of various cultures differ; children's stories celebrate diverse values or styles. Reasons of climate or political history may have brought about the celebration of differentiated human qualities necessary for a group's survival or historical advance. The role of great originating geniuses early in the history of a culture—King Arthur, say—may have attracted the love and imitation of millions through the ages. Music, folk arts, drama, dance, games, the liturgies of church and the state, the sermonic or rhetorical forms of public discourse, and other elements of this sort may continuously have promoted certain forms of behavior and discouraged others. The arts of storytelling may have inculcated narrative expectations that celebrated cleverness, bold action, humility, creative arrogance, wit, endurance, obedience, fidelity, and so on. Finally, the economic or social order of a culture may have inculcated modes of realism—enterprise and openness, say, as opposed to a passion for security—different from those inculcated in a different economic or social system. In all these ways, culture differs from culture. In a kind of shorthand, world travelers or students of comparative culture develop brief, often anecdotal descriptions that attempt to capture the distinctive aspects of each culture. One speaks—to reduce the shorthand to adjectival dimensions—of the "phlegmatic" English, the "orderly" Germans, the "romantic" Latins, the "hot-blooded" Spaniards, the "stubborn" Poles, the "melancholy" Danes, and the like. The danger of stereotyping is great.

In this respect, there is a critical difference between generalizations employed about the distinctive characteristics of cultures and scientific descriptions. Scientific descriptions formulate laws based on individual behaviors. Cultures do not exercise so total a control over individuals; hence, cultural effects cannot be reduced to such descriptions. Cultures do establish distinctive ideals and perhaps even distinctive catalogues of especially abhorred sins. These then exert a kind of attraction and repulsion upon individuals born within a culture. Those who reveal in their own behavior a kind of fulfillment of the highest ideals of the culture are normally singled out for special praise and rewards, and those who do not measure up are, accordingly, less rewarded.

Generalizations about cultural characteristics must, further, observe four other conditions. First, in most complex cultures more than one set of cultural ideals is available; second, cultures are normally open to change, so that new types of cultural heroes regularly emerge; third, the function of cultural ideals is not to describe all members of a society but rather to single out, to promote, and to reward certain forms of behavior; fourth, each individual appropriates the ideals of a culture in a free and distinctive way, sometimes by rebelling against them, resisting them, muting them, or playing counterpoint against them. Without denying the force of distinctive cultural ideals upon the whole everyday life of cultures, it is important to see the wide range of liberty still exercised by individuals within them. It is a mistake to apply to individuals the generalizations that attempt to define the working ideals of a culture; this mistake is properly called stereotyping.

Nonetheless, the power of the distinctive ideals of a culture, together with the mores and manners that support them, makes entrance into a new culture difficult for refugees, emigrants, or others who move from one culture to another. The prospect of exile may hold an understandable dread for fully formed adults. They may doubt their capacity to adapt, and they may fear psychological isolation when the outer conditions of their new world will no longer supply the daily signals that they internalized as children within a different culture. On the other hand, migrants sometimes experience a release in the new culture, which rewards in them qualities of mind, heart, or action that may have been repressed in their culture of origin. Thus does the impact of a culture upon an individual affect the entire soul: every instinct, emotional response, imagination, perception, sensibility, habit of mind. "Assimilation" is often spoken of too lightly.

Generalizations about a culture are dangerous in another way. Many of the ideals or tendencies within a culture are all the more powerful for being tacit. They are most often expressed in practice not as maxims to be memorized, or as codes clearly written out. They emerge, rather, from the tacit distribution of inhibitions and rewards built into institutions, practices, and mores. To put such inhibitions into sentences is often to falsify them. Thus, for example, one may say that Americans are taught to be acquisitive. Putting matters this way, one seems to be indicting Americans for conscious and articulated motives, which many might deny holding, whereas the generalization might merely have been pointing to the unparalleled abundance of unused and unneeded things which many Americans seem to accumulate around them. Yet Jacques Maritain noted in *Reflections on America* that the imputed "materialism" of the American character, an accusation made not only by foreigners but by many Americans as well, actually represents in practice a most remarkable indifference to material things, which because so abundant are held cheap in the calculus of human purposes. In the same way, generalizations about other cultures must be examined with great care.

To put the matter in another way, such generalizations frequently make conscious materials that were in practice unconscious. When such generalizations are carefully formed, they may by that very fact seem to go beyond the materials they point to. The well-established but tacit practices they describe no longer seem to be the same when codified in propositions, for such practices do not function as conscious moral rules, ideals, or approved courses of action. Many aspects of manners, mores, and even morals, once examined and raised before consciousness in propositional form, may come into conflict with other values in the culture. Cultures are such complicated systems of multiple imperatives that they contain many internal conflicts, which are normally resolved only over long stretches of time.

Finally, it must be noted that many aspects of cultural life, just because they have been internalized in tacit and unconscious ways, are difficult to discern in one's own life. It is hard to step outside one's own culture, so as to see it whole. Even when made conscious, aspects of culture such as the distinctively American attitude toward law, for example, are often difficult to articulate in words. It is one of the functions of literature to hold up a mirror to culture in which such secrets of the inner life may be reflected, not by abstraction, but in the full concrete texture of the represented situation. Literature succeeds as an instrument of understanding, where scientific description may fail, by rendering the lived forms of life in anecdotal segments so that tacit understandings and practices may be rendered for inspection through a method different from that of abstraction.

In American life, correspondingly, both literary materials and methods of "participant observation," as employed in so-

ciology, anthropology, and journalism, are among our best
sources for understanding the impact of ethnicity upon our inner lives. Irving Howe's remarkable study *World of Our Fathers* (1976), Michael Arlen's *Passage to Ararat* (1975),
Richard Gambino's *Blood of My Blood* (1974), Alex Haley's
Roots (1976), John Gregory Dunne's *True Confessions* (1977),
and many other books reveal the quite different instincts, attitudes, aspirations, and perceptions that actually motivate diverse individuals in our midst.

Ethnic identity persists among individuals, it appears, by being passed on in unconscious, tacit ways in their early nurture.
The laws of such transmission are not well understood. It appears that in some families the mother and in others the father—
perhaps sometimes in different respects—pass on some of the
values and expectations that he or she internalized from the long
line of human tradition. More study of such matters would no
doubt be rewarding, for it is certain that individuals do not spring
like Venus from the sea, but are social beings. The attractions
and inhibitions acquired by the workings of cultures upon history are passed on through individuals. No one of us represents
all the cultures of humanity, yet each of us carries social meanings and values not invented by ourselves. The reason for studying such sociality in our individual makeup is not to promote
"ethnic pride," for not all that we carry forward is wholly admirable. The primary reason is to obtain self-knowledge.

Normally, our experience with central elements of culture—
with a concept of God, for example—is highly colored by the
culture passed on to us by our parents. Scholars do not take for
granted that the images of God, and the complex of attitudes
deemed appropriate for approaching God, are exactly the same
in every culture, even of those which are generically Christian.
Rather, in different cultures, systems of worship and liturgy, of
preaching and of practice, subtly build up quite distinctive languages of the soul. In some cultures, religion is more closely
identified with morality, in such a way that God is imagined
rather like a great seeing eye of conscience (the "objective observer" of some Anglo-American philosophical theories, for example). In other cultures, particularly in southern and eastern

Europe, religion is more closely identified with nature, in such a way that God is imagined rather as the source of unity in all things. In the former, a person who is religious but not moral may be regarded as "not really religious." In the latter, there is a distance between being religious and being moral, such that even a person who is quite moral may not be perceived as religious, and even a person of less than admirable moral practice may yet be perceived as quite religious. In some cultures history, and in other cultures nature, provides the psychological dynamism of religion. In some the individual, and in others the family or the local community, is the basic unit from which moral values are derived. Similarly, in tacit conceptions of authority and dissent, of masculinity and femininity, of social loyalty and individually defined moral principle, culture differs from culture.

The "voice" and "temperature" of cultures in the home appear also to be communicated from generation to generation to the psyches of children. The constellations within which the various passions and modes of intelligence are distributed appear to vary from culture to culture. Expression of an emotion like anger may be inhibited in some cultures, and regarded as a failure in self-control; in others, anger may be a quite familiar and uninhibited passion. Orderliness may be given high value in some cultures, and low value in others.

How often children are held in the arms, by whom, and in which emotional patterns may establish the rhythm of their own future emotional expectations. How many voices surround them and with what qualities of passion, what is encouraged in their behavior and what is inhibited, the repertoire of facial expression and gesture and information that they absorb—all these are communicated, most often, without theory and apart from conscious decision. So it goes also for the rudiments of religious, political, sexual, and other attitudes. Expectations are established, tonalities become familiar, schemes of approval and disapproval are internalized, emotions are given shape, perceptions are tutored, evil and good are identified.

The history of these transmissions from generation to generation does reflect some change and alteration within cultures, but not much. Almost always, usually through signals below the threshold of consciousness, generation leaps across generation in cultural continuity. Even in rebellion, the sons pass on more of their fathers than they know, the daughters of their mothers. Sometimes in generation-skipping sequences, the life of the grandfather seems to be recapitulated more in that of the grandson than of the son. Because of a long emphasis on the rational and the individual, scholars have done too little work on the patterns of transmitting culture through the generations and on the general theme of cultural continuity.

There are certain central symbolic clusters in personal life in which cultural traditions tend to be concentrated. Even in persons not aware of their own cultural indebtedness, one often finds in the patterns of their tastes, orientations, values, and repugnances clear signals from the past. Imagination and sensibility are especially affected by family culture, but so also is the pattern of perception, the way intelligence works, and desire, and aspiration. One cannot understand the dramatic success of individuals who are Jewish, both in the schools and in the world of enterprise, without understanding as well the specific strengths of the culture that nourished them both in eastern Europe and in the United States. This is particularly striking when one compares the trajectory of the individual lives of eastern European Jewish immigrants with that of those whose ancestors also came from eastern Europe, at about the same time, but who were not Jewish; or with that of other cultural groups.

Among the nodal points for cross-cultural comparison, one could single out at least eight that could illuminate a wide spectrum of other attitudes and behavior: attitudes toward the divine, the sacred, or the holy; attitudes toward nature, history, and moral striving; attitudes toward intelligence, learning, and ideas; attitudes toward the rein to be given passion and emotion, and in which respects; attitudes toward authority, the past, tradition; attitudes toward the individuality or the communality of human living, toward solitude and solidarity, self and family; attitudes toward masculinity and fathering, toward femininity and mothering; attitudes toward the power of goodness and the power of evil in human affairs. Cultures, like individuals, differ remarkably from one another in such matters. One might turn to rites of passage, to sports, to ceremonies of birth and marriage and death, and to other locations in each culture for clues as to how the above-mentioned attitudes are passed on to new generations. There are many methods for studying such attitudes. In many families, attention has for some generations now been drawn to what is "new" and "American" in the experience of individuals, rather than to what is continuous with cultures of the past. That imbalance might now be corrected.

If each of us takes a moment to reflect upon our own deepest associations with such symbols as those mentioned above, we cannot help encountering our radical and fundamental debt to the generations that have preceded us. To be sure, we are free to turn in new directions, to erase or at least to cover over the tracings of the past. We are not imprisoned by our social and cultural inheritance, but we have, in fact, felt its imprint and have been given at least nascent definition by it. Until recently, Americans have not often made explicit connection to their cultural heritage or heritages. To have done so would have been to fly in the face of the strong emphasis in American life upon the principle that we are all individuals, responsible for re-creating ourselves anew. This principle conveys a great and important truth: each of us is responsible for creating his or her own identity. But a companion principle also conveys an important truth: each of us is a social creature, in part shaped by the others of whom we are a part; our destiny is familial as well as individual.

Discussions about values and meaning often go astray in America because the concrete contexts that give flesh and blood to our individual experience of life are left out of account. The eight symbolic clusters mentioned above focus the attention of specific cultures in diverse ways, lead each to interpret the same data within a different horizon of meaning and value, and inculcate in each different sources of attraction and repulsion. Different traditions instruct individuals differently about the power they possess to change things. In some, the tragic sense is strong, or cultural pessimism, or patience; in others, idealism and hope are bright. The differences among us as individuals are often accounted for by phrases such as "to each his own," as though our ethical visions and choices came strictly through individual choice. Actually, it appears, there is in each individual a considerably larger range of cultural principles at work than we seem to notice. Patterns emerge. Traditions come into focus. We are not so independent or so idiosyncratic as we have been led to imagine. There is a general descriptive geography to our moral visions and choices. A kind of general "field theory" of moral symbols powerful among Americans might be developed. Anglo-American, Jewish, black, Italian, and other ethnic cultures have established significant magnetic lodes in this field, which exert contrasting forces upon large numbers of individuals.

The full cultural history of American religion has yet to be written. Accurate and detailed attention to its component historical cultures is still in its infancy. The multicultural materials of American literary history have yet to be fully explored. Particularly interesting are the ways in which a writer in one cultural tradition—a Jewish novelist, say—perceives in his work the secret springs of those who are of a different tradition. In these matters, the way people perceive each other is a valid and important subject of study.

The many divergent ways in which central cultural symbols actually function in the daily lives of Americans have not yet been mapped. The ways in which ethnicity has affected, and still does affect, the inner lives of Americans have not yet been fully explored. One hopes that in religion, philosophy, and literature, as well as in psychology and the social sciences, the materials for such a study will be assembled, and that by the time another generation passes the state of our knowledge will be considerably more concrete and exact than it is at present.

CHAPTER THIRTEEN

Ethnicity and Cultural Diversity

I WAS ASKED TO ADDRESS the subject of ethnicity, a large subject, and one that Senator Daniel Patrick Moynihan calls the most powerful force in the world. The year 1989 will go down as a vintage year, a year to rank with 1776, 1789, and 1848, one which schoolchildren will have to memorize and of which poets will sing. I shall never forget the picture of that young lad in Tiananmen Square in Beijing, in front of the tank: every time it turned he moved in front of it, again and again. I shall never forget the pictures of the students marching in Beijing with the statue of the "Goddess of Liberty," as they called her. The image was quite westernized, as they clearly intended. In Shanghai some miles away, another group of students had a statue modelled directly on the Statue of Liberty. They also knew exactly what they were doing. Nor will I forget a middle-aged man, by the name of Zdenek, in a brewery in Prague in November of 1989 standing on a box before his fellow workers and saying, "We hold these truths to be self-evident that all men are created equal and are endowed by their Creator with certain inalienable rights among which are life, liberty, and the pursuit of happiness."

This chapter is based upon a transcription of an oral, not written, presentation for the Commonwealth of Pennsylvania, given in Harrisburg in 1990.

In other words, 1989 was a year in which citizens from widely different parts of the planet looked to the American experiment that the framers of the Constitution called *Novus ordo seclorum*— The New Order of the Ages. It was, first of all, a new order. There was none like it in the world, not in France, Britain, Turkey, Morocco, nor any of the other places the founders had read about or studied. The 1990s have found people from around the world turning their eyes in the direction of this experiment, exactly as President Washington, in his farewell address, predicted that they would. One day, he said, the peoples of the world would repair to the example of what was begun here.

One thing we have done remarkably well as a country: we have brought together people from every part of the globe, from places where people today are still feuding interminably with each other and killing each other. Here we all live, not without tension and friction and conflict, but nonetheless in peace and with a remarkable capacity for mutual respect. We hold friendship and civic responsibility banquets all over the country, giving one another awards for service to the whole community, in a way that crosses ethnic lines and tries deliberately to recognize people from each of our many different backgrounds. It has been a tremendous achievement, this achievement of multiculturalism. Here, tonight, our meeting itself is a celebration of our nation's motto, "Out of many, one."

We are easily identified as Americans wherever we go in the world, whatever our color, however we try to disguise ourselves in choosing our clothing, or whatever our knowledge of other languages. It takes people around the world only a minute to learn that we are Americans. They often tell us so (sometimes to our embarrassment because we are trying to go incognito). There is something about this country that gets into us and marks us out. We are one, and yet we also well know we are many. We carry with us different memories.

Each of us is born of a single woman. None of us is born as the universal representative. Each of us comes out of a tradition or a mix of traditions, out of a linguistic, religious, cultural heritage, out of a tradition of family life that is different from any other. Family life is one of the most important things that differentiates cultures. The emotions that run through a family tend to vary by culture in interesting, significant, subtle, and often quite powerful ways—all the more powerful because they are hidden and unconscious.

Michael Barone, one of our best writers on American politics, publishes every two years the *Almanac of American Politics*. Quite a young man, he grew up in Detroit and published a magnificent book called *Our Country*. One of its theses is that the most important characteristics of American politics, the feature that shifts elections more than any other feature, is not economics, which is what most of our social scientists think, but culture. He runs through the elections from 1930 through the present and demonstrates this in a most powerful, convincing, and detailed way. But he ends the introduction to his book with a marvelous sentence that has this as its theme: that all around the world people keep looking to this, our country, as their model for what they would like their country to be. What a shock this suddenly is, after decades of anti-Americanism. Over the last 30 years, we have become used to being thought of as the ugly Americans. I am not sure we are going to be able to get used to being suddenly admired by everybody, and imitated from Beijing to Prague. That new twist is going to take some adjustment.

I do not mean that people elsewhere admire our persons or our behavior. Rather, they very much admire the system that allows us to be what we are, even when we are less than we ought to be. Even from afar, they see the basic design of that system—a system that has three parts. The Statue of Liberty represents three liberations. The first people who conceived of it called themselves, and were called by others, liberals. The first liberal flags all had three colors in them, suggesting, perhaps unconsciously, these three liberations. (The first socialist flag had only one color, red, because it is a much simpler system. One party, one small group, makes all the decisions—political, economic, moral, and cultural.)

The first liberation is an economy with greater freedom than any other economy in preceding history. This liberation brought about a liberation from poverty for unprecedented numbers and to an unprecedented degree. America was the first of the nations to which large numbers of the world's poor came. Almost all the immigrants who came were poor; but the second and third generations of those immigrants were not poor. We were the first nation in the world in which a majority was not poor, while France, even 50 years after we adopted our Constitution, was being described by its best writer as a country of *Les Miserables*—"the miserable ones"—living at a level of poverty unimaginable in America. The second liberation, a part we more often honor, was political liberty: liberty from torture and tyranny. The third liberation, more remarkable still, is the liberty to pursue happiness each in his or her own way, although typically in association with others (people do not usually pursue happiness alone). They do it in the way they are taught by their families, the people of their neighborhood, their local community, and their church: through the communities that give them their first meaning of the word "we." Before they embrace the whole human community, people begin by embracing a particular world, a particular tradition within it. This cultural and moral liberation is the one, according to Michael Barone, that is by far the most potent politically.

In 1950, as I was graduating from college, social scientists were saying that ethnicity (and with it religion) was in decline. They held what was called the "secularization thesis." Although people would keep going to church, they said, the real meaning of religion would become thinner and gradually disappear. Ethnicity, tradition, languages, belonging, memory, would also decline. Some of us in those days used to call this the "Coca-Colonization of the world" or the "homogenization of the world." Everybody would use the same products everywhere. In American universities and in the Marxist world, all were saying the same thing: that the only really important factor was economics, and the only important fact was that social change would come from the redistribution of income. Workers of the world would unite, and ethnicity would disappear. Well, that has not happened.

Look at the former Soviet Union. Marxism as an idea and as an ideal has died. Solzhenitsyn said fifteen years ago that nobody can speak of Marx today without a sardonic grin. But ethnicity is alive. Prior to the fall of communism, the Lithuanians were willing to bear the most systematic economic punishments that the Soviet Union could impose in order to be free to be Lithuanian. This was true also of the Armenians, the Georgians, the Azerbaijanis, the Ukrainians, and the others.

Look also to Africa. Because of our history in the United States, we conceive of things dualistically, in terms of race, and do not notice that patterns of culture, memory, and belonging are as various among blacks as among whites. Think of the bitter struggle in Nigeria between the Nigerians and the Biafrans. Think of the enormous struggle in South Africa, not just against apartheid and between the English and the Dutch Calvinists, but also among the tribes and factions among blacks, between Chief Buthelezi and the ANC. One could march all the way around Africa and see the enormous power of culture, language, and history.

Think of Lebanon, tearing itself apart over a boundary line partly for religious, partly for linguistic, partly for cultural and ethnic reasons. Think of Northern Ireland or the restlessness which is gripping Quebec today.

Canada's experiment was quite different from ours. Canada allowed ethnicity to be identified with territorial claims, wherein one ethnic group would claim a whole territory. One of our great blessings is that that did not happen here. You are free to retain whatever memory and associations you like, but not free to make a territorial claim that would exclude others. Ethnicity and belonging are considered a cultural and moral rather than a territorial matter.

To repeat Senator Moynihan's claim again: Ethnicity and religion are surprisingly (at least to the social scientists) turning out to be the most powerful influences at the end of the twentieth century. Far from being diminished, they seem to be more intense than ever before.

There have been many sorrows in central Europe. According to a humorous anecdote attributed to Pope John Paul II, there are today only two possible solutions to the crisis in central Europe: the miraculous one and a realistic one. The realistic solution is for our Lady of Czestochowa suddenly to appear with

Jesus and all the saints and solve the central European crisis.
That is the realistic solution. The miraculous solution is for the
central Europeans to *cooperate* and agree to solve the central
European crisis.

Ethnicity is a powerful force, but it can also be a destructive
force. Everything depends on the kind of system in which it
arises and is nourished, and everything depends on how we nurture and keep alive the strengths of that system. If we misuse a
pluralistic system, we can destroy ourselves over our divisions,
or we can destroy ourselves by enforcing homogenization. The
trouble with being a free people is that there is nobody else to
blame but ourselves. Each generation has to do things right. Each
generation has to relearn the old lessons. That is something ironic
and terrible about the human race: that it is almost impossible to
pass along the necessary wisdom, even to your own children, let
alone across two generations. Free people have to reconstitute
their system all over again, which is why Thomas Jefferson said
that there should be not just one American revolution, but a new
revolution every eighteen and one-third years, which he com-
puted to be the average life of a generation.

About eighteen and one-third years ago, a number of us worked
on a project we called "The New Ethnicity." Irving Levine was
one of the great pioneers in this movement. We owe to him and
to the American Jewish Committee (which sponsored what was
then called "The Project on Group Pluralism") a great deal of
gratitude for their help in getting many of us around the country
together to think about these things in concert. For ethnicity is
something not easy to understand if you stay solely within your
own group. You do not know what it is to grow up or belong in
America if you look at it only in the way your own history suggests. You have to see how different it was for other groups,
how different it was for African-Americans, Italian-Americans,
Jewish-Americans, Slavic-Americans, and Anglo-Americans.

Thus, in the early 1970s, a group of us came together to try to
describe the new ethnicity. Let me say a word about why we
called it "new." In the old ethnicity, in the 1940s, Americans
tended to grow up in neighborhoods where we hardly ever met
people who were different. Go back and reread the novels of

World War II. Every platoon in the war seemed to have a "Billy Joe from Texas," a "Sven from Minnesota," an "Alvin from Kentucky," a "Mario from Scranton," a "Norman from Brooklyn," and so on. Every ethnic group seemed to be represented in that platoon. The story line included the fact that these Americans, people who had never encountered such diversity, were meeting one another for the first time up close. Then, after the war, there came Howard Johnsons, Holiday Inns, superhighways, and suburbs, and in the next two generations we tended to grow up next door to and go to school with many people who were different from ourselves. We did not stay within the same ethnic group. At first it looked as if in the melting pot we would all become the same, but then the great search for "roots" came into being, and the great reality of cultural memory reasserted itself. Even though we were all together and now knew each other, there was still a sense in which each of us had something special, a slightly different point of view to contribute.

That is what made the new ethnicity "new." It was not founded on ignorance of the others; it was founded on knowledge of the others. That very knowledge began to show each of us, in interesting ways, that our own political allegiances, political insights, religion, sense of family history, history of emotions and feelings, the way we understood pain and the rest of it, had its own characteristics. In some families, if men are quiet, that is regarded as strength and dignity. Men who are men do not fuss very much. In other family traditions, men who are quiet are a worry. They should shout and yell and get angry two or three times a day as if by moral obligation. In some cultures, men don't cry, but yet in Russia not a tree grows without a man shedding tears on it, as you can see in the novels of Dostoyevski. Emotional histories differ. In the new ethnicity, people were still crying at different times. Remember Ed Muskie in 1972, presenting himself often as a good Yankee in New England, but when his wife was insulted one day at a crucial moment in the campaign, he cried. There is nothing wrong with a Pole crying or a Slav crying, but Americans are not supposed to cry. That tear going down his face caused a sixteen point drop in his standing before the primary in New Hampshire that year.

There was considerable advancement in ethnic awareness in the 1970s. Very few of our groups had leaders as great as Martin Luther King, Jr., or produced a book that was as powerful as Alex Haley's *Roots*. But what we all had in mind for the new ethnicity was to defuse what many of us thought was going to be a racially and ethnically divided decade. The 1970s, if you look back on it, did turn out to be a fairly bitter decade, but on the ethnic and racial front it went remarkably peaceably. While many people were predicting backlash and racial struggles, those did not materialize. There were signs of racial backlash in at least one of Mayor Rizzo's campaigns in its beginnings, and then people insisted that it be cooled. In Philadelphia, ethnic leadership from many backgrounds worked very hard to bring their communities together. It is now hard to prove that the people in our various groups who tried hard to cooperate actually prevented what did not happen, but that is what all of us intended to do. We wanted to prevent ethnic confrontation, and indeed we did.

There are some new horizons opening up in the 1990s, and I think they go like this. In the last two decades, we have admitted more immigrants into this country legally (let alone the millions who have come illegally) than in any other decade in our history except two. We are living again in the era of immigration. Immigration is not over in the United States. It is entering its biggest years. Moreover, most of the immigrants who came in the 1970s and 1980s were not white. They came predominantly from Asia and Latin America; there were almost as many (I am exaggerating a bit) from Africa as from Europe. Europeans do not come in anything like the numbers they used to. Most of the immigrants who came have succeeded remarkably well. Many high school valedictorians are obviously newcomers to the country. In the Westinghouse Science Awards, something over half of the 40 award winners in a recent year were immigrants or children of immigrants, many of whom did not speak English when they came.

These facts have relieved the American worry of the 1960s and 1970s. Some Americans worried that America used to be a land of opportunity but that that period was now over. It is not over. Immigration has continued, and people have proven that opportunity exists. They have taken splendid advantage of it, and honored us all.

There is another feature. The new immigrants have shown that race is not the central issue of American life, that "non-white" people can do very well indeed, as has a large majority of every single racial group in the United States. A minority in every group is not doing so well, and in some groups it is disproportionately larger than in other groups. Still, we do not talk nearly enough about the success stories in each of our communities.

One sign of this transformation is already apparent. Jesse Jackson was attuned to this when he urged the shift from speaking of "black-Americans" to "African-Americans." I think that was a watershed in recent American history. Subtly but effectively, Jackson took the emphasis off race and began speaking of the black experience in the United States as an African experience in the way we would speak, in my case, of a Slovak experience, or an Italian-American experience. The concept of ethnicity can help us to understand one another by analogy as we learn to look in the experience of others for correlates of things we have experienced ourselves, and to find in each group something different that we have to learn, if we want to understand what it is to be an American. We cannot understand what it is to be an American from our own group alone.

Vast devastation is occurring in our major cities. In the sections in which poverty is the most heavily concentrated, our one hundred largest cities are experiencing a devastation that slavery itself did not cause. Nothing in American history has caused as much anguish as is there now. In the city where I now live, Washington, D.C., 70% of young children are born out of wedlock. That means almost certainly that these children will not have two parents to help them through the many struggles ahead. Typically missed will be the father's presence, both for the sake of discipline and for the sake of introducing the child, particularly a male child, into the world of his friends and his work, giving him the first contacts and names to approach in finding a job, and advice about how to prepare for a job, and how to get through the initial rough spots in it. Each one of us, thinking back, can easily remember how much we owe a father in these respects.

The devastation that drugs are causing on top of this is horrifying. You may have read about "crack babies." Before they even have a chance, they have been deeply injured internally in their nervous systems and in their brains. They number in the thousands. There is in our midst a plague that all Americans need to be concerned about, and we will not be healthy as a country until we all try to help the communities that are hurting the most.

Many of the problems I am describing are spreading to rural areas as well. Beginning in 1985, there were more white children born out of wedlock in rural areas than black or Hispanic. Thus, something dreadful is quietly happening in our midst and injuring the very tissue of the family, which is the nurturing place not only of ethnicity, but of all our values.

There was a report of a task force in New York State on minorities. I wish they had called it "on ethnicity," but it was called "on minorities." This task force made a proposal that I think is misguided. It argued that the ethnic heritage of every one of us is equal and that the school system should treat each ethnic heritage, religion, history, geography, and so forth equally and diminish the influence of what the report called "American European culture." I think it is proper and good that the humanities should be taught in a planetary way, just as when there is a disaster in the world—Chernobyl, a monsoon in India, an earthquake in Nicaragua or Italy—people in the United States get on the telephone to find out whether the members of their families are all right, whether they have survived intact. Our nation is, in a sense, the nervous system of the whole planet. Touch the world any place, and you affect an American family whose relatives live there.

Our educational system, therefore, should deal with Africa, India, China, Korea and all the parts of the earth because our children are going to grow up in an interdependent world. But I also think there must be an emphasis upon the ideas and traditions that grew up in that nexus of the world discribed by such historic cities as Jerusalem, Athens, Rome, Paris, London, and Philadelphia. Those small cities were the early nests that incubated the American way of dealing with pluralism. There is no other place on earth that has taught people of so many different backgrounds to be aware of who they are, to respect others who are different, and to cooperate with others everyday, as we do in this country. We are only able to do that here because of a special kind of system, based on a special heritage of ideas. These ideas are not available anywhere else unless they are borrowed from us. That is why the Chinese students, quite self-consciously, did not worry that they had shaped the face of a western woman on the goddess of liberty. The ideas of liberty that they needed are found in Jerusalem, Athens, Rome, Paris, London, and New York. The Chinese students did not mind using the Statue of Liberty because the *novus ordo* that they wanted to imitate was not available in their own place. We have to cherish certain particular ideas that allow us to live in the pluralism we now share. In that respect (and I say this as one who comes from central Europe, from a Slavic background), I thank God every day that American politics did not come from the Slavic world but from the Anglo-Saxon world. This is the gift of English law to the world. It is a precious gift for Americans. It did not come from everywhere. You will not find it by studying the history of other places. The roots of our system are particular and precious.

I hope you take the point I am trying to make: that there are some ideas, institutions, and a special history that allow us to be many and one at the same time. While we celebrate our diversity and respect each of our traditions, we must, above all, cherish that special one.

Let me conclude with this example. When the British went to battle, they said as Shakespeare has it (*Henry V,* III, i.3), "God for Harry! England, and St. George!" The French pledge allegiance to a language, as in Quebec. The Germans to a *Volk*—a people. But Americans do not pledge allegiance to any one of these things, not to a land, not to a folk, not to a language, and not to a history. When we pledge allegiance to the flag, we pledge allegiance "to the republic for which it stands." That is what holds us together, the republic, the system. Take away the republic, and the deal is off. The republic—the form of our self-government—is what binds us. That republic allows us to celebrate our diversity, so we must give it an honored place.

The system that has made our country what it is has taught us how to be who we are, to respect each other and to love each other, exactly because we are different. It has taught us, above all, to do that most miraculous of all things, to cooperate in solving the concrete problems that weigh upon us, on some of our communities at one time more than on others. At such moments, let us come to the assistance of the most needy ones.

CHAPTER FOURTEEN

How American Are You If Your Grandparents Came From Slovakia in 1888?

Now THAT the theme of "ethnicity" has blazed up again before public eyes, a number of important questions have been raised, a number of objections voiced. What is the meaning of ethnicity? What is the difference between the "old ethnicity" and the "new ethnicity"? Is everybody ethnic? What political implications follow?

One of the most interesting developments is the abrupt rejection of ethnic analysis altogether. This rejection is of three types. Those who have been trying all their lives to *get over* their ethnic origin and join the influential mainstream sometimes see the experience of ethnicity as regressive; sometimes don't even want the subject brought up; have vivid emotional reactions against it; sometimes experience a new sense of relaxation and liberation, in a kind of expanded and (at last) integrated self-consciousness.

A second type of rejection occurs among some who have for a time been living in "superculture," that is, in the influential mainstream of power, wealth, and ideas, apart from any ethnic "subculture." In the 1930s many intellectuals retained not only an ideological but also an experiential contact with lower-middle-class workers. Since the Second World War the population of

This chapter originally appeared in *Soundings* (Spring 1973), pp. 1–20.

superculture has expanded enormously, and now there are millions of educated suburban Americans who maintain almost no contact, ideological or experiential, with ordinary people who work for a living, in blue-collar or white-collar jobs. One sees this gap between cultures on university campuses between faculty and other staff members, or at newspaper offices between the city room and the press room.

It used to be that democracy meant faith in "the common man." But for some time now the common man has come to be perceived as the nation's greatest menace, a racist, a fascist, and— if one is pressed—a pig. All hope is placed in "a constituency of conscience," as opposed presumably to people without conscience. Needless to say, anyone who writes *in support of* the white ethnic is looked upon with puzzlement. What's a nice man like you doing with people like those? This puzzlement sometimes changes to shock, horror, and indignation if the subject is seriously pursued.

Thus, passionate intensity is frequently stirred by the theme of ethnicity, most remarkably among people who believe in the universality of reason or love and simultaneously bewail the blandness and mindless conformity of the suburbs. Perhaps this is because the theme of ethnicity intimately involves each participant. Each is challenged to examine his or her own life for its ethnic materials. Almost by definition, these are more unconscious than not, having been taught informally rather than in explicit words or deeds. Gratitude for being prompted to live the examined life is sometimes keen, but sometimes absent.

This invitation to self-examination, moreover, is not simply a use of the *ad hominem* argument. In a reasonably homogeneous culture, as in England or France, the terms of discourse are reasonably fixed. In a heterogeneous one like ours, the key terms themselves derive from our different historical experiences of America. Words like "moral" used in politics mean something different to a house mother in a dormitory in a small Ohio college, to Philip Roth, to John Courtney Murray, to Shirley MacLaine, to George Meany, to Jesse Jackson. When you see each speaker in his or her own historical context, the words make considerably more sense, even if one continues to disagree. The more sensitive to historical nuance one becomes, the more intelligible various classical arguments—between sectarian and mainline Protestants, for example—become. In the United States, our personal histories retain an influential ethnic and regional component, to which far too little note is methodologically paid. Thus, many of our arguments result not in mutual understanding but in frustration and separation.

A third type of rejection occurs among some who are quite unconscious of any ethnicity on their part at all, either because they're simply white Anglo-Saxons who "don't make anything of it" or because they're "veritable living melting pots," nobody having traced the family's intermarriages for years. Anglo-Saxons who learn English in school, read English literature, have long learned about the superiority of English political institutions, and unconsciously accept Anglo-Saxon rituals and traditions as normative (Thanksgiving dinner without *spaghetti* or *kolache,* for example) are not aware of being ethnic, because the mainstream supports their self-image. Only gradually is the perception dawning that, much as this nation owes the Anglo-Saxon heritage, it is *not* an Anglo-Saxon nation. It is a pluralistic nation. What do you do if your grandmother came to America from Serbia in 1888? The nation is by that increment also made to be Serbian. But when will the cultural impact finally be felt? So many things taken for granted by many in America are unconsciously but effectively ethnocentric. Even the "civil religion" is defined as Anglo-Saxon Protestant—not really even German or Scandinavian Protestant.

Values once highly developed in Anglo-Saxon culture, like those in other groups, are constantly under threat from superculture and its technology—not least that Anglo-Saxon quality par excellence, civility. University students were just yesterday attacking even highly civilized parents as "uptight," "effete," or "subservient." Shouting, for a time at least, was the moralists' vogue. The power of television, the cinema, and high mobility threaten every ethnic culture—which is to say, culture itself. Values and tastes are taught in families and families need, as well, public social supports. We have not yet counted the costs—in anomie, rage, and mindlessness—of allowing families, neighborhoods, and local cultures to bow to commercial forces.

As for those who claim to be "veritable melting pots," one usually finds that the more they talk about their families, the more the "significant others" in their family history come into focus. Certain sympathies, certain ways of looking at things, certain mannerisms of thought or behavior are found to have social antecedents. There is a widespread illusion in America that each individual is alone, entirely invents herself, or wholly creates his own style. Our proverbial historical blindness masks from us the ways in which the experience of past generations continues to live on in each of us, passed on in countless tacit ways in the earliest years of our rearing. The generations are amazingly repetitive in their unpredictable cycles.

In a nation as large and diverse as ours, accurate ethnic perception is crucial for mutual understanding. Regionally, in social class, in race, in religion, and in ethnic culture, we differ from one another. We use the same words but in the context of different historical experiences. Yet we, of all peoples, have been afraid of ethnicity! We have treated ethnicity as a dirty secret about which we should not speak, except softly, in hopes it would go away. Even our usage of the term "ethnic" reflects our emotional and intellectual confusion. The following dictionary sample, especially in usages 3 and 4, suggests amusing biases:

> Ethnic, adj. 1. pertaining to or characteristic of a people, esp. to a speech or cultural group. 2. referring to the origin, classification, characteristics, etc. of such groups. 3. pertaining to non-Christians. 4. belonging to or deriving from the cultural, racial, religious or linguistic traditions of a people or a country, esp. a primitive one: ethnic dances (*The Random House Dictionary*)

"Non-Christian" and "primitive"—these are the images in the background. Not so subtly, "ethnic" is being contrasted with "civilized," from a Western perspective, indeed, from an English perspective.

For good reasons, educated Americans have for a long time hoped that ethnic differences would weaken and disappear. Ethnic conflicts in Europe seem to antedate even the rise of nationalism. Sometimes for generations, nevertheless, ethnic differences seemed not to lead to conflict and a high degree of cosmopolitan interchange was reached. When religious division and nationalism were added to the mix, however, conflicts were brutal and fierce. So it must not be thought that ethnicity is a neutral, unambiguous, or safe part of human consciousness. No part is.

What is ethnicity? For some years a loose sense of "ethnic" has been current, as in "ethnic foods." In New York one could easily conjure up images and smells of Jewish, Italian, Chinese, Greek, black, and other specialties. Would one include turkey, pumpkin pie, plum pudding, or fish 'n' chips as ethnic foods? In the United States, "ethnic" was frequently used as a residual category: those who are *not* white, Anglo-Saxon, Protestant. For example, in describing the Tercentenary Celebration of Yankee City, W. Lloyd Warner writes in *The Family of God,* in a chapter entitled "The Protestants Legitimate Their Past":

> those responsible for the success of the Yankee City Tercentenary were conscious of the need for obtaining the wholehearted collaboration of the organizations and churches of ethnic origin and religious groups. Since almost half the community was of ethnic origin and consciously participated in groups which identified their members with minority subsystems, and since it was hoped to induce the whole community to participate, the leaders of the celebration, recognizing their problem, were anxious to do everything possible to obtain full cooperation from the various cultural and religious minorities.

> Since these groups, including Jews, Poles, Greeks, French Canadians, and others, were all of comparatively recent origin, none being older than about the fourth decade of the nineteenth century, when the Catholic Irish first appeared, to select appropriate symbols for sponsoring ethnic groups and to make assignment of them was a difficult problem for the central committee. Since the interest and main emphasis of those responsible for the subjects chosen was upon periods before the arrival of the new immigrant groups, the problem was even

more thorny. The conception of the celebration and the pageant had to do with the Puritan ancestors and the flowering of New England culture; the themes of the great ethnic migrations and their assimilation—the melting pot, the Promised Land, and the goddess of Liberty welcoming them—democracy for all and every kind of race and creed—such themes were nowhere present. Indeed, those who conceived and presented the pageant saw themselves as teachers initiating the new peoples in to the true significance of the nation.[1]

"Ethnic," then, is a residual category; it is not used of British-Americans, only of "the others." But ordinary usage went further even than that. In America, ethnicity was often viewed as dysfunctional and rather rapidly disappearing. For most groups, "ethnic" meant in effect "meltable." Again, W. Lloyd Warner, writing this time in *American Life*, may be our witness. He describes a Norwegian Lutheran group in a midwestern city, in which the first and second generations of American-born children, as they grow up, are moved by "the desire to lose the stigma of foreignness." They give up ethnic symbols, including the use of Norwegian. The only remaining formal bond of the group remains the moral bonds structured by the church, its services now in English. "The pressure for Americanization comes only from those who have risen in the class structure of Jonesville. Those who remain in the lower class cling to the traditional behavior of the ethnic group." Perhaps because his attention was drawn to the successful classes, or perhaps because his time-frame was quite long (the word he uses is "ultimately"), Warner continues:

The number, size, and importance of ethnic groups and sects in American life decrease almost yearly. Many of them are disappearing, and others yield much of their cultural substance to the influences of the outer American world. All increasingly adjust to the major outlines of American society. There are too many factors involved, including those in the ethnic group, America generally, and the larger world society, to predict accurately whether all these groups will continue to exist or will surrender to the forces of assimilation and acculturation, but it seems likely that most, if not all of them, will ultimately disappear from American life.[2]

This seems to be why, in the last decade, the word "ethnic" came to be used not so much for white ethnic groups from Europe, which were presumed to be rapidly "melting," but as a synonym for "minorities," especially those of color: the blacks, the Latinos, the Indians, in other words, those who visibly were *not* melting. White ethnics were seldom *taught* that they were ethnic. Courses of study about immigrant history—even monographs, or archives, or library collections—were not common; it is amazing how little is known even today. Indeed, strong emotions *against* ethnic identification had been inculcated. For the arrival of over thirty million Catholics and Jews from Southern and Eastern Europe, as Robert Bellah writes:

> profoundly challenged the American national community. At that point a new conception of community based on cultural pluralism might have developed, and indeed some Americans proposed such a solution. But the main line was quite different. The demand for assimilation, the end of hyphenated Americans, 100 percent Americanization, all summed up in the image of the melting pot. This image took on graphic form in an event described by Robert Michaelson. For a festival sponsored by Henry Ford during the early 1920s a giant pot was built outside the gates of his factory. Into this pot danced groups of gaily dressed immigrants dancing and singing their native songs. From the other side of the pot emerged a single stream of Americans dressed alike in the contemporary standard dress and singing the national anthem. As the tarantellas and the polkas at last faded away only the rising strains of the national anthem could be heard as all the immigrants finally emerged. The enormous pressures which created this vast transformation amounted almost to a forced conversion.[3]

Americanization, in short, was a process of vast psychic repression. Anyone with vivid imagination might recreate for himself some feeling for what happened. But even those who in the course of two or three short generations have experienced it have often blocked out its effects from their minds. Again that sensitive Yankee Lloyd Warner describes it objectively:

> The language factor represents a fundamental break between the parent and child, which continually widens as the child grows older. As the schools increase their training of the maturing child in American symbols, his identifications are increasingly with those symbols until more often than not he develops *an active antagonism* to those of his family's origin....

> In school not only does the child learn English and the content of American social symbols, but he learns social attitudes that are *opposed* to his family's and his ethnic group's traditional ways of life.... In Yankee City it was discovered that ethnic children very often *do not want to play with* children of their own ethnic group but prefer those of other ethnic groups and native Yankees—an indication of their subordination of *the ethnic elements in their personalities* and *unwillingness* to be identified with their own group....

> The forces which dominant society exerts upon the ethnic groups are *exerted primarily upon the child,* so that he, rather than the parent, becomes the transmitting agent of social change....

> Although families traditionally have been the central link between the past and the future, thereby assuring cultural continuity and social stability, in the ethnic families the culture that is to be transmitted to the children is *rejected* by them; and the changes that are introduced into that cultural system are resisted by the parents and transmitted through the medium of the children. The result is *disruptive to the family system, to the ethnic group, and to many personalities* that experience it.[4]

The cruelty implicit in this process is intense; on first reading, however, one merely accepts it as normal: the inferior learning from the superior. The psychic destructiveness is overlooked. Still, white Europeans—even if a little darker-skinned or otherwise identifiable ethnically—can "pass" in America. It is much more difficult for those whose racial features are more marked. That, perhaps, was the chief reason why the word "ethnic" for a time became increasingly fixed on the minorities of color. A museum of ethnic history, or a chapter in a sociology book, or a listing in a catalog under "ethnic," I found in my researches, was far more likely to lead me to information on Indians, Latinos, or blacks than on Norwegians, Poles, the Irish, or Greeks.

But there was also another reason. The bias of American intellectual life (and ordinary life as well) is to slight the past, the community, and the imagination, in favor of the future, the individual, and the intelligence. There is a pronounced tendency to underestimate the power of the former and to overestimate that of the latter. Secondly, members of the intellectual community are brought not only into a reasonably affluent social class, but into a class with a significant self-interest in social change. The educated retain relatively little contact, social or intellectual, with lower-middle-class values, aspirations, fears, or insecurities. It is, as Warner suggested, *lower-class* ethnics who remain ethnic longest. The educated undergo far heavier pressures—opportunities?—to "Americanize" than do those who do not go to college, did not (perhaps) go to high school, and do not share in the myths of college communities. The gap between the educated and the uneducated, indeed, may be more significant—and divisive—in our society than the gap between the rich and the poor.

Hence, the intellectual community is liable to neglect a great many important features of American society because of its own sociological position. It has reason, indeed, to be in conflict with other groups in American society: competition for power and status, antagonistic values and modes of behavior, hard questions of freedom and public order. There is a tradition of anti-intellectualism in American life. There is also a correlative tradition of antipopulism: contempt for Main Street, its boosters, and its wavers of flags. We should also add, for completeness, a tradition among our intellectuals of anti-Catholicism—a prejudice with something of an ethnic edge. It is directed not quite so much at English Catholics, who tend to be educated and refined, as at those less graceful and somewhat threatening, heavy-bellied, rather cynical, immigrant working types whose economically progressive politics never quite make up for their way of life.[5] The photos which editors choose to represent these descendants of immigrants today seem related to the cartoons featured in their pages two or three generations ago.

Since 1967, when the American Jewish Committee held its first national conference on "the white ethnic" at Fordham, the word "ethnic" has been gradually moving back toward its broader usage. Most British Americans, I believe it will be found, have hardly ever thought of themselves as "ethnic." But that is perhaps true of many Southern and Eastern Europeans, too. The pressure was almost entirely to think of oneself as "American." "We're all Americans!" That is, "We're all equal; I'm just as good as you are." Whatever the sufferings of the past, they are better forgotten. Concentrate on the future. My favorite uncle once said with gentle wonderment: "We're beyond all that now, aren't we, Michael?" Who wants to remember?

On the other hand, many can't forget. In Newark, in Canarsie, in Forest Hills, in Cicero, in Cleveland Heights, in Warren, and in a hundred other places yet unknown to the media there are large concentrations of "white ethnics" who have normally been the vanguard of the only progressive political party we've got, the Democratic party. In the last few years they have become the fall guy, the villain, in the eyes of many who wish to bring about a greater measure of justice in American society. Richard Daley, George Meany, labor union "bosses," political "machines," cops with little American flags on their uniforms, beer truck drivers, angry crowds.

Well, suppose you want to understand what makes people feel the way they do, think as they do—particularly if you notice odd discrepancies in the usual intellectual descriptions of their behavior. For example, construction workers are pictured as pro-war—but according to a Stony Brook study, no profession in New York City in 1970 was more *opposed* to war than construction workers. Where did FDR, Truman, Kennedy, or Johnson (notably on civil rights) get their majorities? Questions like these raise warning signals about one's own prejudices. What actually is going on among such people? What has their history been like? What in their lives is admirable and beautiful? What are the evils that prey on them? Since all people are evil as well as good, what are their evil tendencies?

Such questions are one part of what is now called "the new ethnicity." For reasons suggested above, the initial focus has been on descendants of immigrants from Southern and Eastern Europe. But if such persons reclaim their own ethnicity, why not others? "Black history" and "Indian history" reopened the study of American history; so did "cold war revisionism." All of a sudden, almost everyone was discovering that the questions "Who am I?" and "Who are we?" led to a much deeper cultural pluralism than we had long been accustomed to imagine. In each of our traditions, good and evil are mixed. Self-discovery does not entail either ethnocentrism or self-glorification. An awakened consciousness of one's social past requires neither chest-thumping nor breast-beating.

During the presidential election of 1972, virtually every national magazine and television news show carried stories on "the ethnic vote." They usually, but not always, meant (as I do in this book) "white Catholic ethnic." For they carried a host of *other* stories specifically on the Jewish vote, the black vote, the Latino vote. In a larger and more accurate sense, of course, all these groups are equally ethnic. Technically and accurately speaking, each of us is ethnic: each human being participates in a particular cultural history (or histories). The fundamental question "Who am I?" includes the question, "Who are we?" This "we" is particular as well as universal, ethnic as well as humanistic. So much is pretty obvious and straightforward.

But practice is not always so obvious and straightforward. Quite commonly, Americans hopelessly misunderstand one another because each fails to note how the contours of his own language and experience differ from those of the other, and neither can find keys to a relevant common culture. We are not skilled in identifying the many senses of reality, styles of exposition, families of symbols, loaded words, and other culturally freighted materials that thrive among us. Some people, of course, observe such cultural cues with great intuitive skill, even without being able to articulate how they do so. The rest of us constantly try—and err. For to catch cues accurately, one must understand both the cultural background and the person. Stereo-types won't suffice.

There are several theses about white ethnics that are conven-tional but wrong. Let me state them and argue against them.

1. *Ethnic consciousness is regressive.* In every generation, ethnic consciousness is different. The second generation after immigration is not like the first, the third is not like the second. The native language begins to disappear; family and residential patterns alter; prosperity and education create new possibilities. The new ethnicity does not try to hold back the clock. There is no possibility of returning to the stage of our grandparents.

Nevertheless, emotional patterns that have been operative for a thousand years do not, for all that, cease to function. Those of white ethnic background do not usually react to persons, issues, or events like blacks, or like Jews, or like Unitarians. In a host of different ways, their instincts, judgments, and sense of reality are heirs to cultural experiences that are now largely unconscious. These intuitive leads, these echoes of yet another language, yet another rhythm, yet another vision of reality, are resources which they are able to recover, if they should so choose.

Jimmy Breslin, for example, has lamented the loss of lan-guage suffered by the American Irish. He urges Irish Americans to read Brendan Behan: "For a style is there to examine, and here and there you get these wonderful displays of the complete lock the Irish have on the art of using words to make people smile." Breslin loves "the motion and lilt that goes into words when they are written on paper by somebody who is Irish." He compares Behan's tongue to the language of the 100,000 Irishmen marching down Fifth Avenue of March 17:

> You can take all of them and stand them on their heads to get some blood into the skull of thinking, and when you put them back on their feet you will not be able to get an original phrase out of the lot of them. They are Irish and they get the use of words while they take milk from their mothers, and they are residing in the word capital of the world and we find that listed below are the two fine passages representing some of

the most important Irish writing being done in the City of New York today.

He then lists business notices from Brady the Lawyer and Walsh the Insurance Man.

Jewish writers are strong by virtue of their closeness to the Jewish experience in America—for example, their sense of story, and irony, and dissent. Mike Royko writes with a hard realism and a blend of humor that is distinctively Slavic; like *Good Soldier Schweik*. Phil Berrigan refers to Liz MacAlister as "Irish," and shares a traditionally tough Irish priest's suspicion of liberal intellectuals.

Authenticity requires that one write and act out of one's own experience, images, subconscious. Such materials are not merely personal (although they *are* personal) but also social. We did not choose our grandfathers.

2. *Ethnic consciousness is only for the old; it is not shared by the young.* It is true that hardly anyone in America encourages ethnic consciousness. The church, the schools, the government, the media encourage "Americanization." So it is true that the young are less "conscious" of their ethnicity. This does not mean that they do not have it. It does not mean that they do not feel joy and release upon discovering it. Often, all one has to do is begin to speak of it and shortly they begin recollecting, begin raising questions, begin exploring—and begin recovering.

Consider the enormous psychic repression accepted by countless families—the repression required for learning a new language, a new style of life, new values, and new emotional patterns, during a scant three or four generations of Americanization. Many descendants of the immigrants who do not think of themselves as "ethnic" experience a certain alienation from public discourse in America, from the schools, from literature, from the media, and even from themselves. Nowhere do they see representations of their precise feelings about sex, authority, realism, anger, irony, family, integrity, and the like. They try to follow traditional American models, of course: the classic Protestant idealism of George McGovern, for example. They see a touch of their experience in *Portnoy's Complaint*. But nowhere at all, perhaps, will they see artistic or political models expressing exactly their state of soul. Nowhere do they find artists or political leaders putting into words what remains hidden in their hearts.

The young are more ripe for the new ethnicity than the old, for the new ethnicity is an attempt to express the experience of *their* generation, not of an earlier generation. It treats past history only as a means of illuminating the present, not as an ideal to which they must return. The new ethnicity is oriented toward the future, not the past.

3. *Ethnic consciousness is illiberal and divisive, and breeds hostility.* The truth is the reverse. What is illiberal is homogenization enforced in the name of liberalism. What is divisive is an enforced and premature unity, especially a unity in which some groups are granted cultural superiority as models for the others. What breeds hostility is the quiet repression of diversity, the refusal to allow others to be culturally different, the enforcement of a single style of Americanism. Our nation suffers from enormous emotional repression. Our failure to legitimate a genuine cultural pluralism is one of the roots of this repression. Our rationalization is fear of disunity; and in the name of unity, uniformity is benignly enforced. (The weapon of enforcement is ordinarily shame and contempt.)

Countless young Italians were given lessons in school on how *not* to talk with their hands; Latin girls were induced to shave their lips and legs; Irish girls to hide their freckles; Poles to feel apologetic about their difficult names; Italians to dread association with criminal activity; Scandinavians and Poles to hate misinterpretations of their taciturnity and impassive facial expression; Catholics to harden themselves against the anti-Catholicism both of intellectual culture and of nativist America.

The assumption that ethnic consciousness breeds prejudice and hostility suggests that Americanization frees one from them. The truth is that *every* ethnic culture—including mainstream America, and, yes, even intellectual America—has within it resources of compassion and vision as well as capacities for evil.

Homogenized America is built on a foundation of psychic repression; it has not shown itself to be exempt from bitter prejudices and awful hostilities.

America announces itself as a nation of cultural pluralism. Let it become so, openly and with mutual trust.

4. *Ethnic consciousness will disappear.* The world will end, too. The question is how to make the most fruitful, humanistic progress in the meantime. The preservation of ethnicity is a barrier against alienation and anomie, a resource of compassion and creativity and intergroup learning. If it *might* disappear in the future, it has *not* disappeared in the present. And there are reasons to work so that it never does. Who would want to live on a thoroughly homogenized planet?

5. *Intermarriage hopelessly confuses ethnicity.* Intermarriage gives children multiple ethnic models. The transmission of a cultural heritage is not a process clearly understood. But for any child a "significant other" on one side of the family or another may unlock secrets of the psyche as no other does. The rhythm and intensity of emotional patterns in families are various, but significant links to particular cultural traditions almost always occur. One discovers these links best by full contact with ethnic materials. It is amazing how persons who insist that they have a "very mixed" ethnic background, and "no particular" ethnic consciousness, exhibit patterns of taste and appreciation that are very ethnic indeed: a delight in the self-restraint of Scotsmen, discomfort with the effusiveness of Sicilians—or, by contrast, a sense of release in encountering Sicilian emotions, a constriction of nervousness faced with the puzzling cues of the culture of the Scots.

Cues for interpreting emotion and meaning are subtly learned, in almost wholly unconscious, informal ways. These cues persist through intermarriage for an indeterminate period. Cues to pain, anger, intimacy, and humor are involved. (Some passages of this book were intended ironically and written in laughter; some reviewers took them seriously.)

6. *Intelligent, sensitive ethnics, proud of their heritage, do not go around thumping their chests in ethnic chauvinism.* Who would want chest-thumping or chauvinism? But be careful of

the definition of "good" ethnics, "well-behaved" ethnics. Many successful businessmen, artists, and scholars of white ethnic background carry two sets of scars. On the one hand, they had to break from their families, neighborhoods, perhaps ghettos, and they became painfully aware of the lack of education and experience among those less fortunate than they. On the other hand, they had to learn the new styles, new images, and new values of the larger culture of "enlightenment." The most talented succeed rather easily; those of lesser rank have quietly repressed many all-too-painful memories of the period of their transition. As surely as their grandparents emigrated from their homeland, each generation has had to carry the emigration farther. Americanization is a process of bittersweet memory, and it lasts longer than a hundred years.

7. *The new ethnicity will divide group against group.* The most remarkable fact about the new ethnic consciousness is that it is cross-cultural. We do not speak only of "Polish" consciousness or "Italian" consciousness, but of "white ethnic" consciousness. The new ethnicity is not particularistic. It stresses the general contours of *all* ethnicity and notes analogies between the cultural histories of the many groups. The stress is not only on what differentiates each group but also upon the similarities of *structure* and *process* in which all are involved. In coming to recognize the contours of his or her own unique cultural history, a person is better able to understand and to sympathize with the uniqueness of others'.

8. *Emphasis on white ethnics detracts from the first priority to be given blacks.* On the contrary, blindness to white ethnics is an almost guaranteed way of boxing blacks into a hopeless corner. A group lowest on the ladder cannot advance *solely* at the expense of the next group. Any skillful statesman could discern that in an instant. The classic device of the affluent and the privileged is to pretend to a higher morality, while setting the lower classes in conflict with one another.

The most divisive force in America today is, ironically, precisely the "new class" of liberal and radical academics, media personnel, and social service professionals that thinks itself so moral. Perhaps out of guilt feelings—or for whatever reason—

they have projected all guilt for "white racism" onto others. And, without undergoing any of the costs themselves, they take sides or plainly appear to take sides in the very sharp competition between lower-class people, white and black, for scarce jobs, scarce housing, scarce openings in colleges, scarce scholarship funds. They take sides not only with blacks against whites but also with militant blacks against other blacks. For almost a decade they have made "white racism" the central motif of social analysis, and have clearly given the impression that vast resources were going for blacks, nothing for others.

It is easy for blacks, at least militant blacks, to voice their grievances on television and in the papers. It is extremely difficult to get coverage of white ethnic grievances. They are not supposed to *have* grievances, it seems, only prejudices. All problems are defined as black-white problems, even when there are obviously real economic issues for real families in straitened circumstances. With all good intentions, therefore, the desire of liberals to give blacks highest priority has become exclusionary and divisive.

One can still give blacks highest priority, but in an inclusionary way that aims at coalitions of whites and blacks on the grievances they have in common. Newark is divided almost wholly between blacks and Italians; Detroit between Poles and blacks. Inadequate schools, the dangers of drugs, insufficient housing, the lack of support for families and neighborhoods—these grievances afflict white ethnics and blacks alike. If these problems are, by definition, problems of race, what sort of practical coalition can possibly grow? If they are perceived as problems of *class* (with ethnic variables) there is at least a practical ground for effective coalition.

In order for a political coalition to work well, people do not have to love one another; they do not have to share the same life-style or cherish the same values. They have to be realistic enough to pursue limited goals in line with their own self-interest. Lower-middle-class blacks and white ethnics share more self-interests in common than either group does with any other. It is on the basis of shared self-interests that lasting political coalitions are built, and on no other.

9. *Ethnicity is all right for minorities, but not for the main-stream.* In America, every group is a minority. Even among white Anglo-Saxon Protestants there are many traditions. What is often called "mainline Protestantism," centered in the Northeast— Episcopal, Congregational, Presbyterian—is only one tradition within a far larger and more complex Protestant reality. The father of Senator George McGovern experienced prejudice in South Dakota because the kind of Methodist fundamentalism he represented was closer in style to the lower classes, not fashionable either among "mainline" Methodists nor among Germans and Scandinavians, who were mostly Lutheran. Each of these traditions affects the imagination in a different way. British Americans from small towns in New England live and work in quite different emotional and imaginative worlds from British Americans who are Brahmins in Boston and New York. Anglo-Saxon Protestants who are dirt-farmers in Georgia, Alabama, or East Tennessee feel just as much prejudice from Northeastern-style settlers as Polish or Italian Catholics: stereotypes of the Southern sheriff and the redneck function like those of the Irish cop and the dumb hard-hat. The Scotch-Irish and the Scots have a vivid ethnic consciousness, as a conversation with John Kenneth Galbraith and Carey McWiliams, Jr., would make plain.

There is no good reason why we do not all drop our pretensions of being *like* everyone else, and attempt instead to enlarge the range of our sympathies, so as to delight in every observed cultural difference and to understand each cultural cue correctly and in its own historical context. Styles of wit and understatement vary. Each culture has its own traditions of emotional repression and expressiveness. Our major politicians are often misunderstood, systematically, by one cultural group or another; the cues they depend on are absent, or mean something else.

"The new ethnicity" has at least three components. First, there is a new interest in cultural pluralism in our midst. It calls for a new sensitivity toward others in their differences. It means looking at America alert to nuances of difference, more cautious about generalizations about "Americans." Second, there is the personal, conscious self-appropriation of *one's own* cultural history—a making conscious of what perhaps one before had not even noticed about oneself. This component is a form of "consciousness raising." It is useful because ways of perceiving are usually transmitted informally, without conscious design or articulation. As one makes progress in appropriating one's own complexity, one finds it necessary to give others, too, more attentive regard. Thirdly, there is a willingness to share in the social and political needs and struggles of groups to which one is culturally tied, as a way of bringing about a greater harmony, justice and unity in American (and world) society. Rather than pretend to speak for all, or to understand all, we can each make a contribution toward what we can do best.

Each of these components requires further comment.

1. Many liberal persons seem to imagine that social progress demands greater unity, and melting away of social differences. The new ethnicity suggests a form of liberalism based on cultural diversity rather than on cultural unity. It argues that diversity is a better model for America, for the self, and indeed for the human race upon this planet. Is the most pressing danger today homogenization or divisiveness? Does the fear of divisiveness breed conformity, fear of difference, repression of genuine feelings? When ethnic cultures and family values are weakened in the pressures of the melting pot, is anything substituted except the bitch goddess success and the pursuit of loneliness? What else might be proposed? How *are* values taught? These questions prompt the new ethnicity.

2. Some persons are expressly aware of their own ethnic background and interpret the signals from divergent backgrounds successfully. They ask, "What's all this fuss about the new ethnicity?" Well, even their awareness may be first awareness rather than second: accurate enough but not very articulate. It is always a delight to see someone in whom a tradition is alive, even if they *show* better than they *tell*. But in America some of our cultural traditions have been brought to a high degree of articulation and others lie virtually dormant. The Slavs, for example, boast no novel like *Studs Lonigan,* or Mario Puzo's *The Fortunate Pilgrim,* or the whole shelf of American Jewish novels, or even the burgeoning black literature. How nourishing for the imagination and the sensibility to grow up

Jewish, with all that intelligence and energy against which to measure one's own experience, rather than Slavic and virtually solitary. Much remains to be done within many traditions: among Appalachians, Missouri Lutherans, Slovaks, Greeks, and others. And even those which seem to be in stronger shape have strange gaps and self-blindness.

3. The political aims of the new ethnicity are not ethnocentrism, nor group struggle; they are, rather, a greater degree of justice, equality, opportunity, and unity in American society. But the *strategy* of the new ethnicity is somewhat different from that of, say, George McGovern or the "new politics" generally. From the point of view of conceptualizers of the new ethnicity like Monsignor Geno Baroni, who worked for many years among blacks in Washington, D.C., the root flaw in the strategy of "the new politics" is that it is unconsciously divisive and self-defeating. It pictures the white ethnic as the enemy. It drives a wedge between the white ethnic and the black and/or Latino. It fails to extend friendship or insight. It fails to share the daily burdens of the actual struggle for justice in jobs, housing, and schools. *Both* the black and white ethnic are defrauded in this society. No doubt the black suffers more; no one denies that. The question is, how can one most practically *help* him? The response of the new ethnicity: By helping *both* the lower-middle-class white ethnic *and* the black together. Otherwise no coalition is possible. Without that coalition, no one advances.

The alternative is that the Republican party will, as President Nixon did, reap the benefits of the breakdown of the alliance between the intellectuals and the white ethnics. A drop in the Slavic Democratic vote from 82 percent to 60 percent is a catastrophe for Democrats; and it does not have to happen. If the university wing of the Democratic party sides with the blacks *against* white ethnics, and sets up a social pattern whereby gains for blacks are possible only as losses for white ethnics (or vice versa), the outcome is plain—and deplorable. The social pattern must be fair to *all* groups. Divisive tactics are fatal.

It is not necessary to idealize white ethnics in order to construct a social scheme within which it would be to their advantage to work for equality for blacks in jobs, housing, and good schools. It is not even necessary to *like* white ethnics. But it does help to understand their history in various parts of America, their spiritual resources, and their chronic weaknesses. Fear of the new ethnicity is very much like the early fear of "black power." Even some blacks sound, with regard to the new ethnicity, like some whites with regard to black pride. Such fears must be proven groundless.

If we knew all we had to know about Poles, Italians, Greeks, and others in America, there would perhaps be no need for the almost desperate tones with which the new ethnicity is sometimes announced. But the fact is, we know very little about them. Our anthropologists know more about some tribes in New Guinea than about the Poles in Warren or Lackawanna. We have encouraged too few of the talented white ethnics to stay with their people and to give voice to their experience. Local political leadership is often at a very low level. Community organizers who spring from the community are all too few. Uncle Toms are many. If there is anomie, fear, or rage in such communities (often there is a great deal of bottled-up political energy and great good will), it is to no one's advantage.

The new ethnicity gives promise of *doing* something creative in such places. The new ethnicity is the best hope of all who live in our major urban centers. What we have without it is not promising at all.

Notes

1. W. Lloyd Warner, *The Family of God* (New York, 1961), p. 144, as it appeared in *Soundings* (Nashville: Vanderbilt University), Spring 1973, pp. 1-20.
2. W. Lloyd Warner, *American Life* (Chicago, 1965), pp. 204-205.
3. Robert Bellah, "Evil and the American Ethos," *Sanctions for Evil,* ed. Nevitt Sanford and Craig Comstock (San Francisco, 1971), p. 181.
4. Warner, *American Life,* pp. 188-90 (emphasis added).
5. When you read the word "immigrant" which ethnic groups figure in your imagination? The millions of British Americans who have arrived here since (say) 1865? Most usage seems to exclude them, as I have here.

One Species,
Many Cultures

BOUNDED BY the slow Danube River on the south and by the rugged Carpathian Mountains on the north, the ancestral land of the Slovak people lies at the axis of Western civilization. For centuries, the vast armies of Attila, Genghis Khan, the Turks, the Germans, and the Russians have risen like a tide toward Europe and in due course have been broken in or near the mountains of Slovakia. In the ninth century, Saints Cyril and Methodius established there the Byzantine influence of the Cyrillic alphabet and the Old Slavonic liturgy; but ambitious German rulers later imposed the Latin language, in order to draw Slovakia back toward the West. The rivers of Slovakia run southward and the cultivation of grapes makes Slovakia a wine-drinking nation; the sensibility of the Slovaks is partly Mediterranean and partly Nordic. For two thousand years, the Slovak people, often to their woe, have abhorred large governmental units and preferred local rule. For a thousand years they have endured almost unbroken political oppression.

Just before the Johnstown flood of 1889, one of my grandfathers came from Slovakia to the United States; within a few

This chapter is reprinted from *The American Scholar,* Vol. 43, no. 1 (Winter 1873–74), copyright 1973 by the United Chapters of Phi Beta Kappa, pp. 113–121.

years, all three of my other grandparents had done the same. During the thirty-nine years from 1875 to 1914, nearly a third of the population of Slovakia emigrated. They left from sheer hunger, to escape military conscription in the hated Hungarian army, to find some way to break the political oppression of Hungarian "magyarization," and to fulfill the ancient Slovak legends and myths of freedom.[1]

The Slovaks, like many other Slavs, tend to be suspicious of governments, activism, and politicians. "Every official has a tail, to sweep in goods," runs a Slovak proverb. Better to concentrate on home, family and work. No other Slavic people is so inventive in song; over 15,000 folk songs of the Slovaks have been catalogued, and a Slavic saying goes: "See a Slovak, hear a song." Nearly all the arts of the Slovaks focus on the home.

The great Slovak names Svatopluk, Janosik, Benovsky, and Stefanik mean little to most Americans. But this is only to say that an ordinary American education is remarkably ethnocentric. About one-third of our population is of Anglo-Saxon ancestry. Yet so far is our nation from fulfilling its own pluralistic destiny that our education is almost entirely Anglo-American. Perhaps the dominance of Anglo-Saxon ethnocentrism in the past necessitates its continued dominance; it has shaped our history. Every American should learn about and, to some extent, assimilate English political history and literature. But is a virtually total concentration on the upper-class culture based in the northeastern section of the nation a sufficient intellectual guide to actual American life, or to the character of the other cultures on this planet?

Not long ago, "the humanities" meant, not humanity, but "Western civilization as seen through English, Protestant, upper-class eyes." Not many of the graduates of Harvard, Princeton, and Yale now in their fifties learned very much in the college days about the other cultures of the world—about Buddhism, or Slavic history, or Jewish family life, or Chinese civilization, or Latin America, or the history of slavery. What they were instructed in as "liberal arts" was not quite fully liberating; what passed before their eyes as "the humanities" was, rather astonishingly, a mirror image of their own ethnicity.

The phrase "our common culture" has in recent years been used with more glibness than hard reflection. A culture is not put on like a suit of clothes. One can mimic a culture, absorb it, even use it as a vehicle of one's own self-expression. If, however, the culture does not flow out of one's own tutored instincts and aspirations, it is not yet one's own and does not yet exhaust one's own intelligence, perceptions, or dreams. So for many millions of immigrants and their descendants—for a majority of Americans—what is currently available as "mainstream culture" does not spring from the heart. Hundreds of thousands of freshmen tapping their feet in classrooms in Providence, Buffalo, Pittsburgh, Detroit, Miami, Houston, and Los Angeles do *not* hear, in the voice of their professors, their own voices—and this is not only because of television, or a generation gap, or the collapsing of "the great tradition." The great tradition itself has been in America too narrowly, too ethnocentrically, perceived.

I concur, there *is* a great tradition. There is a "common" Western culture, distinct from other cultures. But ever since Kant, scholars have sought this tradition in a premature and inaccurately projected "universality." They have tried to emphasize what is *common* in all men, what is *universal,* those qualities in which we all share and are *alike,* those characteristics that do not *divide* but rather *unite* us. A laudable but grievously mistaken impulse.

A profound irony is involved in our common identity as members of the human species. The species to which we belong is a historical species; it possesses consciousness, and this consciousness is at once symbolic and concrete. That is, our species lives not only within the physical atmosphere surrounding this blue and green planet but also within a variety of concrete, historical cultures. We are the species that lives within cultures—within spheres of meaning, sensibility, selective perception, and patterned action. What we have in common is that we are diverse. Our diversity is proof that we are human. We are not so many ants crawling on a soundless orb, nor so many apes obeying laws of natural selection. We generated distinctive cultures. Within cultures, we develop endlessly complex, distinctive individuals. We live within symbolic worlds all our own, both as individuals and as cultures.

In the twentieth century (which is itself, a friend reminds me, a somewhat "culture-bound" concept), the relativity of each of our identities is borne in upon us because we inescapably encounter so many who differ from us. In this relativity we meet a second and novel kind of common identity. What we have in common are our finitude and interdependence. Our diversity does not mean we are intrinsically divided from each other, only that we are intrinsically different from each other. Our future unity lies not in "overcoming our differences" but in seeing how they are analogous: in learning to see that *my* struggle to become a moral human being is rather *like* (not the same as, only analogous to) *your* struggle to become a moral human being.

In a word, the way to become moral is not to become universal, but to become concrete. I need not become the same as you. But my struggle to realize my own moral identity—solely my own, concrete, unique—has many parallels to your struggle to realize your own identity. We face, for example, many similar obstacles: social inequities, ill fortune, self-deception, aging, death. How you face these obstacles in your life illuminates possibilities by which I may, allowing for our differences, conduct my life as well.

A nun may define her life around her chastity, as chosen symbol of God's transcendent love; whereas I, a sensual man, may see in her struggles to protect virginity (of spirit and of flesh) illumination for the perplexities surrounding the central value by which I define my life. The world's literature opens up for me a world of analogy, where flashes of illumination ricochet in unpredictable patterns off a thousand mirrors. The critic of literature who reads Nietzsche after having learned from Goethe may catch different reflections from one who reads him after studying Russell, Hare, and Austin.

What "the great tradition" concerns is wisdom, the voyages individuals take toward moral maturity and moral growth, and the analogous "dilemmas," "ironies," and "tragedies" they encounter. These words, of course, are already heavy with cultural specificity; they conjure up Aeschylus, Kierkegaard, Hesse, and a hundred German scholars. Still, every human life is a structuring of time; each begins with birth, each ends. "Voyage," therefore, is a universal motif. It is the kind of motif that allows for infinite variation, for concrete diversity, for cultural and personal uniqueness. Cultures structure time quite differently. Cultures imagine the model of human fulfillment differently. Yet in every culture individuals voyage from birth to death, and from moral beginnings to moral development.

Many of our present perplexities arise from two confusions. One is a misperception of class, the other a misperception of culture. Some young blacks from Hough may not be literate, but that does not mean that the basic human voyage is closed to them. Both the *Autobiography of Malcolm X* and *Soul on Ice* are classically Greek and Christian in the *metanoia* they narrate, and in the structure of decision and liberation they exhibit. (Note even their chapter headings.) It is a mistake to hold that the fundamental moral struggle is restricted to upper-class Anglo-Saxons—*or* to the "oppressed." Whatever one's social class, the struggle against self-deception (never decisively won), the struggle for clear vision, and the struggle to respect concrete human persons different from oneself is always present.

Bourgeois morality, the morality of appearances and proprieties, must be distinguished from fundamental human morality. "The habit doth not make the monk." One may be an attorney general of the United States without becoming a moral hero to whom others look for illumination on how to become a moral man. It is not easy to be moral simply because one is well-born, nor simply because one is born in a slum. The voyage toward moral development in either case is analogous to the others— essentially different, yet sufficiently parallel to cast mutual illumination. No human life is so different from all others that it cannot shed morally profitable light, thus the fascination of stories even about moral monsters.

When a culture is highly articulated, a "cultivated" person is skilled both in discerning movements of the soul *and* in giving names to them. He will have a full range of references and allusions with which to speak of what he feels. It is not enough, for example, to be "an atheist." Like Sartre? Or like Merleau-Ponty? Or like Malraux? Or like Camus? Like John Dewey? Or like Corliss Lamont? Or like some churchgoer going through empty motions? The state of soul is remarkably various in every case.

Nevertheless, a lack of words does not necessarily indicate an incapacity of soul. It is true (it certainly seems true) that many persons are indeed shallow of soul and contemptuous of introspection. It does not necessarily follow that an abundance of words indicates greatness of soul, or poverty of words, or poverty of spirit. There are some professors, disdainful of the "cultural deprivation" of those they are obliged to instruct, who are sterile of soul; and in some of their students there are depths untongued.

Among some of the Indian chiefs of American history, for example, there is an eloquence, dignity, and precision of speech worthy of the ancient Greeks. Or, to state the matter differently, some of the heroes of Homer utter sentiments worthy of the Indian nations. Want of reading does not disbar human beings from profound moral insight or from classical eloquence. One does not have to read Greek to encounter ancient wisdom. (The American Indians produced no Aristotle; neither has New York.)

On the other hand, a university education in the humanities today is *not* aimed at profound moral insight or classical eloquence. They are lucky indeed whose insight and eloquence are not destroyed by a university education today.

For the culture of the universities today is not the culture of "the great tradition," not the culture of upper-class Anglo-Americans. In some few persons, it may be these things. In most administrators, professors, teaching assistants, and students a university education exhibits a different culture altogether. Let me call it "the culture of the professionals" and attempt to draw attention to its pervasiveness.

Not long ago, a major corporation took an ad in *The Wall Street Journal* to honor one of its employees. Above his picture was a single word, *"Professionalism, "* and below it a definition: *"More than education.... More than experience.... More than training...it's a state of mind. "* Who today are proud to call themselves professionals? Football players, stockbrokers, doctors, lawyers, journalists, gangsters, and professors of literature, philosophy, and other fields. "Professionalism," "state of mind."

These are terms of considerable power. Implied are choices, specializations, narrowing down for purposes of efficiency and effect. Implied, indeed, is the discipline of an entire life, a concentration upon a limited field of expertise. "A state of mind." "A way of life." A major, driving, powerful culture in our midst is the culture of professionals. Football is its major public liturgy, its dramatic expression, its mirror-image festival.

In the daily world of politics, the word "professional" is used in fascinating ways. Of some lifelong politicians, an informed opinion of their performance is "hack" or "fake." By contrast, the most sober and comforting praise for a public figure or for this or that person on his staff is, "He's a real pro." An intermediate word of praise, spoken with a faintly baffled sort of affection, is the phrase, "an old pro." The meaning is that the person in question—Senator Sam Ervin, let us say—lacks some of the technical sophistication and scientific art of modern professionalism, but is, so to speak, an artist of an older style, in a different sort of way, and by God, admirable nevertheless. He "knows his way around," "knows what he's doing," and so one "shouldn't be fooled" by his apparent naivete or folksy style. There are some jobs, among some constituencies, that maybe "the old pro" tackles with a surer grasp than "the real pro."

It's a very good feeling to be called by one's peers "a pro." Certification (college degrees, a tough job assignment) confers the objective status. But not all who have the certification are truly considered by their peers to be "the real pros." Such hints suggest that an accurate discussion of culture must move on several levels.

The first meaning of culture applies to the "state of mind," or the "way of life," of our professional classes. This is the class that manages our institutions of certification—the schools, the universities, the media, and the new institutes of research, development, and consulting. This same class also manages many of our traditional institutions—business corporations, government, foundations, churches, and national organizations. By no means a majority of Americans experience the culture of professionalization. But most of the high-salaried and/or organizing, articulating, managing, and "influential" people do.

"Above" the level of the professional culture lies the "high culture" of family tradition, and/or money, and/or dedication to the classical, recognized arts. Nurture in a certain kind of family tradition—children of Cabots or Lodges, or of concert violinists or professors of the classics—sometimes provides the requisite sensibility. Money that can buy for a new generation the education denied its parents may provide it. (There are many "middle-brow" participants in high culture who enjoy its fruits without being creators.) Finally, sheer talent and desire, an "innate" capacity for the flowering of one's spirit, and the good fortune of schooling of some sort may provide it. Thus, not a few of our ablest artists and scholars today, like Abraham Lincoln and William Shakespeare, although not "well-born," have advanced the reaches of the human spirit.

It is true that the "high culture," once it has been achieved, is in some respects more accessible to the wealthy than to the poor. The wealthy can travel. They have leisure. They are provided with instruction. They finance artists and scholars. They buy the materials, the time spent, and the fruits of artistic endeavor; they are the patrons of art and learning. Yet by their nature the achievements of high culture speak to—and belong to—the human spirit, not to wealth. Instrumentally both a society and individuals require sufficient wealth to gain that freedom from necessity without which there are no liberal arts. Such wealth can be very modest. Even in the caves humans began to draw, and already by the fireside the spirit of Lincoln was being forged. High culture, nonetheless, requires a culture in which leisure is available; it requires wealth. This instrumental tie between wealth and high culture occasions a certain embarrassment in a ruthlessly egalitarian society.

Common speech, we recall, distinguishes several kinds of professional performance. The main force of the word "professional" points toward a specialized commitment: one professes one line of work rather than another. A "hack" is a fellow who has not really mastered all the skills he needs, or else does not really commit the whole of himself to the skills he does possess. A "slick professional," or "operator," or *apparatchik* is a fellow who has the skills but no larger commitment to the whole reality of the world within which he operates: he is "a gun for hire." We respect his skills, but not the spirit of their use.

When we say "real pro," however, we mean that the person has not been distorted by his specialized techniques. We mean that his intelligence and instincts reach out for all the complex, ambiguous, even mysterious elements of the social realities within which he operates. We mean that, both regarding himself and regarding the world of his activities, he maintains a certain realism. He is "in touch." His professionalism is an instrument of his commitment to reality, not a defense against that reality. He is neither an operator, nor a hack, nor a mere specialist.

Hacks are easy to understand but what is the culture of the operator? We are afflicted with operators in America. As testimony to their "cultivation," they may take home movies, or become amateur photographers, or be buffs of considerable artistic skill in one field or another. They may attend concerts or go to all the arty flicks. They may be articulate and even, in some sense, well and broadly educated. Yet there is a sense in which, used in this context, the word "culture" gives off a tinny ring. No doubt anthropologists should study their "culture," too; in a perfectly neutral sense, they represent a "state of mind," a "way of life," as surely as do primitive tribes in New Guinea. But in some way they are rootless, rudderless, without depth. They have made themselves rather into instruments than into ends. The phrase "new barbarians" points to their shallowness. It suggests that smooth, civil persons, persons of considerable education and articulateness, are somehow empty and lacking. Empty of what? Lacking what? No tradition, it seems, lives in them; no long-range, virtually unchangeable, perennial values guide them; their moral universe is without a center; no passionate inwardness directs them. They are, in a sense larger than David Riesman intended, "other-directed." Success, power, expertise—their guides are extrinsic, changeable, consulted for the short term. The social realities of our "temporary society" do not discourage the flexibility such men exemplify. The state, as Plato says, is man writ large; such men are their society writ small.

Operators, then, are quintessentially American; their role has been mythically established in *Huck Finn* and in Melville's

The Confidence Man. They are outsiders, from the city (or the university), traveling salesmen, "experts." But what about the local cultures, those millions who admire and understand "the old pros" but dislike operators? When Senator Sam Ervin quoted the Bible and Shakespeare, he made reverberate a network of trustworthy and illuminating traditions. He played on symbolic strings that have shaped the consciousness of perhaps eighty million Americans. Many, indeed, find the language of a "country lawyer" a good deal more persuasive than the language of the new professionals. To them, they are all the same: the smooth articulateness of John Dean and Gary Hart, of David Brinkley and Professor Galbraith, of Doctor Kildare and Doctor Spock, of Jeb Stuart Magruder and William Coffin. Often today ideology does not divide people (liberal versus conservative) so much as cultural style does. The old pros remain connected to the symbolic worlds of this nation's many diverse cultures; the operators leave and "do not go home again."

Religion, ethnicity, religion, race, and other cultural factors shape symbolic consciousness in different ways. The Irish of Boston are not exactly like those of Minnesota or Texas; contrasts among John Kennedy, Eugene McCarthy, Joseph McCarthy, Richard Daley, and John Connally suggest several of the most significant Irish traditions in the nation. Both George McGovern and George Wallace spring from fundamentalist Scotch Irish traditions, but in regions whose history has been profoundly different. The symbolic worlds within which they speak set off intense but opposite vibrations.

Of the French Canadians of New Hampshire and Maine; the Appalachians of West Virginia and Kentucky; the poor whites of Alabama and the Florida Panhandle; the Anglo-Americans of Wyoming and Idaho; the Oregonians; the Mormons of Utah; the Slavic farmers of Illinois and Nebraska, contrasted with the Slavic miners and mill workers of Pennsylvania, Ohio, and Michigan; the Italians contrasted with the upper-class and the lower-class Jews of New York City; the Anglo-American Protestants who supported George Wallace in the 1968 Indiana primary in proportions far heavier than did German-American

Protestants of similar economic class—of such diverse and criss-cross variety is this nation composed.

Among blacks, there are differences depending on origins in Africa; on the generations of colonial experience whether in the West Indies, or rural Mississippi, or the cities of the South; and on length of time in the urban North. The Spanish-speaking populations of Miami, New York, Chicago, Los Angeles, San Antonio, and Albuquerque are significantly different. The experiences of Oriental Americans—including, without benefit of "Protestant ethic," their astonishing capacity for work and for success— are better admitted into consciousness if one approaches American pluralism from Hawaii and California, rather than from Boston and New York.

The variety of cultural worlds in the United States is a powerful, subterranean influence in our national life. It remains subterranean because it is often repressed, as though it were something "dirty," dysfunctional, and doomed to disappear. In its place, a "national" ideology has been created, divided into three parts. First, there is the ideology of "the American way of life," popular, patriotic, capitalistic, chauvinistic. Second, there is the ideology of the mobile, educated, "committed," professional classes—what one writer has called "the ideocracy." Third, there is the ideology of the neutral, meritocratic, uncommitted, objective professional classes, neither conservative nor liberal, but comfortably in charge. All three of these ideologies, for their own various purposes, try to eliminate cultural diversity. Each carries with it its own ethnic and regional biases. Some, for example, make provision for black, Hispanic, and Indian diversity—and, pressed a little, perhaps, they might expand the list. But the terms of their analyses do not give cultural diversity the prominence reality demands.

It is true, we have seen, that there is a "common culture" in the West, a set of achievements that represents the most profound insights, wrested from suffering, that Western peoples for some five millennia have attained. But it is not true that even highly educated people in any part of the West are well versed in all the subtraditions of this "common culture." A young Italian from New Jersey who attends the University of Notre Dame will have as part of the furniture of his mind and sensibility materials that the young Jew from Brooklyn who attends City College of New York will not share, and vice versa. When I compare, for example, my years of reading in St. Augustine, St. Bernard, Thomas Aquinas, Cardinal Newman, and others, my virtual neglect of Marx, and my dislike of Enlightenment writers like Kant and Mill, with the reading patterns exhibited by, say, Irving Howe, it is vividly clear to me that American intellectual life is profoundly diverse. So it is also with Protestant colleagues of mine in philosophy and religious studies who respond in significantly different ways to materials we jointly consider. Other colleagues have interests and training in the sciences or social sciences; their symbolic world is, again, quite different from mine.

"Where did you grow up? Where did you go to school? What is your religious and ethnic background? What do these mean to you?" These are important questions, not for purposes of stereotyping, but for intelligent and sensitive perception. In order to come to learn and to appreciate the cultural background within which the words of others gain their full and familiar meaning, we must be able to answer such questions. What we have most to gain from each other is generated by our mutual differences. The different horizon, standpoint, and way of perceiving we each bring to our common world are instruments of spiritual wealth.

Consider the following propositions:

1. There is a common Western culture of high intellectual and humanizing potency, instructing all who journey into it in inexhaustible wisdom, insight and spiritual depth.
2. This common culture is composed of many related but divergent traditions, and no one can master all of them.
3. Beyond the boundaries of Western culture, there are also other "common cultures" of great complexity and diversity. In some of these non-eastern riches, westerners are also beginning to share, in ways both superficial and serious.
4. In higher education and in museums and other instrumentalities of culture in the United States, Protestant traditions within the common culture have been favored over Catho-

lic and Jewish traditions. English literature and philosophy
have been favored over Continental literatures and philosophies. Post-Enlightenment materials have virtually driven
pre-Enlightenment materials from the field. Agnostic or
atheistic materials are favored over religious materials. A
rather positivistic ideology of the modern, the progressive
and the "factual" has dominated our dictionaries and ency-
clopedias, as well as our schools, our journalism, and our
business world. (Dictionaries do not list under "rose" one
of its most important cultural meanings: that it is the flower
of love, fate, and war.)

5. Education is commonly regarded, not as a device for
   strengthening and benefiting by local, regional, ethnic, and
   religious differences but for "overcoming" them, for replac-
   ing them with a more or less universal culture. The underlying model for this "universal" ideological outlook is not
   perfectly neutral as regards those who enter into it. Even if
   they are of equal talent, some will find cultural models,
   heroes, texts, and materials related to their own cultural
   background, and others will not.

6. The preferred and most prestigious model for the "high culture" in the United States coincides with the background of
   our most wealthy and powerful citizens. This model illustrates the history of some, at least, of our major institutions, and partially grounds the dominant language of the
   land. Hence, even though it is biased, it cannot be ignored.

Let us attend, first, to proposition 6. Andover, Groton, Milton,
Choate, and the other prestigious private schools nurture a good
part of one major wing of the nation's financial and governmental elites. Yet with every year that passes, in order to understand American reality, students have to go further beyond
the limits of Anglo-American traditions. How can one understand Mailer, Malamud, Trilling, Chomsky, or Howe without
understanding the Jewish traditions of Eastern Europe and
America? How can one understand Kennedy, McCarthy, or
Daley without learning about the Irish experience in America?
Will anyone comprehend Detroit without learning about black

history in America and Polish history in America—two out of every three citizens of that city being either black or Polish, while virtually all the wealth and power of the city's elites remain Anglo-American and Jewish?

Power in America is essentially Anglo-American; hence, it is a condition of survival (and of eventual justice) that all the others penetrate the intricacies of the Anglo-American mind. The Yankee pride in "candor," for example, has generated unique deceptions, especially self-deceptions, whose routes must be painfully traced and plainly marked. Yankee appeals to "morality" and "leadership" and "integrity" require most careful scrutiny; these are the banners of the most powerful elites. Thus, those whose heritage is not Anglo-American have every right (and duty) both to assimilate all that is good in Anglo-American culture, and to be clear-eyed about what assimilation entails.

Irving Howe once quoted in *The American Scholar* the argument of Louis Kampf that "initiating the 'underprivileged' to the cultural treasures of the West could be a form of oppression—a weapon in the hands of those who rule.... High culture itself...tends to reinforce the given alignments of power within the society." Against Kampf, Howe is able to quote Trotsky: "Mastery of the art of the past is...a necessary precondition not only for the creation of new art but also for the building of a new society.... If we were groundlessly to repudiate the art of the past, we should at once become poorer spiritually." Cultural backwardness is not required for political advance.

And yet, what is meant by "backwardness"? In order to be a fully moral man must one be a professor, or at minimum a college graduate? Is it necessary to have read many books? "Man is not saved by dialectics," a Christian aphorism insists. The simple, too, have their own precious wisdom and the learned their patent foolishness. It is not necessary to romanticize either side in order to recognize that there are analogies between the life stories of the uneducated and those of the college trained.

A democracy needs an early discernment system, to spot young persons of talent to remain (if they so wish) in living contact with their own roots. They should be encouraged not to be parochial, and yet to be rooted. Neither our egalitarians nor our meritocrats, it seems, have a sufficiently cultural perspective; both proceed somewhat atomically, somewhat mechanically.

According to egalitarian sentimentality, any student admitted to college through "open admissions" has within him the makings of a student. According to meritocratic arrogance, each student should be judged according to his own performance. The egalitarian forgets that a university is an institution not all citizens are graced with the talent to appreciate; perhaps not one person in ten ought to be admitted to a genuine university. The meritocrat forgets that persons are not individuals merely but also creatures of culture, and that the institutions of high culture in the United States are inequitably and inhumanely ethnocentric.

When as a young Slovak American I read (with eagerness and delight) "English literature," I learned as well a latent message: "*These* are the kinds of people literature is about; not about families like yours, feelings like yours, dilemmas like yours." Literature was not (except by analogy) about myself; it was about those fascinating, foreign "others." In our part of town, when I was very young, we called them "the Americans." (With less than accurate perception, we included the Irish among "the Americans." We seldom dealt directly with Anglo-Americans.)

The heart of the matter comes down to this. There are three main locations of culture. The actual ways of life of ordinary people, in their diverse, loose, and permeable communities are one location. The humanities are, in this sense, not primarily what is written down in books, or celebrated in works of art, but what is lived. Those relatively few artists, scholars, and critical persons in whom a genuinely high culture is alive are a second location. The swarming army of professionals, highly educated but not necessarily in tune with the high traditions of the past, are a third location. Among these new professionals are many who call themselves humanists. Each of these groups is to be taken seriously. Each enhances our own identity. Let us examine each in turn.

We need, in America, a public and popular humanities—a pluralism of stories, myths, accurate histories, detailed studies that touch our various people in all their variety. As a boy, I wish I had learned of the exploits of Janosik as well as of Robin Hood, and had been taught in public and parochial school of the democratic traditions of the early Slovak tribes. I wish I had learned that, after the origins of feudalism, my ancestors endured a thousand-year struggle against oppression that is not yet complete. I wish I had learned officially and fully of the bitter deaths of so many of my countrymen in the mills and mines and strikes of Pennsylvania. (The murder of the Jablonskis of the United Mine Workers was a recent episode in a 100-year war.) My sense of injustice and untruth in America would have come earlier than it did. I would have learned earlier both a tragic sense of life and a fierce desire to remedy injustice. I would have had a way to discern what made me culturally different, and what my peculiar contribution might have been. I would have had personal parallels by which to judge more accurately what America had done to the Indians, blacks, and others in America. (What was I doing, cheering for Custer in *They Died with Their Boots On*?)

We also need, of course, a high culture. We need continuity with the visions and sources of judgment upon us that derive from the great spiritual achievements of our past. In many American towns, counties, and cities, one family, or a small number of families, controls the politics, economics, and media of communication. Against their vulgar power, the arts and critical skills of the high culture are as powerful a threat as human beings have. Indeed even our highest national elites, our best and our brightest, suffer embarrassment compared to the best our race has seen before. I recognize that our elites sometimes use "taste" and "culture" as weapons of intimidation, which only proves their own vulgarity. The proof that a person has attained a genuine high culture is his unself-conscious respect for the moral analogies between his life and those of others. Portrayed in myth and narrative as the nobleman at home with peasants, the saint with sinners, the learned doctor with children and the ignorant, the political leader sharing his people's crusts of bread, this is the excellence by which our culture measures us. It is not exactly an egalitarian standard, for differences of station and talent are not blurred; but it is, at least, a standard of fraternity, and of the human spirit's radical equality in the eyes of God.

Finally, we need the professionals. It is true that concerning the large and important issues, they are almost always wrong. But this is exactly what we should expect; it is their profession to attend scrupulously to a part of the whole; they almost necessarily distort. Yet specialization is no cause for excommunication. Professionals are our brothers, too. We need their powerful skills toward many neglected problems, to mention but one: toward the history and culture of each of the diverse peoples of the United States, toward an accurate history of our actual pluralism.

Note

1.   From 1896 to 1908, 508 Slovaks were arrested and convicted for using the Slovak language in public.

CHAPTER SIXTEEN

The Social World
of Individuals

ONE OF the fascinating features of political life is that there are
"tides" in the affairs of men: that public opinion can be
"swayed"; that certain events can become "turning points"; that
certain leaders can "galvanize" a host of followers; that political facts, feelings, and movements wait for "definition," "direction," "momentum." Political life is remarkably dependent
upon symbolic life. An aggregate of individuals can be bom-
barded with "divisive" symbols and split apart, as for example
in the bitter division on the Democratic Left between the followers of Eugene McCarthy and those of Robert Kennedy in
1968. On the other hand, the same aggregate of individuals
can be left leaderless, apathetic, without energy or direction.
Finally, that same aggregate can be "inspired," united, dedicated to a common task. Individuals can be bound by symbols
that shape a communal life.

According to Aristotle, human beings are political animals;
that they are social is more significant than that they are individual. In his view, ethics is a branch of politics. The character
of the social worlds in which we live is, from a moral point of
view, prior to the character of our individual moral choices. The

Reprinted from Hastings Center *Studies*, Vol. 2, No. 3 (Autumn
1974), pp. 37–44.

character of our social world informs, shapes, enables our individual moral development. Questions of ethics are, in a central dimension, questions of politics and social criticism.

In this respect, an education in the humanities ought to aim at evoking unfamiliar cultural perspectives. At different stages in history, and in different cultures, the relation of the individual to his social world is imagined, perceived, and acted out quite differently. In rough but serviceable terms, we sometimes speak of "The Age of Individualism" in the West, arising out of that complex of cultural movements known as capitalism, Protestantism, and the Enlightenment. The cultural centers of these developments were the first industrial nations: England, Germany, France, the Lowlands, Scandinavia. The temporal span of this age of the "emergence of the individual" extends from the sixteenth century to the twentieth. To study earlier ages in Western culture, or to study other cultures even today, is to encounter quite different symbolic worlds, different especially in their way of relating the individual to society. In a remarkable essay, "Religious Evolution," Robert Bellah has attempted to sketch a conceptual framework for the location of such diverse symbolic worlds; his attempt, naturally enough, gives a kind of superiority to Protestant Christianity. Still, we all do implicitly what Bellah attempted to do explicitly; we relate our own symbolic world to those of others. The emergence of a worldwide culture means that we must learn the rather subtle process of "passing over" from one cultural horizon to another, from one way of life to another.

My thesis in this chapter, then, is modest but perhaps useful. It moves forward in four simple, perhaps well-known, steps: (1) human beings live, move, and have their being in symbolic worlds; (2) symbolic worlds are primarily communal, social, historical, and only in relatively minor measure unique, personal, not participated in by others; (3) in a pluralistic, highly mobile world like that of the United States, a new human type needs to be developed, the pluralistic personality; (4) a method of symbolic realism is required if we are to explain adequately the types of symbolic thinking and acting we experience in ourselves and encounter in others.[1]

1. *The Individual and His Symbolic Worlds*

There are some 210 million citizens in the United States. Few sentences formulated about "the Americans" or "the American People" actually apply to all of them. One of the remarkable features of political discourse in the United States, indeed, is that most political words are perceived differently by individuals and groups that encounter them; such words function differently in different symbolic traditions. (Some examples: the United Nations, welfare, justice, civil liberties, civility, patriotism, loyalty, work, quotas.) Another interesting feature of political discourse in the United States, complementary to the first, is that comparatively few individuals seem to live within one symbolic world alone—one cannot predict with certainty that because an individual has certain group characteristics (religious, racial, ethnic, regional, educational, etc.) his convictions will be a certain type. Political symbols, in a word, are not atomic; they function within systems of interpretation. These systems are social and historical. But most individuals seem to have access to more than one symbol system.

What is a symbol system (a symbolic world)? At least the following "levels" of human consciousness are involved: a sense of reality; a cultural and personal story; a network of images and words; rules for interpreting events, images, and words. By *sense of reality (mythos),* I mean the most fundamental intention of individual or cultural consciousness, prior to perception, thinking, and action. Included within this sense of reality are: criteria for what counts as relevant or evidential; the selective screen through which the overabundance of experience at any instant is given entry and shape; habits of perception and awareness by which individual differs from individual, culture from culture. The sense of reality operates "below" the level of speech or argument, using and guiding them as instruments.

An example or two may help to point to the phenomenon I am trying to isolate, without being satisfied that I have yet done so. Americans overseas sometimes suffer "culture shock." What they have been taught is real, good, important to notice, determinative of the good life or of reality itself, is often devalued by persons of other cultures, deemed strange, odd, insignificant, mistaken, harmful. Perceptions of time, personality, social realities, the sacred, and other aspects of experience vary widely. In Vietnam, the American preoccupation with gaining an "empirical" picture of reality by quantitative measures seemed to some Vietnamese rather "mystical"—that is, irrelevant, unreal, out of touch, and yet obviously powerful, even awesome. An American and a Vietnamese tended to live in "different worlds," internally and environmentally. What one took to be real seemed unreal to the other. Vietnamese tended to look for signals of shifting internal loyalties which to Americans seemed "subjective," "mystical," "impressionistic," but which the Vietnamese took to be the "most real" realities, alongside which everything else seemed irrelevant. The Vietnamese tended to see a cosmic drama affecting individuals, almost against their will, tipping them this way and then that. Americans tended to count armaments, attacks, casualties.[2]

Similarly, even among educated Americans who, by external standards, ought to be living in the same sense of reality, there are remarkable differences of perception and evaluation, of great and perhaps irreducible depth. Even after great efforts to define terms and to articulate the logic of their views, great gaps remain. They "look at" things so differently, "weigh" things so differently, feel that their own judgments are "realistic" in such diverse ways, that one must say that more than merely their "standards" or their "values" differ. Their *address* differs. Their *sense of reality* differs. With sufficient stubbornness and effort, persons who so differ may come to fairly adequate understandings of their mutual divergences, and even find ways of negotiating the differences. But it seems to me important to mark the thoroughness and centrality of such differences by a comprehensive and fundamental term like sense of reality, and not to give a misleading picture of some ideal common ground in which they would both participate.

Secondly, by cultural or personal *stories* is meant the dramatic or narrative structure given to time and history by the individual and by the collectives in which he participates. To have an image of human "progress" and "development," to operate out of a scheme of "evolution," to take "responsibility for the future"—all these are to give time and history a narrative structure. Each world religion interprets the human story differently. Each human person and every human institution necessarily involves itself in at least an implicit narrative: from a past through the present toward a future. There are narratives of repetition and eternal return, narratives of progress, and narratives of decline; narratives of reform and narratives of revolution; narratives of continuity and narratives of aimless wandering. It is our nature to be temporal. We sometimes fail to notice that in the act of structuring our temporality we have decided how we shall perceive events.

Thirdly, our actions, our thoughts, our images are not merely atomic and discreet; they clash with each other and depend upon each other. It is true that we are often inconsistent, that our lives are characterized by flagrant contradictions, that we hold to incompatible symbols. Still, our sense of reality tends to rule out some materials as irrelevant, insignificant, or hostile to our interests. Our culture or personal story makes certain materials empty of meaning, useless, threatening, offensive. Thus, individual *words* or *symbols* are interpreted according to the context in which we situate them. When we first hear of a new proposal—national health insurance, for example—we may not know what we think of it. But as we examine its implications for other words or symbols which we have already made part of our symbolic world, we may come to loathe it—or to make it part of our own purposes.

Finally, connections between the first three "levels" (sense of reality, story, word, and symbol) are established according to processes that, while difficult to reduce to simple *rules,* are fairly orderly. Imagine a medical student whose fellowship was once improperly canceled by an error in administrative procedure; whose whole experience of medical school is impersonal, lonely, and heavily laden with resentment at never visible or tangible authorities; who, in a word, has come to hate bureaucracy. If such a student develops a great antagonism toward "national health insurance," the actual sources of his resistance may or may not appear in the usual logical and ideological forms of argument. Whether he bests his adversaries in argument, or is bested by them, the actual reasons for his position may be hidden from view, and his adversaries may well feel that there is something "irrational" in his performance. Since the discovery of these actual reasons may shed fruitful light on the discussion, there does seem to be an orderly connection between them and his stated arguments. Since the articulation of these reasons—formative of the sense of reality and the story with which he structures his perceptions—may not be easily accomplished, the connection may be difficult to establish.

As rules of thumb for deeply felt arguments, therefore, the following seem useful: Arguments over single words, definitions, or symbols should be "deepened" until (1) the *stories* within which the protagonists employ these words, definitions, or symbols are articulated; or (2) the *senses of reality* within which the protagonists give meaning to these words, definitions, or symbols are made plain. When the medical student's resentment of bureaucratic forms is brought to light, and when one discovers, perhaps, that a major reason for his choice of medicine as a career is its presumed independence of bureaucratic entanglement, the argument assumes new forms. Since a great many arguments go unresolved on one level and never move to more relevant levels, even very general rules for searching out sources of disagreement offer at least modest utility. Even those arguments of others that seem to us irrational may within a different horizon be altogether reasonable. If one's goal is to try to appreciate the reasonableness of other's arguments, general methods for reconstructing the horizon within which they seem reasonable are helpful instruments.

What remains to be shown, then, is that senses of reality, stories, and words and images are in virtually all cases social constructs. The reasons why this is so are mainly two: first, that before individuals begin to perceive, or imagine, or speak, or act, models for their behavior are set before them by the social systems in which they participate; secondly, that it is the function of senses of reality, stories, words, and images to relate individuals to the social systems in which they participate. Suppose that a young man takes personal autonomy, a highly developed individuality, and originality of spirit and expression as the focal points of his personal development. It is unlikely that he would come upon such ideas unaided by a linguistic and moral community in which, from infancy, these ideals had been singled out from other possible ideals. Moreover, were these ideals totally absent among the ideals of the social system in which he participated, then those social systems would constantly warn him, if he persisted, of his lack of realism and effectively discipline him for his deviance. Finally, thrown back solely on his own resources, the individual would scarcely have resources for speaking of his ideals, for conceiving of them clearly, for developing them in their complexity.

Another way of showing how the development of a new sense of reality requires a social effort is to reflect upon our present cultural situation. Not all world cultures instruct their young in the pursuit of their own individuality as do the cultures of Northern Europe. Not all have the relative freedom from roots, cultural traditions, and ancient institutions represented by the United States. In our culture, emphasis upon the independence of the individual from social connections is extreme. The national experience of emigration and uprooting, the symbolic openness of the frontier, the scope given to impulse by enormous wealth, and the centrifugal pressures of success and status have nourished the wild, limitless appetite that Philip Slater has named "the pursuit of loneliness." Even the recent countervailing "quest for community," as Daniel Callahan has observed, reinforces the isolation of the individual. Typically, community is understood from the point of view of the inclinations and conveniences of the self. Community exists for self-fulfillment. Self-fulfillment is not conceived as fidelity to communities.

Even our intellectual life offers few supports to community. Few of our monuments, institutions, holidays, or buildings carry our minds back beyond "the Age of Individualism." Protestant scholarship tends to make a bow toward the period before the Reformation, but establishes its working traditions well within the modern age. Jewish scholarship, too, tends to celebrate the modern age as the age of emancipation. Catholic scholars, unwilling to be identified solely with the ancient and medieval periods, tend to absorb the spirit of the present. Secular scholarship tends to glory in the achievements of modern humanism, science, and democracy. We do not have much ballast, in America, to hold us to a tragic vision of the modern era, a biting skepticism regarding various human "liberations." While the number, kind, and authority of the attacks upon "the Age of the Individual" grow, the overwhelming weight of our practices and symbols falls upon what is individual in us and devalues what is social.

Yet reality has its own methods of instruction. Our individualism is, plainly, of social derivation. Something in the Northern European temper has nourished it; capitalism and industry required it as an ideology; the openness and wealth of America allowed it to grow unchecked. Like many madnesses or aberrations, it blazed across the times unforgettably. But from many quarters now, its limits are being charted and its excesses checked. The finite resources of the earth—not least, the sources of energy—no longer allow us quite so slack a tether. Freud unmasked the struggle between self and society at the very center of the psyche; social scientists point out the many dependencies of the individual; environmentalists insist upon social controls over private enterprise; socialists denounce individualism as the false consciousness of an industrial state; the non-Nordic world demands its due.

Uncertainties felt by individuals indicate that the social worlds they inhabit no longer hold together. The great Protestant captains of our nation once felt that they stood at the helm of human history, riding currents of irresistible progress. They believed that principles like individual liberty unlocked the secret springs of human destiny and power, and they felt that holding fast to such principles justified them in God's sight.

But it is not only the captains of industry that have derived strength from socially shared symbols; even philosophers and men of theory inhabit social worlds. More than they are inclined to notice in themselves, the fund of symbols and images on which they draw is socially derived. Their sense of reality, the narrative form they give to history, the image they have of the relation of the individual to society—these materials they, too, draw from the linguistic and moral inheritance of their time and place.

Thus, it is important to draw attention to the extent to which a treatise like John Rawls' *A Theory of Justice* is an instance of ethnic expression, the drawing out in explicit statement of an Anglo-American sense of reality and an Anglo-American narrative form.[3] It would be possible to draw up long lists of the phrases and metaphors in *A Theory of Justice* that indicate its ethnic derivation and resonance. But, perhaps, a brief enumeration of some characteristics of its worldview will make the point with sufficient power. Explicitly, the tradition within which the book is to be understood is that of Bentham, Mill, and Kant. The basic metaphor of "fairness" is eminently British (it hardly occurs in Spanish, Italian, Greek, or Slavic thought). The argument is clearly *voluntarist;* it hinges upon the conception of an ideal toward which we have the power of making society progressively conform. It is *rationalist;* the fundamental exercise is a search for wholly rational principles in an "original situation" independent of the contingencies of history. At its heart is the image of the *autonomous* individual, the chief *agent* of society and the originating *source* of justice. Society itself is pictured rather as an *aggregate of individuals*, joined by an implicit *contract*. In all these respects, and others as well, the symbolic world of *A Theory of Justice* is Protestant and Anglo-American.

Little or nothing is said of the social bonds between persons that are *not* contractual, rationalist, or based upon autonomy: relations of loyalty, kinship, familial feeling, historical belonging. The basic terms of Rawls' analysis are the individual and society. But between these terms, perhaps more so for some ethnic groups than for others, come other communities, like family and peoplehood (religious, cultural, national). In the Anglo-American view, the individual seems to be perceived as more purely and simply an individual than in other traditions. "You're on your own. Do your thing. Be yourself." Philip Slater points out how historically odd it is—although typical in our culture—to educate children to leave home, to go out on their own, to live separately from their kin.

If we insert into the Rawlsian analysis the many communities in which each individual participates, the calculus of fairness becomes far more complicated than he suggests. Indeed, the basic division of his argument between the ideal world and the non-ideal world becomes impossible to sustain. Rawls follows one classical philosophical strategy: he constructs an ideal world in whose light he then criticizes the flaws of the actual world. But an alternative strategy, equally classical, is to analyze the concrete, historical world in all its dynamism and thickness, and then try to alter it. Here one works not from a pure ideal but from partial sources of illumination; one tries to strengthen a little those tendencies one finds creative and to block those one finds destructive. We are not ever in "the original situation" of choosing a fair social system, and even a stubborn effort of imagination to construct such a situation is somehow (one might say) a false and wasted effort. Human communities of all kinds are, typically, not fair, and the exercise through which Rawls would put us is far too rational, procedural, and blind to the textures of human passion and quirk and contingency to help to express our actual grievances and hurts. Human beings are not the atomic individuals he pictures, nor are their relations in their many communities so organizationally slotted and so administratively smooth as he imagines.

2. *The Many Worlds of the Individual*

If we now try to think concretely about ourselves and the many communities to which we each belong, we discover that we each have several symbolic worlds, several "languages," and that we struggle to keep them all related and yet distinct. In us, state and society and individual do not coincide. We exist as concrete individuals, and yet several rather impressively powerful symbolic worlds dwell serially within each of us. Let me introduce an imaginary colleague among us. I will call him Professor Isaac. He is a literary historian, a native of Brooklyn, a founding member of the Liberal party, a father of three children, a Jew. In recent years, Professor Isaac has begun to alter his own self-image. Not long ago, he would have described himself, by conviction, as a humanist, a professor of literature, a liberal, and—by accident of birth—a Jew. Now he sees certain connections between these other commitments and his Jewishness. Moreover, his political convictions were stirred by Ocean Hill-Brownsville and by recent threats to Israel. On the other hand, although he was brought up in an Orthodox household, Professor Isaac is no longer Jewish in religious or even cultural observance. He is liberal in his sympathies, but not very impressed by recent radical politics. He is not very attracted to the image of America represented by such men as Nixon, Connally, or Reagan; but signs of evangelistic fervor on the left also trouble him—as in Fred Harris, Harold Hughes, and George McGovern. In general, Professor Isaac sympathizes most with more sober liberals of the less evangelical Protestant or Catholic traditions.

All the communities to which Professor Isaac belongs—familial, ethnic, regional, professional—provide the materials through which he understands his experience. Yet none of these communities is wholly self-enclosed. Insofar as Professor Isaac has made himself a master of the Puritan sensibility and the New England mind, he moves comfortably in one symbolic world. He understands the symbolic world of lower-class Orthodox Jews in Brooklyn. He appreciates the symbolic world of more or less assimilated, middle-class professionals in suburban settings. His liberal beginnings provide him symbolic materials that incline him toward socialism. His attachment to individual liberties and democratic procedures and his fear of extremism incline him toward skepticism regarding the radical "movement." His background in humane letters makes him sympathetic to environmentalism, as well as to critiques of scientism, bureaucracy, and corporate amorality. On the other hand, merely romantic or naive criticism makes him uneasy.

It would not be true to say that Professor Isaac's sympathies are universal; they are finite. Not all symbolic worlds are accessible to him, nor is he comfortable within symbolic worlds he knows rather well. But, as we have seen, he does live and move in several symbolic worlds. He has enough symbolic resources to draw upon to make his opinions on any given matter, if not entirely unpredictable, nevertheless interesting.

We are each, I think, in an analogous position. The symbolic worlds each of us draws upon are not identical with those of others. In certain territories, each of us fades a little; in others, we are confident and know all the moves. The symbolic worlds we draw upon have social antecedents and complex traditions. Although our individuality is defined by our personal appropriation of these traditions and by the ways in which we combine them, the character of our perception, thinking, and language is very largely social. Pronounced individuality of mind is relatively rare. Although each of us is notably different from every other and demonstrably unique, the originality and power of our individuality are rather modest.

3. *The Pluralistic Personality*

The actual existence of pluralistic personalities is rather more well-established in our working practice than in our theories. We have been brought up, most of us, under traditions which encourage us (beyond specialization) to try to be "Renaissance men," to try to become as "universal" and "open" as we can, to try to be cosmopolitan, well-informed, and broad of vision. Over against the more parochial views of relatively self-enclosed traditions, such symbols were no doubt both useful and liberating. However, the expansion of human knowledge and our actual encounters with worldwide diversity instruct us in our own finitude. We cannot be universal. We cannot be totally "open" (at least, not in the sense of actually *holding* all positions; we may try to sympathize with views not our own). Consequently, we are in fact learning to mark out rather clearly in self-consciousness the limits of our own symbolic worlds. We see ourselves as one among many. In practice, we are pluralistic personalities without, perhaps, fully developed moral and intellectual symbols to express what we are doing.

Two features of the pluralistic personality deserve elaboration: first, such a person recognizes the limits of his own symbolic worlds; secondly, he tries to "pass over" to the symbolic worlds of those with whom he wishes to cooperate. To "pass over" is to enter empathetically into the sense of reality, story, symbols, and words of another. "Passing over" does not require abandonment of one's own position; it requires the tentative, experimental assumption of the other person's standpoint, for purposes of understanding and communication. When two persons successfully "pass over," each into the other's point of view, they can sometimes invent a new shared "third" world or at least elements of such a world. Thus, long interdisciplinary or intercultural inquiries sometimes bear fruit in new forms of shared discourse.

4. *Symbolic Realism*

If what I have said so far makes sense, then one alternative which some persons try to press upon us is not real. We cannot go back to *Gemeinschaft,* they say; so we must learn to accept our fate as atomic individuals. Yet even when we no longer live in tightly knit ghettos, or ethnic or religious communities, we do not necessarily live in loneliness and atomic solitude. We live, rather, in a limited set of symbolic worlds. It is true that in our public education and even in the solitude of personal reflection, the extreme individualism of our culture does not encourage us to notice the extent to which we live and move and have our being in social symbolic worlds. We tend to exaggerate our independence, our individuality, our isolation. We fail to notice that those instinctive attractions, those tacit likes and dislikes, those deeply satisfying methods and practices—which we often assume to be personal or idiosyncratic—ordinarily have a social history in one or other of the traditions in which we share. Those things that are most important in cultural transmission are usually never spoken of, are seldom conscious, and are remarkably enduring over time.

Under conditions of pluralism, however, we tend to draw upon more than one symbolic tradition. Thus, the traditional consonance between self and society and culture does not always obtain. The self does not live merely within one culture. The self moves into and out of a number of symbolic worlds; or, conversely, various worlds move into and out of the individual. To approach a person as though he were within a certain symbolic world—because at one time or another he has been—is perhaps to misapprehend his present symbolic world. To anticipate that because one had hear him take position X and possibly Y he will certainly assume position Z is perhaps to overlook the fact that another symbolic world, of which we are unaware, enters into his consciousness and inclines him, on some matters, in surprising ways. Sometimes there are keys to understanding the position of others that we search for in vain because of our ignorance of one of the symbolic worlds on which he draws.

The name "symbolic realism" has been attached to this way of looking at human behavior. The word "realism" stresses the need to take seriously each person's (or culture's) "reality." It insists that the solid perception that forms our own sense of reality is some other person's (or culture's) "mere myth." It insists that the address to reality assumed by each of us is, for us, real, even if for others it may be hypothetical. And it suggests that this divergence in senses of reality is itself real: we encounter it almost daily; attempts to believe that all others share our own sense of reality are not corroborated by experience. The force of the word "symbolic" emphasizes that our *interpretations* of experience are ingredients in the structure of experience: that *intentional* forms, socially derived, shape our living and perceiving. Together, the two words "symbolic realism" call attention to the impact upon human life, especially in cultural and political matters, of those expectations and imaginal forms that give human life this concrete shape rather than some other. Such forms give scope to human freedom, and ground our cultural diversity.

One further distinction is necessary. When I speak of the "pluralistic personality," I do not mean the "liberal personality," individualistic, tolerant, open-minded. There are two tendencies in the liberal personality that seem to me deficient; one is an exaggerated sense of individuality and originality; the other, an exaggerated sense of attaining, or approaching, a state of participation in universal reason. The liberal personality tends to be atomic, rootless, mobile, and to imagine itself as "enlightened" in some superior and especially valid way. Ironically, its exaggerated individualism leads it inevitably into an exaggerated sense of universal community. Between these two extremes lie the finite human communities in which individuals live and have their being. These the liberal personality disvalues, and the pluralistic personality values.

The pluralistic personality counters individualism with self-conscious and disciplined participation in specific cultural traditions, institutions, loyalties, and symbol systems. A human being cannot properly pretend to be infinite or universal; he or she necessarily participates in concrete cultural traditions, institutions, loyalties, and symbol systems. In such "narrowness," the liberal personality sometimes finds scandal; but the pluralistic personality finds an accurate assessment of the human ideal. The pluralistic personality recognizes the need to "pass over" into the symbolic worlds of others and finds in such "passing over" a modest form of transcendence and transcultural communion. Where the liberal personality seeks a virtually direct ascent from individual will to universality, commonality, and rationality, the pluralistic personality finds a certain peace in particularity, and seeks in particularity itself a method of "analogous depth"—a method of going deeply into one's own tradition in order find a way to "pass over," by a system of analogies, into the comparable voyages taken by others into their own traditions.

As a theoretical model, the pluralistic personality seems to lead to a more accurate description of the actualities of human community and personality, and also to a more attractive vision of human possibility, than does the liberal personality. For the universality sought by the latter seems unobtainable in practice, and as an ideal tends to mask an ideology of arrogance and homogenization. Diversity of cultures is exactly what is most distinctive about the human species. It flows from human freedom; it expresses human sociality.

The pluralistic personality is cosmopolitan rather than universalist. It rejoices in being different and in noticing differences in others. The temptation of the liberal personality is to consider those who are not liberal, inferior. The temptation of the pluralistic personality is, on the one side, to err by a slippery relativism, refusing to set standards and make judgments, and, on the other side, to be more limited in its "passing over" than it imagines.

Notes

1. In order to specify the intellectual horizon from within which the present effort has been generated, it might be well for me

to mention the books and authors to whom I am, in this respect, most indebted: several essays of Robert Bellah; Hugh D. Duncan, *Symbols in Society* (New York: Oxford University Press, 1969); Murray Edelman, *The Symbolic Uses of Politics* (Urbana, Ill.: University of Illinois Press, 1967); the treatments of symbolism and method in Harold D. Lasswell, *Politics* (New York: World, 1958); Eugene Rosenstock-Huessy, *I am an Impure Thinker* (New York: Argo, 1970); John S. Dunne, for the concept of "passing over."

2.   John T. McAlister and Frances Fitzgerald, both indebted to Paul Mus, have tried to specify these divergent senses of reality. See John T. McAlister and Paul Mus, *Vietnamese and Their Revolution* (New York: Harper and Row, 1970); and Frances Fitzgerald, *Fire in the Lake* (Boston: Little, Brown, 1972).

3.   John Rawls, *A Theory of Justice* (Cambridge, Mass.: Harvard University Press, 1971).

Notes

PREFACE

1. This phrase is the subtitle of my *Belief and Unbelief* (New York: The Macmillan Company, 1965).

CHAPTER ONE

1. David G. McCullough's *The Johnstown Flood* (New York: Simon & Schuster, 1968), stresses the bitterness on the part of workingmen against the millionaires of the South Fork Fishing and Hunting Club, whose dam it was that broke. A Harrisburg newspaperman wrote: "50,000 lives in Pennsylvania were jeopardized for eight years that a club of rich pleasure-seekers might fish and sail and revel in luxurious ease during the heated term," p. 249.
2. R. M. Scammon and Ben J. Wattenberg, *The Real Majority* (New York: Coward-McCann, Inc., 1970), p. 43.
3. *Ibid.*, pp. 43–44.
4. Andrew M. Greeley and Peter H. Rossi have shown that Catholics who attend parochial schools are less prejudiced racially and religiously than those who attend public schools. See their study, *The Education of Catholic Americans* (Chicago: National Opinion Research Center, University of Chicago, 1967).
5. Under headline "Hesburgh Bids Catholic Schools Learn From Youth," *New York Times*, 13 April 1971, p. 20.
6. Mike Royko, *Boss* (New York: E. P. Dutton & Co., 1971), p. 25.
7. *Ibid.*, p. 152.

8. *Ibid.*, pp. 140–141.
9. Louis Harris, excerpted in *Newsday*, April 1971.
10. Samuel Lubell, *The Future of American Politics*, 3d ed. (New York: Harper & Row, 1965), pp. 75–76.
11. Kevin Phillips, *The Emerging Republican Majority* (New Rochelle, N.Y.: Arlington House, 1969), p. 168.
12. *Ibid.*, p. 11.
13. *Ibid.*, p. 88.
14. Scammon and Wattenberg, *op. cit.*, p. 62.
15. For these and the preceding quotes, see William Pfaff, "The New New Politics," *Center Magazine*, May/June 1971, p. 57.
16. Jerome M. Rosow, Assistant Secretary of Labor for Policy, "The White House Report on the Problems of the Blue Collar Worker," in Geno R. Baroni, ed., *All Men Are Brothers* (Washington, D.C.: Task Force on Urban Problems, November 1970), p. 92.
17 Raymond E. Wolfinger, "The Development and Persistence of Ethnic Voting," in Lawrence H. Fuchs, ed., *American Ethnic Politics* (New York: Harper & Row, Harper Torchbooks, 1968), p. 169.
18. From an unpublished paper by Richard J. Krickus, "White Working-Class Youth," p. 3.
19. Scammon and Wattenberg, *op. cit.*, pp. 46–47.
20. Krickus, *op. cit.*
21. *Ibid.*
22. Rosow, *op. cit.*, p. 97.
23. *Ibid.*
24. *Ibid.*, p. 101.
25. Nicholas Pileggi, "Risorgimento of Italian Power," *New York Magazine*, 7 June 1971, p. 33.
26. "The Myth of Middle America," AFL-CIO News, quoted in *All Men Are Brothers*, p. 39.
27. Irving M. Levine in *Newsday*, 5 June 1971, p. 5W.
28. George Romney, "Priced out of the Market," in *All Men Are Brothers*, p. 37.
29. Rosow, *op. cit.*, p. 97.
30. For claims in this paragraph, see the chart found in Andrew M. Greeley, *Why Can't They Be Like Us?* (New York: E. P. Dutton & Co., 1971), p. 77; also Nathan Glazer and Daniel Patrick Moynihan, *Beyond the Melting Pot* (Boston: M.I.T. Press, 1963).
31. Lee Rainwater, Richard P. Coleman, and Gerald Handel, *Workingman's Wife* (New York: Oceana Publications, 1959), p. 118.
32. *Ibid.*, pp. 116–117.
33. *Ibid.*, p. 33.

34. Rosow, *op. cit.*, p. 92.
35: Rainwater et al., *op. cit.*, pp. 149–151.
36. *Ibid.*, pp. 45–46.
37. *Ibid.*, pp. 46–49.
38. *Ibid.*, p. 53.
39. *Ibid.*, pp. 55, 59.
40. *Ibid.*, pp. 60–66.
41. Quoted by Wagner in Section II, "The Human Scale," unpublished outline, *Workshop on Ethnic and Working-Class Priorities* (Washington, D.C.: Center on Urban Ethnic Affairs), 1971. Since the number of employed in 1970 was about 75,000,000, the figure of 25,000,000 persons injured struck me as possibly a typographical error. A phone call to the National Safety Council confirmed the number of workers injured in 1970 was staggering enough: 2,200,000. This many casualties in a war during a one-year period would be considered intolerable.
42. Louis Adamic, *Dynamite* (New York: Chelsea House Publishers, 1958); also Philip Taft and Philip Ross, "American Labor Violence: Its Causes, Character, and Outcome" in Hugh Davis Graham and Ted Robert Gurr, *Violence in America*, A Staff Report to the National Commission on the Causes and Prevention of Violence (Washington, D.C.: U.S. Government Printing Office, 1 June 1969); and J. B. S. Hardman, ed., *American Labor Dynamics* (New York: Harcourt, Brace & Co., 1928; Arno Press and the New York Times Reprint, 1969), pp. 349–356.
43. Senator Henry Jackson, *Newsday*, 10 August 1971.
44. My own assessments are in *A Theology for Radical Politics* (New York: Herder & Herder, 1969) and *Politics: Realism and Imagination* (New York: Herder & Herder, 1971).
45. See Eugen Rosenstock-Huessy, *I Am an Impure Thinker* (Norwich, Vt.: Argo Books, 1970).
46. See Royko's column "The Sensuous Ethnic, by N" in the *Chicago Daily News*, 2 September 1971: "In fact, my background is something like Novak's. His grandparents emigrated here. So did mine. He grew up in a working class, ethnic environment. So did I. He discovered that American history books are all about WASPs, and so did I. But I'm not quite as depressed as Mr. Novak obviously is."
47. For this and the following quote from Pileggi, see Arthur B. Shostak, *Blue-Collar Life* (New York: Random House, 1969), pp. 5–6.

48. Charles Reich, *The Greening of America* (New York: Random House, 1970), p. 297.
49. Royko, *op. cit.*
50 I have expressed this idea more fully in "The Inevitable Bias of Television," an essay written in connection with the Du Pont Awards, Columbia University, N.Y., 1971, and published in Marvin Barrett, ed., *Survey of Broadcast Journalism, 1970–71* (New York: Grosset & Dunlap, 1971).
51. See my "Un-masking Self-Interests, Not of Others, But of Self" in *Christianity and Crisis*, October 1971.
52. Reich, *op. cit.*, p. 294.
53. Mark Zborowski, *People in Pain* (San Francisco: Jossey-Bass, 1969).
54. Mark Zborowski, *Life Is with People* (New York: International Universities Press, 1952).
55. Zborowski, *People in Pain*, p. 55.
56. *Ibid.*, pp. 50; 52–53.
57. *Ibid.*, p. 68.
58. *Ibid.*, p. 102.
59. *Ibid.*, p. 99.
60. *Ibid.*, pp. 225, 197.
61. *Ibid.*, pp. 156–157.
62. *Ibid.*, p. 174.
63. *Ibid.*, pp. 175, 183, 176.
64. *Ibid.*, p. 183.
65. On the other hand, the Germans were the immigrant group most interested in maintaining their independence in America, even to the point of trying to establish their own German State. See John A. Hawgood, *The Tragedy of German-America* (New York: G. P. Putnam's Sons, 1940; Arno Press Reprint, 1970), pp. 93–224.

CHAPTER TWO

1. See Norman Mailer, "The Time of Her Time" in *The Short Fiction of Norman Mailer* (New York: Dell Publishing Co., 1967). In a letter, Garry Wills urged me to re-read this story for this book.
2. See Andrew R. Sisson's chapter "Our Kooky English Language" in his *Applehood and Mother Pie* (Peterborough, N.H.: Orchard Press, 1971), pp. 1–16, for a discussion of the ways in which Continental languages differ from English according to their respective cultural divergencies.
3. Royko wrote in his *Chicago Daily News* column: "I imagine that the ethnic in Buffalo is thinking the same thing that the white Southerner in Birmingham is thinking,

or the Okie oil workers in Tulsa: Another day, another dollar. In fact, that's probably what the guy in Warsaw is thinking on his way to work." There is at least one point Royko overlooks: the bottled-up anger of workers in America.

4. See Victor R. Greene's "Sons of Hunkies: Men with a Past?" *Slovakia*, vol. XVI, No. 39, 1966, pp. 85–86.

5. Lois Wille, "Fear Rises in the Suburbs," a reprint from the *Chicago Daily News*, in *The Anxious Majority* (New York: Institute on Human Relations, 1970), p. 8.

6. One of my first published writings was on the gap between intellectuals and people in *The Nation*, October 1960; I included it in my *A New Generation, American and Catholic* (New York: Herder & Herder, 1964). See also my *Politics: Realism and Imagination.*

7. Daniel Berrigan and Robert Coles, *The Geography of Faith* (Boston: Beacon Press, 1971), p. 9.

8. *Ibid.*, pp. 12–13.

9. Herman R. Lantz (with the assistance of J. S. McCrary), *People of Coal Town* (New York: Columbia University Press, 1958), p. 47.

10. *Ibid.*, p. 179.

11. I especially cherish John McDermott's "The Laying on of Culture" in *The Nation*, 10 March 1969.

12. Louise Kapp Howe, ed., *The White Majority* (New York: Random House, 1970), p. 296.

CHAPTER THREE

1. These long passages are from Louis Adamic, *Laughing in the Jungle* (New York: Harper & Brothers, 1932; Arno Press and the New York Times Reprint, 1969), pp. 11–13.

2. *Ibid.*, p. 26.

3. *Ibid.*, pp. 27–38, for the following incident.

4. *Ibid.*, p. 18, for both passages.

5. *Ibid.*, p. 19.

6. *Ibid.*, p. 294.

7. *Ibid.*, p. 20: "Once upon a time immigrants were called 'dung' in America; that was a good name for them. They were the fertilizer feeding the roots of America's present and future greatness. They are still 'dung.' The roots of America's greatness still feed on them. . . . Life in America is a scramble. More people are swept under than rise to riches."

8. *Ibid.*, p. 298.

9. Recounted by Michael Lerner in Howe, ed., *The White Majority*, p. 206.

10. "Introduction," *ibid.*, p. 6.
11. Winthrop D. Jordan in his *White Over Black* (Chapel Hill: University of North Carolina Press, 1968), p. 46, quotes Cotton Mather addressing the Massachusetts governor and General Court in 1700: "It is no Little Blessing of God, that we are a part of the *English nation*." On the same page Jordan comments: "For Englishmen planting in America, then, it was of the utmost importance to know that they were Englishmen, which was to say that they were educated (to a degree suitable to their station), Christian (of an appropriate Protestant variety), civilized, and (again to an appropriate degree) free men."
12. John Higham, *Strangers in the Land* (New York: Atheneum, 1968), p. 115.
13. For discussions involving emigrants leaving America, see Oscar Handlin, *Race and Nationality in American Life* (Boston: Little, Brown & Company, 1957), pp. 93–138, 255–277.
14. See Nathan Glazer's essay "Ethnic Groups in America: From National Culture to Ideology," in M. Berger, T. Abel, and C. H. Page, eds., *Freedom and Control in Modern Society* (New York: D. Van Nostrand Co., 1954), p. 166.
15. Jordan, *op. cit.*, p. 7.
16. See especially Harold R. Isaacs, "Group Identity and Political Change: The Role of Color and Physical Characteristics," in John Hope Franklin, ed., *Color and Race* (Boston: Beacon Press, 1968), pp. 353–375.
17. Roger Bastide, "Color, Racism, and Christianity," *ibid.*, p. 34: "Sartre has brought out quite well the part the eye plays in racial attitudes, but he does not go far enough. The eye has its substitutes . . . [smell, texture of skin, voice]. This shows that any kind of perception can serve as stimulus to racial attitude."
18. Jerzy Kosinski, *The Painted Bird* (New York: Simon & Schuster, Pocket Book Division, 1966), pp. 159–160.
19. Handlin, *op. cit.*, p. 96.
20. Thus Higham, *op. cit.*, p. 23, quotes Emma Lazarus' famous inscription:

> Give me your tired, your poor,
> Your huddled masses yearning to breathe free,
> The wretched refuse of your teeming shore,
> Send these, the homeless, tempest-tost to me,
> I lift my lamp beside the golden door!

21. David Hume, quoted in Jordan, *op. cit.*, p. 253.
22. *Ibid.*, p. 459.

23. *Ibid.*, pp. 459–460.
24. *Ibid.*, pp. 474–475.
25. *Ibid.*, p. 459.
26. Handlin, *op. cit.*, p. 74.
27. *Ibid.*, p. 96.
28. *Ibid.*, p. 176.
29. *Ibid.*, pp. 159–160.
30. *Ibid.*, p. 97.
31. For these and the previous quotes see Madison Grant, *The Passing of the Great Race* (New York: Charles Scribner's Sons, 1918; Arno Press and the New York Times Reprint, 1970), pp. 87–92.
32. Quoted in Oscar Handlin, *Immigration as a Factor in American History* (Englewood Cliffs, N.J.: Prentice-Hall, Inc., 1959), pp. 183–184.
33. Handlin, *Race and Nationality in American Life*, pp. 101–102.
34. Margaret Mead and James Baldwin, *A Rap on Race* (New York: J. B. Lippincott Co., 1971), pp. 109, 150.
35. Handlin, *Nationality*, p. 112.
36. *Ibid.*, p. 114.
37. *Ibid.*, pp. 104–131, for all these points.
38. For an extended "Chronology of Immigration," see John F. Kennedy, *A Nation of Immigrants* (New York: Harper & Row, 1968), pp. 88–94.
39. On this and the following points see Higham, *op. cit.*, pp. 138–139: "During the 1890's, as the social crisis deepened, racial nativism became more defined and wide-spread. If one may judge, however, from Congressional debates, newspapers and the more popular periodicals, Anglo-Saxonism still played a relatively small part in public opinion. The rising flood of popular xenophobia drew much more upon conventional anti-foreign ideas."
40. *Ibid.*, pp. 250–255.
41. Ralph Perrotta, quoted by Kevin Lahart in *Newsday*, 5 June 1971, p. 4W.
42. See Andrew Greeley, *Why Can't They Be Like Us?*, pp. 135–147; also Greeley and William C. McCready, "The Men That God Made Mad," a chapter in a book on the American Irish to be published by Quadrangle Books.
43. Phillips, *The Emerging Republican Majority*, pp. 72, 74, and *passim*.
44. Higham, *op. cit.*, p. 125.
45. Michael Paul Rogin, *The Intellectuals and McCarthy: The Radical Specter* (Cambridge: Massachusetts Institute of Technology, 1967), p. 49.
46. Handlin, *Nationality*, p. 141: "Often it was a man alone,

an individual, who went, who in going left home, that is, cut himself apart from the associations and attachments that until then had given meaning to his life."

47. *Ibid.*, p. 143.
48. Rogin, *op. cit.*, p. 40: "Unchecked political and economic power had no place in a Lockean world. . . ."
49. Zborowski, *People in Pain*, pp. 49–96.
50. See Robert Warshaw's "The Westerner" in Daniel Talbot, ed., *Film: An Anthology* (Berkeley: University of California Press, 1967), pp. 148–162.
51. Norman Mailer, "A Course in Film-Making," in Theodore Solotaroff, ed., *New American Review, No. 12* (New York: Simon & Schuster, 1971), pp. 240–241.
52. Garry Wills, *Nixon Agonistes* (Boston: Houghton Mifflin Co., 1970), pp. 409ff.
53. Cf. my "Politics as Witness" in *Politics: Realism and Imagination*, pp. 70–74.
54. Radley Metzger, ed., *Collected Speeches of Spiro Agnew* (New York: Audubon Books, 1971), p. 29.
55. Pileggi, "Risorgimento of Italian Power," p. 33.
56. Contrast the content to the tone in Seymour Martin Lipset, *Political Man* (New York: Doubleday & Co., Anchor Books, 1963), pp. 108–126.
57. See Wilson's article "Public-Regardingness as a Value Premise in Voting Behavior," *American Political Science Review*, December 1964.
58. Daniel Bell, *The End of Ideology* (New York: Free Press, 1962), p. 283.
59. See William I. Thomas and Florian Znaniecki, *The Polish Peasant in Europe and America*, vol. 1 (New York: Dover Publications, 1958), pp. 170–171.
60. From the "Acton-Creighton Correspondence" in Lord Acton, *Essays on Freedom and Power*, selected by Gertrude Himmelfarb (New York: Meridian Books, 1955), p. 335.
61. Rogin, *op. cit.*, pp. 299–300.
62. In this respect, the tentative findings of Paul Ehrlich and Jonathan L. Freedman on the effects of overcrowding seem to run against instinctive Anglo-Saxon feelings. *New York Times*, 11 September 1971, p. 27.
63. Handlin, *Nationality*, p. 143.
64. Theodore White, *The Making of the President 1968* (New York: Atheneum, 1968), p. 433: "Agnew had by now made a fool of himself—not so much out of malice or stupidity as, simply, by a coarseness of fiber, an insensitivity which he, as a second-generation American, might above all have been expected to eschew. Coarseness in

'low-level office is sometimes amusing, but coarseness at the head of the American government is almost, in itself, disqualification for leadership."

65. Svend Ranulf, *Moral Indignation and Middle-Class Psychology* (New York: Schocken Books, 1964), p. 198.
66. As suggested by Handlin, *Nationality*, pp. 148–156.
67. On these points, *ibid.*, p. 153.
68. *Ibid.*, p. 132.
69. See Jordan, *op. cit.*, pp. 581–582, and *passim*.
70. Handlin, *Nationality*, p. 140.
71. Stephen Thernstrom, *Poverty and Progress* (Cambridge: Harvard University Press, 1964), pp. 52–53.
72. *Ibid.*, p. 35.
73. *Ibid.*, p. 33.
74. *Ibid.*, p. 56.
75. To see the Anglo-Saxon contribution to American life as one among many does not make its strengths less real. This holds true for its present contribution to Europe as well. 1 read with sympathy and only a modicum of doubt a dispatch from Rome in the *New York Times*, 25 July 1971:

"In other lands it is pointed out that Britain's industrial, technical, commercial and banking skills plus Britain's sizable population will furnish a weighty increment to the producing and consuming potential of the market. But in Italy the primary emphasis is on Britain's moral contribution.

"This Government calculates British membership will firmly thrust Europe forward on a new tide of history . . . With unabashed admiration for Britain's steadfastness, civic sense and long democratic tradition, the highest officialdom considers London will bring into Europe 'the vitamins of Liberty.'

"Rome is wise enough to realize that Mediterranean nations since ancient times have rarely shown an aptitude for sensible self-government and feels this injection from pragmatic Britain is needed by Italy because of debilitating hangover problems from a long tradition of reactionary clericalism and incomplete unification. It thinks the Germans will likewise benefit because of their ugly past heritage and the uneasy lack of confidence produced by continuing partition; and the French because of their rather high-handed Napoleonic and Gaullist traditions.

"There is admiration and respect for the British at top levels here. While the Communists often insult the United States they rarely insult Britain, still secretly respecting its courage during World War II, especially the period of the

Hitler-Stalin pact. Some Marxists say they can never forget that Marx and Lenin were once refugees in London."

76. See Edward George Hartmann, *The Movement to Americanize the Immigrants* (New York: Columbia University Press, 1948).

CHAPTER FOUR

1. Wills, *Nixon Agonistes,* p. 285. Wills' chapter on Agnew is the best available. I rely on it often in what follows.
2. Terry Morris, *Better Than You: Social Discrimination Against Minorities in America* (New York: Institute of Human Relations Press, 1971), p. 6.
3. Lewis Chester, Godfrey Hodgson, and Bruce Page, *An American Melodrama* (New York: Dell Publishing Co., 1969), p. 549.
4. Metzger, ed., *Collected Speeches of Spiro Agnew,* pp. 73, 222, for the preceding two quotes.
5. Wills, *op. cit.,* pp. 292–293.
6. Metzger, *op. cit.,* p. 73.

CHAPTER FIVE

1. See Richard Hofstadter, *Anti-intellectualism in American Life* (New York: Random House, Vintage Books, 1966), pp. 24–29.
2. See Milton M. Gordon, *Assimilation in American Life* (New York: Oxford University Press, 1964), pp. 224–232. Andrew Greeley does not make enough distinctions in separating various families among intellectuals when he speaks of them as a separate ethnic group. See his "Intellectuals as an Ethnic Group," in *Why Can't They Be Like Us?* pp. 120–134.
3. Higham, *Strangers in the Land,* p. 119: "Most progressives, while convinced of the solvent power of democracy, applied it largely to political and economic inequalities. That it might reform relationships among men of varying creeds or colors or cultures did not impress them. On the other hand, some progressives glimpsed an ampler democratic vision. . . . In the cities a few early 20th-century liberals came into close enough contact with the immigrants to see them whole, to learn that poverty and isolation afflicted them in special ways, and to realize that democracy involved a social dimension which was unfulfilled as long as America simply took its foreign peoples for granted. The beginnings lay in the social settlements." See also Hartmann, *The Movement to Americanize the Immigrants.*

4. Thus Kevin Lahart quotes the description of a graduation ceremony of the Ford English School in 1914: "Not long ago this school graduated over 500 men. Commencement exercises were held in the largest hall of the city. On the stage was represented an immigrant ship. In front of it was a huge melting pot. Down the gangplank came the members of the class dressed in their national garbs and carrying luggage such as they carried when they landed in this country. Down they poured into the Ford melting pot and disappeared. Then the teachers began to stir the contents of the pot with long ladles. Presently the pot began to boil over and out came the men dressed in their best American clothes and waving American flags." *Newsday*, 5 June 1971, p. 4W.

5. Many immigrants who came to America were political exiles. In America, they learned to protect their economic and political self-interests. See Adamic, *Dynamite*, and Victor R. Greene, *The Slavic Community on Strike* (Notre Dame, Ind.: University of Notre Dame Press, 1968).

6. In Handlin, *Immigration as a Factor in American History*, pp. 155–156.

7. *Ibid.*, pp. 161–162.

8. Higham, *op. cit.*, p. 123.

9. Robert Coles and Jan Erikson, *The Middle Americans* (Boston: Little, Brown & Co., 1971), pp. 50–51.

10. Marshall Berman, *The Politics of Authenticity* (New York: Atheneum, 1970), p. ix.

11. See "An Interview with Sartre," *New York Review of Books*, 26 March 1970, pp. 22–31; also, Jean-Paul Sartre, *Critique de la raison dialectique* (Paris: Editions Gallimard, 1960).

12. Daniel Bell, ed., *The Radical Right* (New York: Doubleday & Co., Anchor Books, 1964), p. 16.

13. *Ibid.*, pp. 2, 25, for the preceding quotes.

14. *Ibid.*, p. 75.

15. *Ibid.*, pp. 92, 101, for the preceding quotes.

16. *Ibid.*, p. 117.

17. *Ibid.*, p. 119.

18. *Ibid.*, pp. 47, 120.

19. *Ibid.*, for all these phrases.

20. *Ibid.*, p. 126.

21. *Ibid.*, p. 131.

22. Philip Slater, *The Pursuit of Loneliness* (Boston: Beacon Press, 1970), p. 7.

23. Handlin, *Race and Nationality in American Life*, p. 164.

24. Bell, *op. cit.*, pp. 134–135.

25. *Ibid.,* p. 62.
26. Cited by Murray Ross in *The American Way,* October 1971, p. 33.
27. *Ibid.,* for both quotes.

CHAPTER SIX

1. Cf. Hans Magnus Enzensberger's essay, "The Aporias of the Avant-Garde," in Philip Rahv, ed., *Modern Occasions* (New York: Noonday Press, 1966), p. 79. In this section I rely heavily, but not wholly, on Enzensberger's essay; all the quotes below not otherwise marked are taken from it. Also see Jacques Maritain, *Creative Intuition in Art and Poetry* (New York: Meridian Books, Inc., 1955).
2. These two quotes from Marinetti and Breton are also from Enzensberger, *op. cit.,* pp. 96, 98.
3. Richard Chase, "The Fate of the Avant-Garde," *Partisan Review,* Summer 1957, pp. 363–375.
4. See Theodore Solotaroff in the title essay of his *The Red-Hot Vacuum* (New York: Atheneum, 1970), pp. 151–152.
5. Philip Rahv, *Literature and the Sixth Sense* (Boston: Houghton Mifflin Co., 1970), p. 182.
6. *Ibid.*
7. Dwight Macdonald, "Masscult and Midcult," in *Against the American Grain* (New York: Random House, Vintage Books, 1962), pp. 3–75.
8. *Ibid.,* pp. 35–36, for the preceding quotes from Macdonald.
9. Described by Ada Louise Huxtable in the *New York Times,* 11 July 1971, Sec. 8, p. 1.

CHAPTER SEVEN

1. See John Kobler, *Capone* (New York: G. P. Putnam's Sons, 1971), pp. 264–265.
2. See Adamic, *Dynamite,* pp. 9–21; also J. Walter Coleman, *The Molly Maguire Riots* (Richmond, Va.: Garrett & Massie, 1936; New York: Arno Press and the New York Times Reprint, 1969); and Wayne G. Broehl, Jr., *The Molly Maguires* (Cambridge: Harvard University Press, 1965).
3. Norman Mailer, *Advertisements for Myself* (New York: Signet, 1959), p. 381, as is the next quote.
4. *Ibid.,* p. 382. The next quote, as well.
5. Norman Mailer, *The Naked and the Dead* (New York: Signet, 1948), p. 548.

6. Mailer, "The White Negro," in *Advertisements for Myself,* p. 336.
7. Mailer, *The Naked and the Dead,* p. 360.
8. *The Merchant of Venice.*
9. Alfred Kazin, *Starting Out in the Thirties* (Boston: Little, Brown & Co., 1965), pp. 45–47.
10. Solotaroff, *Red-Hot Vacuum,* in "Philip Roth: A Personal View," p. 311. Further quotes in this section are from the same essay.
11. *Ibid.,* p. 325, and for the next quote as well.
12. Philip Roth, *Portnoy's Complaint* (New York: Bantam Books, 1969), pp. 20–21.
13. Solotaroff, *Red-Hot Vacuum.*
14. This and subsequent quotes in this section are from Mailer's "The White Negro," and "Reflections on Hip," in *Advertisements for Myself,* pp. 302–322, 323–334.
15. Solotaroff, ed., *New American Review Number 12,* p. 241. This quote fascinates me. I cite it twice.
16. See Lionel Trilling, "Authenticity and the Modern Unconscious," *Commentary,* September 1971, pp. 39–50.
17. Mailer, *Advertisements.*
18. See Noam Chomsky's "Introduction" to Daniel Guerin, *Anarchism* (New York: Monthly Review Press, 1970), p. xi. The following quote is from the same page.
19. Chomsky cites Buber's *Paths to Utopia* and Fourier at *ibid.,* p. xiii.
20. *Ibid.*
21. *Ibid.,* p. vii.
22. *Ibid.,* p. x.
23. Kosinski, *The Painted Bird,* pp. 147–148.
24. Quoted by Pileggi in "The Risorgimento of Italian Power," p. 36.

CHAPTER EIGHT

1. In the *New York Times,* 12 July 1971.
2. See *Civilization and Its Discontents, the Complete Psychological Works of Sigmund Freud.* Standard Edition, vol. XXI (London: Hogarth Press), p. 141.
3. Marcus Raskin, *Being and Doing* (New York: Random House, 1971), pp. 37–38. The next quote is from p. 38.
4. *Ibid.,* pp. xv–xvi.
5. *Ibid.,* p. xvi.
6. Norman Mailer, *Cannibals and Christians* (New York: Dial Press, 1966), p. 4.
7. Lubell, *The Future of American Politics,* p. 81.
8. Adamic, *Laughing in the Jungle,* p. 118.

9. See Adamic's description of his mother's faith, p. 73.
10. Quoted in Roger B. Nelson's "Hitler's Propaganda Machine" in *Current History*, June 1933, p. 289.
11. See Ortega y Gasset in *The Revolt of the Masses* (New York: W. W. Norton & Co., 1957).
12. See Gabriel Marcel, *Man Against Mass Society* (Chicago: Henry Regnery Co., 1962).
13. See H. L. Mencken, "On Being an American," in *Prejudices*, A selection made by James T. Farrell (New York: Random House, Vintage Books, 1955), p. 99.
14. On these points, see Robert Dahl, *After the Revolution?* (New York: Yale University Press, 1970).
15. Robert E. Park and Herbert A. Miller, *Old World Traits Transported* (New York: Harper and Brothers, 1921; Arno Press and the New York Times Reprint. 1969), p. 110.
16. For example, see Thomas and Znaniecki, *The Polish Peasant in Europe and America*, vol. 2, p. 1518; also Park and Miller, *ibid.*, p. 126.
17. Quoted by Garry Wills in *Nixon Agonistes*, pp. 521–522.
18. *Ibid.*, p. 502.
19. See Peter L. Berger's wry remarks: "Much of politics, of course, is too ordinary to invoke commitment of any depth. Most of the rest is crime, illusion, or the self-indulgences of intellectuals. . . . Intense political commitment is usually bad. It is bad in its motives. It is bad in its consequences. . . . In most of human history, politics has been left to the few whose vocation it was supposed to be, leaving the many to go about their own (possibly much more interesting) business." *Movement & Revolution* (Garden City, N.Y.: Doubleday & Co., Anchor Books, 1970), pp. 13, 16.
20. Dahl, *op. cit.*, p. 8.
21. Rogin, *The Intellectuals and McCarthy*, p. 275.
22. *Ibid.*, pp. 6–7.
23. *Ibid.*, footnote on p. 15.
24. Coles and Erikson, *The Middle Americans*, p. 44.
25. Shostak, *Blue-Collar Life*, p. 217.
26. John C. Leggett, *Class, Race and Labor* (New York: Oxford University Press, 1968), pp. 126, 129.
27. Shostak, *op. cit.*, pp. 218–219.
28. Robert Dahl, *Polyarchy* (New Haven: Yale University Press, 1971).
29. Michael Harrington, *New York Times Book Review*, 8 August 1971, p. 5.
30. See Lipset, *Political Man*, pp. 87–126.
31. *Ibid.*, p. 87, for these and the following quotes.

32. Thomas Luckmann, *The Invisible Religion* (New York: The Macmillan Company, 1967).
33. Cited by Lipset, *op. cit.*, p. 110.
34. *Ibid.*, footnote.
35. Kurt Vonnegut, *Cat's Cradle* (New York: Dell Publishing Co., 1970), p. 66.
36. See Morton Mintz and Jerry S. Cohen, *America, Inc.* (New York: Dial Press, 1971).
37. "The Shape and Role of Ethnic Groups in American History: An Overview" in Paul Peachey and Sister Rita Mudd, eds., *Evolving Patterns of Ethnicity in American Life* (Washington, D.C.: National Center for Urban Ethnic Affairs, June 1971), p. 19.
38. Quoted by Handlin, *Immigration*, pp. 102, 103.

CHAPTER NINE

1. Wills, *Nixon Agonistes*, p. 593.
2. See Michael Harrington, *Toward a Democratic Left* (New York: The Macmillan Company, 1968), pp. 73–74.
3. *Ibid.*, p. 74.
4. See Thernstrom, *Poverty and Progress*, p. 205.
5. See Dahl, *After the Revolution?*, p. 155.
6. *Ibid.*, p. 69.
7. See *Newsday*, 7 September 1971, pp. 3, 11.
8. See Herbert J. Gans in *New Generation*, Fall 1970, p. 10.
9. See Lantz and McCrary, *People of Coal Town*, p. 49.
10. Tom Wicker in the *New York Times*, 28 September 1971, p. 39.
"... prisoners are substantially in the power of the guards at most times, and since many guards are insensitive and brutal, the prisoners, too, live in fear."
11. See, for example, *The Middle Americans*.
12. See the *Washington Post*, 19 August 1971, for the report on these and the findings that follow. A Gallup poll of mid-March 1969 reported that sixty-seven percent of the American people would vote for a Negro for president. Seventy-eight percent of Catholics said they would. In 1958 the figure had been thirty-eight percent of all Americans. See John D. Lafton, Jr., Republican National Committee, in Letters to the Editor, *New York Times*, 30 September 1971.
13. *The Middle Americans*, p. 46.
14. Being honest involves being able to recognize motivations. Robert W. Terry, associate director of the Detroit Industrial Mission, charts three basic positions whites have

towards blacks in *For Whites Only* (Grand Rapids, Mich.: Wm. B. Eerdmans Publishing Co., 1970):

Basic Orientation	Main Professed Value	Who Is the Problem?	Why?	Value Acted Out	Relation with Blacks
White conservative	Self-determination	Black Power groups	Breakdown of law & order	Domination	Punishment
White liberal	Respect	Black institutions	Societal sickness	Closure	Paternalism
New white	Pluralism	White culture	Cultural white racism	Pluralism	Collaboration

15. See Greene, *The Slavic Community on Strike*, pp. 143–144.
16. See Coleman, *The Molly Maguire Riots*, pp. 44, 40. For further details on the Mollies, see Broehl, *The Molly Maguires*, and F. P. Dewees, *The Molly Maguires* (New York: Burt Franklin, originally published 1877).
17. See Greene, *op. cit.*, pp. 138ff.
18. *Ibid.*, p. 155.
19. See Fred J. Cook's story "Chance Killings, or Deeper Problem?", *New York Times*, 29 August 1971.
20. Herman Melville, quoted in Horace M. Kallen, *Cultural Pluralism and the American Idea* (Philadelphia: University of Pennsylvania Press, 1956), in the footnotes on p. 179.
21. Max Rafferty, "The Passing of the Patriot" (reprinted by America's Future, Inc.), pp. 2–7.
22. See William F. Buckley, Jr., *New York Times Magazine*, 1 August 1971, p. 9.
23. See Kallen, *op. cit.*, p. 63.
24. Buckley, *op. cit.*, p. 39.
25. Ben Halpern, *Jews and Blacks* (New York: Herder and Herder, 1971).
26. *Ibid.*, pp. 168–169ff.
27. See Handlin, *Race and Nationality in American Life*, p. 59.

CHAPTER TEN

1. John Stuart Mill, *On Liberty*, as edited by Currin V. Shields (Indianapolis: Bobbs-Merrill Co., 1956), p. 89.
2. See Paul Mus and John T. McAlister, Jr., *The Vietnamese and Their Revolution* (New York: Harper & Row, 1970).

3. Mill, *op. cit.*, pp. 88, 90, for these and the preceding quotes.
4. Halpern, *Jews and Blacks*, pp. 39–40.
5. L. Paul Metzger, "American Sociology and Black Assimilation: Conflicting Perspectives" in *American Journal of Sociology*, January 1971, pp. 628–629, 643–644.
6. See Greeley's discussion of alternatives in "The New Ethnicity," *Dissent* (to appear).
7. Nie and Currie, cited by Greeley, *ibid.*
8. Richard Sennett, "Break Up the Family," in the *New York Times*, 19 July 1971, for these and the next two quotes.
9. Nathan Glazer, "The Limits of Social Policy," *Commentary*, September 1971, p. 52.
10. *Ibid.*, p. 53.
11. *Ibid.*, p. 54.
12. *Ibid.*
13. Mus and McAlister, *op. cit.*, pp. 21–24.
14. Bell, *The End of Ideology*, p. 238. The preceding quote is cited by Bell on p. 229.
15. See Peter Binzen, *Whitetown U. S. A.* (New York: Random House, 1970), pp. 36–78.
16. But note the rise in anti-Catholic feeling among Jews. See Greeley, *Why Can't They Be Like Us?*, p. 199.
17. See Halpern's discussion, *op. cit.*, p. 30.
18. *Ibid.*, pp. 18–26.
19. In Handlin, *Immigration as a Factor in American History*, pp. 100–101.
20. Hank Messick, *Lansky* (New York: G. P. Putnam's Sons, 1971).
21. See John Franklin Campbell's "The Death Rattle of the Eastern Establishment," *New York Magazine*, 20 September 1971, pp. 47–48.

Bibliography

Abell, Aaron I. *American Catholicism and Social Action: A Search for Social Justice 1865–1950.* Garden City, N.Y.: Hanover House, a Division of Doubleday & Co., 1960.

————, ed. *American Catholic Thought on Social Questions.* New York: Bobbs-Merrill Co., 1968.

Acton, Lord. *Essays on Freedom and Power.* New York: World Publishing Co., Meridian Books, 1955.

————. *Lectures on Modern History.* New York: World Publishing Co., Meridian Books, 1961.

Adamic, Louis. *Cradle of Life.* New York: Harper & Brothers, 1936.

————. *Dynamite.* New York: Chelsea House Publishers, 1958.

————. *Laughing in the Jungle.* New York: Arno Press and the New York Times, 1969.

————. *A Nation of Nations.* New York: Harper & Brothers, 1945.

Adorno, W. W.; Frenkel-Brunswik, Else; Levinson, Daniel J.; and Sanford, R. Nevitt. *The Authoritarian Personality.* New York: Harper & Row, 1950.

Allport, Gordon W. *The Nature of Prejudice.* Reading, Mass.: Addison-Wesley Publishing Co., 1954.

Almond, Gabriel A. *The American People and Foreign Policy.* New York: Frederick A. Praeger, 1960.

Balch, Emily Greene. *Our Slavic Fellow Citizens.* New York: Arno Press and the New York Times, 1969.

Baltzell, E. Digby. *The Protestant Establishment.* New York: Random House, 1964.

Barron, Milton L., ed. *Minorities in a Changing World.* New York: Alfred A. Knopf, 1967.

Bell, Daniel. *The End of Ideology*, rev. ed. New York: Free Press, 1962.

———. ed. *The Radical Right.* Garden City, N.Y.: Doubleday & Co., Anchor Books, 1964.

Bennett, Levone, Jr. *Confrontation: Black and White.* Baltimore: Penguin Books, 1965.

Berger, Bennett M. *Working-Class Suburb.* Berkeley: University of California Press, 1968.

Berger, Monroe; Abel, Theodore; and Page, Charles H., eds. *Freedom and Control in Modern Society.* New York: D. Van Nostrand Co., 1954.

Berger, Peter L., and Neuhaus, Richard J. *Movement and Revolution.* Garden City, N.Y.: Doubleday & Co., Anchor Books, 1970.

Berman, Marshall. *The Politics of Authenticity.* New York: Atheneum, 1970.

Berrigan, Daniel, and Coles, Robert. *The Geography of Faith.* Boston: Beacon Press, 1971.

Binzen, Peter. *Whitetown, U. S. A.* New York: Random House, 1970.

Blythe, Ronald. *Akenfield: Portrait of an English Village.* New York: Dell Publishing Co., 1969.

Bourne, Randolph S. *War and the Intellectuals.* New York: Harper & Row, Harper Torchbooks, 1964.

Broehl, Wayne G., Jr. *The Molly Maguires.* Cambridge: Harvard University Press, 1965.

Campbell, Angus; Converse, Philip E.; Miller, Warren E.; and Stokes, Donald E., eds. *Elections and the Political Order.* New York: John Wiley & Sons, 1967.

Capek, Thomas. *The Czechs in America.* New York: Arno Press and the New York Times, 1969.

Chester, Lewis; Hodgson, Godfrey; and Page, Bruce, *An American Melodrama.* New York: Dell Publishing Co., 1969.

Coleman, J. Walter. *The Molly Maguire Riots.* New York: Arno Press and the New York Times, 1969.

Coles, Robert, and Erikson, Jan. *The Middle Americans*. Boston: Little, Brown & Co., 1971.

Dahl, Robert A. *After the Revolution?* New Haven: Yale University Press, 1970.

————. *Polyarchy*. New Haven: Yale University Press, 1971.

————. *Who Governs?* New Haven: Yale University Press, 1961.

Dewees, F. P. *The Molly Maguires*. New York: Burt Franklin, originally published 1877.

Dinnerstein, Leonard, and Jaher, Frederick Cople, eds. *The Aliens*. New York: Appleton-Century-Crofts, 1970.

Duncan, Hugh Dalziel. *Symbols in Society*. New York: Oxford University Press, 1968.

Edelman, Murray. *The Symbolic Uses of Politics*. Urbana: University of Illinois Press, 1967.

Endleman, Shalom. *Violence in the Streets*. Chicago: Quadrangle Books, 1968.

Epstein, Benjamin R., and Forster, Arnold. *The Radical Right*. New York: Random House, Vintage Books, 1967.

Foner, Philip S. *American Labor and the Indo-China War*. New York: International Publishers, 1971.

Franklin, John Hope. *Color and Race*. Boston: Beacon Press, 1969.

Fromm, Erich. *Escape from Authority*. New York: Harper & Row, Harper Torchbooks, 1964.

————. *Escape from Freedom*. New York: Avon Books, 1965.

Fuchs, Lawrence H., ed. *American Ethnic Politics*. New York: Harper & Row, Harper Torchbooks, 1968.

Glazer, Nathan, and Moynihan, Daniel Patrick. *Beyond the Melting Pot*. Cambridge: M.I.T. Press, 1963.

Glock, Charles Y., and Siegelman, Ellen. *Prejudice U. S. A.* New York: Frederick A. Praeger, 1969.

Gordon, Milton M. *Assimilation in American Life*. New York: Oxford University Press, 1964.

Graham, Hugh Davis, and Gurr, Ted Robert. *Violence in America*, A Staff Report to the National Commission on the Causes and Prevention of Violence. Washington, D.C.: U.S. Government Printing Office, June 1969.

Grant, Madison. *The Passing of the Great Race*. New York: Arno Press and the New York Times, 1970.

Greeley, Andrew M. *Why Can't They Be Like Us?* New York: E. P. Dutton & Co., 1971.

Greene, Victor R. *The Slavic Community on Strike*. Notre Dame, Ind.: University of Notre Dame Press, 1968.

Guerin, Daniel. *Anarchism.* New York: Monthly Review Press, 1970.

Halpern, Ben. *Jews and Blacks.* New York: Herder & Herder, 1971.

Handlin, Oscar. *The American People in the Twentieth Century*. Boston: Beacon Press, 1963.

———. *The Americans*. Boston: Little, Brown & Co., 1963.

———. *Immigration as a Factor in American History*. Englewood Cliffs, N.J.: Prentice-Hall, 1959.

———. *Race and Nationality in American Life*. Boston: Little, Brown & Co., 1957.

———. *The Uprooted*. Boston: Little, Brown & Co., 1951.

Handman, J. B. S., ed. *American Labor Dynamics*. New York: Arno Press and the New York Times, 1969.

Hansen, Marcus Lee. *The Immigrant in American History*. New York: Harper & Row, Harper Torchbooks, 1964.

Harrington, Michael. *Toward a Democratic Left*. New York: The Macmillan Company, 1968.

Hartmann, Edward George. *The Movement to Americanize the Immigrant*. New York: University of Columbia Press, 1948.

Hartz, Louis. *The Liberal Tradition in America*. New York: Harcourt, Brace & World, 1955.

Hawgood, John Arkas. *The Tragedy of German-America*. New York: Arno Press, Inc., 1970.

Headley, Joel Tyler. *The Great Riots of New York: 1712–1873*. New York: Bobbs-Merrill Co., 1970.

Higham, John. *Strangers in the Land*. New York: Atheneum, 1968.

Hofstadter, Richard. *Anti-intellectualism in American Life*. New York: Random House, Vintage Books, 1966.

Howe, Louise Kapp, ed. *The White Majority*. New York: Random House, 1970.

Hudson, Winthrop S. *Nationalism and Religion in America*. New York: Harper & Row, 1970.

Hughes, Emmet John. *The Church and the Liberal Society*. Notre Dame, Ind.: University of Notre Dame Press, 1961.

Jordan, Winthrop D. *White Over Black*. Chapel Hill: University of North Carolina Press, 1968.

Kallen, Horace M. *Cultural Pluralism and the American Idea.* Philadelphia: University of Pennsylvania Press, 1956.

Kazan, Elia. *America! America!* New York: Popular Library, 1961.

Kazin, Alfred. *Starting Out in the Thirties.* Boston: Little, Brown & Co., 1965.

Kennedy, John F. *A Nation of Immigrants,* rev. and enlarged. New York: Harper & Row, 1964.

Kobler, John. *Capone.* New York: G. P. Putnam's Sons, 1971.

Komarovsky, Mirra. *Blue-Collar Magazine.* New York: Random House, Vintage Books, 1967.

Kornhauser, William. *The Politics of Mass Society.* New York: Free Press, 1959.

Kosinski, Jerzy. *The Painted Bird.* New York: Houghton Mifflin Co., a Pocket Cardinal Edition, 1966.

Lantz, Herman R., with the assistance of McCrary, J. S. *People of Coal Town.* New York: Columbia University Press, 1958.

Leggett, John C. *Class, Race and Labor.* New York: Oxford University Press, 1968.

Leinwand, Gerald. *Minorities All.* New York: Washington Square Press, 1971.

Lieberson, Stanley. *Ethnic Patterns in American Cities.* Glencoe, Ill.: Free Press, 1963.

Lipset, Seymour Martin. *Political Man.* Garden City, N.Y.: Doubleday & Co., Anchor Books, 1963.

Lopreato, Joseph. *Italian Americans.* New York: Random House, 1970.

Lubell, Samuel. *The Future of American Politics,* 3d ed. New York: Harper & Row, 1965.

Luckmann, Thomas. *The Invisible Religion.* New York: The Macmillan Company, 1967.

McAlister, John T., and Mus, Paul. *The Vietnamese and Their Revolution.* New York: Harper & Row, 1970.

McCullough, David G. *The Johnstown Flood.* New York: Simon & Schuster, 1968.

Macdonald, Dwight. *Against the American Grain.* New York: Random House, Vintage Books, 1962.

Mailer, Norman. *Advertisements for Myself.* New York: New American Library, a Signet Classic, 1959.

————. *Cannibals and Christians.* New York: Dial Press, 1966.

————. *The Naked and the Dead.* New York: New American Library, a Signet Classic, 1948.

————. *The Short Fiction of Norman Mailer.* New York: Dell Publishing Co., 1967.

Marcel, Gabriel. *Man Against Mass Society.* Chicago:. Henry Regnery Co., 1962.

Marden, Charles F., and Meyer, Gladys. *Minorities in American Society.* New York: Van Nostrand Reinhold Co., 1968.

Maritain, Jacques. *Creative Intuition in Art and Poetry.* New York: Meridian Books, 1955.

May, Henry F. *Protestant Churches and Industrial America.* New York: Harper & Row, Harper Torchbooks, 1967.

Mead, Margaret, and Baldwin, James. *A Rap on Race.* Philadelphia: J. B. Lippincott Co., 1971.

Mencken, H. L. *Prejudices,* A Selection made by James T. Farrell. New York: Random House, Vintage Books, 1955.

Metzger, Radley, pub. *Collected Speeches of Spiro Agnew.* New York: Audubon Books, 1971.

Minogue, Kenneth R. *The Liberal Mind.* New York: Random House, 1963.

Mintz, Morton, and Cohen, Jerry S. *America, Inc.* New York: Dial Press, 1971.

Morgan, Edmund S., ed. *Puritan Political Ideas.* New York: Bobbs-Merrill Co., 1965.

Morris, Terry. *Better Than You.* New York: Institute of Human Relations Press, The American Jewish Committee, 1971.

Nimmo, Dan, and Ungs, Thomas D. *American Political Patterns.* Boston: Little, Brown & Co., 1969.

Ortega y Gasset, Jose. *The Revolt of the Masses.* New York: W. W. Norton & Co., 1957.

Park, Robert E., and Miller, Herbert A. *Old World Traits Transplanted.* New York: Arno Press and the New York Times, 1969.

Phillips, Kevin P. *The Emerging Republican Majority.* New Rochelle, N.Y.: Arlington House, 1969.

Portal, Roger. *The Slavs.* New York: Harper & Row, 1969.

Pye, Lucian W., and Verba, Sidney, eds. *Political Culture and Political Development.* Princeton, N.J.: Princeton University Press, 1965.

Rahv, Philip. *Literature and the Sixth Sense*. Boston: Houghton Mifflin Co., 1970.
———, ed. *Modern Occasions*. New York: Noonday Press, 1966.
Rainwater, Lee; Coleman, Richard P.; and Handel, Gerald. *Workingman's Wife*. New York: Oceana Publications, 1959.
Ranulf, Svend. *Moral Indignation and Middle-Class Psychology*. New York: Schocken Books, 1964.
Raskin, Marcus G. *Being and Doing*. New York: Random House, 1971.
Reich, Charles A. *The Greening of America*. New York: Random House, 1970.
Rexroth, Kenneth. *An Autobiographical Novel*. New York: New Directions, 1969.
Riesman, David. *Individualism Reconsidered*. New York: Free Press, 1954.
Rogin, Michael Paul. *The Intellectuals and McCarthy: The Radical Specter*. Cambridge, Mass.: M.I.T. Press, 1967.
Rose, Thomas, ed. *Violence in America*. New York: Random House, Vintage Books, 1969.
Rosenstock-Huessy, Eugen. *I Am an Impure Thinker*. Norwich, Vt.: Argo Books, 1970.
Roth, Philip. *Portnoy's Complaint*. New York: Bantam Books, 1969.
Royko, Mike. *Boss*. New York: E. P. Dutton & Co., 1971.
Sartre, Jean-Paul. *Critique de la raison dialectique*. Paris: Editions Gallimard, 1960.
Scammon, Richard M., and Wattenberg, Ben J. *The Real Majority*. New York: Coward-McCann, 1970.
Segal, Bernard E., ed. *Racial and Ethnic Relations*. New York: Thomas Y. Crowell Co., 1966.
Sennett, Richard, ed. *Classic Essays on the Culture of Cities*. New York: Appleton-Century-Crofts, 1969.
———. *Families Against the City*. Cambridge: Harvard University Press, 1970.
———. *The Uses of Disorder*. New York: Alfred A. Knopf, 1970.
Sexton, Patricia Cayo and Brendan. *Blue Collars and Hard Hats*. New York: Random House, 1971.
Shils, Edward. *The Torment of Secrecy*. Glencoe, Ill.: Free Press, 1956.

Sholokhov, Mikhail. *And Quiet Flows the Don.* New York: New American Library, a Signet Book, 1959.

Shostak, Arthur B. *Blue-Collar Life.* New York: Random House, 1969.

Simko, Michael. *Mila Nadaya.* Philadelphia: Dorrance & Co., 1968.

Simpson, George Eaton, and Yinger, J. Milton. *Racial and Cultural Minorities.* New York: Harper & Row, 1963.

Sinclair, Upton. *The Jungle.* New York: New American Library, Signet Classic, 1906; Afterword, 1960.

Sisson, Andrew R. *Applehood and Mother Pie.* Peterborough, N.H.: Orchard Press, 1971.

Slater, Philip. *The Pursuit of Loneliness.* Boston: Beacon Press, 1970.

Solotaroff, Theodore, ed. *New American Review, Number 12.* New York: Simon & Schuster, a Touchstone Book, 1971.

————. *The Red-Hot Vacuum.* New York: Atheneum, 1970.

Stanton, William. *The Leopard's Spots.* Chicago: University of Chicago Press, 1960.

Talbot, Daniel, ed. *Film: An Anthology.* Berkeley: University of California Press, 1967.

Terry, Robert W. *For Whites Only.* Grand Rapids, Mich.: William B. Eerdmans, 1970.

Thernstrom, Stephen. *Poverty and Progress.* Cambridge: Harvard University Press, 1964.

————, and Sennett, Richard, eds. *Nineteenth-Century Cities.* New Haven: Yale University Press, 1969.

Thomas, William I., and Znaniecki, Florian. *The Polish Peasant in Europe and America,* vols. 1 and 2. New York: Dover Publications, 1958.

Thompson, E. P. *The Making of the English Working Class.* New York: Random House, Vintage Books, 1963.

Tomasi, Silvano M., and Engel, Madeline H., eds. *The Italian Experience in the United States.* Staten Island, N.Y.: Center for Migration Studies, 1970.

Vizinczey, Stephen. *The Rules of Chaos.* New York: McCall Publishing Co., 1969, 1970.

Walker, Daniel, dir. *The Walker Report: Rights in Conflict.* New York: Bantam Books, 1968.

Ware, Carolyn F. *The Cultural Approach to History.* Port Washington, N.Y.: Kennikat Press, 1940.

White, Thèodore H. *The Making of the President 1968*. New York: Atheneum, 1969.

Whyte, William Foote. *Street Corner Society*. Chicago: University of Chicago Press, 1943.

Wills, Garry. *Nixon Agonistes*. Boston: Houghton Mifflin Co., 1970.

Wytrwal, Joseph A. *America's Polish Heritage*. Detroit: Endurance Press, 1961.

Yinger, J. Milton. *A Minority Group in American Society*. New York: McGraw-Hill Book Co., 1965.

Zborowski, Mark. *People in Pain*. San Francisco: Jossey-Bass, Inc., 1969.

Index